Gold, Dollars, and Power

The New Cold War History
John Lewis Gaddis
*Editor*

# Gold, Dollars, and Power

*The Politics of*
*International Monetary Relations, 1958–1971*

Francis J. Gavin

The University of North Carolina Press
*Chapel Hill and London*

Portions of the text have previously appeared, in slightly different form,
in the following articles, all by Francis J. Gavin:
"The Gold Battles with the Cold War: American Monetary Policy and the Defense of
Europe, 1960–1963," *Diplomatic History* 26, no. 1 (Winter 2002): 61–94;
"The Myth of Flexible Response: American Strategy in Europe during the 1960s,"
*International History Review* 23, no. 4 (December 2001): 847–75;
with Erin Mahan, "Hegemony or Vulnerability?: Giscard, Ball, and the Gold Standstill,"
*Journal of European Integration History* 6, no. 2 (December 2000): 61–84; and
"The Legends of Bretton Woods," *Orbis* 40, no. 2 (Spring 1996): 183–96.

The paper in this book meets the guidelines for permanence and durability of the
Committee on Production Guidelines for Book Longevity of the Council on Library
Resources.

Library of Congress Cataloging-in-Publication Data
Gavin, Francis J.
Gold, dollars, and power: the politics of international monetary relations, 1958–1971 /
Francis J. Gavin.
p. cm.—(The New Cold War history)
Includes bibliogaphical references and index.
ISBN 978-0-8078-2823-6 (cloth: alk. paper)
ISBN 978-0-8078-5900-1 (pbk. : alk. paper)
1. International finance—History. 2. Gold—History. I. Title. II. Series.
HG3881 .G315   2004
332.4'5'09046—dc21
2003012092

07 06 05 04 03   5 4 3 2 1

For Catherine Marie

# Contents

Acknowledgments   xi

Abbreviations   xiii

Introduction. Gold, Dollars, and Power   1
*Money, Security, and the Politics of the U.S. Balance of Payments, 1958–1971*

1.   Bretton Woods
     and Postwar International Monetary Relations   17

2.   The Costs of Commitment   33
     *Eisenhower, Europe, and the American Balance-of-Payments Crisis*

3.   The Gold Battles within the Cold War   59
     *Kennedy's International Monetary Policy*

4.   Reform, Restrictions, or Redeployments?   89
     *The Balance of Payments and the Franco-German Revolt, 1963*

5.   LBJ Takes Over   117
     *Battles with de Gaulle and Proposals for Reform, 1964–1966*

6.   Defend Europe or the Dollar?   135
     *Money and Security, 1964–1967*

7.   The End of Bretton Woods   165
     *The Devaluation of Sterling and the 1968 Gold Crisis*

8.   Nixon and the New Era in Global Monetary Relations   187

     Conclusion. No Way to Build an Empire   197

     Appendix A. Analyzing the Numbers:
     Breaking Down the U.S. Balance of Payments for 1960–1961   203

     Appendix B. Charts and Graphs   209

     Notes   215

     Bibliography   247

     Index   259

# Illustrations

Movie poster for *Goldfinger*  2
Delegates at Bretton Woods  19
Keynes and White at Bretton Woods, 1944  29
JFK with French finance minister Giscard d'Estaing  79
Cartoon: JFK and Adenaur  96
JFK with Douglas Dillon  100
De Gaulle on *Time* magazine cover  123
LBJ with FRG chancellor Ludwig Erhard  150
LBJ with Walt Rostow and Secretary of the Treasury Fowler  170
Cartoon by Bill Mauldin  183
Nixon and his economic team  189
John Connally  194
Cartoon by Herblock  199

# Acknowledgments

This book could not have been written without the warm and generous support of many individuals and institutions. I want to thank Arthur Burke, Matthew Connelly, Michael Creswell, Michael Desch, Evan Feigenbaum, Eugene Gholz, Robert Kane, Jonathan Kirshner, Bruce Kuklick, Erin Mahan, Tarek Masoud, John Mearsheimer, Paul Pittman, Walt Rostow, Bryan Saliamonas, Mary Sarotte, Thomas Schwartz, Jim Stein, Jeremi Suri, and Tom Zeiler for their most helpful comments and suggestions on various parts of this book. I have been lucky to have very good research assistants. Celestino Gallegos, Rahel Kahlert, Amanda Kempa, and especially Michael Gerson were tireless in their efforts. Portions of this research were presented to the Business, Government and International Economics group at the Harvard Business School, the International History Department at the London School of Economics, the Institute for Strategic Studies at Yale University, the LBJ School of Public Affairs, the American Foreign Policy Program at SAIS–Johns Hopkins, and the John M. Olin Institute at Harvard University. I am grateful for the feedback I received from the participants in these talks. Parts of this manuscript have appeared previously, and I thank *Diplomatic History*, the *International History Review*, the *Journal of European Integration History*, and *Orbis* for their permission to use the material in the book.

While completing the dissertation at the University of Pennsylvania, I received funding from the Annenberg Foundation, the Mellon Foundation, and the Roy F. Nicols fellowship. The University of Pennsylvania Department of History, the John M. Olin Institute, Harvard's Center for European Studies, the Miller Center for Public Affairs at the University of Virginia, the Policy Research Institute at the LBJ School of Public Affairs, and the Dwight D. Eisenhower, John F. Kennedy, and Lyndon B. Johnson presidential libraries provided generous travel and research funds. I thank the University of Texas Cooperative Society for awarding me a subvention grant. Steve Miller and the Belfer Center for Science and International Affairs at the John F. Kennedy School of Government provided a wonderful environment to work on the manuscript in fall 1998. Two institutions deserve special thanks. As anyone who has spent time there knows, Sam Huntington and Stephen Rosen provide an incredibly welcoming and exciting environment at the John M. Olin Institute of Strategic Studies at Harvard. And it is hard to imagine a more collegial and intellectually stimulating environment than the LBJ School of Public Affairs at the

University of Texas, and its sister organization, the LBJ Presidential Library. The professors, archivists, visiting researchers, and students at LBJ are a constant source of inspiration. In particular, I want to thank former library director Harry Middleton, LBJ School Dean Edwin Dorn, Professor Jamie Galbraith, and Elspeth and Walt Rostow for their generous support and friendship since I arrived in Austin.

Several people deserve special mention. My parents and siblings have provided an incredible foundation of love and support over the years. Art Burke has been a great friend in good times and bad. Natalie Britton has been amazing. The wonderful staff at the University of North Carolina Press—and, in particular, Charles Grench, Brian MacDonald, Pamela Upton, and Amanda McMillan—has spared no effort to successfully conclude this project. Randall Woods generously provided detailed suggestions and helpful encouragement to improve the manuscript. Michael Parrish, previously of the LBJ library and now a distinguished professor in the Department of History at Baylor University, helped this project enormously over the years. Walter McDougall was a constant source of intellectual excitement and encouragement, both during my time at the University of Pennsylvania and later. John Lewis Gaddis generously (and graciously) labored over several versions of this manuscript with kindness and penetrating insight, and his suggestions have made this a much better book. I am especially grateful to Drew Erdmann for his enthusiastic support and friendship over the years. Finally, as everyone who has worked with him knows, Marc Trachtenberg is the model of what a great scholar and mentor should be. There are no words to describe his influence on me personally and professionally.

# Abbreviations

| | |
|---|---|
| CEA | Council of Economic Advisers |
| CRU | Collective Reserve Unit |
| DEA | Department of Economic Affairs |
| EEC | European Economic Community |
| EPU | European Payments Union |
| FRG | Federal Republic of Germany |
| G-10 | Group of Ten |
| GDR | German Democratic Republic |
| IMF | International Monetary Fund |
| JCS | Joint Chiefs of Staff |
| MLF | multilateral force |
| NATO | North Atlantic Treaty Organization |
| NPT | Non-Proliferation Treaty |
| NSC | National Security Council |
| OECD | Organization for Economic Cooperation and Development |
| SACEUR | Supreme Allied Commander, Europe |
| SDR | special drawing rights |

Gold, Dollars, and Power

*Introduction*

# Gold, Dollars, and Power

*Money, Security, and the Politics*
*of the U.S. Balance of Payments, 1958–1971*

We are at a most important moment in postwar history. Both the
Communist world and the noncommunist world are in considerable disarray.
The outcome—whether in Vietnam or the gold crisis—depends on how
free men behave in the days and weeks ahead. . . . If the free nations of the world
fail to cooperate intensively and if the Congress fails to vote a tax increase,
we could set in motion a financial and trade crisis which would undo much that
we have achieved in these fields and endanger the prosperity and security
of the Western World.
—Walt Rostow to President Johnson, 19 March 1968

In 1964 the James Bond thriller *Goldfinger* was released in movie theaters
throughout the United States and Great Britain. In the Ian Fleming novel
on which the film was based, the sinister Goldfinger, ably assisted by
Pussy Galore, plotted to steal the American gold supply from Fort Knox.
The movie added an interesting twist to the book's improbable scenario.[1]
In the film, Bond is understandably skeptical that Goldfinger can physically remove tons of gold from the most secure building in the world.
Goldfinger tells agent 007 that he does not have to remove it *physically*.
Instead, he only needs to get inside Fort Knox and install a timed nuclear
device supplied by the People's Republic of China. The bomb would irradiate all the gold inside the building and make it unusable. Bond recog-
nizes the fiendish genius behind Goldfinger's sinister scheme. With a
large part of the world's gold supply irradiated, Goldfinger's private hoard
would escalate in value. More frightening from Bond's perspective was
the impact on the global payments system. With the American gold supply rendered unusable, international liquidity would seize up, and the
Western trade and monetary systems would collapse. A catastrophic depression would ensue, and the Chinese would exploit the collapse of the
free-world economy to achieve an easy victory in the Cold War. Fortunately, this calamity is averted by a timely combination of Bond's usual
quick thinking and an unlikely last second shift in political (and sexual)
sentiments by Ms. Galore. Together, James and Pussy save the free world
from monetary chaos and political disaster.

The target chosen by the film for the economic decapitation of the
West is revealing. It was not a large factory or a valued natural resource

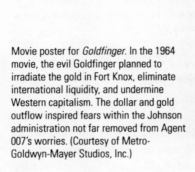

Movie poster for *Goldfinger.* In the 1964 movie, the evil Goldfinger planned to irradiate the gold in Fort Knox, eliminate international liquidity, and undermine Western capitalism. The dollar and gold outflow inspired fears within the Johnson administration not far removed from Agent 007's worries. (Courtesy of Metro-Goldwyn-Mayer Studios, Inc.)

that fueled machinery, transportation, or a weapons system. It was not even a financial center, such as Wall Street or the City in London. It was a pile of heavy, yellow metal, a regulated commodity with a fixed price and few nonmonetary uses, expensive to guard and difficult to move. Would destroying this resource really paralyze the free-world economy? Policy makers and economists of the time certainly thought so, as memos detailing scenarios as grim as Goldfinger's plot were circulated within the Johnson administration throughout late 1967 and 1968.

Three days before the 1967 Christmas holiday, presidential aide Joseph Califano sent a telegram to Lyndon B. Johnson summarizing the findings of an emergency study produced by the cabinet committee on the balance of payments.[2] This committee had been told to produce a serious and far-reaching program to bring the ballooning payments deficit of the United States down to equilibrium. Since 1958, when the payments deficits had first caught the attention of the Eisenhower administration, countless committees and high-level officials had crafted proposals to arrest the outflow of American dollars and gold. But this task became urgent when Great Britain, in the face of massive speculation on the currency markets, was forced to devalue sterling on 17 November 1967. The president's closest advisers believed that unless the American deficit was drastically reduced, speculators would attack the dollar next. A run on the dollar could force the United States to suspend its promise to convert dollars into gold, ending the commitment that had served as the cornerstone of the postwar international monetary regime. If the pledge to redeem dollars for gold was not honored, many economists feared that forces of economic disorder would be unleashed, producing a worldwide depression equal to the economic collapse of the 1930s.

The recommendations of the committee were severe.[3] Its suggested program included border taxes and export subsidies, steep travel taxes, increased offset payments from allies, limits on overseas lending by American banks, and mandatory controls on capital investment abroad. For an embattled president entering an election year, this plan was nothing short of political suicide. It would anger everyone from the banks and the multinationals to the average American tourist. The proposal would provoke an outcry overseas, especially in Western Europe, and might be met with retaliatory actions that could wipe out any potential balance-of-payments gain. The Atlantic alliance, strained to the breaking point in 1966 and 1967 by internal crises, would be pressured further by the committee's policies. Acrimonious monetary relations had been an irritant in relations with each of the three European powers—Great Britain, France, and West Germany—in the past eight years and the balance-of-payments program might exacerbate these tensions toward a rupture. Furthermore, the plan reversed the cardinal tenet of postwar American foreign economic policy: to promote open markets and free trade around the world, even if it meant accepting unfair discrimination against American goods and capital to accomplish this goal.

Johnson was furious. The president recognized that he was in a no-win situation. If he avoided action, the United States could run out of gold, with unknown but potentially devastating consequences to the free-world economy. But if he successfully implemented his program, the consequences for the international monetary system might be just as bad. In addition to the unpopularity of the measures, Johnson believed that a complete end to American deficits would drastically reduce world liquidity. The Bretton Woods system was not a gold standard, but a gold exchange standard, and the dollar served as the primary reserve asset in the system. A portion of the American deficits provided much of the international liquidity that financed world trade. "The world supply of gold is insufficient to make the present system workable—particularly as the use of the dollar as a reserve currency is essential to create the required international liquidity to sustain world trade and growth."[4]

LBJ lamented the bitter irony of the payments crisis, believing that the deficit was largely caused by the requirements of America's leadership role around the world: "[A]t the same time, our strength is required for so

many extraneous situations: Vietnam, world wide defense, German in-
stallations, aid to underdeveloped countries, military aid abroad, etc."
The president was told that if the United States ended all these commitments, the payments deficit would disappear and the dollar would stabilize. But enacting these policies would have economic and political consequences that would be felt worldwide. "If all these or even some of them
were eliminated, our monetary structure–balance of payments would be
as strong as any nation. Dollars held by other countries would return. The
risk of loss of gold would evaporate or, in fact, our gold stocks would
increase."

Johnson believed he was caught in the same dilemma that had faced
both Kennedy and Eisenhower before him. The American payments deficit could be ended but the political and economic cost would be enormous: a return to isolationism in the United States, and financial ruin for
the free world. "Our role of world leadership in a political and military
sense is the only reason for our current embarrassment in an economic
sense on the one hand and on the other the correction of the economic
embarrassment under present monetary systems will result in an untenable position economically for our allies."[5] The president felt he was
being asked to choose between America's wide-ranging commitments—
both military and economic—that had been painstakingly built since the
end of the Second World War and the health of the international monetary system, which was the foundation of postwar economic prosperity.
But his advisers told him that he had no choice: if he failed to act, the
world monetary system would collapse. On 1 January 1968, he outlined
the provisions of the balance-of-payments program to the public.[6]

There was muted praise for the program from overseas financial cen-
ters, but most others were outraged. The American public found it hard to
understand how U.S policy makers had gotten the nation into such difficulty. Milton Friedman, in a widely read *Newsweek* column, roundly con-
demned Johnson's program: "How low we have fallen! The United States,
the land of the free, prohibits its businessmen from investing abroad and
requests its citizens not to show their faces or open their pocketbooks in
foreign ports. The United States, the wealthiest nation in the world, an-
nounces that its foreign policy will no longer be determined by its national interest and its international commitments but by the need to
reduce government spending abroad by $500 million."[7]

In spite of the negative political repercussions of the program, the
administration was relieved that its harsh balance-of-payments policy
seemed to work. During the first weeks of 1968, the currency and gold
markets calmed and the dollar strengthened. But by the end of January,

the drain of gold from the treasury resumed, slowly at first but increasing as the winter wore on. The Johnson administration was alarmed. Within months, the American gold stock would be depleted. What was going on?

The White House was paralyzed that winter by crisis after crisis: the Tet offensive in Vietnam, the seizure of the USS *Pueblo* by North Korea, the resignation of Defense Secretary Robert McNamara, worsening race relations, Eugene McCarthy's impressive showing in the New Hampshire primary. Congress refused to pass the budget and tax program the administration thought was critical to strengthen America's international economic position. At a time when the country seemed on the verge of a complete meltdown, the last thing that Johnson needed was to witness the collapse of the dollar on his watch. Clearly, the severe balance-of-payments program was not working. It was in this panicked atmosphere that a memorandum from the economist and Johnson confidante, Barbara Ward Jackson, circulated in the White House.

The predictions of the memo were dire. In it, Jackson argued that the president's painful program would not be enough to save the international monetary system. The dollar was weak, and sterling, despite a 14 percent devaluation, was even weaker. Jackson warned that many of the circumstances that led to the Great Depression were evident in present trends. If quick action were not taken, the economic and political outcome would be disastrous:

> A situation is brewing up in the world economy with some dangerous overtones of the 1929/31 disaster. If a crisis were to occur, the economic consequences might be so considerable a dislocation of world trade that depression and massive unemployment could appear in Europe and deflation spread quickly to the developing continents. This in turn would have profound political effects. The Russians might scent the long-hoped-for failure of capitalism and revert to hard-line adventurism and hostility. Despair in the poorer countries would cancel out present disillusion with China and its cultural revolution. The world could tip dangerously away from its present not wholly ineffective "coexistence."[8]

What more could the president do? A worried Johnson handed this memorandum to the chairman of the Council of Economic Advisers, Gardner Ackley, and his national security adviser, Walt Rostow, for comments. Both agreed that a worldwide economic collapse was not out of the picture. Ackley responded with a memorandum the next day: "Surely there is a *risk* of a critical deterioration of the world economic situation—

one that could even lead to a world depression if prompt action were not taken to reverse it."[9] Rostow agreed "international financial problems could get out of hand with very serious deflationary consequences for the world economy."[10] Rostow said it was time to get really tough with the Europeans, especially the Germans, and recommended sending a delegation led by Secretary of State Dean Rusk to force cooperation out of the allies. But the Germans had been cooperating since 1961 with a series of offset arrangements. More important, they had not purchased gold from the United States in years, despite large payments surpluses. The West German government had even taken the extraordinary step, in 1967, of publicly agreeing never to purchase gold from the U.S. Treasury in order to encourage other surplus countries to hold their dollars. Because other European countries had been pressured before, without result, there was little reason to think that they would help the United States now. The only options left were considered drastic, policies that in the past had been considered unthinkable: increasing the dollar price of gold, closing the private gold market, or ending the dollar's connection to gold altogether, in effect, allowing it to float against other currencies. The Johnson administration did not find any of these options appealing.

By mid-March, the gold outflow had reached crisis proportions and the administration was forced to act. Johnson asked the British government to close the London gold market and called for an emergency meeting of the world's leading finance ministers and central bankers in Washington, D.C. After a weekend of tense negotiations, the administration won approval for its plan to terminate the gold pool and eliminate market pressures by separating the intergovernmental gold market (where the price of gold would remain thirty-five dollars an ounce) from the private market (where prices would fluctuate, and presumably rise).[11] The leading world central bankers, excluding France, agreed not to buy or sell gold on the open market, and also agreed to initiate the controversial special drawing rights (SDR) plan by the end of the year.[12] The creation of an intergovernmental gold market meant that the American gold supply would be protected from the forces of the private market. It would be much easier for the United States to convince foreign governments not to buy gold than to constrain private holders of dollar liabilities. These actions essentially began the process that ended the brief and fitful life of the Bretton Woods monetary system. And all of it unfolded without Goldfinger or the Chinese doing a thing.

This extraordinary episode in international monetary relations generates many important questions. How had this financial crisis emerged?

Why weren't the drastic measures taken to limit the payments deficit and gold outflow effective? Did American policy makers correctly assess the causes and potential effects of the payments imbalance? Was the payments imbalance caused by the vast overseas requirements of its leadership role, as American leaders claimed? How much of the crisis was driven by political and diplomatic issues as opposed to purely economic factors? Why did American policy makers strive so hard to preserve an international monetary system that was clearly flawed? These questions make up the heart of an essentially untold story, the history of the strategic, political, and economic consequences of the attempt by American policy makers to understand and solve the seemingly intractable problem of the payments imbalance and gold outflow.

Between 1958 and 1971, the primary objective of U.S. foreign economic policy was to find a way to control the American balance-of-payments deficit and stem the loss of gold from the U.S. Treasury. Many of the policies that were enacted or considered in order to solve the payments problem and ease the gold drain conflicted with the larger goals of American foreign policy, strategy, and domestic economic policy. This clash created enormous tensions within both the U.S. government and the Western alliance, and affected a whole range of policies, from American troop deployments overseas to U.S. investment in Europe. Despite these political tensions, American policy makers feared an economic catastrophe if the payments deficit was not reduced and the gold outflow ended. Many policy makers, correctly or not, drew parallels with the international monetary conditions of the 1930s and feared that a failure to correct the problem could unleash an international economic collapse and political disaster.

Four successive administrations were obsessed with trying to end the U.S payments imbalance and gold outflow without jeopardizing America's vast political and military commitments around the world. Each administration produced controversial programs to limit or end the deficit, all to no avail. These plans had an enormous influence on U.S. foreign economic policy and a no less important effect on American grand strategy during a crucial period of the Cold War. Yet, despite the obvious importance of this subject, there has never been a full-scale diplomatic or economic history of the attempt by American policy makers to understand and solve the vexing problem of the balance-of-payments deficit. This study fills that void. In the process, I make several arguments about the history of international monetary relations, interalliance dynamics, and the nature of U.S. foreign economic, strategic, and diplomatic policy during the Cold War. These arguments, made throughout the book, fall into three sometimes overlapping categories.

## Economic Policy, Strategy, and Politics

Why was the world's most powerful state so afraid of what might happen with respect to seemingly second-order issues as gold reserves, offset payments, and exchange rates? The key is to understand that these issues were more than just economic questions. Fundamental questions of power politics and strategy were also at stake. This study demonstrates that there was a triangular relationship between the strategic objective of "dual containment," aimed both at the Soviet Union and the Germans; the economic objective of avoiding another Great Depression; and the political objective of sustaining domestic support for continued American involvement in Europe. The U.S. balance of payments was central to all these concerns, in a way that has never been recognized by the historical literature. This underscores a crucial methodological point. We cannot look at questions of economic policy, strategy, and foreign policy in isolation from each other.

### International Monetary Relations, Nuclear Weapons, and the German Question

International monetary policy had an important bearing on the central issue of the Cold War: the German question. One of the fundamental foreign policy issues facing the United States in the 1950s and 1960s was how to keep West Germany locked into the political and military status quo established by the NATO system. In order to "keep the Russians out, and the Germans down," the NATO system required a large American troop presence in West Germany. The Americans had to be kept in.

But many top American policy makers identified America's generous political and security policy in Europe—chiefly the decision to station six army divisions in West Germany—as the root cause of America's monetary woes. What if concerns about the balance of payments forced the Americans to bring these troops home? Would American policy makers risk an economic catastrophe if they maintained these troops? Sharply reducing the number of American forces abroad was to many policy makers the most tempting target for balance-of-payments relief. Would domestic support for this large conventional force dissipate in the face of détente, economic malaise, and European intransigence? How top American policy makers struggled with these questions is a central theme of this book. The answers to these questions had consequences that went well beyond international monetary relations.

*Bringing the Troops Home from Europe*

It is hard to underestimate the economic and domestic political pressure on American policy makers to pull U.S. troops out of Europe during the late 1950s and 1960s. Surprisingly, Eisenhower, Kennedy, and Johnson all expressed a strong desire to "redeploy" out of Europe in order to strengthen the U.S. balance of payments. This is one of the most important findings of this study. But if the Americans significantly reduced their conventional force structure, the NATO system would be undermined. The Soviets might become emboldened to become more aggressive toward Western Europe. And without American protection, the West Germans might follow a more independent political and military path, one that might include a nuclearization of their armed forces. This would be deeply unsettling to America's allies and adversaries alike.

*The Myth of Flexible Response*

The Kennedy-Johnson period witnessed the most important *rhetorical* shift in U.S. strategy during the Cold War: from massive retaliation to flexible response. The new strategy was supposed to enhance deterrence by providing the president with flexible nuclear options and increased conventional capabilities to deal with any number of military crises in Europe. But how seriously can we take this strategy when its key rhetorical supporters, most significantly President Kennedy and Secretary of Defense Robert McNamara, wanted to pull troops out of Western Europe to improve the U.S. balance of payments? In fact, Chapters 3, 4, and especially 6 will reveal that there were wide gaps between the *rhetorical* emphasis on a conventional strategy and the *operational* desire to reduce America's conventional commitment to NATO.[13]

## Bretton Woods Reconsidered
*An Ineffective and Crisis-Prone Monetary System*

It has long been an article of faith that the Bretton Woods regime was the most effective, stable international monetary system in modern history. In actuality, the conventional wisdom concerning the Bretton Woods period is deeply flawed, a point that emerges throughout this study. The Bretton Woods agreements did not create financial stability, economic interdependence, and international cooperation, as is often claimed. Instead, monetary relations in the postwar world were marked by crisis and chaos, intrusive capital controls, and nonconvertibility. Domestic interests and grand strategic considerations, not supranational institutions and enlightened rules as is often claimed, guided monetary relations.

This made global monetary relations highly politicized—far more so than they are today—and, more often than not, antagonistic. Speculators enjoyed enormous potential benefits with little risk and could, in a matter of weeks, bring the system to its knees.

### Vulnerability, Not Hegemony

Even if the Bretton Woods system was often unstable and inefficient, wasn't the system designed to benefit the United States by forcing the rest of the world to finance its overseas empire by holding dollars? This is certainly the conventional wisdom. The Bretton Woods system was "a prerequisite for continued American global hegemony."[14] "America's allies acquiesced in a hegemonic system that accorded the United States special privileges to act abroad unilaterally to promote U.S. interests."[15]

The real story is rather different. American policy makers had no great love for the Bretton Woods system. The United States ran a payments deficit; the Europeans (and, to a lesser extent, the Japanese) were in effect financing that deficit and were thus enabling the Americans to live beyond their means. But the Americans did not view this as a source of strength: the growing European dollar balances, which, under the rules of the system, could be cashed in for gold at any time, were a kind of sword of Damocles hanging over their heads. The U.S. government felt vulnerable, and it did not like it. Kennedy best expressed this vulnerability when he told his advisers that if the system was not reformed, the Europeans might come to the conclusion that "my God, this is the time . . . if everyone wants gold we're all going to be ruined because there is not enough gold to go around."[16] Many American policy makers were quite willing to sacrifice the advantages of Bretton Woods in order to end this vulnerability.

### U.S. Reform of Bretton Woods Considered

This points to another, previously unrecognized fact: the United States seriously considered abandoning the Bretton Woods system far earlier than previously acknowledged. This contradicts the long-held belief that "because it was interested in preserving the privileges it derived from the operation of the Bretton Woods regime," the United States would not "condone a structural reform" of the system that threatened "the continued preeminence of the dollar."[17]

The United States was, in fact, quite willing to sacrifice the so-called seigniorage privileges that the system bestowed on the dollar in order to end its vulnerability. Dramatic proposals to recast and reform the global payments system—which would have ended the dollar's privileged role—were seriously considered as early as 1962. Proposal followed proposal until July 1965, when the Johnson administration publicly committed itself to reform of the system. Eisenhower even suggested replacing gold with uranium as the reserve asset for the system. Most of the plans circulating both within and outside of the U.S. government went well beyond the Bretton Woods framework. When these proposals were not adopted, it had less to do with sacrificing the benefits of seigniorage and more to do with the fear of the unknown. Would structural changes bring chaos, disorder, and even depression? But after the March 1968 gold crisis and the failed November 1968 meeting to save the franc, it was pretty clear what little remained of the Bretton Woods system would not last for long.

### Richard Nixon's "Destruction" of Bretton Woods?

Most historians and political scientists identify Richard Nixon as "the destroyer of Bretton Woods."[18] And the closing of the gold window has been described as a shock, a sudden reversal of American monetary policy, all the more surprising as the Bretton Woods system was the economic cornerstone of America's imperial ambitions. But this study demonstrates that Bretton Woods was terminally ill by the time Nixon took office. In fact, it could be argued that the system began breaking down as soon as it came into being—after most Western Europeans adopted current-account convertibility for their currencies at the end of 1958. The system lurched from crisis to crisis, and there was not one year between 1958 and 1971 when the dollar and gold problem was not the most pressing issue of American foreign economic policy.

Furthermore, the dollar and gold problem was a serious predicament well before either the Great Society programs or the U.S. escalation in Vietnam. During 1965–66, and even 1970, the dollar and gold problem was far less pressing than in 1960 or 1963. While the costs of Vietnam certainly worsened the U.S. balance of payments, most American policy makers identified the $3 billion spent in Western Europe to meet NATO commitments as the real culprit.

### A Different Cold War
#### A Multipolar Struggle between Adversaries and Allies

The key geopolitical event during the period covered in this book was the Cold War rivalry with the Soviet Union. Yet remarkably, Western relations with the Soviet Union played an almost secondary role in the gold story. The conflicts over gold, monetary reform, and even conventional troop levels turned more on the intra-alliance conflicts within NATO than the bipolar conflict with the Russians.

For example, the Americans could, and often did, threaten to bring their troops home if the Germans did not tow the American line on any number of issues. This threat to bring the troops home, which the balance-of-payments deficit made real, helped pressure the Germans into a number of positions they would otherwise have avoided—for example, forgoing their independent nuclear force, distancing themselves from de Gaulle, and agreeing to pay offset costs and hold dollars instead of gold. On the other hand, the Federal Republic of Germany could signal its displeasure with America's European agenda or its arms control policies by reducing offset payments or hinting that surplus dollars could be turned in for gold. Balance-of-payments issues were often the field where larger political differences between the United States and Great Britain, France, and especially West Germany were played out. These relations were far more acrimonious than most accounts of the period reveal.

*Geopolitics Trumping Economics . . . but Not for the Reasons You Think*

Throughout this period, there is a repeated U.S. pattern of sacrificing economic for geopolitical interests. This surfaces most clearly when American policy makers, despite great pressure and desire, failed to make large-scale troop reductions from NATO. After the Cuban Missile Crisis, few top American policy makers worried that the Soviets would attack Western Europe. And despite their *public* statements, few top policy makers believed that increased U.S. conventional forces were critical to defense and deterrence in Europe. But the troops remained, despite their balance-of-payments cost, because of their stabilizing influence on the explosive set of issues surrounding the German and nuclear questions. This dynamic— American policy makers calculating they could not pull troops out of Europe to ease dollar and gold problems, not because of the Soviet threat but because of the German problem—calls into question the traditional neorealist interpretation of a Cold War struggle in Europe dominated solely by the bipolar struggle between the Soviets and Americans. It also challenges interpretations of the Cold War that focus solely on American economic interests.

*America's Ambivalence toward Economic and Political Empire*

America's Cold War foreign policy has often been described as imperialistic and hegemonic. At its most extreme, this interpretation explains America's postwar encounter with the world as a relentless search for markets, resources, and political domination. More benign versions of this interpretation portray America's Cold War empire as informal, cre ated by invitation.[19] Europe, because of its history, wealth, and strategic importance, has been identified as the focus of American empire. There has been much debate over whether America's dominance was a good or bad thing for the world. But few have contested the notion that the United States enthusiastically created, maintained, and dominated transnational political and economic institutions or regimes in order to maintain its hegemony on the European continent.

The two most visible manifestations of the American Cold War empire in Western Europe were, on the economic side, the Bretton Woods monetary order and, on the political side, the NATO alliance. According to political scientist Robert Gilpin, the United States maintained hegemonic power "based on the role of the dollar in the international monetary system and on the extension of its nuclear deterrent to include its allies."[20] But, as we will see, many American policy makers felt burdened by both the Bretton Woods system and their large NATO commitments and wanted to curtail, if not end, both. Clearly, there was great ambivalence to both the economic and strategic legs of America's so-called empire.

## The "Lessons" of the Past

Were the dark fears of the Eisenhower, Kennedy, and Johnson administrations about the balance-of-payments deficit justified? As detailed in Chapter 1 and Appendix A, their macroeconomic worries were probably exaggerated. And while the post-1971 flexible exchange rate regime has often been turbulent, it did not bring the disaster and depression many policy makers had feared. International capital flows, which have fueled growth throughout the world, have risen exponentially since the end of Bretton Woods. Although the world has seen a fair share of global monetary chaos, the feared nightmares of trade wars, "beggar thy neighbor policies," and international deflation never materialized. And flexible exchange rates have largely solved the two structural problems that worried American policy makers most during the 1960s—adjustment and liquidity.

It is important to remember, however, what caused these fears among top U.S. policy makers during the 1950s and 1960s. Most Cold War statesmen, whether Democrat or Republican, came of age during the Depression. The events that had turned a deep recession into a global disaster— the collapse of the Creditanstalt bank in Austria, sterling going off gold in 1931, the failure of the 1933 London Economic Conference, the devaluation of the dollar—were seared into the collective consciousness of most policy makers. To most, it was a simple equation—monetary chaos and devaluations unleashed beggar-thy-neighbor policies and economic nationalism; economic nationalism produced dictatorships; and dictators unleashed world war.

Diplomatic historians have demonstrated the enormous power that historical interpretations of the origins of the First and Second World War had during the Cold War. The Sarajevo and Munich analogies provided policy makers and scholars with simple but influential analytical tools to make sense of the military and political competition between the East and West. The Great Depression analogy offered an equally powerful framework to understand international economic relations in the postwar period. Decades of scholarship have revealed that the Sarajevo and Munich analogies provided vastly oversimplified and misleading accounts of the origins of the First and Second World War. The Great Depression analogy used by most postwar policy makers was equally simplified and perhaps even more misleading than the Sarajevo and Munich analogies. But the lessons that postwar policy makers took from America's foreign economic policy during the 1930s, whether correctly understood or not, had an enormous influence on how the balance-of-payments deficit and gold outflow problems were understood and attacked. This study underscores how these generational lessons influence policy debates.

## Outline of the Book

This study focuses on the intersection of monetary and security issues in America's relations with Europe between 1958 and 1971. Fundamental political and military issues surrounding the difficult struggle with the Soviet Union, the health of the Atlantic alliance, and the dilemmas created by the German question dominated American relations with Europe during this period. Of course, these events commanded the foreign policy attention of all four administrations, and these topics were often the backdrop for discussions and debates over the U.S. balance of payments and concerns about the outflow of gold. In other words, monetary issues were not discussed in a vacuum but were inextricably linked to the larger political and security issues of the time. This rule worked in reverse as well. Concerns about monetary relations often affected larger issues of grand strategy and policy toward Europe. The balance-of-payments and gold issues must be understood within their larger political and strategic context.

The first chapter of this study examines the economic issues behind the American balance of payments and the outflow of gold. After discussing the origins and actual workings of the Bretton Woods agreements, the chapter describes postwar international monetary relations in a way that varies significantly from the conventional wisdom. The second chapter concentrates on American concerns over the balance of payments during the last years of the Eisenhower presidency. The balance-of-payments deficit became a major concern at almost the exact same time that Khrushchev began pressuring Berlin, and the outbreak of the 1960 gold crisis took place at a time of extreme East-West and interallied tension. The dollar and gold crisis took Eisenhower completely by surprise, and the administration's reaction often ranged from befuddlement to outright panic. In addition, the military and strategic environment of the alliance was going through changes, both evolutionary and sudden, that had important ramifications for the U.S. balance of payments. The third chapter, which highlights the first two years of the Kennedy administration, focuses on how the new administration dealt with these strategic and political pressures and also reveals the debate over how to tackle the dollar and gold problem. The argument between those in the administration who wanted a dramatic reform of the international payments system and those who preferred a slower, more cautious strategy is revealed for the first time. The fourth chapter confronts the monetary issues behind the near Franco-German revolt in 1963 against American policy in the wake of the Cuban Missile and Berlin crises, the multilateral force (MLF) proposal, and the Skybolt affair.

The fifth through eighth chapters of the study focus on the period 1964–71, a time when East-West anxieties lessened considerably but intra-alliance tensions, particularly between the United States and Western Europe, increased significantly. The fifth chapter chronicles the balance-of-payments strategy of the Johnson administration between 1964 and 1966, highlighting its efforts to reform international monetary relations by replacing the dollar with special drawing rights as the world's reserve currency. The sixth chapter demonstrates how the linkage between security and money strained the U.S.–West German relationship during the mid-1960s. This strain threatened key military and political arrangements that had stabilized Central Europe and provoked the worst crisis between the United States and the Federal Republic of Germany during the Cold War. The trilateral negotiations, which explicitly linked dollar and gold concerns to troop levels and had the explosive question of the Nuclear Non-Proliferation Treaty (NPT) as a backdrop, are examined in detail. The seventh chapter describes the collapse of the Bretton Woods system, beginning with the sterling devaluation in November 1967 and ending with the separation of the private and intragovernmental gold markets in March 1968. The final chapter looks at Nixon's decision to end dollar-gold convertibility formally in 1971.

*Chapter One*

# Bretton Woods and Postwar International Monetary Relations

The Bretton Woods Agreement of 1944 was the most ambitious and far-reaching monetary arrangement between sovereign states in history. British and American financial officials, led by John Maynard Keynes and Harry Dexter White, hoped to set up a system that would maintain stable, fixed exchange rates; allow national currencies to be converted into an asset over which they had no issuing control (gold); and provide an effective mechanism to adjust exchange rates in the event that a fundamental balance-of-payments disequilibrium emerged. When "nonfundamental" deficits emerged, the deficit country would pay with a reserve asset (gold or a key currency convertible into gold), or seek short-term financing from the International Monetary Fund (IMF), which would supply the currency needed.[1]

This system differed greatly from a traditional gold standard, where the domestic money supply—and hence the domestic price level—was directly determined by the national gold stock. Under the gold standard, a balance-of-payments deficit would be paid for through the export of gold, resulting in a decrease in the domestic money base and a deflation of prices. The decreased purchasing power would lower that country's imports, and the increased international demand for that country's lower-priced goods would increase exports, automatically correcting the payments deficit. Conversely, an influx of gold would increase the domestic monetary base and domestic prices, boost imports, and discourage exports, thereby eliminating a payments surplus. According to standard market theory, any balance-of-payments disequilibrium would be adjusted more or less automatically, eliminating the need for government interference. In reality, this system worked as well as it did because capital flows from London—and, to a lesser extent, Paris—kept the system functioning smoothly.[2]

White and especially Keynes believed that the interwar experience had demonstrated that an adjustment process that relied on deflating the economy of a deficit country was draconian in an age when national governments promised full employment and a wide array of social spending. Decreasing the monetary base in a deficit country would lead to a fall in national income, unleashing unemployment and necessitating large cuts in government spending. To avoid such a politically unacceptable system, the Bretton Woods regime allowed nations to import and export gold without penalty. Deficits would be corrected through IMF assistance and small, IMF-approved changes in the exchange rate. While the Bretton Woods agreement was hailed as the hallmark of international cooperation, it provided national economic and political authorities a large measure of immunity from the international pressures of the market. National governments were quick to sacrifice measures that would bring about payments equilibrium in order to achieve important domestic goals.

Because it was generally believed that the existing gold stock was too small to sustain the growing demand for international liquidity, the Bretton Woods agreements established a two-tiered system in which certain key currencies—those convertible into gold, such as the dollar and eventually sterling—could be used in lieu of gold to settle international transactions. It was believed that this would conserve the use of gold and dramatically increase the amount of liquidity available to finance international transactions. This meant that international liquidity requirements would be supplied by the balance-of-payments deficits of the key currency economies. Keynes recognized that Great Britain would face postwar deficits, and he wanted a system that did not penalize sterling. Ironically, he also feared American surpluses and wanted to guarantee that the United States fulfilled international liquidity needs.

But it was unclear how large these deficits had to be to fulfill international reserve needs. If the key currency economies had no deficit, or too small a deficit, then the world would have to rely on gold alone to finance trade. Without key currency deficits, liquidity would dry up and international transactions disappear. But if the key currency country ran payments deficits that were too large, the resulting inflation would test the value of the key currency and set off a large-scale conversion of the currency into gold. This would remove valuable liquidity from the system and set off a fierce competition for gold, with deflationary effects on the international economy. Capital controls, trade restrictions, and currency blocs might ensue. This made the meaning of British and, to a greater extent, American balance-of-payments deficits somewhat ambiguous. The system was designed to make deficits necessary, but it was never clear how large or how small a deficit was needed to supply liquidity without undermining confidence in the value of the dollar. This ambiguity—were U.S deficits dangerously high?—was to haunt the system throughout the late 1950s and 1960s.

What were the larger motives of the founders of the plan? It has often been noted how remarkable it was that Keynes and White, despite the

Delegates gathered from around the world at a small resort in New Hampshire to build a new international economic order from the ruins of war. What emerged from the Bretton Woods conference were two new institutions— the International Monetary Fund and the International Bank for Reconstruction and Development. (Courtesy of the IMF)

vastly different economic priorities of the countries they represented, were able to come up with such an extraordinary compromise.[3] Indeed, Keynes's original plan envisioned a "currency union" in which countries would have to pay a penalty on their surplus payment balances. Additionally, debtor nations would have unrestricted and virtually unlimited access to the resources of the clearing fund without having to seek international approval or make domestic adjustments to correct payments disequilibrium.[4]

This system has often been portrayed as an attempt to move away from the vicious economic competition of the late nineteenth and early twentieth centuries. White and Keynes were driven, it has often been suggested, "by a humanitarian desire to prevent the kind of financial stresses and economic dislocations that might lead to future wars." A noted policy analyst summed up the conventional wisdom: "In short, Keynes and White were convinced that international economic cooperation would provide a new foundation of hope for a world all too prone to violence. 'If we can continue,' Keynes observed, 'this nightmare will be over. The brotherhood of man will have become more than a phrase.'"[5]

Keynes's motives may have been less benign. Not only would his blue-print protect Great Britain's planned full-employment policies from balance-of-payments pressures, but it would also present a convenient and politically painless way to get money out of the United States in the guise of international reform:

> It would also be a mistake to invite of our own motion, direct financial assistance after the war from the United States to our-selves. Whether as a gift or a loan without interest or a gratuitous redistribution of gold reserves. The U.S. will consider that we have had our whack in the shape of lend-lease and a generous settle-ment of consideration. . . . We in particular, in a distressed & ruined continent, will not bear the guise of the most suitable claimant for a dole. . . . On the contrary. If we are to attract the interest and enthusiasm of the Americans, *we must come with an ambitious plan of an international complexion, suitable to serve the interests of others sides ourselves.* . . . It is not with our problems of ways and means that idealistic and internationally minded Ameri-cans will be particularly concerned.[6]

White rejected Keynes's currency union plan as too radical, but the British came up with a substitute in the scarce-currency clause, which permitted extensive capital controls and trade discrimination against ma-jor surplus countries. Roy F. Harrod, a British Treasury official and Keynes protégé, even suggested that the scarce currency not be discussed in pub-lic, for fear that the U.S. Congress might figure out its true implications: "[I]n view of the need for 'good handling' the less public lucidity there is on this matter the better." Keynes agreed, arguing that "the monetary fund, in particular, has the great advantage that to the average Congress-man it is extremely boring."[7] Regardless, there was a heated debate in Congress over the scarce-currency clause.[8] While the clause was included in the agreement, the Americans interpreted it very narrowly, a fact that created much bitterness in Britain. In later years, the British blamed many of their economic woes on the narrow interpretation of Article VII by the Americans:

> In particular, United States policy in the Fund has been directed . . . to making the "scarce currency" clause a dead letter. We thought originally that this clause might give some real protection against a dollar shortage; indeed, Lord Keynes' conviction that this was so was one of the main factors which led His Majesty's Government and Parliament to accept the Loan Agreement. Once the clause

comes into operation, it gives wide freedom for discriminatory exchange and trade controls against the scarce currency; and then there is real pressure on the country concerned to play its full part in putting the scarcity right, e.g. by drastic action such as we want the United States to take to stimulate imports.[9]

In the end, the British had little to complain about. By the late 1940s, America's political goal of promoting European reconstruction and eventual integration led the United States to permit extensive dollar discrimination while furnishing billions of dollars of aid. Furthermore, to the surprise of many, the United States ran consistently large balance-of-payments deficits throughout the postwar period. The problem was not, as Keynes and White had feared, too little liquidity. The opposite was the case. By 1958 there was a growing sense that the flood of postwar dollars had become too large, and that measures had to be taken to choke off the persistent American payments deficit.

### The Flaws of the Bretton Woods Plan

In its final form, the Bretton Woods Agreement was unworkable because it lacked a mechanism to adjust persistent payments imbalances between countries. Exchange rate stability could only be maintained by providing ever increasing amounts of liquidity, a process that created enormous political difficulties and ultimately undermined confidence in the system.

Why were the fixed exchange rates unstable? The plan, unlike a pure gold standard, affirmed the primacy of domestic economic goals, which included the maintenance of full employment economies, over strict balance-of-payments concerns. But exchange rate stability can only be sustained when there is comparable price stability between countries—a near impossibility. If prices change markedly because of inflation or deflation in a given domestic economy, then currency exchange rates must shift accordingly or else their initial par rates will quickly be rendered meaningless. When exchange rates are not changed to reflect price changes, disequilibriums in the balance of payments quickly emerge. Such a situation would be especially problematic if the initial par values were already out of line, which was often the case under Bretton Woods, because nations were given wide discretion to establish their own rates.

The ensuing balance-of-payments disequilibriums were a constant source of monetary instability. For example, if Great Britain's inflation rate was 6 percent, and the United States pursued policies that resulted in 4 percent inflation, then the exchange rate would have to be adjusted to avoid a payments disequilibrium. But this obviously contradicted the goal of exchange rate stability, and without market-determined rates there was no easy mechanism to adjust the exchange rate without creating havoc. Deflating the domestic economy to bring the balance of payments into balance was not politically realistic. Furthermore, the system actually rewarded speculators, who knew the direction of any revaluation and could simply put pressure on a vulnerable currency until a nation exhausted its reserves or its will to defend the old exchange rate. Speculators made a fortune during the devaluation of sterling in 1949 and 1967. The only option to avoid damaging devaluations involved capital and trade controls. Every major country, including the United States, had to install capital controls in one form or another during the Bretton Woods era in order to maintain its exchange rate.

A second flaw, less well recognized but equally serious, was the method of providing liquidity in the Bretton Woods system. Liquidity is simply another word used to describe reserve assets that are transferred from debtor to surplus countries to cover their payments gap. In order to offset a negative payments balance and maintain a fixed exchange rate, governments had to supply some universally accepted asset over which they had no issuing control. Until 1914 this asset was, at least in theory, gold. Because the Bretton Woods planners believed that there was not enough gold to supply world liquidity (reserve) needs, key currencies such as the dollar and sterling would be used to supplement or replace gold to settle international transactions. As this study reveals, however, the liquidity issue has been largely misunderstood.

The failure to make sterling fully convertible in 1947 meant that the dollar alone served the reserve-asset, or liquidity, function. This meant that the dollar was demanded by foreign nations both as a reserve asset and to finance much of the world's trade. These factors, in conjunction with the economic recovery of Europe, helped produce a sizable deficit in the American balance of payments. But it was not like the payments deficit of any other nation. Some of these excess dollars were actually desired by the rest of the world, not to purchase American goods and services but for reserve and international settlement purposes. In other words, some of the deficit might not have been a deficit at all, as those excess dollars were sought after, at least for a time, by central banks and entities involved in financing trade. This fact has not been widely recognized in the nontechnical literature. But it is a key element behind the political and economic ambiguity of the American balance-of-payments deficit during the postwar years.

The dollar's unique role in world trade and reserve creation meant that to a certain degree a deficit in the American balance of payments was desirable and even necessary for the international economy. But how much of a payments deficit was needed to supply global liquidity was difficult, if not impossible, to determine. Initially, most foreign central banks preferred to hold dollars because they earned interest and had lower transaction costs than gold. But as American dollar liabilities—created by the yearly payments deficits—increased, confidence in the gold convertibility of the dollar fell. After convertibility was established by the major economies of Western Europe, central banks began to buy increasing amounts of gold from the United States with their excess dollars.

This brought up a larger question: how stable and cooperative could a system be that only worked if the world's largest economy ran persistent deficits in its balance of payments? Much has been made of the advantages and disadvantages this system conferred on the American economy. When foreign central banks held dollars for reserve and transaction purposes, it enabled American consumers to receive foreign goods and services without having to give anything other than a promise to pay in return. It was like automatic credit or, if the reserves built up indefinitely, like getting something for almost nothing. This arrangement, which is the benefit of seigniorage, could be maintained as long as the dollar was "as good as gold," or when holding dollars in the form of short-term interest-bearing securities was probably preferable to buying gold. The danger emerged when overseas holders of dollars worried that the dollar was not as good as gold or, for noneconomic reasons, preferred holding gold to dollars.

## The Dilemmas of the Dollar as a Reserve Currency

Under the Bretton Woods system, overseas central bankers could turn in their excess dollars for gold at any time. But at some point, the ratio of dollar liabilities to American-held gold would increase to a level that might cause a loss of foreign confidence in the dollar and a run to the U.S. Treasury gold window. American policy makers saw this as a threat to the economic well-being and foreign policy of the United States. After 1958 U.S. officials often felt they had to sacrifice important domestic policy goals and strategic imperatives in order to maintain the dollar's value. What really angered these policy makers was their belief that much of the deficit was caused by U.S. expenditures overseas made to defend Europe and Asia from the Soviet Union. Many foreign central bankers worried that the loss of American gold could bring down the international monetary system and wreck the world economy. A worldwide preference for gold over dollars would decrease the amount of liquidity, or reserve assets, needed to finance and balance ever expanding world trade. A mass conversion to gold would force the United States to suspend convertibility, which would wipe out the dollar's value as a reserve and transaction currency. It was feared that competition between central banks for scarce gold could subject the international economy to paralyzing deflation. These officials believed that the resulting collapse of liquidity could freeze world trade and investment, restoring the disastrous conditions that paralyzed the world during the 1930s, creating depression and world war.[10]

What is especially interesting from a political standpoint is the fact that the United States could be pressured for political reasons by the countries within the system. Although the United States accrued benefits from the system, its pledge to covert dollars into gold made it vulnerable in ways other countries were not, especially as the ratio of gold to dollars decreased over time. To some extent, Great Britain ran a similar gold exchange standard before 1914 with very low gold-to-sterling ratio, but international monetary relations were far less politicized before World War I. If France held a large supply of dollars as reserves and wanted to express dissatisfaction with some aspect of American foreign or economic policy, it could convert those dollars into gold. Converting dollars into gold gave surplus countries an important source of political power.

The system trapped reserve countries in another way. If a nonreserve country ran a persistent deficit in its balance of payments, it could devalue its currency to improve the terms of trade of its exports. Because the dollar was priced in terms of gold, if it was devalued, other countries could simply shift the value of their currencies so that no real devaluation could take place. The only true devaluation option that the United States had was to suspend the convertibility of the dollar into gold. The rest of the world would be left with a choice. Overseas central bankers could use their own reserves to maintain the previous exchange rate with the dollar. Or, they could float their currencies and allow the foreign exchange markets to determine their correct value. For various reasons, this was an option few American policy makers wanted to consider during the 1950s and 1960s. For their part, most European surplus countries dreaded either option.

Why was there such a fear—both in the United States and abroad—of abandoning fixed exchange rates and moving to a market-determined, free-floating exchange rate regime? It is hard to underestimate the powerful influence of the received wisdom concerning the history of monetary relations between the wars. In the postwar period, it was a widely held belief that the economic collapse of the 1930s was caused by the lack of international monetary cooperation. In the minds of most postwar economists and policy makers, capital flight, caused by free-market speculation, had ruined the gold exchange standard, which in turn destroyed international liquidity and froze international trade and financial transactions. The collapse of the rules of the game unleashed a vicious competition, whereby countries pursued beggar-thy-neighbor policies of competitive devaluations and trade restrictions. To most, the culprit behind the international economic collapse was a free market out of control, fueled by pernicious speculators who had no concern for the large effects of their greed-driven actions. According to this conventional wisdom, the economic collapse had severe political consequences: autarky, dictatorships, and eventually war. For many postwar policy makers, a market-driven international monetary system was no longer compatible with stability and international cooperation. Any situation that remotely looked like a repeat of the 1930s was to be avoided at all costs. Bretton Woods–era planners and policy makers fervently believed that in the postwar world the market had to be tamed and national interest replaced with international cooperation that would be fostered by enlightened rules and institutions. Strangely, few seemed to understand how chaotic and inefficient the Bretton Woods system eventually became. Massive American aid, trade and exchange controls, and constant intervention obscured the system's failings. This understanding of the recent past that produced the Bretton Woods blueprint, though flawed, had a profound impact on the postwar planners in most Western countries (including the United States) and thrived well into the 1970s.[11]

Ironically, the Bretton Woods system fostered an image of Western unity and cooperation. The Bretton Woods monetary system could not function without constant government intervention and transnational collaboration. Between 1958 and 1968, when the Bretton Woods system was supposedly at its height, a whole series of agreements, regimes, rules, and institutions were needed to ensure the system worked. These arrangements and institutions included swap agreements, the gold pool, the General Agreement to Borrow, the special drawing rights (SDRs), and Working Party Three, to name the most important. The IMF, nearly moribund since its creation, was brought to life in the 1960s to help the system function. Each of these new organizations or arrangements was created out of necessity; without them, the whole monetary system might have collapsed. Ironically, these institutions and regimes made it appear as if the West was unified and cooperative. In fact, the system guaranteed that Western Europe (and Japan) had a stake in what the United States did, and vice versa, because the reserve currency at the heart of the system was the dollar, a dollar whose convertibility into gold at a fixed price was considered fundamental to the prosperity of the Western economies.

Why did policy makers in America and Western Europe work so hard to prop up a faltering monetary regime? More than anything else, they were afraid of the unknown. Although the system was inefficient and prone to crisis, monetary relations, no matter how strained, were far better than during the interwar period. Furthermore, Western monetary relations were interwoven into a complex fabric that included key political and military relationships. No one knew what would happen to this fabric if the Bretton Woods system collapsed, and few were anxious to find out.

## Bretton Woods and the "Adjustment" Process

Before looking at the politics of international monetary relations between 1958 and 1971, we must define our terms. Most important, what do we mean when we use the term "the balance of payments"? The balance of payments is simply a summary statement of all the economic transactions between the residents of one country and the rest of the world during some specified period of time. While this definition appears to be clear-cut, it seems to exclude the possibility that over an extended period of time a country can run a deficit in its balance of payments. Similar to the practice of double-entry bookkeeping, most balance-of-payments theories state that all accounts must eventually achieve equilibrium, with total debits equaling total credits. In principle, a country cannot run a payments deficit with the rest of the world for an indefinite period of time. Yet we know that the United States ran a payments deficit during all but one year between 1950 and 1968. How was that possible? In order to understand this mystery, we must explore how a nation's deficit or surplus can be eliminated.

In order to preserve or restore a balance in international payments, imbalances between a country and the rest of the world must be brought into equilibrium through an *adjustment* process. The adjustment process can take many different forms, depending on the rules of the international monetary system. There are two monetary systems where the adjustment mechanism is automatic, at least in theory: a gold standard and a system of freely floating exchange rates. The nineteenth-century gold standard eliminated payments deficits and surpluses automatically through changes in a country's aggregate demand brought about by importing or exporting gold. The present system of free exchange rates eliminates prospective payments imbalances through market-driven shifts in exchange rates. In both systems, payments imbalances are brought into equilibrium through processes that are largely automatic and independent of any governmental interference. The adjustment process in gold standard and free exchange rate regimes tends to be less politicized.

But this is not how payments imbalances were adjusted in the Bretton Woods system. A crippling flaw of the Bretton Woods plan was its lack of an effective adjustment procedure. Domestic economies were protected from demand fluctuations produced by gold or other reserve movements, and the system of fixed exchange rates prevented the market from determining the equilibrium price for a nation's currency. Because there were inevitably great differences between national monetary policies, some method was needed to adjust for the changes in the relative value of currencies produced by differential rates of inflation and savings. But exchange rate variations were difficult, because they unsettled foreign exchange markets and it was impossible to get countries to agree to shifts because they feared the adverse effects on their terms of trade. Quite understandably, countries were equally reluctant to sacrifice full employment and social policy goals to benefit their balance of payments. This left no effective means to close balance-of-payments gaps automatically. As the economist Robert Stern has stated, "[S]ince the functioning of the pegged-rate system may appear to avoid rather than expedite adjustment, it might be more fitting to characterize this system . . . as the 'international disequilibrium system.'"[12]

## The Bretton Woods System and the Liquidity Problem

The liquidity issue was a much discussed issue throughout the 1960s. Liquidity, which was merely a euphemism for reserves, was the vehicle for financing balance-of-payments deficits in the Bretton Woods system. The greater and more persistent the imbalances, the more reserves, or "liquidity," were needed to make the system work. Government leaders, unwilling to adjust exchange rates or alter domestic priorities to improve their country's balance of payments, clamored for more liquidity to finance payments deficits. But it was rarely pointed out that this liquidity would be unnecessary if there was an efficient, effective, and automatic process for adjusting imbalances. As a noted economist had pointed out:

> A final point of criticism worth mentioning is that the need for international monetary reserves is greatly increased under the pegged-rate system in comparison to other systems because of the lack of an efficient balance of payments mechanism. That is, the longer the period during which balance of payments deficits are financed without adjustment occurring, the greater will be the reserves required. It will be necessary furthermore to establish

institutions, both national and international, to carry out the
international financial policies involving the provision and use
of international reserves for balance of payments purposes.[13]

During the 1950s and 1960s, when both policy makers and academics
recognized that the international monetary system was flawed, proposals
for reform emphasized the need for more liquidity instead of changes in
the adjustment mechanism. Suggestions ranged from increasing the resources of the IMF to inventing a whole new form of liquidity, called
special drawing rights, or SDRs. In 1958, the major Western European
nations eased capital controls and allowed for convertibility of their currencies into dollars. Trade and capital flows increased dramatically. This
made liquidity a more important issue than before. Larger trade and capital flows increased the payments imbalances that inevitably arose in a
fixed exchange rate regime. More reserve assets were needed by central
bank authorities to defend their exchange rate. As the 1960s went on, the
problem worsened as currency markets increased in size and complexity.
Western countries managed, but never solved, these balance-of-payments
difficulties through capital controls, trade restrictions, and agreements
and institutional arrangements such as the General Agreement to Borrow,
currency "swap" arrangements, and the gold pool.

## A Rough Start for Bretton Woods

These flaws meant that the Bretton Woods blueprint for exchange rate
stability, hard convertibility, and international cooperation through the
International Monetary Fund would prove untenable from the start.
Great Britain attempted to make sterling convertible into gold and dollars,
as stipulated by the Bretton Woods agreement. By the summer of 1947, the
attempt proved a dismal failure, despite an enormous stabilization loan
given by the United States after the cessation of Lend-Lease. There was an
immediate run on the pound, and within months, Britain ran down the
proceeds of the loan.[14] Sterling convertibility was suspended, and no
other major currency would attempt anything approaching full convertibility until the end of 1958. Sterling's collapse exposed the weaknesses of
Bretton Woods, and convinced American policy makers to provide direct
aid to Great Britain and Western Europe through the Marshall Plan.[15] It
also persuaded the Americans to accept widespread trade discrimination
and monetary controls aimed at the dollar and dollar goods, in clear
violation of the terms and spirit of Bretton Woods. Some monetary restrictions were lifted in 1958, but much of the trade discrimination against
American goods continued long after convertibility was achieved.

Keynes and White at Bretton Woods Conference, 1944. Keynes and White were hailed for negotiating the Bretton Woods agreements to stabilize and rebuild the postwar international economy, but their global monetary arrangements were soon tested and found wanting. (Courtesy of the IMF)

The pretense of exchange rate stability was abandoned in 1949, when Great Britain undertook a massive devaluation of sterling in order to make its exports more competitive and to write down wartime debts. Great Britain did not seek the approval of the IMF or any of its major non-Commonwealth trading partners except for the United States. The 1949 devaluation outraged the political and economic leaders of Western Europe, and threatened to undo the tentative movement toward European economic integration. The lesson learned by other nations was that there was no international punishment for a unilateral devaluation if national interests warranted it. If one of the countries that designed the Bretton Woods system flouted its rules, how could other nations be expected to tow the line?

The International Monetary Fund, which was supposed to be both the source of liquidity for temporary payments imbalances and the enforcer of Keynes's and White's international monetary rules, was almost entirely excluded from the decision. In actuality, the IMF was emasculated in the 1940s and 1950s, with little authority or voice in international economics. Desperately needed liquidity was supplied to the world by direct American aid, through programs like the Marshall Plan, Point Four, and the Military Assistance Program. In fact, signatories of the Marshall Plan were strictly forbidden from using the IMF to correct payments imbalances. The Marshall Plan actually created a monetary system for Western Europe—the European Payments Union (EPU)—which provided for extremely limited intra-European convertibility and discrimination against dollar transactions. It was only much later that the IMF became a player in world monetary relations, when the United States used the IMF as a vehicle to make an enormous loan for Great Britain after the Suez crisis.

Disequilibrium characterized the postwar monetary system throughout the so-called Bretton Woods period. During the early postwar period, there were large payments imbalances between the devastated economies of Western Europe and the United States, made worse by the fact that currency par values were often established in an arbitrary manner. Once exchange rates were set, changes came in dramatic and disruptive devaluations whose direction was always known in advance. Deficits and monetary turbulence were managed through extensive trade and capital controls that discriminated largely against dollar goods. In order to fill the large payments gap, the United States provided enormous amounts of aid. The adjustment process during the postwar period was not automatic but had to be managed by governmental policy and controls. This made the Bretton Woods period different from the gold standard and the free exchange rate period in one important respect: because the adjustment process could only be accomplished by government intervention and policy, the system was highly politicized.

The often abrasive clash between economic and political interests in the postwar monetary system is one of the major themes of this study. But even accounting for the politicized nature of the adjustment mechanism, one still would have expected some rough measure of American payments equilibrium over time. Throughout most of the postwar period, and particularly during the period between 1958 and 1971, the United States continuously ran large payments deficits. How was it possible to run chronic payments deficits, year after year, when payments equilibrium should have been the rule? A detailed answer to this complicated and somewhat technical question can be found in Appendix A, where the balance-of-payments statistics for 1960, the year of the first gold crisis, and 1961, the first year of the Kennedy administration, are broken down into their component parts and analyzed. In effect, a part of the official U.S. payments deficit was not a real deficit at all, because overseas companies, individuals, and central banks often held dollars voluntarily, instead of using them to buy American goods and services. The dollar was a reserve currency, useful for the market interventions required by a fixed exchange rate system, and when they were held (and not spent) by overseas entities, they added to the U.S. balance-of-payments deficit.

This study makes clear, however, that not all of these deficit dollars were held voluntarily. The United States often exerted enormous pressure on countries with payments surpluses to hold their dollars and limit their purchases of American gold. Sometimes incentives were offered—medium-range bonds with attractive interest rates and guarantees against devaluation. In other cases, overt political pressure was used, as when the United States linked its continuing military presence to the Federal Republic of Germany's reserve management policies.

Whether these dollars were held voluntarily for their reserve and intervention functions or whether surplus countries such as West Germany and Japan were coerced into holding dollars instead of gold, it was clear that from a statistical point of view, the U.S. balance of payments would always have some level of deficit. But as deficit dollars piled up overseas in an amount that eventually exceeded the value of gold that the United States held, confidence in the promise to convert deficit dollars into gold at thirty-five dollars an ounce eroded. What would happen if those central banks holding dollars, voluntarily or not, decided they no longer wished to do so? Would the dollar fall and the international monetary system collapse? Would the United States be forced to ignominiously withdraw from overseas military commitments that increased its balance-of-payments deficit? As we shall see, these questions vexed U.S. policy makers for well over a decade and drove economic and political policies that had a fundamental effect on issues ranging from international monetary policy to military strategy in Europe.

*Chapter Two*

# The Costs of Commitment

## Eisenhower, Europe, and the American Balance-of-Payments Crisis

> The world balance of payments was rather like a game of poker; if one player held all the chips the game came to an end.
> —Prime Minister Harold Macmillan, 11 August 1960

In early October 1960 the president's special assistant Clarence Randall circulated a memorandum written by Karl Brandt of the Council of Economic Advisers concerning economic relations between the United States and Western Europe. The Eisenhower administration was struggling to stem the unremitting flow of gold that had been leaving the United States since late 1957. Subtle attempts by the administration to prod the surplus countries of Europe to correct the underlying payments imbalance had failed; in fact, there were fears that the gold drain would only worsen. According to Brandt, this situation could not be allowed to continue: "[I]t is obvious that in the coming years we will be in great straits to keep our balance of payments in such shape that we can maintain free convertibility of a hard dollar and stick to a liberal trade policy." The obstinacy of the European surplus countries was especially galling, given that the United States had "spent some $80 billion to get the Europeans on the road toward rising productivity, expansion, and hard freely convertible currencies." Brandt likened the situation to the failure of the 1933 London Conference, which led to competitive devaluations and onerous trade restrictions. He warned that unless the European surplus countries, particularly West Germany, were forced to undertake serious corrective measures, the economic nationalism and political instability of the 1930s would return. The consequences would be more than economic collapse: "If this should arise again, it would do its part to blow up NATO and start the march on the slippery downgrade in the Cold War."[1]

What was this financial emergency really about, and how had the American balance-of-payments deficit and gold drain emerged? And why did the Eisenhower administration fear that the gold crisis could cause the collapse of the Western Alliance and defeat in the Cold War? By any measure, the United States in 1960 possessed overwhelming economic strength, commanding a larger share of the world's wealth than any modern nation-state in history. America convincingly exhibited this wealth by dispensing billions of dollars in aid to its allies, while stationing hundreds of thousands of troops in foreign countries and providing a robust nuclear shield for its sprawling worldwide alliances. Yet as his administration ended, President Dwight D. Eisenhower feared that America's vast military and economic commitments had made the dollar and its gold guarantee vulnerable. "The budget and balance-of-payments problems could destroy the defenses of the U.S."[2]

It seemed logical to many in the Eisenhower administration to blame the payments imbalance and gold loss on America's overseas commitments, because the United States had a large current-account surplus throughout this period. Eisenhower and his top aides feared that if these commitments were not reduced or eliminated, the payments balance would continue to deteriorate and the gold outflow would worsen until the international monetary system was destroyed. The resulting economic collapse could fracture the NATO alliance and hand the Soviet Union a victory in the Cold War without a shot being fired.

If the Eisenhower administration, rightly or wrongly, identified American aid and military obligations as the source of the gold crisis, why weren't these commitments reduced or eliminated? This was certainly the advice of top administration economic officials, notably Secretary of the Treasury Robert Anderson. In a National Security Council meeting at the height of the gold crisis, Anderson put the situation in the bluntest terms. "We could not afford such aid and if we continued it, we would face the worst collapse you ever saw."[3] President Eisenhower was sympathetic to this view and had often commented that American aid and forward military deployment in Western Europe had originally been meant to be temporary. Eisenhower thought it galling that the countries with the largest payments surpluses, taking the largest share of gold from the U.S. Treasury, were the same European countries American troops were defending. The Europeans were "close to 'making a sucker out of Uncle Sam.'"[4]

Despite dire predictions of financial collapse, bringing home American troops stationed overseas proved difficult. Complex strategic considerations were actually pulling American policy makers in the opposite direction. Soviet pressure on the status of Berlin had convinced many analysts that the United States had to strengthen its commitment to a robust forward defense of Western Europe. This evolving strategy envisioned a move away from the concept of fast and massive American nuclear response in the event of global war. Instead, many administration planners hoped to provide NATO with a wider range of military options, including vigorous conventional responses. This strategy would require a substantial increase, rather than a decrease, in the number of American troops stationed overseas. If these troops were, as many in the Eisenhower administration believed, the primary cause of the payments imbalance and ensuing gold drain, then it was obvious that financial imperatives would clash with strategic considerations.

Surprisingly little scholarly attention has been given to the important implications of the balance-of-payments deficit on both the economic and strategic policies of the Eisenhower administration during its last two years.[5] Yet the payments imbalance and gold drain influenced American foreign policy at one of the most dangerous periods of the Cold War. The Eisenhower administration placed the utmost importance on finding a policy that would correct the imbalance, avoid the end of dollar convertibility, and prevent the breakdown of the world payments system. Large U.S. troop withdrawals from Europe would accomplish this goal. At the same time, the administration recognized that countering Soviet threats during the Berlin crisis would require military strength and Western political unity, which required no withdrawals and perhaps troop increases that would worsen the deficit. Eisenhower was trapped. The president believed that a failure to solve the payments crisis could have disastrous political consequences, including the end of an American military presence in Western Europe and capitulation to the Soviets over Berlin. But the same outcome could result from any payments-inspired troop pullback from NATO.

## From Confidence to Concern:
## The U.S. Balance-of-Payments Deficit in the Late 1950s

No one doubted the financial power of the United States during the first six years of the Eisenhower administration. Perhaps the most convincing display of America's international monetary strength came during the Suez crisis. Faced with the depletion of its gold and dollar reserves and the possibility of devaluation, the British were forced to turn to the United States for financial support. The Eisenhower administration explicitly linked any monetary bailout to a complete withdrawal of British forces from the Suez. Great Britain's capitulation was caused not by a defeat on the battlefield or a military threat from an adversary, but by a financial ultimatum from an ally:

> Mr. Humphrey has just got back and telephoned the Economic Minister. He again emphasized that any financial support was subject to agreement on the political front.

> In this respect he wanted to stress the point that an under-
> taking to evacuate all our and French troops by a definite date
> would almost certainly be the determining factor in the judg-
> ment of the President and State Department. He, Humphrey, did
> not think that some such phrase as "expeditiously" would meet
> the situation. . . .
>    Humphrey went on to say that if and when the green light was
> given we could look forward to massive support.[6]

The unique factors behind the weakness of sterling masked the problems of the American dollar and, in particular, the international monetary system. The United States had come to the relief of sterling before and
would do so again throughout the 1960s. Nonetheless, the Eisenhower
administration was convinced that international monetary worries were,
if not the unique province of the British, not something the United States
would ever have to worry about. This sense of American predominance
obscured notice of the increasingly large balance-of-payments deficits
and resulting loss of gold that the United States suffered throughout the
late 1950s.

The administration considered international monetary problems a
purely British concern as late as February 1958. Offering arguments that
would be used against them in later years, U.S. officials rejected British
claims that the international monetary system was in disrepair. According to U.S. secretary of the treasury Robert Anderson, Great Britain's problem "was how to increase its ability to earn." This could only be done with
prudent fiscal management that avoided inflation. Permanent Under-
secretary of the Treasury Sir Leslie Rowan replied that Britain's problems
were indicative of a worldwide liquidity crisis. Rowan blamed Britain's
deficit on the world's exclusive use of gold, dollars, and sterling to finance
trade. "Wider use of the German DM was necessary." A. W. Marget of the
Federal Reserve Board strongly disagreed, arguing that he "did not see any
overall liquidity problem, though there were of course problems for indi-
vidual countries, caused primarily by their own unwise internal policies."[7] Ominously for the Americans, Rowan pointed out that the United
States itself was in deficit and losing large amounts of gold, most of which
was ending up in the hands of West Germany. The meeting ended without any agreement about future monetary cooperation, and in fact, the
U.S. side did not believe that future meetings would be useful.

Official American opinion quietly shifted as the loss of gold worsened
throughout 1958. In October, the Treasury Department prepared a memorandum detailing the gold outflow with suggestions for possible courses

of action. While warning that the payments deficit could not be ignored, the memo was calm and suggested nothing more than tighter fiscal policy to avoid inflation. The memo firmly rejected radical solutions, such as increasing the dollar price of gold.[8] Treasury Secretary Robert Anderson reasserted his confidence in the health of the international monetary system in a short year-end memo to President Eisenhower.[9] The memo applauded Western Europe's actions making its currencies convertible for nonresidents. Anderson saw this as a hopeful sign that currency and trade discrimination against American goods would end soon, allowing American exports to increase.

Instead, European convertibility exacerbated the gold drain, as central banks increased the ratio of gold to dollars in their reserves throughout 1959. By March 1959 Secretary Anderson admitted that the gold drain was getting worse but still advised against radical solutions. Anderson believed that promoting confidence, in the form of a commitment to maintain the dollar price of gold and continued fiscal discipline, would suffice. But others were not so sure. Increasingly, certain administration officials believed that the root of the problem lay in the policies of Western Europe. According to the American representative on the IMF, European trade and exchange discrimination against dollar goods was worsening the U.S. balance-of-payments deficit.[10] If American goods were not allowed to compete in Europe's increasingly lucrative markets, the deficit would only worsen.

Others were less concerned about the present payments deficits than with the long-term buildup of dollar liabilities. Henry C. Wallich of the Council of Economic Advisers asserted that even if Americans improved their export position, an international monetary system based on a dollar with a gold guarantee would be vulnerable. "Our real problem, as I see it, is not any immediate threat to our gold reserves. The threat is the persistent build-up of short-term liabilities against an unchanging gold reserve." Wallich was the first adviser within the administration to suggest that the problem might lie within the structure of the world monetary system. "For the very long-run, this raises the question whether a world currency system based upon growing world dollar holdings, which in turn are based upon a static U.S. gold reserve, should not be buttressed by some other elements, such as a greatly strengthened IMF."[11]

Few others in the administration were interested in any far-reaching reforms.[12] During a 4 June 1959 National Security Council (NSC) meeting, Anderson cautioned that there had been "very significant change with respect to our balance of payments situation even since 1956." Focusing on the foreign exchange costs of U.S. military commitments abroad, the treasury secretary warned "that if the balance of payments disparity continues for any considerable number of years, we in the U.S. would be in for real trouble. We have bitten off rather more obligations than we can chew even in the opinion of some foreign experts."[13]

A State Department paper written in July 1959 and circulated among top administration officials in August painted an even bleaker picture. "Continued large balance-of-payments deficits such as we are presently incurring cannot be permitted to continue for much longer."[14] In 1958 the United States lost $3.4 billion in gold and liquid dollar assets, while Western Europe gained $3.7 billion. The paper suggested three remedies: first, increasing the current-account surplus, especially with Western Europe; second, reducing U.S. military expenditure in Western Europe; and, third, increasing the flow of long-term capital from Western Europe toward less developed Third World countries. The key to any solution was to avoid restrictive or discriminatory measures such as import quotas or capital restrictions: "As the postwar experience of Western Europe amply demonstrates, restrictive or discriminatory methods serve to suppress and conceal the symptoms of imbalance. They do not promote, and usually impede, sound adjustments in the balance of payments, which can only come about through the pressures of competitive market forces operating within a framework of sound fiscal and monetary policy."[15]

These remedies, however, were hardly realistic. The United States already had a large surplus on its current account that was bound to decrease as European productivity increased. This increase in productivity, combined with recent action making most Western European currencies convertible on current account, was likely to increase capital investment from the United States. This left only one feasible alternative: reducing America's expensive overseas commitments. Anderson warned that "we have reached the point where it is necessary to reexamine the kinds of things we are doing, including the problems we generate for ourselves. . . . Export increases as large as could reasonably be hoped for would still be insufficient to solve the problem."[16] The allies, according to Anderson, had to bear a much larger share of the military costs and the United States had to reexamine all of its military expenditures overseas. Without a concerted effort to prune these programs, the balance-of-payments deficit could not be reduced, and Anderson and others in the administration feared that the dollar would remain weak, gold would flow from the United States, and the stability of the international monetary system would be threatened.

Yet even as Anderson was suggesting a significant reduction in American troops abroad, other voices within the NATO alliance and the Eisenhower administration were considering policies that would have the opposite effect. The outlines of a new Western military strategy were beginning to emerge, which if adopted would maintain and perhaps significantly increase the same programs that Secretary Anderson believed were causing the payments deficit. This created a conflict between military priorities and financial imperatives that sparked an intense debate within the Eisenhower administration over the direction and cost of American strategy in Europe.

### The Tensions between Strategy and Finance

The deteriorating payments balance was not only a financial concern. The loss of gold influenced how the Eisenhower administration thought about American and NATO military policy. Dramatic changes in the military and political environment were forcing a painful reassessment of how the United States should defend its vital interests and at what cost. The strategic debate that ensued had a deeply unsettling effect on the alliance. Balance-of-payments considerations played an important role in this discussion. In order to explain how strategic concerns affected the balance of payments, and vice versa, a brief explanation of the geopolitical and military environment of the 1950s is required.

The most vital overseas interest of the United States during the 1950s was the defense of Western Europe and its vast economic resources. The proximity of the Soviet Union's overwhelming military power made this mission difficult. There was little chance that the United States and Western Europe could match Soviet conventional capability without bankrupting their economies, and President Eisenhower believed that it was foolish to try. Eisenhower believed that the days of large, conventional land wars of attrition were over. Any conflict with the Soviet Union would inevitably become nuclear. How likely was it that either side could refrain from using its most powerful weapon in a fight to the death?

The existence of nuclear weapons profoundly changed the political and military calculations that went into a decision to go to war. If a conflict would automatically become nuclear, there would be enormous incentive to strike hard and fast with atomic weapons in order to knock out the opponent's retaliatory capability. This meant that any conflict over vital interests with the Soviet Union could escalate quickly into general, or full-scale, nuclear war. This philosophy was embodied in the NATO military doctrine of the 1950s, which predelegated the authority to use nuclear weapons to military commanders in the battlefield and envisioned a rapid and massive nuclear escalation. In such a scenario, NATO would only need enough conventional capability to hold a Soviet offensive in check for a limited duration, until the United States could launch both tactical and strategic nuclear attacks from its atomic arsenal. Because this strategy deemphasized a conventional response, the United States thought it best to spend its military dollars on nuclear delivery capability.[17]

Eisenhower strongly believed that America's conventional-force commitment was a _temporary remedy_ to Western Europe's weakened state after the Second World War. The former supreme allied commander had tried since the beginning of his administration to find a way to "redeploy," or withdraw, American troops stationed in Western Europe. Maintaining troops in a foreign country was an enormous budgetary expense that, as the 1950s wore on, was seen as one of the primary causes for the worsening balance-of-payments deficit. Eisenhower believed a permanent American commitment would allow the Europeans to take the United States for granted and give them an excuse to lessen their own defense efforts. But any move to withdraw U.S. troops from Europe could gravely damage the alliance and arouse fears about the political status of Germany.

Concurrent with the payments crisis was a shift in the military environment between the Western alliance and the Eastern bloc. The whole NATO strategy was predicated upon the United States responding with its nuclear arsenal. But the credibility of this commitment would be tested when the Soviet Union developed a survivable second-strike force. By the late 1950s, it was seen as only a matter of time before the Soviets developed this ability. If the hard and fast nuclear strike envisioned by NATO strategy left the Soviet Union with enough retaliatory capability to devastate the United States with a second strike, would the United States hesitate before launching its weapons? In other words, would the United States trade New York City for Paris in a crisis with the Soviets? Policy makers in Europe and the United States were struggling to construct a new military and political strategy that would overcome this dilemma. Given the new military environment, most experts felt that NATO would have to augment its "shield" forces, meaning its battlefield capability, rather than increase its "sword," or nuclear deterrent forces. The goal was to provide NATO with a wide array of military options short of general nuclear war. But such a strategy would require an expensive buildup of ground troops, which would be difficult at a time when these forces were identified as a major cause of the American payments deficit and gold outflow.

This dilemma emerged during a meeting between Eisenhower and the Supreme Allied Commander, Europe (SACEUR), Lieutenant General Lauris Norstad. The president said he was "very anxious to find ways of

carrying on our overseas activities without draining our own gold reserves." Eisenhower felt that "there is a strong reason for the United States
to start pulling some of its forces out of Europe. We went there in 1951 to
cover the period until the Europeans could form forces of their own. . . .
The British, Germans, and others are taking advantage of us." When Norstad demurred, Eisenhower responded forcefully. "We must do something
along these lines, since the United States lost $4.3 billion in gold last
year."[18]

General Norstad took a firmer line on the idea of American troop redeployments in a meeting with the president several months later. The subject of a possible reduction of U.S. forces in NATO had been "badly handled." Norstad "protested violently" because there had been no chance
to prepare the European governments for the announcement. The Europeans were finally moving in the direction of increasing their own forces,
and an American reduction would ruin these hard-won gains. "If we decrease our forces, following the Khrushchev visit, this action will be
taken as a deal with the Soviets, removing the need for security and
the Europeans will cut back."[19] Norstad pleaded with the president to
wait until the political situation had changed before bringing American
troops home.

Eisenhower was unmoved by Norstad's arguments. For five years, the
president had been urging the State Department to "put the facts of life
before the Europeans concerning the reduction of our forces." The American troops had been sent as a stopgap measure during a time of European
weakness, and these countries now had the resources to do much more.
Eisenhower stressed that the United States was paying for the whole strategic deterrent force, all space activities, most of NATO's infrastructure
cost, and large naval and air forces. Why should it also pay for six divisions, especially when these troops were threatening American financial
strength? "For us the problem is one that is both budgetary and involves
the flow of our gold." When Norstad contended that the savings in the
U.S. balance of payments produced through a troop withdrawal—$200–
$300 million, according to Secretary of Defense McElroy—would not be
worth the collapse of morale in Western Europe, Eisenhower exploded.
"Our gold is flowing out and we must not weaken our basic economic
strength." It was time for the Europeans to take up the slack. The French
should no longer use Algeria as an excuse. The Germans had to do more.
"Their dollar balances are rising."[20]

NATO leaders were not the only group that was concerned by the
president's views on U.S. troop withdrawals and their connection to the
balance of payments and military strategy. Sharp bureaucratic divides

emerged during the president's contentious meeting with the state, defense, and treasury secretaries and other officials on 24 October 1959.[21] Secretary of the Treasury Anderson warned the group that if the payments deficit continued, confidence in the dollar would erode and a crisis could emerge. The United States did not have the cushion it once had to withstand a monetary crisis. "Mr. Anderson thought we could live with some adverse balance of payments but that we must reverse the present trend." Increasing exports could help a little but would take time. "Mr. Anderson expressed the view that if a decision could be reached to reduce forces in Europe and bring dependents home, this would make a great difference in the balance of payments."

The difference within the administration over redeployment reflected more than just different degrees of concern over the dollar and gold problem. It also revealed deep differences over alliance military strategy. The president "did not believe that limited war was possible in Europe and thought that the NATO shield could be symbolic and did not require the present five divisions." Others in the room agreed. "Mr. McElroy commented that as long as the U.S. was committed to the principle that any war with the Soviet Union was general war, the need for NATO defenses diminished." If there was a troop withdrawal, it should be justified by strategic imperatives, especially during a time of acute tensions over Berlin. Removing troops for financial reasons would seem like an admission of weakness. "Mr. Anderson agreed with the Secretary's suggestion that he, Mr. Anderson, did not want balance of payments given as a reason for any such decision but rather that there be a review of our military posture with conclusions that were militarily desirable. Mr. Gates said he did not see how we could balance our budget unless we completely revolutionized our military strategy."[22]

Secretary of State Herter was horrified by unilateral discussions of troop withdrawals. Unless "it were possible to obtain the agreement of General Norstad and other military people to a revision of NATO strategy, it would blow NATO higher than a kite." The State Department certainly wanted to revise NATO strategy but not in the direction of a stronger reliance on a nuclear deterrent. After reading the memorandum of the 24 October conference, Assistant Secretary of State for Policy Planning Gerard Smith sent a letter to Herter that reflected the State Department's frustration with Anderson's position. Smith was infuriated that the administration would try to justify troop withdrawals because of NATO strategy: "I gather that the real argument for force withdrawals is based on economic pressures and that the military arguments are more or less rationalizations. If economic factors require us to weaken American military influence abroad, I think it is most important that we not fool ourselves by rationalizing such retraction as being warranted by the military situation."[23]

Smith attacked Secretary McElroy's assumption that the United States was committed to the principle that any war with the Soviet Union would be a general war. This strategy had been coming under increasing fire for several years. "Almost two years ago Foster Dulles on a number of occasions told the Secretary of Defense and the President that he believed this principle was obsolescent and that we should be developing a new strategic concept and military posture to implement it." Smith and others in the State Department believed that any modification of NATO strategy that reduced the importance of shield forces and allowed the United States to redeploy troops could only result in a move toward a tripwire strategy. "I believe that any move which will increase our dependence on the strategic bombing deterrent would be contrary to the new emphasis on maintaining balanced forces which the president approved only a few months ago."[24]

While the president did not support a tripwire strategy, he did support the withdrawal of *American* troops. Eisenhower thought the time had come for the Europeans to fill out the shield part of the alliance force structure with their own troops, while the Americans maintained the strategic nuclear component. The president also believed that the Europeans would never do this unless the Americans actually pulled troops out of Europe. And while Eisenhower was genuinely concerned about the balance-of-payments costs of the troops, he also saw the gold and dollar crisis as an opportunity to make it clear to the Europeans that the day was coming, sooner than they probably thought, when they would have to take up the burden of the alliance's conventional forces.

Many in the State Department, including Smith, did not support Eisenhower's military strategy. They feared that America's military and political position in Europe would be undermined by a temporary financial problem. The payments crisis and gold outflow might be bad, but, according to Smith, they were temporary fluctuations and could be fixed without denuding America's military strength. Smith thought it was foolish to risk the consequences of troop redeployments in order to correct the payments imbalance:

> There seems to me to be no greater problem facing this Government than whether or not to warp our military doctrine and stunt our military establishment to meet temporary economic pressures. We face the alternative of whether to run an *uncertain* risk

of some loss of confidence in the dollar or the *certain* risk of loss of confidence in America's determination to make common cause with its allies and maintain a rational and credible deterrent to communist aggression. If this happens, the standing of the American dollar and a great deal more will inevitably be prejudiced.[25]

In sum, there were three positions within the administration. Smith and others in the State Department wanted to bolster the American conventional commitment to Europe. The Treasury Department wanted to bring troops home to reduce the balance-of-payments deficit. The president, while deeply concerned about the deficit, also sought a major withdrawal for larger political reasons. Eisenhower had always believed that the American troops in Western Europe were a temporary expedient and should be removed as soon as the Europeans had economically recovered and could defend themselves. To the president's mind, that time had now come. Even if the Americans could afford to defend Europe, why defend people who would not defend themselves? "We can import troops, but we cannot import a heart, and people lose heart if they feel that everything depends on us. We must not minimize the overall seriousness of the situation."[26] The threat to the international monetary system made reducing U.S. forces abroad all the more urgent. If troops stationed in Western Europe were threatening the financial health of the free world, Eisenhower was not going to stand idly by and do nothing. "We can't sit still and see our monetary system destroyed. People have to realize this fact."[27]

Eisenhower wondered if the Berlin crisis presented an opportunity to bring U.S. troops home from Europe. The president had "no objection to new measures in Berlin and Germany. For example, it is time to pull out some of our forces now located in Europe" because of the "balance of payments difficulty the United States is experiencing at the present time." Instead of confronting the Soviets, Eisenhower emphasized getting "tough with Britain, Germany, and France to get them to take up more of the load." American policy should force the Europeans to "furnish the Commander for the European NATO Command," while the United States withdrew all but "one of our divisions there." Eisenhower believed that "we should put no more military assistance into Europe. They are now able to support themselves."[28]

By the end of 1959, however, Eisenhower decided to postpone dramatic troop withdrawals. "We should stress that what we are seeking to do is keep our economy strong—upon which all of NATO depends—and at the same time be faithful to our commitments. He repeated that we cannot make a budget for FY '61 that contemplates a pullout." The president reluctantly charged military officials to make whatever savings they could in the balance of payments without significantly reducing the U.S. conventional-force presence in Western Europe. Less than a year later, however, an unexpected monetary crisis would throw the administration into a panic and place the question of troop withdrawals squarely before the president.

## The Gold Crisis of 1960

Despite the efforts of the Eisenhower administration, the program to reduce the payments deficit had no discernible effect in 1960. More troubling was the increased loss of gold. The situation continued to be monitored by the Treasury Department and the Council of Economic Advisers, but no major changes in policy were announced in the first half of the year. During the late summer months of 1960, however, the London gold market became jittery. Reopened only in 1954, this market had grown quite large. Its increasingly volatile movements, which reflected growing concern over the strength of the dollar, forced the Eisenhower administration to consider drastic actions that would have been inconceivable two or three years earlier.

Several factors were driving up the price of gold from thirty-five to forty dollars an ounce on the London market. The burgeoning balance-of-payments deficit left currency traders afraid that the amount of dollars held in foreign countries would surpass the amount of gold held by the U.S. Treasury. Rumors spread that the United States would devalue the dollar. The dollar-gold outflow was made worse by the fact that West Germany and Great Britain had higher interest rates than the United States and were attracting substantial short-term capital from the United States. The Federal Reserve had actually been cutting its interest rates throughout the summer in a countercyclical action to ease a recession in the United States. Increased capital outflow left the U.S. balance of payments in worse shape despite a dramatic improvement on the current account during the first half of 1960.[29] Another destabilizing factor was the rapid move out of the dollar into gold because of the increased international tension. Investors worried throughout the summer and fall that the Berlin crisis might break out into hostilities. Finally, world currency markets were concerned about the American presidential election. As it became more likely that John F. Kennedy could win in the November election, the financial world feared that a Democratic administration would ease monetary policy in order to promote economic growth. Domestic inflation would undermine the value of the dollar and make gold more attractive.

The London gold market exploded on 25 October 1960, rising to a price of $40.60 per ounce and creating a crisis atmosphere in the financial world. With such a high price, Anderson stressed that the United States might "have to pay out gold for practically all of our balance of payments deficit." Given the large dollar liabilities from previous American deficits, a run to convert dollars into gold would threaten the whole structure of the gold exchange system.[30] Eisenhower believed it was time for the Western allies to come to America's aid. The United States had repeatedly bailed out the Europeans, and they should return the favor. President Eisenhower demanded that discussions begin immediately, since he believed he would have more influence over the Europeans than either presidential candidate: "These discussions should be pressed as much as possible while he is in office because of the relationship he has established with the British, French, and General de Gaulle on the basis of mutual integrity and trust."[31]

On 7 October 1960, Eisenhower sent a letter to West German chancellor Adenauer that practically begged for help. The letter asked West Germany to cooperate with the United States in a solution to the American payments deficit. After mentioning the role the Marshall Plan and other aid packages played in rebuilding Europe, the president pointed out that present-day economic reality had changed. In particular, Eisenhower said it was time to reconsider the American troop deployment to Europe: "At that time, I myself testified before our Congress, as Commander of the NATO Forces, that the need for military assistance would be temporary. Ever since, the American people have hoped that the burden of our foreign expenditures, economic and military, would eventually be lifted or at least substantially reduced by the cooperation of other nations."[32] In spite of the ongoing Berlin crisis, Eisenhower claimed that he would defend the viability of the dollar no matter what the cost, and that no overseas commitment could be seen as sacrosanct. A "failure to make prompt, decisive and substantial progress" on America's payments deficit may "set in motion cumulative events of a serious disruptive character, deleterious to world trade and prejudicial to the position and prestige of both our countries as leaders of the free world. Once set in motion these disruptive forces would be difficult to restrain."[33]

Adenauer essentially ignored the president's plea, and pretended not to understand the economic issues involved. The chancellor argued that it would be impossible for West Germany to pay for the stationing costs of American troops, especially in the year before a German national election. Adenauer brandished his old threat of a Social Democratic Party victory, which could be possible if the Americans pushed the issue. "A loss of the election by us would mean the end of the European policy as hitherto pursued."[34] It would also end discussions concerning nuclear weapons for the German army, which Adenauer believed were required for NATO to remain viable. "The NATO army would be finished in such case where an essential contingent such as the German one is not equipped with nuclear arms." Adenauer pointed out that he had recently received a report from the West German ambassador in Moscow indicating that Khrushchev had the firm intention of "bringing about decision in the German question during the coming year."

Adenauer's response made it clear that he believed resolving the balance of payments was a minor concern compared with providing the Bundeswehr with nuclear weapons and strengthening the Western alliance for a future confrontation with the Soviets over Berlin. Furthermore, Adenauer knew that Eisenhower would not be president much longer, and there was little to gain from negotiating with a lame duck. But despite what appeared to be an outright rejection of the president's proposal, the administration took heart from the fact that the chancellor agreed to a high-level meeting with Secretary of the Treasury Anderson and Under Secretary of State Dillon in late November to discuss the issue.

As the 1960 presidential election approached, the administration was still torn between those who wanted massive troop cuts to stem the dollar and gold crisis and those who thought the Berlin crisis required increased American forces. This conflict came out during a late October meeting of the NSC and the Treasury, Defense, and State Departments called to discuss the U.S. military assistance program.[35] Ironically, the State Department's Douglas Dillon argued against U.S. troop cuts, a position he would reverse when he became secretary of the treasury. "Simultaneous reduction of U.S. forces and military assistance would cause such a loss of confidence in NATO that it would have the gravest possible effects on the structure of NATO." President Eisenhower disagreed. "If the balance-of-payments got out of hand, there would be a disintegration of confidence in the world. We should see what we could do about this problem and should provide assistance in kind to the limit of our ability."

Halfway through the meeting, Secretary of the Treasury Anderson launched into a diatribe. He was "astounded by the comments that had been made on the balance-of-payments."

> If this proposed program were put into effect, he could not assume responsibility for the security of the dollar. . . . We talk about what other countries will do but they have a good thing going and know it; they are not going to give it up as a result of persuasion by

us. They are not that loyal to NATO nor do they feel that kind of
obligation to us as a result of our Marshall aid. These countries
were not going to support the dollar.[36]

When Dillon protested that none of the military assistance money was going to Germany or France, the key surplus countries, Anderson responded
by saying that the United States could no longer afford to give out any
foreign assistance whatsoever. "He again emphasized that continuing on
this course would bring us the greatest holocaust we had ever seen."

Secretary Anderson argued that the real strategic dilemma went beyond the issue of the balance of payments. If the Europeans were unwilling to help, and were willing to risk the destruction of the international
monetary system for their own perceived gain, why was the United States
spending such huge amounts at such great risk to defend these countries?
With the dollar under threat, Anderson believed that the whole concept
of stationing troops in Europe should be questioned. In his lifetime "we
had not been faced by a problem as serious as the one facing us today.
Moreover, this was a unique experience; it had never happened to the U.S.
before."[37]

The debate over military assistance continued after the meeting, and
both Secretary of State Christian Herter and Secretary of the Treasury
Anderson sent memoranda to the president decrying the other's position.
Herter claimed that "reducing or eliminating the relatively low levels of
military assistance in these four countries would lead them to infer that
U.S. interest in NATO and the defense of the Far East was diminishing and
that a 'Fortress America' concept was being seriously considered."[38] Anderson was equally blunt:

> I can say that our NATO and other military alliances are very
> weak reeds for the defense of the Free World if our financially
> able allies are not willing to increase their defense expenditures as
> their financial abilities increase and the financial problems of the
> United States become critical—in large part owing to the tremen-
> dous amount of assistance we have given these countries in reach-
> ing their present healthy situation. If our alliances are weak, the
> time has now come to reappraise them.[39]

The crisis intensified in the week leading up to and after the election.
In a meeting with the president and other top officials on 9 November
1960, Anderson announced that the gold reserves of the United States
were about to slip below $18 billion "for the first time in many, many
years."[40] With great reluctance, he admitted that it might be necessary to

reduce the 25 percent gold cover for currency required by the Federal
Reserve Act. But this would be a dangerous course. It "would set off the
biggest monetary debate in our history with terribly damaging effects."
Anderson suggested two other remedies equally unpalatable to the Eisenhower administration. The United States could increase the dollar price of
gold—or, in other words, devalue the dollar. Or it could let the dollar
fluctuate on the open market and replace the fixed exchange rate system
with a free or flexible exchange rate regime. The former would be ineffective, because in the dollar-based system everyone else could revalue their
currencies, negating the dollar devaluation. The second option, it was
feared, could lead to competitive devaluations and chaos in the markets.

Eisenhower interrupted and asked whether or not it would be possible
to replace gold with uranium as our major reserve. "We now have $21
billion worth of refined uranium and plutonium. This has great future
value as a source of power." He wondered "if this could be substituted for
gold." Anderson politely dismissed this possibility, but suggested a final
option, one certain to be controversial with the State and Defense Departments. "We can cut down and in some cases eliminate the stationing of
dependents of military and civilian personnel abroad. We can reduce our
troops overseas." In Anderson's view, it was important to take some of
these measures before his trip to Europe. "We are at the point where we
must cut our troops in Germany, without waiting to see what the Germans are willing to contribute."

In a postelection meeting held at Augusta, Georgia, on 15 November,
the president agreed with many of Anderson's comments and approved
an order bringing home the dependents of overseas military and embassy
personnel. Eisenhower obviously felt anxious about having to make such
a move, and again reminded his top officials that he had always intended
the positioning of U.S troops in Europe be temporary:

> The President reminded the group that he had been preaching for
> eight years that we had been too easy with Europe. He pointed
> out that when he went to Europe as SACEUR in 1951 he had told
> everyone that the measures we were taking were emergency mea-
> sures only. In this regard the President quoted the late Secretary
> Dulles as having urged him continually to maintain the current
> force levels in Europe. Secretary Dulles had said that morale would
> collapse if one soldier were pulled back from the line.[41]

Eisenhower recognized that all the efforts of eight years would be for
nothing if the international monetary system broke down even before
President-elect Kennedy was sworn in. The president instructed Ander-

son to push the balance-of-payments issue on his trip, especially with Adenauer and de Gaulle.

## The Failure of the Anderson-Dillon Mission

After the election, it was decided that a key element of the administration's policy to improve the balance of payments would be to pressure the West Germans to increase their contribution to the defense of Europe, primarily by offsetting the cost of American troops stationed in their country by purchasing goods in the United States equal to the dollar costs of the troop commitment. Because a considerable part of the payments imbalance was run with West Germany, it was thought entirely reasonable that the Germans pay for what the administration identified as the main cause of the American payments deficit: U.S. troops assigned to NATO. A German offset not only would help relieve the payments deficit and gold drain but would allow the United States to avoid redeploying its troops during a period of increasing tensions over Berlin. A failure to win an offset from the Germans would provide powerful ammunition to American financial officials, particularly Anderson, who questioned the wisdom of maintaining such expensive commitments during a period of financial instability.

Secretary of the Treasury Robert Anderson and Assistant Secretary of State Douglas Dillon traveled to West Germany in late November to negotiate an offset with Chancellor Adenauer and other high-ranking officials. But since the Germans refused to consider the idea of paying support costs for American troops, the discussions proved futile. "The Chancellor was unwilling to discuss the question of U.S. cost of troops stationed in the Federal Republic on the grounds that this was a political impossibility."[42] This stunning refusal to negotiate came despite the fact that Anderson made it clear to Adenauer that a failure by Germans to provide offsets could have disastrous consequences for the international monetary system. The United States would take whatever policy measure was necessary, no matter how painful, to avoid such consequences:

> We made clear to the Chancellor and his associates that in view
> of these circumstances and in view of the key position which the
> U.S. dollar occupies in the international financial system we will
> be required by irresistible logic to make whatever decisions we
> deem appropriate both in our domestic policies and in our inter-
> national policies, including both military and economic matters
> as are necessary and appropriate to our firm resolve that we will
> not allow the dollar to deteriorate.[43]

Other than a token offer to prepay debt owed the United States, the Germans did not offer any meaningful aid. Dillon informed Herter that for "practical purposes there is very little relief either to the budget or balance of payments that will result from our discussions."

The Eisenhower administration had held high hopes that the Anderson-Dillon mission would produce favorable results. The failure of the mission to bring about meaningful negotiations, let alone an offset agreement, was a bitter blow to the president. The German government in Bonn rejected outright the idea of paying the costs of American troops. This rejection made the lame-duck administration look weak and confused.[44] This image of weakness was compounded by the announcement on 14 November by the Ford Motor Company that it planned to purchase those units of its British subsidiary that it did not already own for $358 million. Ford had pursued this transaction despite a stern warning from Anderson that it might lead to exchange controls.[45]

In a meeting with the president after they had returned, Anderson and Dillon tried to put the best spin on the trip that they could. Upon the advice of the American ambassador to Germany, they had not pulled their punches with the German government. They made it clear that balance of payments and gold outflow were directly linked to the cost of stationing American troops in West Germany: "Mr. Anderson said they had met with the Chancellor on Monday. They had outlined the balance of payments situation to him and the problem of our gold outflow. They had made clear the necessity for actions to defend the dollar and had brought out that support costs in Germany represent a $600 million gold burden to us. They had stressed that we cannot run a $4 billion deficit in balance of payments annually."[46]

The Germans were unmoved. One problem, according to Anderson, was that Adenauer pretended that he had no understanding of the balance-of-payments issue, which may have been a ruse. At least the Germans had been put on notice that this issue was of paramount importance to the United States. When Adenauer asked whether the United States was considering redeploying American troops, Anderson replied, "President Eisenhower is resolved to do whatever the United States has to do to protect the dollar."[47] Despite this threat, Adenauer refused to consider any move that would add to his budget or prejudice his party's chances in the 1961 election. Adenauer even stated that he was convinced he would be better off waiting for the new Kennedy administration:

> Mr. Dillon said that Chancellor Adenauer had told him that the Germans simply could not possibly pay support costs. Adenauer

added that a Bundestag member who was recently in the United States had talked with President-elect Kennedy, and quoted Kennedy as saying that he would not ask the Germans to pay troop costs. Mr. Dillon observed that anything the Germans really do they will want to do for the new administration, so as to get maximum credit with them.[48]

Despite these attempts to emphasize the positive, the mission was generally perceived as a disaster. The tone of these documents is one of frustration and resentment. It appeared that Eisenhower's deepest fears regarding the American commitment to defend Western Europe were coming true. The Americans were risking a nuclear holocaust to defend people who didn't seem to care if the United States went bankrupt while trying to maintain the security of the free world. The German rejection at a time of American need amplified Eisenhower's belief that Western Europe took the commitment of the United States for granted.

Eisenhower considered a large U.S. troop withdrawal, both before and after the failed Anderson-Dillon mission. In late November, Anderson pushed Eisenhower—"we should not let the Germans off the hook, that we may take our troops out."[49] Two days later, Eisenhower seemed to have made up his mind. If Germany and other allies refused to do their part, "on our own part, one move we can make is to redeploy troops."[50] During his December meeting with President-elect Kennedy he stated that he was going to warn the NATO community that the United States would redeploy troops unless the payments deficit was solved.[51] Yet despite his own inclinations and pressure from Secretary Anderson and others to return the troops, Eisenhower backed down. While the president had deep personal doubts about the American troop commitment, his administration reluctantly concluded that maintaining strength during the Berlin crisis was the highest national priority. As worried as the Eisenhower administration was about the balance-of-payments crisis, and as angry as Eisenhower was at the European allies for refusing to help, redeployment in the midst of the Berlin crisis could have undermined vital American interests. With a new president a month away from entering office, Eisenhower felt he could defer the decision.

But a second, and perhaps more important, reason came from within the bureaucracy of his own government. Many in the Eisenhower administration, if not Eisenhower himself, had embraced new strategic policies that would require increases, rather than cutbacks, in overseas commitments. This strategy emerged, in large measure, to confront the confounding dilemmas posed by the Berlin crisis. These forces in the administration worked to prevent any redeployment scheme. These advocates refused to let a deficit in the U.S. balance of payments undermine the new strategy.

## The Clash between Strategy and Finance: Dollars, Berlin, and Flexible Response

Despite his oft-stated goal of withdrawing American troops from Europe, Eisenhower found it hard to stomach redeployment in the face of Soviet pressure over Berlin. Throughout the fall of 1960, the Soviets and East Germans had increased their harassment over the status of Berlin. The Soviet strategy seemed to be a series of half measures and minor irritations, which, individually, could not really be contested by the Western alliance, but which in sum would eventually lead to the GDR taking over Berlin.[52] The crisis also exposed the lack of unity among the Western partners.[53] By the fall of 1960, for example, American military officials already thought that the Western response in the face of Soviet pressure had been entirely too weak.[54] A public spat over the American balance-of-payments deficit and an ignominious withdrawal of U.S. troops would send the wrong signal to both the Soviets and America's European allies. Despite the perceived threat to the dollar and the international monetary system, in the end Eisenhower refused to play hardball with the Europeans, especially the Germans, at the height of one of the most dangerous crises of the Cold War.

Even Eisenhower was beginning to realize the enormous strategic problems that a large American withdrawal might cause. In August, President Eisenhower met with Robert Bowie to discuss a study on the future of NATO. Bowie began by saying that there was "an urgent need for a new look at the strategy of NATO in light of the Soviet nuclear development."[55] To meet this challenge, Bowie suggested two courses: first, develop a multilateral nuclear program for the NATO allies and, second, significantly augment the shield forces that would provide the forward defense of Western Europe in the case of a Soviet attack.

Eisenhower agreed with Bowie's first suggestion but was confused by the second. Why augment the expensive shield forces, especially at a time of such financial difficulty, when any war with the Soviets would be a general nuclear war?

> In fact, he said he cannot see any chance of keeping any war in Europe from becoming a general war. For this reason he thought we must be ready to throw the book at the Russians should they jump us. He did not see how there could be such a thing as a limited war in Europe, and thought that we would be fooling our-

selves and our European friends if we said we could fight such a
war without recourse to nuclear weapons. If massive land operations such as the Ludendorff offensive in early 1918 in World War I
were to occur, he was sure that nations would use every weapon
available to them.[56]

Bowie explained that given the changing nuclear environment, the point
of augmenting the shield forces was more psychological and political
than military: "If the Europeans think that they are in a situation where
they cannot resist at all if they do not use all-out nuclear attack, the
probability becomes great that they would not resist and accordingly not
prevent Soviet encroachment. What he is suggesting is that we should be
careful that we would not end up deterring ourselves."[57]

Bowie proposed increasing NATO's conventional capability, including
the American ground troops that were putting such pressure on the U.S.
balance of payments. Eisenhower bristled at the suggestion. "Since the
costs of developing and maintaining such a force would be quite large we
come to a matter of priorities. Our gold outflow has been such that we
cannot take on too much of a burden supporting the development of
conventional forces." But Eisenhower admitted that his views on NATO
strategy and nuclear war put him in the minority. "He recognized that
perhaps there has been a gap in his own thinking regarding this question." During a National Security Council meeting held on 25 August to
discuss nuclear sharing, Eisenhower stated that all of Bowie's suggestions
deserved full consideration. "The President remarked that Mr. Bowie had
convinced him that many current ideas, including some which he (Eisenhower) had held, were not sacrosanct."[58]

In November, the National Security Council discussed NATO strategy
again as it prepared for the NATO Ministerial Meeting in December. In a
discussion of nuclear sharing, the debate over U.S. shield (conventional)
forces came up again. Eisenhower's Bureau of the Budget director Maurice
H. Stans argued that a proposed deployment of medium-range ballistic
missiles to Europe should allow for a reduction, not an increase, in American conventional forces. Secretary of Defense Thomas Gates said that "he
disagreed with any concept that conventional forces were needed for a
limited war in Europe."[59] While Eisenhower did not dispute the need for
troops, he emphasized that any increases should be borne by NATO countries other than the United States.[60] But the President did not demand
U.S. troop withdrawals. This shift in attitude was made clear during the
American delegation's trip to the NATO summit in mid-December. The
secretary of state, Christian Herter, emphasized two things in his presen-

tation: the need to rethink NATO strategy and the importance of correcting the U.S. balance-of-payments deficit. Herter asked for help with the
U.S. balance of payments but, unlike Eisenhower, did not threaten U.S.
troop withdrawals.[61]

Herter's speech clearly demonstrated that many in the administration,
if not the president himself, had accepted the logic of a new NATO strategy that demanded a more "flexible response." Not all conflicts with the
Soviet Union should be met with a full nuclear strike. "In case of attack,
NATO forces should be able to meet the situation with a response appropriate to the nature of the attack."[62] Herter quoted General Norstad's
statements that this would mean having forces with "a substantial conventional capability" and distanced himself from the Eisenhower policy
when he supported Norstad's statement that "the threshold at which
nuclear weapons are introduced into the battle should be a high one." To
accomplish these goals, the shield forces that had been deemphasized in
Eisenhower's strategy would have to be augmented: "Unless all NATO
shield goals are substantially achieved, NATO Military Commanders will
not have that flexibility of response that will enable them to meet any
situation with the appropriate response."[63]

That the strategy of flexible response, long associated with the vigor of
the Kennedy administration, was laid before the allies in the waning days
of the Eisenhower administration is all the more amazing given the serious consideration given only one month earlier to the idea of redeploying American troops to ease the balance-of-payments deficit.[64] Herter's
speech to NATO did argue that the United States was doing more than its
share, that it was time for the recovered nations of Western Europe to
increase their defense burden, and that the United States was determined
to correct "the international payments situation, which has an importance beyond the financial field." A statement alluding to a possible redeployment to improve the U.S. balance of payments was reluctantly
included after much debate and President Eisenhower's insistence. Despite a watered-down statement, the momentum for large U.S. troop
withdrawals from Europe had passed. But the deficit problem had not
gone away and, in fact, worsened. New policies would have to be found to
counter what was believed to be a grave threat to the international monetary system and the productive functioning of the Western economies.

## Eisenhower Advises Kennedy

Both President Eisenhower and Secretary of the Treasury Anderson briefed
Kennedy on the balance-of-payments issue in December, and Paul Nitze,
who headed a Kennedy transition task force on national security, was

informed of the results of the ill-fated negotiations with the Germans. As was to be expected, Anderson's presentation to the president-elect was blunt. The payments problem was enormous and also unique. No American administration had ever confronted such an issue. Anderson emphasized that the problem could not be papered over by cosmetic repairs; critical decisions were necessary: "Nothing which affected our balance of payments should be considered sacrosanct; nor should any course of action be permitted to achieve a new attractiveness simply because it is easy."[65]

Kennedy appeared to understand the magnitude of the problem. But could he really contemplate the withdrawal of American troops, as suggested by Anderson? It would be one thing for General Eisenhower to take such a potentially disastrous move, but the world's reaction to Kennedy pulling American troops out of Germany would be much different. Additionally, Kennedy had campaigned on the need to remain militarily vigorous, including an increase in limited war and conventional capabilities. The new president did not want to be forced to withdraw American troops from Europe at the start of his new administration, especially as the Soviets were certain to test the mettle of Eisenhower's successor early.

Kennedy had commissioned a transition task force to provide a comprehensive analysis of the American payments deficit.[66] The report recognized two different elements of the deficit. The basic deficit was the net outflow of dollars on account of transactions in goods and services, long-term foreign investment, and aid. The second deficit was composed of short-term capital flight of the type that threatened the dollar during the gold crisis. According to the task force, the president faced a choice. He could end the deficits through "restrictionist" measures, such as import restrictions and the reduction of foreign military and economic aid (as proposed by Anderson). Or the chief executive could solve the dollar and gold problem by expanding the economy through an increase in American exports. Not surprisingly, the report recommended the expansionist solution. The task force suggested easing capital restrictions, unilateral tariff reduction, and generating increased revenues from tourism.[67]

None of these measures would produce immediate results, and American exports had already increased significantly between 1958 and 1960. The report echoed the calls of Anderson for the surplus countries, like Japan, Italy, the Netherlands, and especially Germany, to do more. It was unclear, however, why the Kennedy administration would succeed where Eisenhower had failed. The task force also recommended working through the newly transformed Organization for Economic Cooperation and Development (OECD):

> We should seek explicit recognition of the proposition that any
> member country's expenditures for common defense purposes, or
> to provide assistance to the less developed countries, should not
> result in a deficit in its balance of payments through the further
> accumulation of reserves by other members. Any surplus country
> accumulating foreign exchange as a direct result of such expendi-
> tures by other members should accept a responsibility to take
> measures to increase its imports of goods and services, expand its
> foreign aid, and, in the case of NATO countries, increase its contri-
> butions to the common defense.[68]

But Kennedy, like Eisenhower, would find it very difficult to get America's
NATO allies to embrace this concept.

By the end of Eisenhower's presidency, the American balance-of-payments deficit and gold outflow unleashed a heated debate over some of
the most fundamental issues of U.S. grand strategy and foreign economic
policy. Many in the Eisenhower administration felt that the American
troop commitment was the primary cause of the dangerous weakening of
the dollar. At the height of the gold crisis, it seemed as if the health of the
U.S. economy and viability of the international monetary system were
being threatened by America's commitments abroad. Logic dictated that
some reduction in these commitments be considered, or that the countries of Western Europe defray the balance-of-payments costs of these
commitments. But neither policy proved feasible. Eisenhower was a lame-
duck president with little power over his allies, and, in the end, troop
reductions were strategically and politically impossible given the crisis
atmosphere surrounding Berlin. But the dollar and gold crisis had not
been solved, and this sharp divide between strategic considerations, alliance politics, and America's monetary burdens would resurface time
and time again in the years to come.

Chapter Three

# The Gold Battles
# within the Cold War

### *Kennedy's International Monetary Policy*

On more than one occasion, President John F. Kennedy told his advisers "the two things which scared him most were nuclear weapons and the payments deficit." George Ball claimed that Kennedy was "absolutely obsessed with the balance of payments."[1] Kennedy's sensitivity to the nuclear danger is well documented and completely understandable. But his fear over the consequences of the American balance-of-payments deficit has not been adequately recognized. Why did he compare a technical problem of international monetary economics to the dangers of a nuclear war?

As the next two chapters demonstrate, these two problems were inextricably linked during the Kennedy years. It is impossible to understand Kennedy's Cold War strategy during this period, particularly in Europe, without coming to terms with the balance of payments and the gold question. Likewise, these monetary issues make no sense unless they are understood within their political and security context.

Although there is no shortage of scholarship on the Kennedy administration, the U.S. balance-of-payments deficit and gold outflow has been ignored or marginalized in the historical literature. For example, the standard account of American strategy and foreign policy during the Kennedy years, Michael Beschloss's *The Crisis Years*, does not even mention the issue in more than 800 pages of text.[2] Those historians who have addressed America's monetary policy during the Kennedy period treat the issue as strictly a question of foreign economic policy, unrelated to the core power politics of the period. One historian characterizes Kennedy's monetary policy as "an aggressive but ultimately futile defense of American economic hegemony." Other historians and political scientists have suggested that the Kennedy deficit was a symbol of American decline, produced by a combination of economic malaise at home and imperial overstretch abroad.[3] This assessment, however, has been largely rejected in the professional economics literature.[4] All of these accounts fail to consider how the dollar and gold problem was central to the most important security questions of the day. The whole spectrum of the Kennedy administration's policy toward Europe, ranging from the German question to to nuclear-sharing policy, cannot be understood without reference to American monetary policy.

Nowhere was the inextricable link between monetary and security policy clearer than on the question of America's military posture in Europe. It has long been assumed that the United States was committed to a strong American troop presence in Europe.[5] Because of Kennedy's criticism of Eisenhower's emphasis on nuclear weapons, and his own administration's advocacy of the so-called flexible response doctrine, it has been an article of faith among historians that the Kennedy administration sought to strengthen and enlarge this conventional-force commitment.[6] But, in fact, the Kennedy administration seriously considered plans to withdraw U.S. troops from Europe.

Kennedy, like Eisenhower before him, identified America's generous political and security policy in Europe—chiefly the decision to station six army divisions in West Germany—as the root cause of America's monetary woes. The payments deficit and the foreign exchange costs of this commitment were roughly equal, a fact that neither Kennedy nor his advisers thought coincidental. The new administration did not want to deflate the American economy or impose trade or capital controls to correct deficits in the balance of payments. Therefore, it made perfect sense to focus on the foreign exchange costs of America's NATO commitment. Furthermore, the countries that benefited most from American protection—France and West Germany—pursued policies that ran counter to U.S. economic and strategic interests. By 1962 Kennedy was convinced that the West German chancellor Konrad Adenauer and the French president Charles de Gaulle would use their newfound monetary leverage to compel changes in America's political and security policies in Europe.

This struggle over the U.S. troop commitment and the nature of America's relations with Europe during the Kennedy years was at the heart of what might be called the "gold battles" within the Cold War. On the surface, these appeared to be contentious but simple disputes over burden sharing within the alliance. Simply put, the balance-of-payments cost of America's commitment was putting the dollar and the U.S. gold supply at risk, and the Americans pushed their European allies to do something to relieve this burden. The Europeans responded unenthusiastically and blamed the gold drain on America's economic profligacy. In reality, the gold battle within the alliance during the early 1960s was one of the most important components of a complex and bitter political struggle— between the United States on one hand, and France and West Germany on the other—over the direction of the Western alliance and its Cold

War strategy. While the dispute was at heart over political and strategic matters—Adenauer and de Gaulle were deeply disturbed by Kennedy's nuclear-sharing and Berlin policies—the field of battle was often economic and monetary. Negotiations and discussions about payments deficits and gold holdings, which included serious threats of American troop withdrawals, often masked a deeper struggle over the leadership and direction of the NATO alliance.

Almost everyone involved in this battle understood that a large American troop withdrawal from Europe would have profound effects on international political stability. At the end of the day, would the president order the troops back home? This question was the starting point for the second gold battle, namely the sharp and at times acrimonious bureaucratic struggle within the Kennedy administration over how to resolve the problems posed by the U.S. balance-of-payments deficit and gold outflow. There were essentially two sides in this conflict. The Department of the Treasury, led by its secretary, Douglas Dillon, and Under Secretary Robert Roosa, strongly advocated troop withdrawal plans. They saw the dollar and gold crisis as one of the most important economic and political issues facing the Kennedy administration, and believed that troop withdrawals were the easiest and most sensible policy option to resolve America's monetary problems. Dillon repeatedly warned the president that a failure to resolve the payments problem could lead to international monetary chaos abroad and deflation and possibly depression at home. Surprisingly, the Defense Department, and in particular Secretary of Defense Robert McNamara and his lieutenant Roswell Gilpatric, allied themselves with the Treasury Department's campaign to bring American troops back home. From a military standpoint, they were convinced that six U.S. divisions were needlessly expensive and that the Europeans should provide the bulk of NATO's conventional forces.[7]

The State Department, led in this struggle by Under Secretary of State George Ball and former secretary of state Dean Acheson, vehemently opposed even the smallest reduction in American ground forces in Western Europe. They understood that American troops served a political as well as a military role and feared that a troop withdrawal would undermine West Germany's confidence in the NATO alliance and America's commitment to defend Europe. A redeployment of U.S. troops could initiate a chain of events that might produce any number of outcomes inimical to America's strategic interests, including nuclearization of the West Germany military, a Franco-German alliance to shut the United States out of Europe, and an intensified conflict with the Soviets over the status of Germany. Instead, with the support of the Council of Economic Advisers, the State Department advocated plans to reform and recast the international monetary system, even if it meant curtailing or eliminating the dollar's role as a reserve currency. Those who opposed a major redeployment hoped that a new and improved payments system would eliminate the monetary pressure to withdraw American ground forces from Western Europe.

### The Reluctant Emperor:
### Kennedy and the Balance of Payments, 1961–1962

The gold and dollar problem did not catch the incoming Kennedy administration by surprise. During the campaign, it had been speculated that a liberal Kennedy administration would pursue loose monetary and fiscal policies in order to encourage domestic economic recovery. This fear contributed to the weakness of the dollar on the London market, a fact the Republican nominee, Richard Nixon, tried to exploit. There were even rumors that Kennedy would follow Franklin Roosevelt's example and devalue the dollar. Kennedy's campaign moved quickly to squelch this speculation, and on 31 October Kennedy issued a public statement declaring his commitment to maintain the dollar price of gold at thirty-five dollars an ounce.[8]

Ironically, this public concern was unwarranted, as the incoming president wanted to convince the public—and especially Wall Street and the international banking community—that he would not pursue unrestrained fiscal and monetary programs. During their first transition meeting, Kennedy agreed with Eisenhower when he warned that the United States was carrying "far more than her share of free world defense." Eisenhower explained that the gold drain made it imperative that his successor start bringing American troops home from Europe.[9] Several weeks later, Kennedy commissioned a committee to come up with a policy on the dollar and gold crisis.[10] A key recommendation was the early appointment of a secretary of the treasury who "enjoys high respect and confidence in the international financial world" and would restore confidence in the dollar. A Kennedy transition adviser, Richard Neustadt, agreed, and suggested tapping someone from the financial community who also had experience with foreign policy. To the dismay of many New Frontiersmen, Kennedy passed over economic liberals like John Kenneth Galbraith and Averell Harriman and chose the conservative Republican and Wall Street stalwart Douglas Dillon. Kennedy risked alienating his closest supporters to demonstrate his concern for the stability of the dollar. When Senator Albert Gore Sr., a Tennessee Democrat (and a presumptive candidate for the treasury position himself), told Kennedy that selecting Dillon signaled a continuation of the stagnant policies of the Republicans, Kennedy was unmoved. "Albert, I got less than 50 percent of the vote. The first requirement of the Treasury job is acceptability to the financial community."[11]

Dillon's selection was revealing in other ways. The president selected the progrowth liberal economist Walter Heller as the chairman of the Council of Economic Advisers. Heller advocated looser fiscal and monetary policies to stimulate higher domestic growth, which might weaken the dollar and increase the gold outflow. By putting advisers with diametrically opposed views in the top economic policy-making spots, Kennedy guaranteed that he would never be railroaded into a decision.[12] Heller would argue with Dillon, just as the European-minded George Ball in the State Department would square off against Robert McNamara, whose analysis of the troop withdrawal issue was informed more by quantitative analysis than by concerns about European political sensitivities. Kennedy also strived to break down what he saw as the bureaucratic inertia that had plagued the Eisenhower administration, and he relied on key White House advisers from a pared-down National Security Council to make sense of the conflicting opinions offered by cabinet secretaries. White House assistants Walt Rostow and Carl Kaysen, both economists, were especially important in this role. This whole policy-making process had the advantage of guaranteeing that Kennedy would hear all sides of an argument. But it occasionally prevented his advisers from unanimously supporting a policy option. Kennedy feared choosing the wrong international monetary policy and often deferred making difficult choices for as long as he could.[13]

During its first months, the Kennedy administration developed a monetary policy that mirrored aspects of Eisenhower's strategy but which differed dramatically from its predecessor's tactics. It had three components. First, those countries that gained foreign exchange as a result of U.S. defense efforts were pressured to offset this gain by spending surplus dollars on military equipment from the United States. Surplus countries were also asked voluntarily to hold surplus dollars earned through U.S. defense commitments and not use them to purchase U.S. gold. The second part of the Kennedy strategy involved constructing elaborate, multilateral defenses against speculative attacks on the dollar. Concurrently, the administration considered plans and proposals to reform the global payments system. Finally, the Kennedy administration initiated serious trade negotiations aimed at lowering European tariffs.[14] The administration expected European, and especially West German, cooperation for all three of these policy initiatives. If the Europeans proved unwilling to ease the dollar and gold outflow, the administration would not back away from threats to pull U.S. troops from NATO.

## American Monetary Policy and Germany:
## The Origins of Offset

In their debates over America's international monetary policy, it is clear that many key administration officials viewed the deficit as a product of U.S. defense efforts in Europe. Kennedy, in particular, thought it only natural that those who had benefited from American protection should contribute to the solution of the dollar and gold outflow. The United States had protected Western Europe during a time of weakness and danger. Most Western European countries now held dollar surpluses. No country had gained more from American efforts than West Germany, and no country was more susceptible to American pressure. The foreign exchange cost of the American troop presence in Germany made up a large part of the payments deficit, and unlike short-term capital flow, tourist expenditures, or foreign direct investments, it was an account government officials could directly control. The Kennedy administration focused its efforts on getting West Germany to cooperate.

The strategy of seeking offsets initially proved difficult and acrimonious. Kennedy wanted to establish the principle that every dollar spent in Germany defending Europe should be used by the Federal Republic to purchase American military equipment—hence the term "offset." This would serve two purposes: relieve the American payments deficit and increase the West German Bundeswehr's capacity to fight a conventional war. The Germans resented both of these aims. They felt singled out, because the U.S. troops were defending all of Western Europe but the Federal Republic was the only country offering significant balance-of-payments relief. And the West German leadership disliked any change in strategy that emphasized fighting the Soviets with conventional rather than nuclear forces. The offset arrangement would also make West Germany even more dependent upon the United States by foreclosing arms arrangements with European, and especially French, suppliers. Finally, there was the fear that by building up West German conventional forces the Kennedy administration was making it possible for the United States to withdraw its own conventional forces in the future.

According to Werner Knieper, a Ministry of Defense official, "a long-range FRG commitment on military procurement in the U.S. was . . . not acceptable—not even 'in principle' "[15] By guaranteeing large-scale procurement in the United States, the Ministry of Defense risked alienating important French and British suppliers. Knieper complained that large purchases in the United States would undermine the joint European weapons production programs the Eisenhower administration had encouraged. The German attitude might be different if either Pershing or Polaris missiles were included in any purchase list, but Knieper admitted that such decisions would have to be made at a much higher level.[16]

The new administration strongly rejected the German viewpoint. A sense of how Kennedy would deal with this issue was conveyed in a memo to Secretary Rusk expressing disappointment at how the West Germans were handling the offset negotiations. "As the Chancellor is interested in power it would seem to me that I should give Mr. Brentano a sense of our disappointment with their progress."[17] If the West Germans thought that the incoming administration was going to drop the issue, they were in for a shock.[18] The Transition Report on the Balance of Payments had emphasized the need to obtain German cooperation on reducing the deficit, and the administration made obtaining offsets a high priority.[19]

After a meeting between the Departments of Defense, State, and Treasury, the Kennedy administration put a new spin on the issue. The new approach would proceed from the basic assumption that "a general condition of economic imbalance exists in the Western world which can only be rectified by continuing and concerted measures which members of the Alliance should take, within their respective capacities, to fulfill their responsibilities." Special emphasis would be placed on the need for "sustained increase in German contributions to the common defense and for aid to less developed countries consistent with Germany's capacity to support a larger share of the common burdens."[20]

Instead of posing the issue as a temporary imbalance caused by American excess and cyclical conditions, Foreign Minister Brentano was told that the United States faced "a short-term reserve and a long-term, basic balance of payments deficit." These problems were not the fault of the United States. The deficit existed "only because the U.S. is carrying such heavy burdens of defense for the whole free world." This put the world economy in a disequilibrium that unjustly burdened the United States, while unfairly benefiting the Federal Republic of Germany. The Americans claimed that the German payments surplus was the mirror image of the American deficit. The German proposals were completely inadequate because they related only to the alleviation of the short-term reserve problem and not the basic disequilibrium created by U.S defense burdens. In other words, the FRG negotiators were told that the deficit was not America's fault, and if they were not prepared to help, the political consequences could be severe.[21]

On the equally contentious issue of gold purchased with surplus dollars, the linkage was far less subtle. The president told the Germans that "a sustained accumulation of gold and other international reserves by any one country is disruptive to the international community . . . one nation's gain can only be another nation's loss."[22] In essence, the Americans were telling the Germans that they better hold surplus dollars in their reserves and not purchase U.S. gold. The threat worked: the Federal Republic transformed its reserve management policy by holding surplus dollars and forgoing gold purchases. But there was no formal arrangement, and there was always the possibility that West Germany could turn in dollars for gold if relations with the United States soured.

The administration successfully pushed the FRG on several fronts connected with the balance of payments. The Germans increased their foreign aid program. They also prepaid $587 million of their postwar debt. Trade restrictions against American poultry were liberalized. The deutschemark was revalued by 5 percent.[23] But on the most important part of offset, military procurement, negotiations were far more difficult. Several working groups were established to increase German purchases in the United States and to establish joint logistics operation, but FRG officials were wary of establishing any permanent link between the deficit and weapons procurement.

The erection of the Berlin Wall dramatically changed the offset negotiations in several ways. For the West German government, this was not the time to question the American commitment, as was the case in some circles, by quibbling over weapons procurement. The intensification of the crisis brought a rapid improvement in the offset negotiations.[24] "We are approaching the strongest bargaining position since the negotiations began. Our negotiating leverage is increased by the possibility of major deployments to assist in the defense of Berlin and Germany."[25]

Worry over the dollar and gold outflow deepened with the renewal of the Berlin crisis. The payments deficit would worsen considerably if the contemplated call-up of reserves and the buildup of American troops and supplies were carried out. A deployment of six or even three new divisions to Europe, as some in the administration were recommending, would cause the payments deficit to explode. Worse, the political crisis was shaking confidence in the dollar, and it was feared that another gold crisis could emerge. To cover the additional payments cost of the buildup, Walter Heller suggested a "reverse lend-lease."[26] According to the plan, the Germans would finance the additional troop cost directly out of their budget. At first, the payment would retire the remaining German debt to the United States. After that, it would take the form of a long-term, low-interest loan. The United States would set up a counterpart fund to the

German financing of the troop costs, which would be used to finance German military purchases in the United States. A major benefit to the plan was the strong incentive West Germany would have to make most of its military purchases in the United States. This plan was to augment, not replace, the hope for regular offset, which was still being negotiated.

Heller's plan was popular, especially with the president, who wrote in the margins of his memo that "this should be pursued now with Germans."[27] But the proposal was tabled for fear that it might undermine the offset negotiations between FRG defense minister Franz Joseph Strauss and U.S. under secretary of defense Roswell Gilpatric. A full offset agreement was reached between Gilpatric and Strauss in October, and it included a provision to examine how to reduce the costs of any crisis-induced troop buildup to the American balance of payments.[28] Most important, the agreement established a link between the American troop presence and the continued, full offset of U.S. foreign exchange costs. But if this linkage was embraced by the Kennedy administration, it was not yet fully accepted in West Germany, a fact that would cause much tension in the next two years.

### International Monetary Policy: Treasury versus the CEA

Although politics often drove Kennedy's international monetary policy, it should be emphasized that there was a real fear of what the economic outcome might be if the problems affecting the balance of payments were not solved. Economists and policy makers, from within and outside the administration, warned of the potentially disastrous consequences of a new gold crisis. The president was told that if strenuous measures were not taken to correct the payments imbalance and gold outflow, a repeat of the 1931 financial disaster could not be ruled out. Kennedy himself took these warnings seriously. But the lack of a consensus within the administration on the nature of and the solution to the payments problem hampered Kennedy's ability to tackle the issue.

Initially, the Treasury Department, led by Secretary Douglas Dillon and Under Secretary Robert Roosa, took the lead. While the Defense and State Departments were pressuring West Germany and other allies to make offset arrangements with the United States, the Treasury Department pursued a more conventional course. Douglas Dillon headed an effort to identify ways to reduce the U.S. payments deficit, primarily by reducing net government outlays overseas and increasing American commercial exports. Robert Roosa, under secretary for international monetary affairs, initiated a series of cooperative arrangements with the leading central banks and finance ministries to expand liquidity, stabilize the dollar, and prepare a strong, coordinated, and multilateral defense should another gold crisis arise. Roosa and Dillon considered these measures part of an innovative strategy to strengthen the existing international monetary structure, which they believed was the foundation of American economic strength. But when the payments deficit did not dramatically improve and treasury officials resisted radical solutions, critics accused Dillon and Roosa of "ad-hocery" and began to call for a fundamental restructuring of worldwide monetary relation.

Dillon was particularly concerned about the causes of the deficit that were under the direct control of the government. The secretary of the treasury was a vocal supporter of obtaining offsets from all the allies whose payments benefited from American expenditures. He was quite happy with the amount agreed to in the negotiations with the FRG; not fully understanding the unique pressures that could be applied to West Germany, he even held out great hope that similar arrangements could be worked out with other surplus countries, such as France, Italy, Belgium, the Netherlands, and Japan.[29] He naively believed it would be possible to achieve a $325 million yearly offset agreement from France. Ultimately, a small offset of $100 million was worked out with Italy, but little more was offered by anyone else.

Dillon also focused on the reduction of military expenses overseas. Somewhat surprisingly, Secretary of Defense Robert McNamara supported these efforts and pledged to reduce overseas military expenditures from $3 to $2 billion a year. This required an enormous effort if there were not going to be troop withdrawals. McNamara required all procurement to be done in the United States as long as it was within 50 percent of the local price. This amounted to a sort of de facto devaluation and traded real budgetary cost increases for balance-of-payments savings, which demonstrated how convoluted policy could become. Additionally, foreign aid was increasingly given in goods and services, and dollar disbursements were often tied to purchases of American goods.

Under Secretary Roosa initiated a series of informal, multilateral operations to strengthen the dollar, reduce the American gold outflow, and dampen speculative attacks. Under Roosa's direction, the Treasury Department began to intervene directly in the foreign exchange markets. Roosa negotiated bilateral agreements with European bankers to hold each other's currencies, perform forward transactions in currencies, and borrow dollars or other currencies when needed.[30] Operation "Twist" sought to raise short-term interest rates (and avoid capital flight from the United States) without raising long-term rates (which could deflate the domestic economy). It was hoped that these technical manipulations would provide the means to dampen speculative attacks or reverse destabilizing short-term capital movements.[31]

Probably the most important of these arrangements was the gold pool agreement. Switzerland, West Germany, Italy, the Netherlands, France, Belgium, and Britain all agreed, in conjunction with the United States, to utilize a portion of their gold stocks to hold down the price of gold on the market in London. When the price rose, the gold pool agreed to sell gold until the price returned to thirty-five dollars an ounce. It was hoped that this formidable consortium would deter speculation in gold. A cartel of this sort went a long way toward discouraging the market from bidding up the price of gold, and it succeeded for a time in preventing a repeat of anything like the London gold crisis of October 1960.[32]

Despite the sophistication of these efforts, the policy pursued by the Treasury Department appeared to many a temporary expedient. Debt prepayment, swap agreements, operations in foreign exchange and gold markets, and increased IMF subscriptions all provided "barrier" defenses against another gold crisis, but they did not confront the causes of the payments deficit or solve the problem of increasingly unwanted dollars held by foreign central banks. Even the calls for increased burden sharing and offset missed the point. It was unrealistic to expect large offsets from countries other than West Germany unless the administration threatened troop withdrawals. If the administration ordered redeployment, the United States could realize enormous payments relief, but the Europeans were willing to bet that that would not happen any time soon. It was the same frustrating dilemma that had infuriated Eisenhower: the Europeans only responded when threatened, a fact that certainly did not cement alliance solidarity.

Some in the administration contended that even if Dillon's policies were successful, and even if burden-sharing agreements were reached, the dollar would remain vulnerable to speculative attacks in a way other currencies (with the exception of sterling) would not. These attacks could paralyze American foreign policy and undermine the domestic economy. Paradoxically, some in the administration believed that solving the payments deficit would create worse problems. Policies to reduce the deficit would require deflationary measures that could unleash a worldwide liquidity crisis. If true, then the Treasury Department's efforts to strengthen the monetary structure were misplaced. Perhaps U.S. problems were produced by a flawed international monetary system that guaranteed problems and that had to be replaced.

This alternative view was first presented to the president in a memo from the Council of Economic Advisers.[33] The CEA claimed that many people, both at home and abroad, believed the U.S. international monetary policy was a series of ad hoc expedients. These observers did not see the gold panic of autumn 1960 as a problem unique to the dollar. The CEA argued that the Europeans and the U.S. Treasury incorrectly characterized this crisis as the inevitable result of American overspending abroad. The policies recommended by the Treasury Department—strengthening the U.S. balance of payments—amounted to little more than what the CEA called "dollar salvage" operations.

The CEA argued that the crisis was not a symptom of American weakness or declining power but rather evidence of a flawed international monetary structure. Given the high regard with which the Bretton Woods system was generally held, this was an extraordinary statement for the president's closest economic advisers to make. They argued that fundamental weaknesses of the system made it possible for short-term, privately held capital movements to wreak havoc on the dollar and American gold supply. The American deficit on foreign direct investment and short-term capital accounts outweighed the deficit on the government account, and the capital accounts would only become larger and more volatile as the global economy expanded. The government could use its reserves to counter imbalances produced by capital movements but had to rely on a limited gold supply to do so. Beyond that, the central banks of the world could supplement their reserves with dollars (and to a lesser extent sterling), but this produced problems common in any gold exchange scheme, widely discussed at the time because of the publication of Robert Triffin's book, *Gold and the Dollar Crisis: The Future of Convertibility*.[34]

The CEA contended that burden-sharing exercises should be pursued regardless of the U.S. payments position. Alliance military expenditures should be determined by relative national wealth, not the balance of payments. In the same vein, it was inefficient to tie foreign aid to purchases in the granting country. Finally, the last place to discuss these issues was at the IMF; it was a cumbersome organization bureaucratically committed to traditional positions. Negotiations to create a new monetary system should take place among the key countries of the Atlantic community whose monetary stability mattered. The CEA believed that the OECD would provide the right forum.[35]

The balance-of-payments deficit prevented the CEA from implementing its expansive economic policies, a source of great frustration to Heller and his associates. The CEA's progrowth plans included lowering interest rates, increasing government spending, and reducing taxes, all of which were likely to enlarge the payments deficit. Walter Heller referred to this as the "cruel dilemma." You could have economic expansion or you could reduce the payments deficit and stop the gold outflow, but you could not do both. The CEA, as opposed to the Treasury Department, feared anemic domestic growth more than another dollar crisis. In fact, the council believed that only through a full-employment, full-capacity economy could the United States permanently bring the deficit down. But it would take at least two years for that to happen, and in the meantime, a gold crisis was likely. Reforming the Bretton Woods international monetary system might allow the administration to pursue domestic growth without fear of the consequences of such policies on the U.S. balance of payments.

Heller recommended that the administration should restore the U.S. economy to full employment by 1963 and accept that the deficit would not be eliminated in that time.[36] In the interim, measures should be taken to protect the dollar. For Heller, the key was not the payments deficit but the gold outflow. If a way could be found to finance the deficit without losing large quantities of gold, then there would be no crisis, regardless of the size of the payments deficit. This would entail some sort of agreement with the most likely recipients of these deficit dollars, foreign central banks in Western Europe.

How could the administration ever get the Europeans to agree to such a scheme? They were already holding more dollars than they wanted. Heller suggested gold guarantees and loans from the IMF to the United States. The chairman warned Kennedy that many people would tell him that favoring full employment was dangerous, but he reminded the president that there was a historical parallel to this situation:

> In 1925 Winston Churchill . . . resolved a somewhat similar dilemma the way bankers wanted him to, i.e. in favor of a "sound" pound sterling and its world prestige, and against the domestic economy. The consequences (foreseen by Keynes in the "Economic Consequences of Mr. Churchill") were: Britain had unemployment and depression long before 1929–1930; labor was alienated by deflationary policy, and there was a bloody general strike in 1926; in the end the pound sterling was devalued anyway.[37]

Through 1961 Kennedy deferred to what critics labeled the monetary conservatism of Douglas Dillon and ignored the pleas of the CEA. But by the summer of 1962, when it became clear that the Treasury Department's efforts were not going to eliminate the U.S. payments deficit, CEA found support from George Ball at the State Department and Carl Kaysen at the White House. This group focused less on the payments deficit and more on what they perceived as the structural flaws in the international monetary system. They agreed with the Treasury Department that offset payments and burden-sharing initiatives should be continued, but pointed out that, with the exception of West Germany, these negotiations were producing very little relief. This group chafed at the idea, circulated by the central bankers and finance officials of Europe, that America's overseas military outlays were somehow "sinful"—they were sure that the prime ministers and presidents of these same countries would disagree. They advocated moving negotiations to the highest *political*, as opposed to *financial*, levels, where fundamental reforms of the system could be negotiated.

Over the next year, a whole series of plans for dramatic international monetary reform was debated. The administration discussed such controversial ideas as a gold standstill, reserve ratios, gold guarantees, massive European loans, and even dollar devaluation or the suspension of the gold guarantee. Of course, nobody expected the allies, particularly the Europeans, to like these ideas. But some in the administration were willing to make an explicit link between Europe's accepting these plans and America continuing its military presence.

The Treasury Department was alarmed that such radical plans could even be discussed. Led by Dillon, it fought furiously to prevent their implementation. They believed that any successful solution to America's payments deficit and gold outflow depended on friendly cooperation that strengthened the system, not coercive negotiations to alter international monetary relations in a dramatic fashion. The Europeans would never go along, and mere suggestions of radical solutions would rock the currency and gold markets and threaten confidence in both the dollar and the global payments system.

But what if the quiet cooperation assumed by the Treasury Department did not come about? What if the European countries, led by France, tried to dislodge America from Europe and the dollar from the international monetary system? The United States could probably manage the balance-of-payments deficit with the support of the major surplus countries for a few more years, but without such help, another crippling gold crisis was inevitable. By simply refusing to help, France or West Germany could shake the confidence of the dollar and unloose debilitating capital flight from the United States. The payments deficit and dollar liabilities acted as an Achilles' heel for the United States, potentially leaving American foreign policy hostage to the monetary policy of the European surplus countries.

## Tensions with France

By early 1962 the Kennedy administration's balance-of-payments strategy seemed in place. The Federal Republic of Germany had signed an offset agreement, trade negotiations had begun, and Robert Roosa had negotiated a whole series of sophisticated defenses for the American dollar and gold supply. But two problems remained: the deficit was still dangerously large; and Kennedy's monetary policy relied on the goodwill of the European surplus countries, most notably West Germany and France, which had the largest surpluses. And by the spring of 1962, America's political relations with both these countries had deteriorated sharply. How much sense did it make to base America's monetary policy on continued cooperation from two allies who were increasingly hostile to Kennedy's security policies in Europe?[38]

There were two related reasons for the deep political tensions between the United States, France, and West Germany: America's Berlin policy and its attitude toward independent national nuclear forces.[39] On Berlin, Adenauer and de Gaulle feared that the policy developed by Kennedy during the summer of 1961 was simultaneously too belligerent and too accommodating toward the Soviets. The administration had ordered a military buildup and authorized direct negotiations with the Soviets. Adenauer and de Gaulle feared that the American policy might lead either to a war through miscalculation or to dangerous concessions to the Soviets that would undermine West European security. Both the French and West German governments went to great lengths in the first half of 1962 to block any negotiated settlement with the Soviets over Berlin.

The second issue of dispute, America's attitude toward independent national nuclear forces,[40] was a complicated story, reaching far back into the Eisenhower years, but in essence both Adenauer and de Gaulle believed that Kennedy was revising America's military strategy toward both a greater reliance on conventional forces and a greater centralization of nuclear decision making in the hands of the American president. Both Adenauer and de Gaulle hated both aspects of a policy that eventually involved what came to be known as the flexible response doctrine.[41] The Europeans feared that the administration's new emphasis on conventional forces would undermine the credibility of America's promise to use its strategic nuclear weapons against a Soviet attack. If the United States was the only NATO country with strategic nuclear weapons, then Western Europe would be completely dependent on the Americans. Most Euro-

peans did not believe America's proposed multilateral force would resolve
these questions, as long as the Kennedy administration insisted on an
American veto over the firing of the weapons.

It turns out the change between Eisenhower's and Kennedy's security
policies was nowhere near as dramatic as the Europeans supposed, a point
expanded upon in the next chapter. Both the flexible response doctrine
and the multilateral force had their origins in the Eisenhower administration. Many of the Kennedy administration's strategic changes were driven
by the unique dilemma presented by the Berlin crisis. Furthermore, as we
shall see, Kennedy and McNamara were not automatically hostile to the
French nuclear program.[42]

These caveats, however, should not blur the far-reaching conflict that
developed between the Kennedy administration, France, and West Germany over the direction of NATO strategy. And from Kennedy's perspective, a European attack on America's weakened monetary position
seemed a logical way to undermine U.S. security policies. Douglas Dillon
told the president "that it must be realized that France's dollar holdings
represented a political as well as an economic problem."[43] A widely circulated State Department memo summarized a French newspaper article
that warned de Gaulle "would be fully prepared to play the diplomatic
trump card he holds in form of substantial French holdings of dollars." If
America's policy toward Europe clashed with French interests, "de Gaulle
would pressure Kennedy by purchasing gold from the United States."
Unless France was accepted as an equal, the French leader "would not
hesitate to make himself felt by resorting to devices liable to cause grave
embarrassment to United States," even at the cost of weakening free-
world strength.[44]

The deep strain in Franco-American relations and the link between
monetary and security policies were revealed in a remarkable meeting
between Kennedy and the French minister of state for cultural affairs,
Andre Malraux. The president warned Malraux that if de Gaulle preferred
a Europe dominated by Germany, then Kennedy would bring the U.S.
troops home and save $1.3 billion, an amount that "would just about
meet our balance of payments deficit." If France wanted to lead a Europe
independent *from* the United States, then Kennedy would "like nothing
better than to leave Europe." The United States was not trying to create a
Pax Americana, and had no taste for empire building:

> The President said that we have no sense of *grandeur*, and no tradi-
> tion of leadership among the nations. Our tradition is fundamen-
> tally isolationist. Yet since World War II, we have carried heavy

burdens. In our international balance of payments we have lost $12 billion, and the drain on our gold continues. We engaged in a heavy military buildup, and we have supported development of the Common Market. . . . We find it difficult to understand the apparent determination of General De Gaulle to cut across our policies in Europe.[45]

The French leader accused the United States of undermining its leadership by dictating to its allies. By entering into negotiations with the Soviets over Berlin and publicly stating that France should not have an atomic force, the administration risked a breakdown in the alliance. The Americans should stay out of European affairs except in the case of war.[46] The president responded furiously: "We cannot give this kind of blank check." The United States was not going to defend Europe, weaken the dollar, and remain politically silent. It would be very difficult for the United States to continue its security guarantee if France and West Germany organized Europe in such a way as to leave America on the outside. "We shall not hesitate to make this point to the Germans if they show signs of accepting any idea of a Bonn-Paris axis."[47] But de Gaulle dismissed the possibility that the United States could withdraw from Europe.[48] A Franco-American showdown appeared imminent. France, fully aware of America's balance-of-payments problems, seemed willing to use its monetary power in any political dispute.

Would France attack the dollar? Many high French officials believed that the international monetary system was rigged in favor of the Americans. The famous international monetary economist and close de Gaulle adviser, Jacques Rueff, had argued that the current gold exchange regime should be replaced by a pure gold standard.[49] Rueff was to influence de Gaulle's decision to attack the dollar publicly in a famous press conference in February 1965.[50] The French foreign minister, Couve de Murville, argued that the dollar should be devalued. But it is unclear whether de Gaulle considered attacking the dollar in the summer of 1962.[51] France's ambassador to the United States, Herve Alphand, told de Gaulle that Kennedy was receiving all sorts of dangerous advice on monetary policy from his advisers. Controls and a gold embargo were being considered. Alphand speculated that since Kennedy did not understand the economics of the issue, he would do what was politically expedient, which in the end might harm France's interests. Kennedy wanted a secret negotiation with de Gaulle to settle these issues on the highest political level. When asked how he should answer the president, de Gaulle told Alphand to wait, suggesting there was no point talking to Kennedy now.[52]

## Giscard and French International Monetary Policy

What was France's international monetary policy? Like their American counterparts, French officials were also deeply divided over this question.[53] The Fifth Republic's Ministry of Finance was, like the U.S. Department of the Treasury, essentially conservative. First under Wilfrid Baumgartner, and later under Giscard d'Estaing, the ministry was far more "Atlanticist" than other parts of the government.[54] For example, France, unlike other European countries, had not converted the bulk of its dollar reserves into gold. In 1961 the United States sold no gold to France but $970 million of gold to other European countries.[55] Although Baumgartner did not agree to the Kennedy administration's plan to expand international liquidity, he did participate in the ad hoc arrangements designed by Roosa, including the swap and gold pool. Baumgartner's December 1961 resignation left U.S. Treasury officials wondering if quiet but effective French monetary cooperation would soon end.[56]

Unfortunately for the Americans, the finance minister was not the only French official with an opinion about international monetary policy.[57] French prime minister Michel Debré believed that the United States depended upon "easy money" that exported inflation abroad and led to American overinvestment in the French economy. Foreign Minister Couve de Murville wanted the dollar price of gold increased. Olivier Wormser, director general of economic affairs at the Ministry of Foreign Affairs, connected Kennedy's and Prime Minister Harold Macmillan's desire to stabilize the dollar and the pound to Britain's bid to join the Common Market.[58]

The most influential French voice arguing against both the Bretton Woods system and America's international monetary system was the renowned French economist, Jacques Rueff. Rueff's views were forged during the interwar period, when he believed that international deviation from the gold standard had caused the global financial meltdown. Rueff first gained de Gaulle's trust in late 1958 and 1959, when the French president relied on him to stabilize France's economy. Rueff's domestic plan called for sacrifices—higher taxes, a devaluation of the franc by 17.5 percent, strict budgetary policy, removal of the automatic tying of wages to a cost-of-living index, selective trade liberalization, and reduced government subsidies. The currency was replaced with a new franc at a rate of one hundred to one. Though painful, Rueff's reforms tamed France's inflation and won de Gaulle's respect.[59]

In 1961 Rueff turned his attention to the international monetary system. In a series of lengthy letters to de Gaulle, published in *Le Monde* in early June 1961 and reprinted in the *London Times*, Rueff encouraged de Gaulle to bypass Parliament, invoke emergency presidential powers, take measures to end the dollar's role as an international reserve currency, and force a devaluation of the dollar. Rueff argued the gold exchange standard was a "prodigious collective error that allowed the United States to avoid the consequences of its economic profligacy." Rueff also urged conversion of France's dollar reserves into gold as an indication of displeasure with U.S. abuses of the reserve-currency system, which accelerated French inflation.[60] In private, Rueff dismissed claims that America's payments deficit was produced by Cold War security commitments. Rueff argued that U.S. foreign economic and military aid programs were a small proportion of GNP, far less than the cost borne by France during its conflict in Algeria. As a practitioner of strict fiscal and monetary orthodoxy, he believed that a sharp increase in the discount rate would eliminate the U.S. deficit overnight, as the French government had proved in 1958.[61]

Would Rueff come to dominate France's international monetary policy? And what would be the attitude of Baumgartner's young successor, Valery Giscard d'Estaing? Like his predecessor at the Ministry of Finance, Giscard did not share Rueff's animosity toward the United States and felt that it was in France's national interest to stabilize the international monetary situation. In fact, Giscard authorized his subordinates, Claude Pierre-Brossolette, André de Lattre, and Pierre Esteva, to do what they could to combat Rueff's influence on French foreign economic policies.[62] The Kennedy administration was encouraged by a successful visit by Walter Heller and James Tobin to Paris in May 1962. The two economists were welcomed by Giscard and held detailed discussions about the causes of the robust growth in the French economy.[63] Heller and Tobin also tried to convince Giscard that the administration was taking measures to end the payments deficit and stabilize the domestic economy. The successful visit reinforced McGeorge Bundy's comment that "in the current state of Franco-American relations, any friendly contact is a good thing."[64]

At the same time, however, pressure from within the French government obliged Giscard to shift France's reserve management policies toward more gold purchases. With its own payments surplus increasing, France purchased $45 million worth of gold in the first quarter of 1962 and $97.5 million during the second quarter. France also repaid its post–World War II debt of $211 million.[65] Giscard also complained that American investment in France was leading to the loss of control over key segments of the economy and warned that "measures might be taken by the French government to establish safeguards against such a possibility."[66]

Furthermore, Giscard argued that in the future, international monetary issues should be discussed within the OECD, and not the IMF. In exchange for French cooperation within the OECD, the Americans would have to accept certain limits on their freedom of action—a kind of "surveillance multilatérale."[67] Giscard calculated that using the OECD instead of the IMF would give the French government a platform to criticize an overly expansionist U.S. domestic budget, which many within France identified as the primary cause of the American payments deficit.[68]

Given the overall climate of mistrust between France and the United States during the spring and summer, Kennedy administration officials initially suspected a veiled threat when French finance minister Valéry Giscard d'Estaing reminded them that only cooperation "on a grand scale" could help the Americans with their dollar drain and prevent a speculative attack.[69] Giscard claimed that the United States could not handle a real run on the dollar without support from those European central banks that held large quantities of dollars. But he did not present a specific proposal, and the Americans did not want to appear weak by asking what he had in mind. Although the U.S. deficit had decreased, gold purchases had increased, and the dollar market was weak. Giscard's hints fed into the administration's suspicions of French intentions and combined with worsening gold outflow figures to stimulate a top secret, high-level intergovernmental effort to end America's monetary woes.

Responding to rumors of French blackmail over the dollar, Under Secretary of State George Ball sent a memo to Kennedy recommending that the administration take preemptive action in an upcoming meeting with Giscard. "I am seriously concerned about the tendency of our allies to view the present world financial problem as a case solely of dollar weakness rather than as a common problem for the Atlantic partnership." It was time to move away from the position that the payments deficit was a narrow, technical problem to be negotiated between the U.S. Treasury and European central bankers, whose views Ball described as "pre–Herbert Hoover."[70] In its efforts to move toward payments equilibrium and arrest the gold outflow, American policy was increasingly "reminiscent of Dr. Schacht"—that is, of the series of bilateral deals and clearing arrangements that the Nazi government had negotiated in the mid-1930s. Unless an explicit link was made between American military policy and the balance of payments, the United States would be vulnerable to "blackmail" by the Europeans. Ball argued it was time for fundamental, systemic reform of the Bretton Woods edifice.

On 20 and 21 July 1962, Giscard met first with Kennedy and later with Ball, Bundy, and Tobin. The president and these advisers conveyed their

JFK with French finance minister Giscard d'Estaing. During his summer 1962 visit, Giscard surprised American policy makers by suggesting France would help the United States with its monetary problems. Giscard's visit initiated a fierce debate within the administration over whether to launch dramatic international monetary reform. (Courtesy of the John F. Kennedy Library and Museum)

concern over the deficit and gold outflow, and their desire to "manage" these issues on the "political" level. Ball said the administration did not have any formal plan, but felt that in principle some sort of political agreement should be reached to stabilize payments among the major industrial countries. A multilateral, political solution would demonstrate the solidarity of the Atlantic partnership and squelch calls for protectionism in the United States. What the United States had in mind, Ball said, was an agreement regarding the ratio of gold to dollar holdings.[71]

Thus, the administration was pleasantly surprised when the French finance minister agreed with most of what the Americans said about the problem and appeared to want little in return. Giscard had a relatively free hand to negotiate with the United States during the summer of 1962. Better still, he wanted any arrangements to be conducted with minimal publicity because it would strengthen his hand against Rueff and not draw de Gaulle's attention.[72] The finance minister stated that the key was to avoid any unilateral action by either side. He thought that it was important for the creditor countries to establish a common payments policy while the United States reduced its payments deficit. Such an agreement might suspend gold takings and establish fixed reserve ratios. France was certainly willing to hold its dollars for a time, as long as others agreed as well. He thought Great Britain might protest but would cooperate, given its desire to join the Common Market.

The administration was delighted that Giscard appeared to understand American difficulties. Giscard's statements alleviated the fear of a Franco-German monetary bloc. A French-led initiative to reform the payments system would end the embarrassment of continued ad hoc measures that made the United States look weak. In order to be prepared for such negotiation, the administration launched an enormous effort to study and debate exactly what form an international monetary agreement should take. An interdepartmental committee on the balance of payments was created, and a "gold budget" established.[73]

Giscard was hopeful that he could convince de Gaulle to accept a gold standstill arrangement because it could satisfy the general's long-term objective of curbing the hegemony of the dollar. Ball had suggested that after a two-year grace period, the G-10 nations could modify or construct a new international financial structure. While Giscard did not intend to end the use of the dollar as a reserve currency, he did hope to give the franc a place in a broadened monetary scheme that used additional currencies as reserves. He wished to establish a *unité de réserve composite* or Collective Reserve Unit (CRU), which would be tied to gold. The creation of a CRU would address French concerns about curbing global inflation while meeting demands for expanded international liquidity.[74]

### The Debate over Monetary Reform within the Kennedy Administration

The Kennedy administration hoped that there was now an opportunity to solve the gold outflow problem within a political, multilateral context. Giscard seemed to accept the need for a standstill agreement to give the United States time to bring its payments into equilibrium and begin thoroughgoing reform of the international financial system. The U.S. Treasury held over $16 billion of gold, but legally $12 billion was required to back domestic currency. There was much talk about rescinding the laws behind the domestic cover, and the Federal Reserve could take certain actions in a crisis that would release the gold without legislative action. But Congress would want a protracted debate on the issue, and the public discussion would upset the markets and possibly set off another gold crisis.

More important than the gold cover issue was the supply of dollars held by surplus countries, both officially and in private hands. These liabilities totaled over $20 billion, which could be turned in at any time. While this was more than the gold supply backing them, it was not, by the historical standards of gold exchange regimes, a dangerous ratio. Interest rate policy and central bank cooperation could handle a run on the dollar. But if this cooperation was not forthcoming, then the dollar liabilities would be like a loaded gun aimed at the American gold supply. A Franco-German bloc could exploit these overhang dollars to expose American monetary weakness and perhaps force political concessions. Therefore, it was important to take the opportunity afforded by Giscard's suggestions to create a mechanism to prevent a large American gold outflow.

Encouraged by the French finance minister's cooperative spirit, Kennedy's closest advisers began considering dramatic departures from traditional international monetary policy. Gold guarantees, gold standstill agreements, and raising the dollar price of gold, in concert with others or unilaterally, were all debated. The Department of State even prepared a draft memo for the president should he want to end the American policy of redeeming gold on demand.[75] Carl Kaysen sent Kennedy an essay by Keynes proposing an international payments system that dispensed with gold altogether. Kaysen wrote the president: "The great attention paid to gold is another myth. . . . As you said of the Alliance for Progress, those who oppose reform may get revolution."[76]

Perhaps the most discussed proposal was from George Ball. In his memo to the president, entitled "A Fresh Approach to the Gold Problem," Ball maintained that the issue was fundamentally political, not economic.[77] Unfortunately, few people in Europe, Wall Street, or even the U.S. Treasury Department understood this. For them, the gold outflow and payments deficit were signs of American profligacy, correctable through deflationary policies at home and massive cuts in military aid expenditures abroad. By pursuing Roosa's policy of "improvised expedients" and taking the posture of supplicants seeking credits, offsets, and debt prepayments, the administration had created a picture of weakness that eroded America's authority and bargaining power with the Europeans. Ball warned that "this is no way to run the government of any nation—much less to exercise the leadership of the Free World."[78]

Ball argued that the answer to this problem was simple. The strength of the dollar should not be dependent on the "daily whims of private and official 'confidence' but on a structure of long-run reciprocal assurances by governments." The Europeans must be made to understand that such an agreement was in their best interest as well. Western Europeans, Ball claimed, would be just as hurt by a dollar crisis as the United States. More important, they must recognize that the continued American defense of Europe depended upon safeguarding the dollar.[79] Without such reforms, President Kennedy would be forced to take aggressive, unilateral action to improve the balance of payments, including withdrawing American troops from Europe and imposing controls on capital and restrictions on tourism. Ball argued that such policies would not be in America's interest.

Instead, Ball advocated a multilateral agreement negotiated at the *political* level, which would "insulate ourselves from the danger of excessive gold losses" while the administration pursued less costly policies to "restore equilibrium" over a reasonable period of time. If this policy was not pursued, the United States would continue to be vulnerable to the "confidence" game. More important, as long as the current rules were maintained, the U.S. would remain "subject to the blackmail of any government that wants to employ its dollar reserves as political weapons against us."[80] Ball told Kennedy that if the United States were to "become more heavily involved in Southeast Asia," the "West Coast of South America," or the "Congo," the Europeans might be tempted to "exploit our own problems, NATO's difficulties, and our own problem with the gold flight for political purposes."[81] A multilateral gold standstill arrangement would limit America's vulnerability to this kind of pressure. Why would the Europeans agree to such a plan? Ball hinted that the United States could exploit its own political leverage. "Central bankers may regard our expenditures to defend the Free World as a form of sin," he argued, "but the political leaders of our Western allies do not."[82]

Ball provided a general outline of a temporary arrangement to stop the gold outflow. Its provisions included a massive increase in treasury swaps with foreign central banks, a long-term loan with a consortium of European allies, large withdrawals from the IMF, and fixed gold ratios for central bank portfolios. The United States would have to redistribute some of its gold and perhaps guarantee overseas dollar holdings. Ultimately, Ball believed the United States should seek a "thorough-going" revision of the Bretton Woods system, "multilateralizing" responsibility for the creation of liquidity as Giscard suggested during his visit. The under secretary of state was fully prepared to sacrifice the "hegemonic" role of the dollar if a new system reduced America's vulnerability.

The key to any plan was convincing the Europeans to maintain the same or a smaller proportion of their reserves in gold. James Tobin of the Council of Economic Advisers produced a plan to accomplish this.[83] To meet Giscard's demand for similar conversion policies among the European nations, Tobin suggested that the leading industrial countries determine a uniform ratio of gold to foreign exchange to which all countries would have to adhere. This would require countries with gold in excess of this ratio to sell a part of their gold for foreign exchange. Instead of only using the dollar and sterling as reserves, the currencies of all participating countries would be acceptable. French demands that the franc be treated as a reserve currency on par with the dollar would be satisfied. Each country would provide a gold guarantee for its currency against devaluation. Tobin laid out several different ways this could be done, but they would all involve America's selling gold for foreign exchange and retiring dollar liabilities. Some European countries would also have to sell or buy gold. Over time, the nongold component of reserves would decrease, and the currencies of the participating countries would increasingly share the burden borne solely by the dollar. Removing the wide variations in gold ratios would make the international monetary mechanism more predictable and manageable.

The president was keenly interested in these plans, and commissioned a small, interdepartmental group to draft an interim international monetary agreement based on Ball's and Tobin's ideas. The group, drawn from the Departments of State and Treasury and the CEA, produced a plan that would protect the American gold supply and strengthen the dollar. The report claimed that cyclical forces would combine with measures already taken to end America's balance-of-payments deficit within a few years. The heart of the plan was a proposed standstill agreement between ten members, called the Paris Club, and Switzerland whereby the participants would agree not to convert the official dollar balances they held at the start of the agreement into gold. In order to accommodate increases in the dollar balances of the participants over the two years of the plan, $10 billion would be mobilized from a variety of financial sources. This would include $1 billion of American gold sales, a $5 billion drawing on the IMF, $2.5 billion in swaps and direct borrowings from Europe, and up to $1.5 billion in forward exchange operations undertaken by the Treasury Department.[84]

The purpose of this agreement was twofold: to get the countries of Western Europe to "extend more credit to the U.S. than they might voluntarily" and to dampen speculative attacks on the dollar. Even with the plan in place, there were all sorts of potential difficulties. The two years had to be used to eliminate the "basic" deficit, and there would certainly be large-scale reshuffling and uncertainty when the arrangement ended. To make the plan work, it had to be acceptable to the Europeans and, in fact, had to be initiated by the Europeans, so that it did not look like an act of American weakness. The report did not suggest how the Europeans could be brought to accept, let alone propose, such a plan.

Walter Heller, the CEA chair, was extremely enthusiastic about the interdepartmental proposal. It would "eliminate the whims and prejudices of currency speculators and bankers from the making of U.S. policy." The administration could end the basic deficit in an orderly way, without deflation or drastic cuts in programs crucial to American foreign policy. An international, interim agreement would give the United States far more protection than the techniques used by the Treasury Department, which were employed on a "secret, day-to-day, piecemeal, ad-hoc basis."[85] An interim agreement would also give world leaders time to scrap the Bretton Woods regime and come up with a world payments system that defended all currencies against speculative attack, internationalized the burdens of providing international money, and provided for an orderly increase in liquidity. Carl Kaysen, the National Security Council officer responsible for international monetary affairs, and Kermit Gordon, a member of the Council of Economic Advisers, went so far as to argue that devaluation could remain a potentially profitable action for the United States, even after the guarantee was paid off.[86]

Douglas Dillon was infuriated by these analyses. In a cover memo to a report written by Henry Fowler, Dillon claimed that Ball's interim reserve scheme was simply a reflection of the State Department's "reluctance to squarely tackle the more difficult but fundamentally necessary job of obtaining a more adequate sharing of the burden by our European friends."[87] The Treasury Department argued that Ball was treating the symptom, the gold outflow, and not the disease—the continuing balance-of-payments deficit. The interim reserve scheme would give a green light to loosen up on all the disciplines that the administration had established to cure the payments imbalance. Fowler agreed that international discussion on the balance of payments should be raised to the highest political level, but the focus should be on increased burden sharing within NATO, not reserve composition. The U.S. balance of payments would never move to equilibrium unless the Europeans started paying a greater share of NATO's military costs.[88]

Dillon was even more caustic in his attack on the interim agreement, despite the fact that a treasury representative, John Leddy, had helped write the report. In essence, the actions proposed would close the gold window for $7.9 billion of official dollar balances, an abandonment of traditional gold policy similar in scope to the U.S. devaluation of 1933.[89] The Kennedy administration would be reneging on its promise not to change its gold policy, which would shake private financial markets and scare those countries not participating in the agreement. Dillon believed that using the word "standstill" would evoke memories of the German standstill agreement of 1931, an event associated with the world economic collapse. A formal gold standstill arrangement would mean that "it would no longer be sensible" to "expect foreign monetary authorities to continue to hold dollars as an international reserve currency," thereby eliminating the "important substantive advantages" the United States enjoyed under the Bretton Woods system.[90] The plan assumed that the Europeans would agree to such a scheme, an idea Dillon found preposterous. The secretary of the treasury found an ally in Federal Reserve Board chairman William Martin, who said the plan for a standstill monetary agreement would "hit world financial markets as a declaration of U.S. insolvency and a submission to receivers to salvage."[91]

Dillon also forwarded a report by his under secretary, Robert Roosa, to rebut the charge that the Treasury Department's actions had been ad hoc. Roosa argued that the agreements that had been reached in the past two years between the United States and its allies had been very successful. It had not been a policy of ad hoc expedients, as many had claimed, but a well thought out and innovative plan to strengthen the Bretton Woods system. It only appeared ad hoc because many of the discussions held between financial officials were secret. These arrangements, however, made the global payments system much better prepared to absorb the shocks of any future financial disturbance. The gold pool, swap agreements, forward exchange operations, and increased IMF borrowing privileges allowed the United States to rebuff any attack on the dollar. According to Roosa, some of the ideas being discussed, both inside and outside the administration, were foolish. Devaluation, gold guarantees, or a gold standstill would damage or destroy a world payments system that had greatly benefited the United States and its allies.[92] Dillon believed these policies more appropriate for the currency of a Third World country, not the United States, and publicly tried to sabotage the idea. Kaysen was infuriated when Dillon testified before the Congressional Joint Economic Committee on 17 August and called gold guarantees a "dangerous experiment . . . a poor idea and not to be seriously considered." Dillon also ruled out changing the value of the dollar. McGeorge Bundy was worried that Dillon's public statements would preclude the changes in international monetary policy that the administration was considering.[93]

Surprisingly, the reformers were unconcerned with Dillon's contention that the United States might lose the benefits of "seigniorage" in a new international monetary system. During a meeting on 20 August 1962, Ball told the president that "we're not persuaded that it is at all vital to the United States that we do return to a situation in which the dollar would be the principal reserve currency . . . we can see many disadvantages as well as advantages." Kennedy appeared to agree with Ball's analysis. "I see the advantages to the Western world to have a reserve currency, and therefore it's an advantage to us as part of the Western world, but what is the national, narrow advantage?" When Dillon tried to spell out these benefits, Kaysen pointedly asked, "[Y]ou wouldn't describe this as an advantage right now, would you Doug?"[94]

The president seemed to side with the reformers against Dillon. Kennedy argued that now was the time to negotiate a monetary agreement with the Europeans because "we have much more political strength with them now than we'll probably have two years from now." The Europeans "are much more dependent upon us militarily than they might be" before they "get together" to organize their own defense.[95] The administration wanted the Europeans to agree that for "a two year period . . . they're not going to ask" for gold while "our balance of payments situation improves and while we work on other arrangements."[96] The president concluded that the administration should "pursue" the gold standstill arrangement, "because I think this is really the area where we may be able to make some progress." Kennedy wanted the Europeans to agree that in the future "they are all going to go easy on the taking of gold."[97]

Kennedy dispatched Assistant Secretary of State C. Griffith Johnson and Assistant Secretary of the Treasury John Leddy to explore the possibilities of a European initiative to limit foreign purchases of U.S. gold and to strengthen the international monetary system. Kennedy suggested that an acceptable arrangement would be for the Common Market countries and the United Kingdom each to set an absolute target for gold holdings, as opposed to a ratio, which could be controversial and might involve *increasing* the amount of gold held by certain countries. Another solution would be to limit the amount of gold taken from the United States to a small percentage, perhaps 30 percent, of the overall payments deficit. But regardless of the plan, Kennedy insisted that it should look like a voluntary European initiative. Any evidence of U.S. pressure could shake the confidence of financial markets and lead to a run on American gold.[98]

Giscard appeared ready to negotiate. While always wary of the British and any deals between *les Anglo-Saxons* that excluded France, he did invite the G-10 finance ministers to participate in discussions at the upcoming IMF–World Bank meeting. Anxious to maneuver without arousing de Gaulle's intervention, he asked the G-10 ministers to limit accompanying officials to two persons and to conduct their meetings without publicity.[99] But even with these precautions, Giscard and the Americans found it hard to engage in serious negotiations. For example, when Leddy and Johnson asked Giscard what British chancellor of exchequer Reginald

Maudling's thoughts were on the subject, Giscard replied that "the two were in agreement that there should be high level secret discussions of the subject." Giscard did not tell Johnson and Leddy what the "subject" actually was. Was it the hoped-for initiative to limit gold takings? Giscard did not say, and the American representatives thought it imprudent to ask. Later, British representatives asked the Americans what Giscard had said and, after being told, observed that "the whole affair was mysterious." The next day, French officials said the same thing.[100]

President Kennedy was scheduled to speak in late September to the central bankers and finance ministers of the G-10 at the IMF–World Bank meeting. The purpose of the meeting was to tell the Europeans that the underlying cause of the American deficit was its disproportionate share of Western military and aid expenditures. This group had heard this message many times before, but the meeting would give the president the chance, as Kaysen put it, to "give them a real feeling of how central it is to your thinking. This is something that you can convey directly in a way no one else can." Kaysen urged Kennedy to tell his audience that the administration recognized the fact that "there is more than one way the system might evolve in relation to the central role of the dollar, and we do not foreclose consideration of alternative schemes of improvement for the payments system." In other words, the United States was not wedded to the Bretton Woods structure and its supposed privileges. A better system could be created that reflected the new economic strength of the Europeans. This new system would give the Europeans an "expanded role in the international monetary system."[101]

Dillon argued, however, that it was too risky to act without the hoped-for French or European initiative suggested by Giscard. "A statement by you that we are prepared to study new ideas and welcome new initiatives would in all probability be misinterpreted . . . as indicating a lack of confidence on your part in our ability to handle our balance of payments problem within the framework of the existing monetary system. This could have dangerous and immediate effects this fall." Lacking a formal proposal from the French, Kennedy's speech was closer to Dillon's than Kaysen's approach, hinting that the administration was open to international monetary discussions but offering no concrete American plans. The American team adopted this position because of the fear that "open pressure on the French might lead them to think that political questions could be successfully interjected."[102]

The momentum for monetary reform subsided considerably after the IMF meeting. By the time Kennedy returned to the dollar and gold outflow issue, America's political relations with France had deteriorated markedly. Without assurances that other European nations would restrict hoarding of gold, the French government began increasing its conversion of dollars to over $100 million in each of the first two quarters of 1963.[103] More important, after 1962, Rueff and others who were against monetary cooperation with the Americans increased their influence with de Gaulle. Worse, one of Kennedy's greatest fears—a Franco-German political bloc that used its surplus dollars to compel changes in America's political strategies in Europe—seemed to become a reality as the year 1963 began.[104]

With France and the United States in vehement disagreement over *how* to reform the global payments system, meaningful change was elusive. But it is important to note that the Kennedy administration was not wedded to the Bretton Woods system and felt more vulnerable than hegemonic under its rules. While they were not sure what they wanted exactly, key officials, including President Kennedy, were willing to contemplate fundamental changes to the system, *even* if this meant sacrificing the dollar's central role in the global payments system. What is perhaps even more surprising is that the French were not monolithically determined to oppose the Americans in this area in the early 1960s. Even de Gaulle was open to options that went beyond a pure gold standard, as long as the "exorbitant privileges" of the dollar were curtailed.[105] In the end, to characterize America's and France's attitudes toward the Bretton Woods system in terms of hegemony or empire is a vast oversimplification. There were ambiguities and contradictions in policies on both sides of the Atlantic, as the United States and Western Europe struggled to understand how to pursue their narrower national interests without precipitating a worldwide monetary calamity.

## Chapter Four

# Reform, Restrictions, or Redeployments?

*The Balance of Payments
and the Franco-German Revolt, 1963*

In January 1963 Secretary of the Treasury Douglas Dillon received two urgent memos from the president. The first dealt with Dillon's estimates for American gold losses for 1964. "I am concerned about the figures that you sent me on the gold drain for 1963. Won't this bring us in January 1964 to a critically low point? What are the prospects that we could bring this under control by 1964?" Two days later, the president warned Dillon that "our present difficulties with France may escalate. If things become severe enough it is conceivable that they will take some action against the dollar—to indicate their power to do something if nothing else." Kennedy wanted a plan to deal with any French action, including options of taking "extreme steps if that should prove necessary."[1] Less than a week later, the president warned the National Security Council that "De Gaulle may be prepared to break up NATO . . . the French may suddenly decide to cash in their dollar holdings as a means of exerting economic pressure of us."[2]

Why had this interallied tension exploded into a full-blown public dispute, only weeks after the successful resolution of the Cuban Missile Crisis? Only six months earlier, the French finance minister had expressed sympathy for the administration's efforts to combat the American payments deficit and had suggested a unified Western response to forestall a global monetary crisis. The Kennedy administration had hoped that a European-led initiative would lead to an international monetary plan that might include a gold standstill, reserve ratios, and large-scale funding of dollar liabilities. Despite the vehement objections of Douglas Dillon and the Treasury Department, President Kennedy wanted to explore opportunities to improve the global payments system. While the payments deficit remained dangerously high, there was a hope that some sort of multilateral plan would provide the time and space the administration sought to bring the American balance of payments into equilibrium.

Two events, de Gaulle's press conference on 14 January and the announcement, only nine days later, of the Franco-German treaty, provoked a political crisis that shook the foundations of the Western alliance.[3] Both appeared to signal a Franco-German revolt against U.S. policy toward Europe and an effort to undermine and weaken American influence on the continent.[4] And both appeared to threaten key elements of U.S. foreign economic policy, including trade negotiations, the American gold supply, the position of the dollar, and the German offset arrangement. The long-feared European revolt had finally appeared, and Kennedy wanted to be prepared should France, alone or with West Germany, move to weaken America's monetary position. Proposals for radical reform of the global payments system, rejected in 1962, were actively reconsidered in 1963. Policies that had once been deemed out of bounds, such as restrictions on the capital markets and massive troop redeployments, were now closely reexamined for their balance-of-payments potential.

## American Policy toward Europe Examined

Although much of the struggle with France and West Germany in 1963 focused on the U.S. payments and gold outflow, the underlying issue was geopolitical, emerging from fundamental questions surrounding American policies toward the security of Western Europe. As Marc Trachtenberg has convincingly argued, the "Franco-German revolt" centered upon the two basic, intertwined issues of the Cold War in Europe: the German and nuclear questions. NATO had been created with two goals in mind: to deter and if necessary defeat a Soviet attack on Western Europe, and to bind West Germany firmly within the Western alliance. In order to accomplish the first goal, it was necessary to marshal German military power. But this had to be done without provoking fears of a resurgent, revanchist Germany. These fears could be muted if the Germans were prevented from obtaining nuclear weapons. Over time, however, West Germany might chafe at such blatant discrimination, especially since Britain and France were atomic powers. How could the West German Bundeswehr be expected to face a Soviet military armed with nuclear weapons if it had no atomic weapons of its own?[5]

The solution to this problem, at least through most of the 1950s, was the American security umbrella. The United States offered the protection of its own nuclear forces to Western Europe and especially West Germany, a promise guaranteed by a large presence of American troops on the front lines. These troops were there both to protect and, if necessary, restrain the Germans. This protection tied the FRG firmly to the West, and helped prevent a Stresseman-style foreign policy in which Germany could play the Eastern bloc and Western alliance off each other. The American troop presence also allowed West Germany safely to rearm under the watchful eye of the United States, without unduly provoking European or Soviet fears of German revanchism.

But the American security guarantee had two problems. Almost as soon as it was extended, the United States sought to undermine it by contemplating large troop withdrawals from Western Europe. This led to the second problem, the credibility of the commitment to defend Europe with nuclear weapons. In an age where strategic nuclear parity with the Soviets was on the horizon, this commitment appeared shaky. At the moment of truth, could the United States be expected to trade New York for Bonn or Paris? The American nuclear guarantee was stronger if large numbers of U.S. troops would be threatened if the Soviets invaded. Furthermore, these troops might provide for a credible military response short of full-scale nuclear war. This is why the constant mention of the balance-of-payments cost of these troops was so unsettling to many Europeans, especially Germans.

The confusion surrounding the American commitment produced varying degrees of concern and even alarm in Western Europe. Eisenhower had tried to get around this by moving toward giving the Bundeswehr de facto control over nuclear weapons. But doing this understandably alarmed the Soviet Union, the European allies, and eventually the Kennedy administration. A nuclear-armed West Germany might drag NATO and the Warsaw Pact into a global war in its desire to reunify with East Germany.[6] The Kennedy administration undertook a number of policies (such as installing permissive action links centralizing control of nuclear weapons) that reversed Eisenhower's policies. While this may have calmed the fears of German control over nuclear weapons, it did nothing to improve European confidence in the U.S. commitment to defend Europe with nuclear weapons. It also shook German confidence in America's leadership and reliability.

A related issue was the move toward European integration and eventual political unification. The United States had been an ardent supporter of binding the nations of Western Europe together, first economically and eventually politically and militarily, so that their combined power could be efficiently exploited. This would create a European power bloc strong enough to face the Soviet Union alone, allowing the United States to bring its troops home. But the United States wanted Britain in this arrangement so that it might combine with France to counterbalance German power within Western Europe. A European entity dominated by West Germany would arouse deep suspicion and fear. The trick was to exploit German power, but in a political and military framework that made it impossible for the FRG to act alone or to acquire weapons of mass destruction. But de Gaulle, whose feelings about European integration and unification were ambivalent at best, moved to build a different Europe than the one the United States envisioned. Most significantly, he hoped to use the Common Market as a springboard to return France to great-power status. To do this, however, he had to deny Great Britain's entry. In de Gaulle's mind, Britain was simply a "Trojan horse" for American power. If de Gaulle's vision of French power was to be realized, then it was critical to weaken and eventually remove American influence from the continent and exploit German uneasiness over U.S. leadership and commitment.

Both of these issues lurked near the surface of almost all aspects of U.S. policy toward Europe in the first two years of the Kennedy administration. But they were rarely voiced aloud until the fateful December 1962 Nassau conference between President Kennedy and British prime minister Harold Macmillan that produced the Skybolt decision. When the U.S. Defense Department decided to cancel the Skybolt missile program, a dual U.S.-U.K. project created to enhance the British nuclear deterrent, a potentially deep rift emerged. Without Skybolt, Great Britain might be forced out of the nuclear club. Of course, there were many in the U.S. State Department who would have been very happy to see this happen. European integration would be simpler and the problem of discriminating against the Germans in nuclear weapons would be easier if there were no independent national nuclear forces in Europe. The American-sponsored multilateral force (MLF) would have much greater appeal. Ultimately, however, President Kennedy decided that the United States could not embarrass and humiliate its closest ally. If the Macmillan government believed it was a vital national interest that Great Britain possess an independent nuclear deterrent, then the United States had to be prepared to offer a substitute.

The substitute was the Polaris missile. Fired from a submarine, this weapon was far more advanced than Skybolt. With Polaris, Great Britain could hope to maintain a robust and independent deterrent well into the 1970s. But if the British were to have such an advanced weapon, the French could not be made to feel they were being treated unfairly. A similar offer was prepared for the French, which represented a shift in U.S. nuclear policy. Would anything meaningful in the way of nuclear weapons be offered to the West Germans? Noises were made about the MLF, and the British had to promise their Polaris forces to a combined NATO force (from which they could withdraw), but at heart there was no way around the fact that the Germans were going to be discriminated against in the nuclear arena. Adenauer would be angry, of course, but with the

French and the British back on board with U.S. policy, there would be little the FRG could do except follow along.[7]

The Kennedy administration hoped that it could negotiate a deal with de Gaulle that might end the acrimony that had plagued Franco-American relations in the past. But before serious negotiations could begin, de Gaulle rejected the offer during his press conference on 14 January 1963. At the same press conference, he rejected Great Britain's application for membership in the European Economic Community (EEC). Clearly, the two issues were related in de Gaulle's mind—the Skybolt offer proved that Britain was still subservient to the United States and therefore unsuitable for de Gaulle's vision of Europe. Whether de Gaulle fully understood the American offer (particularly the phrase "similar arrangement") is a subject for debate. But the muted anti-Americanism that had been straining the alliance was now completely out in the open.

Both issues, the nuclear question and European integration, had important consequences for the U.S. balance of payments. The foreign exchange cost of the American troops in Western Europe was often the largest deficit account in the overall U.S. balance of payments. It was also an account that, unlike trade or capital accounts, could be directly controlled by government policy. With the payments deficit seemingly out of control, bringing American troops home seemed the most reasonable thing to do. This feeling was only increased when the Europeans purchased American gold with these deficit dollars or failed to provide adequate funding for their own military commitments to NATO. Many American policy makers, especially President Eisenhower and even Kennedy, felt that the Europeans would never do more to defend themselves as long as the Americans were there to do it for them. But if these troops were removed or significantly reduced, the American nuclear guarantee would be severely weakened and the pressure on the FRG to develop an independent nuclear capability would increase.

The evolution of the EEC had direct balance-of-payments consequences as well. The United States had allowed the Common Market to erect tariffs and trade restrictions that blatantly discriminated against American goods. This was done in the hope that intra-European trade flows would economically bind the continent together, thereby making it easier to establish political and military ties, and eventually union. Of course, this discrimination hurt the trade account of the U.S. balance of payments, but this price was well worth paying if the Common Market developed into a true United States of Europe. But if de Gaulle's plans were realized, the Common Market might be used against American interests. The United States would still suffer on its trade account to Western Europe, but instead of a United States of Europe, the Common Market could become a tool to destroy the Atlantic alliance and forward de Gaulle's dreams of French hegemony in Western Europe.

De Gaulle's press conference made it clear that he was trying to undermine American policy toward Europe. The announcement of a Franco-German Treaty so soon after de Gaulle's attack made it appear as if the FRG supported France's anti-American policy. A Franco-German bloc did not have the military or political power to force a change in American policy, but it might have the economic power or, to be exact, the monetary power. West Germany and France held more dollars in their reserves than any other country, and their balance-of-payments surplus would grow if the Common Market increased its tariffs and restrictions against American goods. By using their strong payments position and large dollar reserves, France and Germany could expose America's monetary weakness. They could run down the U.S. gold supply and shake confidence in the dollar. In the panicked days following the press conference and the announcement of the treaty, the Kennedy administration was almost paranoid in its fear that the Europeans were trying to force the United States out of Europe.

## International Monetary Policy Reviewed

De Gaulle's press conference threw the administration into a panic. To what lengths would the French president go to undermine American influence on the continent? A deal with Russia? A Franco-German power bloc? An attack on the U.S. monetary position? Kennedy ordered a complete reassessment of American policy toward Europe. The president was keenly aware of American financial weakness. "The U.S. military position is good but our financial position is vulnerable."[8] The threat of a Franco-German monetary attack, or even an attack by France alone, provoked a reevaluation of U.S. foreign economic policy. In his typical fashion, the secretary of defense crisply laid out the choice the administration faced in dealing with de Gaulle. The United States could "disengage entirely from Europe." Or the administration could "tie ourselves much more closely to the European powers other than France." McNamara explained that there were "certain actions we could take in the immediate future which would contribute to either of the two courses of action he described."[9]

To make matters worse, the balance of payments for 1962 was far poorer than had been expected. The commercial trade surplus had fallen from $3.2 billion to $2 billion. The deficit figures would have been even higher if not for European debt repayments of $666 million, a source of financing that was a rapidly wasting asset, and $250 million in fifteen- to sixteen-month borrowings from surplus countries. The predictions made by the Cabinet Balance of Payments Committee in October 1962, that the 1964 deficit would be "only" $1 billion, had been "overly optimistic." Most alarming was the loss of gold. Surplus countries were "becoming less prepared to increase their dollar holdings, much less to increase the ratio of dollars to gold in their reserves." The State Department predicted that 1963 gold losses would be "fairly heavy," and the United States would find itself financing an increasing percentage of its deficit in gold sales in future years. What was urgently needed was "time and protection" to allow the administration to achieve payments equilibrium without having to resort to actions that might permanently damage fundamental U.S. interests.[10] But how was this to be accomplished?

The president linked the continued presence of American troops in Europe to a resolution of U.S. payments difficulties. In an NSC meeting soon after de Gaulle's press conference, Kennedy declared that "our balance of payments problem is serious, it is not now under control, and it must be righted at the latest by the end of 1964." The Europeans must be prevented from "taking actions which make our balance of payments worse." It was time to exploit what power the United States had to achieve its objectives. Kennedy pointed out that the United States maintained large forces in West Germany and the administration must oppose actions that hurt American economic interests. "We cannot continue to pay for the military protection of Europe while the NATO states are not paying for their fair share and living off the 'fat of the land.'" It was time to "consider very hard the narrower interests of the United States."[11] The United States no longer had any source of financial pressure it could exert on the Europeans and had to exploit its military power before the Europeans went nuclear. "This sanction is wasting away as the French develop their own nuclear capability."[12]

Dillon pushed Kennedy to order troop withdrawals. "He felt that if the French did attack our financial stability we should consider ways of responding by actions in the military and political areas." Later in the meeting, Dillon suggested that "we examine the question of how many forces the U.S. must have in Europe." The secretary of the treasury wondered "whether the withdrawal of U.S. troops would be the disaster some say it would . . . especially if Europe could defend itself against a Soviet attack." Kennedy appeared to agree. "Congress might well conclude that we should not help Europe if de Gaulle continues to act as he has been."[13] At a later meeting, when Dean Acheson suggested that the administration promise the Europeans that for some specified period of time the United States would not remove American troops in Europe for "peripheral"

JFK and Adenauer. Kennedy was convinced that the French and West Germans were getting a "free ride." The president told his National Security Council, "We cannot continue to pay for the military protection of Europe while the NATO states are not paying for their fair share and living off the 'fat of the land.'" (From *Time*, 18 May 1962)

reasons such as the payments deficit, the president dismissed his idea outright. "He said that the threat of withdrawing our troops was about the only sanction we had, and, therefore, if we made such a statement, we would give away our bargaining power."[14]

From a purely economic standpoint, redeploying American troops should have been an uncomplicated issue. It could have been argued that after the American "victory" in the Cuban Missile Crisis, the danger of a Soviet move against Berlin was small. Kennedy was now convinced that the Soviets were not going to risk thermonuclear war to invade Europe, and he found arguments that they would go for some sort of limited land grab in West Germany preposterous.[15] If large troop deployments abroad threatened the strength of the dollar and the health of the global payments system, then it made perfect sense to reduce them. Kennedy could hardly support domestic deflation, restrict American tourism abroad, and prohibit capital exports by American banks and industries in order to finance unneeded U.S. troops in Europe.

The issue of troop redeployments was not simply an economic concern. Strategically, a large withdrawal of American troops could signal that the United States was abandoning the flexible response posture. The political aspect of redeployment revolved around the German question. If the Americans withdrew troops, West Germany would feel uncertain about the American commitment to defend it with its nuclear arsenal, thereby increasing pressure to acquire its own national deterrent. If West Germany sought nuclear weapons, the tentative European "détente" which was emerging between the United States and the Soviet Union in 1963 would unravel.[16] The president would have to choose between the strong economic and domestic political appeal of troop withdrawals and the complicated but indisputable strategic-political logic of a continued American troop presence.

The bureaucratic gold battle was resumed with vigor. Instead of troop withdrawals, the State Department once again proposed high-level political negotiations to reform the international monetary system and protect the American dollar and gold supply. The chairman of the Policy Planning Council, Walt Rostow, argued that America's difficulties were the product of the dollar being "a unique reserve currency which leaves us vulnerable to sudden withdrawals." Rostow wanted to "spread the burden" of maintaining a reserve currency to the surplus countries of the world and explicitly rejected the sorts of deep cuts in overseas expenditures that Dillon thought crucial to bringing the American payments account into equilibrium.[17] Dillon strongly disagreed and argued that Rostow's plan would put the United States "in a position similar to Brazil or Argentina, who, when they cannot pay their debts, go to their creditors and get an agreement to stretch out the debt over a period." Dillon charged that Rostow's ideas represented the philosophy of those who did not want to make the reductions in overseas expenditures that were absolutely necessary if confidence were to be restored to the dollar. "It is only natural that they search for ways to make this very real problem go away without interfering with their own projects, be they extra low interest rates in the U.S. or the maintenance of large U.S. forces in Europe."[18]

Presented with diametrically opposed advice, and uncertain what to do, Kennedy once again hesitated. A mistake on the dollar and gold question would be politically disastrous. Domestically, monetary and trade battles with Europe and Japan could increase unemployment and start an economic downturn. In foreign policy terms, Kennedy understood that he would take the political heat if the United States continued to lose gold. "I know everyone thinks I worry about this too much," he told his speechwriter Ted Sorenson. But the balance of payments was like "a club that de Gaulle and all the others hang over my head." In a crisis, Kennedy complained, they could cash in all their dollars, and then "where are we?"[19] America would be forced off the continent in the most humiliating way.

### Acheson and Ball versus Dillon and McNamara

Kennedy decided to select someone from outside the administration to help him choose from among the conflicting options to deal with the balance-of-payments deficit and gold outflow—a method the president often used to cut through tough intra-administration disputes. Kennedy selected former secretary of state Dean Acheson, a choice that indicated the importance of the issue. Acheson had written the influential "Green Book" early in the administration, a document that set out the Kennedy administration's NATO policy. Many of the recommendations in the report, including more centralized control of NATO's nuclear weapons and increased conventional forces, had been enthusiastically embraced as official U.S. policy.

As part of the overall review of American policy toward Europe, Acheson's task was to recommend how the president should solve the balance-of-payments question. Kennedy told Acheson that the administration "had respect for people who had diametrically opposite views, and the language that they used seemed very confusing to him."[20] Acheson was to go into the problem much as a "layman" would, determine whether the president's advisers were really all that far apart, identify what was driving them apart, and find a way to bring them together.

Acheson spent two weeks accumulating information and questioning top administration officials, with the assistance of Richard Cooper and Mort Goldstein from the State Department. One of the most interesting documents Acheson received was a memo from James Tobin of the CEA, which confronted the basic questions of the economics of international payments without alarm. "Why do we have fixed exchange rates, and why do we attach so much importance to maintaining the gold value of the dollar?" If the purpose of the system was to promote ever increasing trade and capital movements, then it hardly made sense "to preserve an exchange rate with 'Schachtian' measures," which included exchange and trade controls. If such restrictionist policies had to be implemented, it was proof that the dollar was no longer as good as gold. "Neither God nor the Constitution set the value of the dollar in gold or other currencies, and the world would not end if it were changed." Tobin recommended measures similar to those of Ball and Rostow: large withdrawals from the IMF and long-term political loans from Europe and Japan. But if the deficit proved intractable, "we should be prepared to devalue the dollar."[21]

Tobin's memo influenced Acheson. In a cover letter of his report to Kennedy, Acheson used almost the same words when mentioning the possibility of devaluation.[22] Given his role in promoting the monetary agreement two decades ago, Acheson had surprisingly concluded that "the Bretton Woods arrangements have been outgrown; outdated."[23] Acheson rejected the Dillon approach: "We should also not try to patch the problem over with bandaids. We should take new, constructive action which would deal with the great overhanging balances of dollars which the rest of the world is using as their monetary reserves at the present time."[24]

Acheson blamed the American payments deficit on a flawed international payments system, not overseas spending. In fact, Acheson predicted that the present system could be faced with a much different crisis within the next five years—a lack of liquidity caused by the American payments account moving toward *equilibrium* or even *surplus*. Acheson believed that the actions already taken would combine with long-term wage and price trends to end the U.S. deficit by 1967. Drastic actions, such as capital controls and steep reductions in overseas expenditures, could end the deficit sooner but were against the national interest. The critical task ahead of the administration was to find a way to finance $10 billion of deficits over the next five years without provoking a run on gold or a loss of confidence in the dollar. Acheson recommended a scheme similar to the one Ball had proposed the previous summer. Of the $10 billion, $3 billion would be financed by gold sales, $2 billion through IMF drawings, $1 billion through increases in private working balances abroad, and $4 billion borrowed from surplus countries through five-year bonds.[25]

Acheson discussed his proposal with the president on 27 February. The former secretary of state suggested that the whole point of his plan "was to get a period of time in which it would not be necessary to use small expedients with troublesome side effects." Given this breathing space, the United States could get its house in order and determine whether the Europeans were prepared to carry their fair share of alliance military burdens. If they were not, the United States could make "careful plans for rearrangements of our own commitments." Acheson believed that both the French and West Germans would participate in the partial financing of the American deficit; in fact, the French would welcome the chance to cooperate in this field. "The United States was facing these difficulties not because things are going badly, but because they are going well, and that the proposed program is in their interest as well as ours."[26] It is hard to understand why Acheson was so optimistic about the prospects for Franco-German cooperation in this scheme.

Kennedy complained that his main problem was getting the Departments of State and Treasury to agree on a policy. Acheson said the dispute within the administration was caused by the fact that Rusk took little interest in the problem and that Ball "took a breezy attitude which was very frightening to Mr. Roosa."[27] In fact, the two sides were not so far

JFK with his secretary of the treasury, Douglas Dillon. Dillon warned that initiating the international monetary reform proposals offered by Ball, Acheson, and the CEA could incite a run on the dollar. Instead, Dillon advocated deep cuts in the number of U.S. troops stationed abroad. (Courtesy of the John F. Kennedy Library and Museum)

apart, and Acheson pointed out that many of the ideas in his proposal had come from Roosa.[28] Acheson suggested that Kennedy call a meeting and let everyone air out their differences. At the end of the meeting, the president would make a final decision that everyone would have to sign on to. The president readily agreed. But the meeting did not turn out at all as Acheson had hoped. Acheson complained that Dillon staged a filibuster for over an hour. At the end of the meeting, the president reluctantly agreed to allow the Treasury Department to study the payments problem in more detail, despite Acheson's claims that they already knew all they were ever going to know about the problem.[29]

Dillon's filibuster did not end the pressure for a more dramatic monetary policy. In April, Walter Heller sent a memo to the president summarizing the findings of a Brookings Institution report. In 1962 the

CEA, Treasury Department, and Bureau of the Budget had commissioned Brookings to undertake a thorough study of long-term American payments prospects. According to Heller, the report suggested "the present system is basically inadequate" and recommended that the administration formulate plans for improvements in the international monetary system "without delay."[30] Like Acheson's report, the Brookings study stated that long-term trends were favorable but that significant financing would have to be found to cover the U.S. deficit over the next five years. The study recommended IMF drawings and loans from Europe.

The president again tried to eliminate the disagreements over American payments and gold policy within the administration. Kennedy called a meeting with the Cabinet Committee on the Balance of Payments "for a thorough discussion of the alternative proposals for further actions to reduce or finance the anticipated balance of payments deficit in the next two years."[31] George Ball was asked to discuss his proposal to negotiate large, long-term financing of the U.S. deficit, as well as his plan to restrict the sales of foreign securities in the United States. The CEA was asked to lay out its plan for large IMF drawings. Treasury was told to discuss its recommendation to tax or restrict American tourist expenditures abroad. All the other proposals, plans, and suggestions that had been put before the president in the past year were also open for discussion.[32]

Both Dillon and Ball presented detailed plans to Kennedy before the meeting. Dillon, as usual, cautioned against any dramatic moves that could shake international confidence in the dollar and provoke a massive move from the dollar into gold. The solution was to be found in drastic cuts in overseas expenditures, as well as vigorous export promotion and reduction in travel by Americans abroad. All other solutions were simplistic panaceas that could dramatically worsen the situation.

> While this action program is . . . essential, it is every bit as important that we refrain from actions that would weaken or destroy confidence in our ability to handle the situation. Frankly speaking, a number of the suggestions that have recently been put forward are likely to have just such an effect. Specifically, there is great danger in any attempt to limit capital flows, resort to the IMF, except on an emergency basis, or to ask for governmental assistance from other countries.[33]

Ball pointed out that Dillon was using optimistic numbers that assumed large cuts in overseas expenditures and wage-price stability. But what would happen if the payments deficit was worse than the government anticipated? The committee predicted a deficit of $8 or $9 billion (less than Acheson or the Brookings report). Financial techniques employed by the Treasury Department could finance $4 to $5 billion. Another $1 to $1.6 billion in savings could be realized by further cuts. This would get the United States through the next two years, but what about after that?

> Even on this optimistic assumption, there would be little, if any, financing left over for the 1965–66 period, except through further gold sales.
>
> I do not think this is good enough. During the past two years, we have consistently erred on the side of excessive optimism. At this point we should take a dour Scottish view of the future. . . . Now is the time to strengthen our defenses, since it will become more and more difficult and dangerous to take Spartan actions if events start to turn out badly.[34]

Ball recommended high-level political negotiations with the Europeans to acquire $4 billion in supplemental financing. This could be done through direct governmental credits; better yet, $2 billion could come from the IMF. High-level emissaries would be sent to Europe to lay the groundwork before the president's trip to the continent in late June and early July. The supplemental financing scheme would be placed in the context of shifting more political, military, and economic responsibility to the recovered countries of Europe. Ball suggested that the Europeans would be attracted by the chance to "share world authority as well as world responsibility,"[35] or what Rostow called the desire to "reemerge as big boys on the world scene."[36] This scheme for "full Atlantic partnership" could be linked to other initiatives, including the MLF and favorable trade negotiations. The time gained with this supplementary financing could be used to revise the international payments system in a dramatic fashion. Perhaps a new, nonnational medium of exchange and liquidity could be created to supplement or replace the dollar and gold.[37]

Ball and Dillon confronted each other in a tense meeting with the president on 18 April. Ball again stated that Dillon's numbers were too optimistic, and that prudence dictated a more pessimistic assumption. "If we are forced to take measures to defend the dollar under pressure it will be dangerous from the point of view of national interest."[38] Furthermore, the growth of the world's economy was making the international payments system obsolete. The under secretary of state predicted a liquidity crisis when American payments were brought into equilibrium. If the administration was not going to initiate high-level political negotiations to secure financing for the deficit, then Ball reluctantly suggested restrictions on access to American capital markets to stem the dollar outflow. Such restrictions would certainly be better than "large troop redeployments" or "regressive taxes on tourism."[39]

Dillon complained that restricting access to capital markets would produce little in real payments savings, yet it risked provoking a massive outflow of capital. Ball's proposal was "reckless."[40] If Kennedy implemented the recommendations of the Cabinet Committee, which included large cuts in overseas expenditures, then the United States could finance its payments deficit for some time. Roosa underscored this point. He defined the problem faced by the United States as that "of any other borrower—how to keep our credit standing good."[41] This could be done with a sound financial policy and reducing unnecessary overseas expenditures. Roosa also dismissed the possibility of obtaining political loans in the amount and for the length of time suggested by Ball.

After this meeting, the president circulated a memo to the Cabinet Committee on the Balance of Payments.[42] In it, Kennedy instructed the Treasury Department to continue to finance as much of the payments deficit as possible along the lines already established, minimizing the drain on American gold supplies. The question of political loans was shelved for the time being, but the president did direct treasury officials to prepare public opinion for an American request for financing from the IMF. The Long Range International Payments Committee was charged with studying proposals to increase international liquidity and reform the global payments system, in addition to considering ways to increase member quotas in the IMF. In addition, the interest equalization tax was developed to discourage the use of U.S. capital markets by foreign borrowers.

The most important part of the memo, however, was the plan for deep cuts in overseas expenditures. Although some savings could be reached through the cuts in overseas aid and the so-called gold budget, most of the savings would have to come from steep reductions in military expenditures abroad. "Secretary McNamara should proceed to develop recommendations . . . after consultation with State . . . on specific actions which can be completed by end CY 1964 with the target of a gross reduction . . . of between \$300–\$400 million below FY 1963."[43] This could only be accomplished by cutting the number of troops stationed overseas or, in other words, by redeployment. The secretary of defense had no qualms about doing this: "[T]he only way to improve our position was to reduce troop deployments."[44] McNamara was not optimistic about the Germans' continuing to offset U.S. expenditures in full through military purchases. "We must be prepared to meet the contingency of decreased income from that source."[45] In the months that followed, McNamara and his associates in the Defense Department would go further. Supported by Dillon, the Defense Department proposed deeper force cuts that could significantly affect the American troop presence in Europe.

### The Myth of Flexible Response under Kennedy and McNamara

Had not the United States, only a year earlier, announced a new strategy for defending Western Europe that required *more* conventional forces? Obviously, major U.S. troop withdrawals would undermine the so-called flexible response strategy, and many within the administration were puzzled by the president's desire to pull troops out of Europe. State Department official J. Robert Schaetzel asked how the United States could demand a "greater European contribution to a flexible strategy" while initiating steps "toward a détente with the Soviet Union" and at the same time "move unilaterally toward significant cutbacks in our present commitments and drift back toward the plate glass doctrine."[46] Carl Kaysen pointed out that a McNamara plan to withdraw troops from the Far East would require American strategy to shift toward "an immediate nuclear response." Wouldn't troop cutbacks in Europe require the same shift in strategy?[47] White House official David Klein pointed out the possibility of American troop withdrawals from Europe made the Kennedy administration appear Gaullist: "We are calling for the creation of the MLF, with the proviso that the contributions to the conventional forces will *not be reduced*. But then we go on to say, *either* you put more into the conventional pot, and support our strategy, *or* we'll pull back and support your strategy. And then before the Europeans can respond, we go on to the *or* of the *either-or* condition, and come out looking like good Gaullists."[48]

At first glance, Kennedy's demand to withdraw troops, and McNamara's eagerness to follow through on this command, is puzzling. But recently declassified documents and transcribed recordings reveal that many Kennedy administration officials, including Kennedy and McNamara, did not buy into several of the core *strategic* arguments surrounding the flexible response doctrine when it came to America's role in Europe. This was clear from McNamara's first budget, which provided no additional money for new nonnuclear forces in Europe. The supporters of a more "flexible" strategy were outraged. Maxwell Taylor said that he was "sorry to note the intention to cut back the level of conventional forces."[49] Dean Rusk complained that the defense budget "actually projects a cutback in force levels, principally in the Army, below those currently approved."[50] Carl Kaysen pointed out that McNamara's five-year budget plan kept "limited war" forces static until fiscal year 1969. Kaysen asked

McGeorge Bundy, "[I]s this the New Look which corresponds to the President's program?"⁵¹ Despite intense lobbying, McNamara "showed no great increase in his receptivity" to increase permanently America's conventional force strength, either in his 1961 budget or any that followed.⁵²

Kennedy was even less interested in permanently stationing more U.S. troops in Europe. With the dollar and gold outflow worsening, Kennedy told the Joint Chiefs that Europe was getting a "free ride" on both the political and defense side and that "this situation with our NATO allies had to be changed this year."⁵³ Two months later, he ordered them to examine "how much we can reduce our forces in Europe in the next twelve months."⁵⁴

By 1962 Kennedy appears to have concluded that the only *military* reason for the large numbers of American troops was the threat to West Berlin. Because the city lay well within East Germany, NATO would have to initiate military action to restore Western access in the event of a new blockade. America's nuclear forces, on the other hand, could do little to maintain the viability of West Berlin. The situation was anomalous, almost bizarre. Kennedy felt that the strategic requirements for the defense of Western Europe were much simpler than the requirements for maintaining access to West Berlin. If the Berlin crisis could be resolved, then Kennedy believed he could bring large numbers of American troops home.⁵⁵

What if the Soviets invaded Western Europe? The president made it clear that *any* Soviet move against Western Europe would "lead promptly to nuclear warfare." For that reason, "the nuclear deterrent would be effective."⁵⁶ The Americans "would be forced to use nuclear weapons against the first Russian who came across the line."⁵⁷ Kennedy told Eisenhower in 1962, "[I]f we did not have the problem, I say, of Berlin and maintaining access to that autobahn of ours, then you can say that any attempt to seize any part of West Germany, we would go to nuclear weapons." In order to maintain access to Berlin, you cannot suddenly "drop nuclear weapons the first time you have difficulty." Kennedy concluded that the unique and perplexing challenge the West faced in Berlin was the only "valid reason" for "our emphasizing the necessity of their building up conventional forces."⁵⁸

Kennedy fully understood that reducing the size of American conventional forces in a particular theater meant that nuclear weapons would be used sooner. During a 25 September 1962 meeting to discuss American strategy in the Far East, Maxwell Taylor told the president that if the Chinese crossed the Yalu River the United States would use nuclear weapons in Korea "at once." McNamara actually advised lowering the nuclear

threshold so that the United States could reduce its conventional presence and "free substantial Korean forces" that were being paid for with
American aid: "In the long run it would greatly reduce our military assistance program because we're supplying air power to Korea and Taiwan,
and we will have to supply it to Thailand if we continue the present
policy, which wouldn't be required if we understood that we could use nuclear weapons, particularly nuclear weapons delivered by U.S. aircraft."[59]
When Bill Bundy argued that this was the opposite of the American strategy for Europe, Kennedy disagreed. The president argued that the only
reason that American strategy was slow to use nuclear weapons in Europe
was the fear of proliferation and the anomaly of Berlin. Kennedy concluded, "[I]f you didn't have the Berlin problem, you just had a thin line,
you would use nuclear weapons almost from the beginning if they came
in force." Six months later, when McNamara claimed there might be a
military need for conventional forces in Europe for contingencies other
than Berlin, the "President did not seem persuaded."[60]

Proponents of flexible response wanted enhanced conventional forces
for other limited-war contingencies besides Berlin that would fall below
the threshold of general war. It was often argued nonnuclear options
would be needed to deal with what strategists called the "hostage city"
scenario. But Kennedy dismissed the idea that the Soviets would ever
launch a limited attack to seize a West German town like Hamburg. "But,
of course, they never will." To Kennedy's mind, there was a "great deal of
doubt in the Soviet Union about whether or not we would use nuclear
weapons and . . . it would be unlikely that the Soviet Union, with this
doubt in their minds, would take up a venture such as the seizure of a city
in Western Germany."[61] As the president told his National Security Council in 1962, it was the "credibility of our nuclear deterrent" that held the
Soviets back—because "they think we might use the bomb if they pushed
us hard enough."[62] Only the "geography of Berlin," which would force the
West to "make the first military move . . . detracted from the credibility of
our threat of nuclear war" and made it necessary to "use our conventional
forces."[63] Kennedy told the British chief of defense that the "Berlin situation distorted the whole Western military posture," and that all of NATO
would only need "ten divisions in Central Europe" if not for the need to
maintain access to the city.[64] The British took Kennedy's statements so
seriously that the military undertook a study of how many conventional
forces NATO would need if President Kennedy's premises—a nuclear stale-
mate and a trusteeship arrangement for Berlin—came to pass.[65]

Kennedy's and McNamara's disregard for the so-called flexible response doctrine went beyond a desire to reduce America's *conventional-*

force presence in Western Europe. Only weeks before McNamara belittled small independent nuclear forces at the NATO meeting in Athens, the secretary of defense was actively pushing a pro-sharing line within the administration.[66] McNamara told the president that nuclear sharing with the French "would be justified on *balance of payments reasons alone*."[67] During the Cuban Missile Crisis, Kennedy directed that the French be offered nuclear assistance.[68] As we have seen, Kennedy also authorized a shift in policy during the Nassau conference with the British in December 1962. Perhaps most surprisingly, given the awful state of Franco-American relations during the summer of 1963, the Kennedy administration was ready to give the French "Polaris or Minutemen missiles . . . [o]r Polaris submarine technology" if the French signed the partial test ban treaty.[69] Carl Kaysen, who was intimately involved in the test ban negotiations, claimed that the administration was even willing to give the French "nuclear warheads for their bombs" if they supported the treaty.[70] The contradictions between rhetoric and reality on a series of other issues related to the flexible response doctrine—controlled response, damage limitation, tactical nuclear weapons—are even more startling.[71]

## Redeployment, Offset, and the German Question

After the president rejected the plans put forward by Acheson, Ball, Rostow, and Brookings to finance the payments deficit with large European loans, large troop withdrawals seemed inevitable. McNamara and his underlings plunged into redeployment schemes with unexpected zeal. In late May, the State Department received reports that there was widespread concern in European capitals over rumored U.S. troop cutbacks; along with the reports came warnings that dramatic withdrawals would be politically disastrous.[72] The State Department complained that the secretary of defense "seems to assign almost primordial importance to the military balance of payments aspects alone."[73] Rusk warned the Defense Department that major troop withdrawals from Europe would "be contrary to U.S. interests," and that balance-of-payments concerns did not appear to warrant such withdrawals, at least not until all other solutions were exhausted.[74]

In response to a request by Rusk, the State Department produced a detailed report examining the political and strategic consequences of troop withdrawals from Europe. The authors of this comprehensive report admitted that there were compelling reasons to support withdrawals. Western Europe should contribute more resources to its own defense. Carefully managed withdrawals might even pave the way to similar troop reductions by the Soviet Union. But in the end, large, unilateral U.S. troop withdrawals would harm American national interests. The administration's efforts to "induce the Europeans to accept a broad-spectrum strategy designed to avoid . . . recourse to nuclear war" would be undermined. A withdrawal would play right into the hands of de Gaulle, corroborating the French president's thesis "that Europe cannot depend upon the U.S. to help defend it." The pressure to create national nuclear forces would increase. And the Soviet Union could be tempted into a more aggressive posture if the United States withdrew large numbers of forces.

According to the report, it would not take a complete withdrawal to produce these harmful consequences. Returning only one to three divisions, numbers that were being considered by McNamara, would be enough. "Once . . . as much as a full division was removed from Europe we would begin to see some of the problems described." A one- or two-division American reduction might produce a three- to six-division reduction in European forces. NATO could be left with only twelve to fifteen divisions in the central region, enough for a "tripwire" strategy but far short of the forces required for a robust conventional response. "Such a reduction would make it easier for the Soviets to conduct quick seizure operations with quite limited forces, so that the West would be presented with the necessity for a nuclear choice at a low level of conflict intensity." Because of their small numbers and crude delivery capabilities, the independent nuclear forces created by European countries would likely be targeted against cities instead of military objectives, notably increasing the risk of global war involving civilian populations in the United States and Europe. The report concluded that these enormous risks were hardly worth the "10 to 20 percent" reduction in the payments deficit that troop withdrawals would bring.[75]

McNamara presented his proposed cuts to the president on 16 July. Most involved trimming the fat and did not involve whole-scale redeployment of combat troops from Europe. But McNamara made it clear that he was not finished. He told Kennedy that he was investigating "certain of our forces committed to NATO and deployed overseas, keeping in mind the possibility of redeploying some forces to the United States and in turn demonstrating frequently our ability to deploy to Europe in support of NATO commitments."[76] The State Department was shocked to learn that "the Department of Defense program to reduce overseas military expenditures . . . was considered by the president as only a beginning" and that further steep cuts could "only be achieved by withdrawing combat forces."[77]

Despite over two years of intense effort, the Kennedy administration had failed to reduce the U.S. balance-of-payments deficit, and in August and September the dollar weakened. The president instructed his advisers to "give this problem our most urgent attention."[78] The pressure for large troop withdrawals increased. McNamara was ordered to present plans for further reductions in overseas military expenditures. The Treasury Department was to prepare a contingency plan for direct capital controls. The State Department was directed to examine how the Kennedy Round trade negotiations would affect U.S. exports and to prepare for the emergency use of countervailing duties.[79]

McNamara submitted plans shortly thereafter that would return 30,000 U.S. ground forces from Europe, in addition to redeploying important tactical air forces. Secretary of State Rusk protested vigorously, repeating the arguments laid out in the State Department study of the political impact of troop withdrawals.[80] The president accepted Rusk's arguments, at least for the time being, and approved cuts in the amount of $190 million (McNamara's total package, if accepted, would have realized $339 million), most of which were in non-European areas. But the president also "indicated his desire that a political base be established which would make it possible at some later stage to reconsider the disapproved actions."[81]

The Defense Department wasted no time in publicly trying to establish this political base. The military planned a deployment exercise called "Big Lift" to demonstrate America's ability to transport large numbers of combat troops to the European theater quickly and efficiently. Some worried that this operation signaled a move to redeploy American troops out of the European theater. The deputy secretary of defense, Roswell Gilpatric, noted in a widely discussed speech that "[b]y employing such a multi-base capability the U.S. should be able to make useful reductions in its heavy overseas military expenditures without diminishing its effective military strength or its capacity to apply that strength swiftly in support of its world-wide policy commitments."[82] Within the same week, an article written by former president Eisenhower for the *Saturday Evening Post* called for all but one of the American divisions in Europe to be brought home. The timing of Gilpatric's speech, Eisenhower's article, and Operation Big Lift led the *Washington Post* to declare that the Pentagon was seeking a major showdown on strategy with its NATO allies at the next conference in December.[83]

The State Department warned Gilpatric that his speech would "create serious political problems for us" and proposed certain deletions and changes. To their surprise, "Mr. Gilpatric would not accept the proposed deletions."[84] It turned out that McGeorge Bundy had already signed off on the speech, presumably with the president's approval.[85] While Alexis Johnson acknowledged that Gilpatric was acting on the president's instructions to "pave the way" for future withdrawals, he protested the technique and the timing. The West German government, already nervous about the real motives of Operation Big Lift, would get the wrong message. Johnson told Rusk that "before a governmental decision is made on the advisability, militarily and politically, of making any major force withdrawal, a much more thorough consideration of the issue at the top level is required."[86] But these were exactly the signals Kennedy wanted to send to the West Germans. The Dillon-McNamara approach seemed victorious in the domestic-political gold battle. Large U.S. troop withdrawals from NATO-Europe appeared imminent.

### West Germany and the Gold Battles

What about the international component of the gold battle? The key here was the attitude of West Germany, especially toward the offset arrangement. Relations with the Federal Republic had been quite strained. By 1962–63, Adenauer had distanced himself from America's NATO policy and fully embraced de Gaulle. To Kennedy, deploying large numbers of American troops in Europe was pointless if the French and the Germans were combining to undermine U.S. interests on the continent. In September 1962 the president told the British defense minister that if the Franco-German bloc were cooperating on a nuclear program, as he suspected, then perhaps the United States would simply "haul out" of Europe. If the Germans produced atomic weapons, the United States would "have to consider whether they should regard themselves still committed to their own obligations for keeping troops in Europe."[87]

This political conflict with the West Germans emerged in discussions over the offset arrangement. The Americans expected a complete offset of the foreign exchange costs of troops stationed in West Germany as an absolute requirement for the American presence.[88] But the West German leadership did not accept this linkage. When American representatives complained that the Federal Republic was not fulfilling its obligations under the 1961 offset agreement negotiated by FRG defense minister Franz Joseph Strauss and U.S. under secretary of defense Roswell Gilpatric, German foreign minister Gerhard Schroeder claimed that neither "the Chancellor nor he knew the details of the problems which had arisen."[89] During the spring of 1963, Ambassador George McGhee was warned that the offset agreement faced difficulties in the future.[90] McGhee complained in July that the German military was unwilling to commit to more than $1 billion for 1964–65, at least $300 million short of the amount needed to fully offset the payments costs of U.S. troops. These difficulties made U.S. officials wonder if the FRG was trying to avoid a commitment to full offset in the next agreement. McNamara, for one, did not expect West German military expenditures to keep pace with the balance-of-payments costs of the American troop commitment. But it was crucial that the administration "get the dollars out of them."[91] Only a full offset arrangement would accomplish that.

By the summer of 1963, Kennedy decided to put tremendous pressure on the Germans to accept the link between full and continued offset and the maintenance of six American divisions in West Germany. All the public movements—Operation Big Lift, Gilpatric's speech, press leaks— were meant to make it clear to the Germans that Kennedy meant business. But if the Federal Republic did not pick up these hints, then direct threats would be used. The Spanish dictator, Francisco Franco, told the German ambassador to Spain that the American president had said "the question of the American balance of payments constituted one of his greatest concerns." If he did not resolve the dollar and gold problem, Kennedy would be forced to "change his whole policy" and "dismantle the military support of Europe."[92] In May, Bundesminister Heinrich Krone was explicitly told that the United States would be forced to withdraw to rectify its balance of payments.[93]

During a tense but revealing meeting with Adenauer, Kennedy forcefully argued that "economic relations, including such matters as monetary policy, offset arrangements and the Kennedy Round of trade negotiations," were "possibly even more important to us now than nuclear matters," because the nuclear position of the West was strong enough to deter any attack. "Trade was important to us only because it enabled us to earn balances to carry out our world commitments and play a world role."[94] West German cooperation was expected for all of these economic initiatives. In a September meeting with West German foreign minister Gerhard Schroeder, the president stated that "the U.S. does not want to take actions which would have an adverse impact on public opinion in Germany but does not wish to keep spending money to maintain forces which are not of real value."[95]

The most explicit threat came in a meeting between McNamara and his German counterpart, Kai-Uwe von Hassel. The secretary of defense told von Hassel that the deficit and the cost of stationing troops abroad was roughly equal and that "frankly . . . America cannot carry this burden any longer if it couldn't reduce this deficit." Von Hassel told McNamara that the Federal Republic would probably come up at least $300 million short during the next two years because West Germany was beginning its own weapons production. Von Hassel said this was unfortunate but that there was little he could do. McNamara responded with alarm. "According to the American view it is absolutely essential to leave the military units in Germany. But this is simply impossible if the offset is not found for this . . . the Americans have no choice whatsoever here."[96]

What could the Federal Republic do? The American threat to withdraw troops forced the West German government to make fundamental policy choices that would affect German security for years. But Adenauer for one no longer believed that the Americans were reliable allies who could be trusted.

Following the law of alliance politics, this intra-NATO struggle worsened as the Soviet threat to Berlin receded. America's tensions with its allies came out into the open.[97] Soviet pressure had in the past forced the United States, France, and West Germany to muffle their dispute, but in the wake of the Cuban Missile Crisis, Washington and Moscow appeared ready to try to negotiate some sort of arrangement to reduce the danger of war in Central Europe. As 1963 wore on, it became clear that if the Soviet Union agreed to lay off Berlin, then the United States would offer the Soviets political concessions, like de facto recognition of East Germany and a promise to keep the Federal Republic of Germany nonnuclear. These concessions would undermine the foundation of Adenauer's foreign policy, which had been based on nonrecognition of East Germany, equality with its Western allies, and seeking reunification through a policy of strength. U.S.-Soviet arrangements that stabilized the status quo would imply accepting the division of Germany. Furthermore, if Berlin was no longer a problem, then Kennedy believed there would no longer be any military need for six U.S. divisions in West Germany. The president was convinced that the deterrent effect of America's strategic nuclear forces would prevent a Soviet attack on Western Europe.[98]

The Kennedy administration's move to reach some sort of accommodation with the Soviets in 1963 caused consternation among West German policy makers.[99] Adenauer responded by embracing de Gaulle's policy of independence from America, but in the end he did not have the support of his own government. It became clear to many within the West German government that a policy based on a Franco-German bloc would only mean dependence on another, albeit much weaker, ally, one that had even more incentive to sell out its interests to the Soviets.[100] In the end, there was little choice but to accept a NATO policy based on American leadership.[101] The alternatives to a strong alliance with the United States, backed by six American divisions, were not very promising. This meant accepting a lot of compromises that were distasteful. The key now was to make sure that the Americans did not get so fed up with the Europeans that they pulled their troops out. And this meant that America's monetary policy had to be supported. There could be no more hints of monetary collaboration with the French, no more rumors that surplus dollars would be turned in for gold, and, most important, the offset arrangement had to be fulfilled and renewed. The American demands for German monetary cooperation would have to be met.

In October, Rusk traveled to West Germany. In a meeting with Defense Minister von Hassel, Rusk stated that the administration's policy of maintaining troops in West Germany depended on two things: NATO meeting its force goals and a continuation of the offset arrangement. "If our gold flow is not brought under control, the question could become an issue in next year's elections. The continuation of Germany's payments under the offset is vital in this respect."[102] The new West German government understood what was at stake and, with few other options, accepted these conditions. Flanked by Rusk, the new chancellor, Ludwig Erhard, gave a major speech in Frankfurt in which he publicly acknowledged a quid pro quo between security and money. Erhard admitted that the American payments deficit arose from the U.S. policy of "rendering the major portion of economic and military aid to the free world."[103] This was a major shift for Erhard, who had previously stated that the American payments deficit could only be reduced through basic internal adjustments in the U.S. economy. Negotiations for a new, full offset arrangement began soon thereafter.[104]

The administration had gotten what it wanted from West Germany.[105] The Federal Republic had rejected the Adenauer–de Gaulle policy, and West Germany had, among other concessions, grudgingly accepted the link between offset and American troop deployments in Europe. The Kennedy administration decided that it had to end any threat—at least for the time being—of major troop withdrawals. In Frankfurt, Rusk formally promised an end to the talk of redeployment. "We have six divisions in Germany. We intend to maintain these divisions here as long as there is need for them—and under present circumstances there is no doubt that they will continue to be needed."[106] The president also surprised many observers when he publicly disavowed any intention of removing American divisions from West Germany.[107] In December, a full offset arrangement was reached, and the settlement was announced as an agreement of "great value to both governments," which should be "fully executed and continued."[108] The international and domestic gold battles appeared over. The troops would remain as long as the Federal Republic towed America's political line and offered full offset through military purchases.

## The Transatlantic Bargain

What had happened? The panicked atmosphere, both in Germany and in the State Department, surrounding Operation Big Lift, the Gilpatric speech, the Eisenhower article, and the president's mixed signals appeared to have brought the troop withdrawal issue to a head. The White House produced a national security memorandum that ended speculation and guaranteed the six-division presence in Germany "as long as they are required."[109] The president ordered that Operation Big Lift be presented as an exercise to demonstrate the army's ability to supplement, rather than replace, its divisions in Europe. The memo also instructed policy makers to end the divisive public discussion of the issue. This commitment also seemed to be linked to a continued full offset by the Germans of the foreign exchange costs of the troops.

Withdrawing U.S. troops from Europe would have been the easiest and quickest way to reduce the balance-of-payments deficit. But the political consequences would have been severe. Fears about the effect of an American troop withdrawal on the "German question"—and not its impact on the flexible response strategy against the Soviets—terrified policy makers who argued against U.S. redeployments. In 1963 the West Germans had reluctantly agreed to arrangements that "precluded independent nuclear forces" so long as the United States guaranteed their security.[110] "The objective of German security policy is assurance that her borders will be defended by adequate and appropriate forces. As long as the German government and people are convinced that the United States will defend Germany, Germany does not need nuclear weapons." This fragile arrangement was based on the extension of the American "commitment to the defense of Europe"—a commitment that "should not and cannot be lightly made."[111]

This political and strategic decision was extremely important. By guaranteeing the security of West Germany, the Kennedy administration helped to stabilize Central Europe, reaffirm the American-German alliance, and preserve the possibility of a meaningful flexible response force structure for NATO. It calmed the nerves of leaders on both sides of the Atlantic, which had been badly shaken by the year of crisis within the alliance. But the security guarantee incurred a cost to the U.S. balance of payments. Throughout 1963 the administration had debated all sorts of measures to ease the gold drain and strengthen the dollar—proposals for reform, plans for capital restrictions, and strategies of troop withdrawals. By the end of 1963 none of these strategies had been selected, yet the payments deficit and gold outflow continued unabated. The offset agreement would help, of course, but it was a volatile arrangement that would soon be in trouble. And absent a more comprehensive burden-sharing formula in which all of NATO participated, American military expenditures overseas would continue without compensation.

There were those in the administration who were alarmed that the balance-of-payments issue was being swept under the carpet. John Kenneth Galbraith, the ambassador to India and an important economic adviser to the Kennedy campaign during the presidential transition in 1960–61, was asked to review the administration's balance-of-payments program in the late summer of 1963. Galbraith's apocalyptic reports warned of disastrous economic and political consequences unless dramatic measures were taken to end the payments deficit. Galbraith even warned of a Republican Party conspiracy to scare the dollar into crisis and swing the 1964 election to its candidate.[112] Another report called for a complete moratorium on long-term capital outflows, increased tariffs, redeployment, restrictions on tourism abroad, and requiring recipients of foreign aid to purchase dollar-denominated goods.[113] The administration's economic policy makers harshly criticized the reports. Dillon called Galbraith's assertions "an amazing mixture of truth and fantasy which is difficult to entangle."[114] Gardner Ackley pointed out that Galbraith's proposals said nothing about the dollar liabilities and that his program was likely to unleash a massive conversion of dollars into gold by central banks and private holders scared by such draconian proposals.[115] James Tobin reminded the president that if things got as bad as Galbraith predicted, the United States could always devalue or suspend the convertibility of dollars into gold.[116] The dollar and gold issue was put to the side, at least for the time being.

America's Cold War confrontation with the Soviet Union in Europe reached its most intense and dangerous point during the Kennedy period. Kennedy tried to construct a security policy that met the Soviet challenge with strength but left room for negotiations and respect for each other's interests. But America's two most important continental allies, France and West Germany, felt threatened by Kennedy's policies and openly challenged his administration's Cold War strategy in Europe. Concurrently, the Kennedy administration faced a grave crisis in its balance of payments. These two crises—one political, the other monetary—were inextricably connected in the minds of the participants. The French and the Germans signaled their unhappiness with Kennedy's security policies by cashing in dollars for gold or by abrogating arrangements, such as offset, that were meant to ease the U.S. dollar and gold drain. The administration, on the other hand, believed that the dollar and gold problem could be solved in one of two ways: with cooperation from the European surplus countries, namely France and West Germany, or by reducing government expenditures abroad. Because most of these government expenses were related to NATO expenses, this meant large withdrawals of U.S. conventional forces in Western Europe.

Many of the most troubling issues of American policy toward Europe were quieted before President Kennedy was assassinated in November. But the balance-of-payments deficit and gold outflow problem had not been solved. The optimistic predictions made by Acheson, the CEA, and Brookings that domestic growth and European inflation would correct the payments imbalance were to prove completely wrong. Over time, the weakness of the dollar acted like a cancer on foreign economic policy and grand strategy alike, threatening to undermine the important political and strategic understandings that had been reached in 1963 to stabilize Central Europe.

## Chapter Five

# LBJ Takes Over

## Battles with de Gaulle and Proposals for Reform, 1964–1966

The biggest problem I've got outside of Vietnam is balance of payments.
—President Lyndon B. Johnson to Senate minority leader Everett Dirksen,
18 March 1965

American imperialism, no domain escapes it. It takes all shapes, but the most
insidious one is that of the dollar.
—Charles de Gaulle to Alain Peyrefitte, 27 February 1963

In both domestic and foreign policy, the Johnson administration abandoned the cautious approach of the Kennedy administration and pursued bolder initiatives, both for good and ill. Although the groundwork for dramatic changes in civil rights, fiscal policy, the antipoverty agenda, arms control, and the war in Southeast Asia were laid by the previous administration, Johnson and his advisers took a far more aggressive tack in each area. The same was true for international monetary policy. While the new president did not take a day-to-day interest in the balance-of-payments question like his predecessor, he followed the lead of those advisers, like his Council of Economic Advisers, who advocated international monetary reform. Furthermore, Henry Fowler's Treasury Department, unlike Douglas Dillon's, did not impede, obstruct, or water down the reformers' plans for change. The new administration's tactics were different as well. Instead of quiet, behind-the-scenes negotiations with West European monetary leaders, the Johnson administration publicly announced a groundbreaking plan calling for a Bretton Woods–type conference to create a new, nonnational form of liquidity called special drawing rights (SDRs). The French, who wanted a payments system based entirely on gold, fiercely resisted this proposal for more than two years, setting the stage for remarkable and bitter international monetary negotiations.

American policy makers placed great hopes in the SDR proposal, believing that this new reserve asset would quell the monetary instability that had plagued Western countries during the first half of the decade. But problems beyond French resistance arose to complicate America's dollar and gold problem. When the Johnson administration announced its SDR program in the summer of 1965, the U.S. balance of payments was better than it had been since the late 1950s. But inflationary pressures caused by

the war in Southeast Asia and Johnson's Great Society programs were severely weakening the position of the dollar. Worse, sterling was suffering
crisis after crisis, in the process exposing the vulnerability of the global
payments system. By the time the SDR proposal was approved, after intense American lobbying, it was too late. The SDRs, which were supposed
to create liquidity, could do nothing about the weakening of the dollar and
sterling caused by excess U.S. and British balance-of-payments deficits.

## The G-10 Liquidity Study and the Kaysen Report

The Kennedy administration, which had toyed with various international monetary reform plans, appeared ready to embrace proposals for
change by the second half of 1963. Several factors were at work. First, the
president was deeply frustrated that the balance of payments remained a
problem despite the considerable efforts his administration had made to
correct the deficit. Kennedy's attitude was also deeply colored by his misgivings about Western European surplus countries—particularly France
and West Germany—that held large dollar reserves that could be turned
in for gold at any time. The commitment made by the administration in
Dean Rusk's Frankfurt speech, to maintain six divisions in Germany for
as long as they were needed, meant that troop withdrawals, previously
the most appealing policy to end the U.S. balance-of-payments deficit,
were a less viable option for relief. If the troops that caused much of the
dollar drain could not be recalled, then extra efforts had to be made
to decrease U.S. vulnerability through offsets, gold standstills, and international monetary reform schemes.

Two Kennedy administration initiatives to deal with the balance-of-
payments problem set the stage for the Johnson administration's asser-
tive economic policies. The first was the Task Force on Foreign Economic
Policy, which looked at a wide range of topics, including tariff reductions,
trade with the Soviet bloc, measures to reduce the payments deficit, and
international monetary reform. The second initiative was the Long Range
International Payments Committee, which was chaired by Roosa (and
later Fred Deming), and tasked with evaluating plans to create alternative
types of liquidity.[1]

The initial results of this study group exposed differences between the
American and European positions over the liquidity issue. The French
initiated an effort to establish collective balance-of-payments discipline
through multilateral surveillance, a position that the United States found
unacceptable. The French also criticized what they termed the privileged
role of the dollar as a reserve currency. In the end, all the United States
accomplished during the negotiations was a modest increase in IMF quo-

tas. But the groundwork was established to continue, at a higher level, official discussions concerning the so-called liquidity creation process. When the French suggested a new form of international reserve, the Collective Reserve Unit (CRU), the Americans saw an opportunity. The reserve instrument proposed by the French would be closely linked to gold and was meant to displace the dollar as the main form of liquidity in the system. But as Walter Heller pointed out, the American negotiators believed that stripped of its anti-American and restrictive features, "the CRU might possibly be turned into a constructive reform; a way of adapting the gold-dollar system to the needs of the 1960s; and an acceptable alternative to a strengthened IMF."[2] The French eventually regretted the CRU proposal, preferring a system that relied entirely on gold.

Official American attitudes toward international monetary reform really started to change because of two events: the release of the Kaysen Report on Foreign Economic Policy and, more important, General de Gaulle's February 1965 press conference attacking the gold exchange standard. The Kaysen Report was delivered to Johnson in late November, after his landslide election, and was discussed and debated within the White House throughout December. In many ways, the report reflected Johnson's desire to set himself apart from his predecessor with bold and aggressive policies. The task force had been told to "disregard narrow problems of feasibility in terms of domestic political tactics."[3] The report covered all aspects of foreign economic policy, calling for more open trade (even with the Eastern bloc), the dismantling of American tariffs and restrictions on imports, large increases in foreign economic and development aid, and "mobility assistance" programs for domestic industries hurt by increased imports. It also reasserted the need to promote fiscal and monetary policies that guaranteed full employment. One might wonder how all these goals could be achieved while the U.S. balance of payments remained a serious problem—such inflationary policies were sure to increase the payments deficit—but this disconnect between expansionary domestic policies and their effect on America's foreign economic position was common in the mid-1960s. In retrospect, it is clear that the report proposed a dollar and gold strategy that did little to face up to the contradictions between the desire for domestic growth and the need to reign in the flow of dollars overseas. While not explicitly stated, the report seemed to suggest that the burdens of adjusting the balance of payments could be shifted to surplus countries under the guise of international reform. Ironically, John Maynard Keynes had proposed the same strategy at Bretton Woods in 1944, only to have his plan rejected by the Americans because of its inflationary bias.

The report identified three tasks for American monetary policy: ending the payments deficit, managing the large accumulations of dollar claims held abroad, and "designing suitable international monetary arrangements to meet the needs of the world economy as the volume of international trade and payments grow." The key to the first problem, the payments deficit, was to maintain price and wage stability. This would be difficult during the anticipated economic boom the administration hoped to engineer. The report offered no concrete solutions to this problem. The report simply suggested that the boom would eventually increase American exports and attract capital to domestic activities. The administration should continue to address the balance of payments through policies already under way.

The authors of the report recommended getting the Europeans to finance dollar liabilities in long-term debt instruments, a policy that George Ball had proposed in both 1962 and 1963 before his idea was rejected by the Treasury Department and President Kennedy. The report suggested that as much as $5 to $7 billion in these liabilities be financed in ten- to fifteen-year loans, an amount and a term far longer than anything European central bankers had previously considered. But most important, the report contended that "the present gold exchange standard . . . will not without reform prove adequate to the needs of the world economy." The administration should strenuously push for the types of reforms that the task force believed were in the country's best interest. In particular, the report stressed the need for "a more orderly and controlled process of reserve creation" and a more automatic process for providing adequate international credit for nations with balance-of-payments difficulties. The goals of funding the dollar liabilities and reforming the system were indivisible, and the report contended that "there was no time to lose" in pursuing both objectives.[4] The Kaysen report was quite influential and was widely discussed within the administration.[5]

## De Gaulle's Attack and the U.S. Response

Monetary reform on American terms became more urgent when French president Charles de Gaulle denounced the Bretton Woods monetary system in his press conference on 4 February 1965 and called for a return to a pure gold standard. De Gaulle invited other countries to follow France's example and turn in their surplus dollars for gold. The French policy was not a complete surprise. In a move personally approved by de Gaulle, French monetary policy had become increasingly intransigent in 1964, and France obstructed the American position in the G-10 monetary negotiations. But the severity and public nature of de Gaulle's attack caused great concern. The French added $1.5 billion in gold to their reserves between 1965 and the end of 1966, most of which was drawn from the United States. Because of the large overhang of dollars already in European central banks, de Gaulle's actions forced the Johnson administration to make international monetary reform a higher priority than ending the American payments deficit.[6]

What were the reasons for de Gaulle's public attack on the dollar? As we have seen, French finance minister Giscard appeared willing to cooperate with American monetary officials in 1962. But formal negotiations were never initiated. By early 1963 Franco-American political relations soured, and de Gaulle attacked American economic policies in general and their international monetary policies in particular. De Gaulle laid out his views to Alain Peyrefitte soon after his *double-non* of January:[7] "The United States is not capable of balancing its budget. It allows itself to have enormous debts. Since the dollar is the reference currency everywhere, it can use others to suffer the effects of its poor management. It exports its inflation all over the world. This is not acceptable. This cannot last."[8]

The core issue, to the French president's mind, was the danger of American investment on the continent. De Gaulle believed that these deficit dollars allowed U.S. companies to take over European companies cheaply. America was so large that "we will be able to hold out only if we are armed." How else could France avoid "being submerged by monsters such as General Motors or IBM?"[9] De Gaulle demanded that U.S. capital be kept from "savagely pushing aside the management in French companies."[10] Otherwise, there would be nothing to "stop IBM" from deciding to close its "plants in France in the interest" of its company.[11] Americans "export their inflation all over, and to our disadvantage." They want to "invest abroad no matter what, and that doesn't cost them very much." By allowing the Americans to run endless payments deficits, "we are paying them to buy us!"[12] While many Europeans seek U.S. capital, they "don't want to face the fact that this capital, it is the dollar printing machine that created it, and that at the same time they also receive orders."[13]

The danger of U.S. investment went well beyond economics; the issue was fundamentally geopolitical. De Gaulle told Peyrefitte that "without financial independence, there is no such thing as independence."[14] After having granted its colonies their independence, it was time to "bring about ours." "Western Europe has become, without being aware of it, a protectorate of America. It is now a question of ridding ourselves of its domination."[15] When Peyrefitte told de Gaulle that other Europeans were more than happy to make concessions to the United States, the president exploded. "Europe must decide to be Europe." It must overcome its "inferiority complex toward America, which is her daughter, after all."[16] Otherwise, the United States would dangerously dominate world affairs. "The views of the Pentagon on the world strategy, the views of American business (he pronounced it bu-zy-ness) on the world economy are imposed on us."[17]

How could this so-called American imperialism be stopped? Two years before his press conference denouncing the Bretton Woods system, de Gaulle foreshadowed his move.

> Americans are within a process of taking over all of the economic, financial, military and political networks in the world. It is an invasion that spreads like the flow of a river. Should the Americans want to, they could not oppose it. In fact, there is not a chance that they would want to. Who puts up a barrier? It is not the river. . . . That duty, therefore, falls on us. You will see, our example will be followed in the end if we do it in a dazzling fashion. . . . With dazzle but without arrogance.[18]

How would France dazzle? "If we were to go back to the gold standard, the currencies would be on track." If France began to convert its dollars into gold, then "everyone would do the same." In a purely gold-based system, politicians could "no longer manipulate currencies," even when their "governments are subject to electoral or social pressure." A gold standard "would force governments to be reasonable, the American government and all such others."[19]

The key was timing the "dazzling" policy. When would de Gaulle unveil his plan to undermine the Bretton Woods system? In September 1963, after complaining to Peyrefitte that "the world monetary system is not working properly," de Gaulle promised his close advisers he would not "dazzle" the world with "revolutionary proposals" at the annual IMF meeting after both Prime Minister Georges Pompidou and Finance Minister Giscard begged the president "not to knock over the flowerpot." "I recognize that it is not immediately necessary to let the Americans know" France's plans.[20] The following year, during the 1964 IMF meetings, the finance minister moved closer to an outright attack on America's international monetary policies than at any time before. De Gaulle was pleased that "Giscard said openly in Tokyo what most whisper, that is, that not all is for the best in the current system of international monetary regulations." The French president made it clear that "this monetary system cannot go on."[21]

De Gaulle decided the time was right in early February 1965. The day before his famous press conference, the French president told Peyrefitte

Time magazine cover on de Gaulle and the World Monetary Crisis. The day before his famous press conference, the French president told his aide Alaine Peyrefitte that he was going to announce that "the Gold Exchange Standard has become null and void." When Peyrefitte asked if the Americans and English would see this as an act of "aggression," de Gaulle claimed, "They will react but that doesn't matter very much." In the end, it was up to the Americans to "straighten out their balance of payments." (*Time*, 29 November 1968; © TimePix)

that he was going to announce that "the gold exchange standard has become null and void." When Peyrefitte asked if the Americans and English would see this as an act of "aggression," de Gaulle brushed these worries aside. "Many global companies are expropriated for the benefit of Americans, with capital they get from their inflation. . . . They will react but that doesn't matter very much." In the end, it was up to the United States to "straighten out their balance of payments."[22]

Not surprisingly, de Gaulle's attack was well received in France. Peyrefitte reported that the "journalists are split between the dazzle of this brilliant lecture, the stupor of seeing this military man leap into a technical subject he should not know anything about, and the irony of seeing him go merrily against the dollar fortress, unassailable by definition." Most impressed was de Gaulle's tutor in economics, Jacques Rueff. When Peyrefitte asked if he was proud of his student, the economist said he was filled with "awe." "Never had he heard the dollar, the gold exchange standard, and the internal monetary system discussed with such clarity, depth, and mastery."[23]

The Americans, of course, were less pleased by de Gaulle's public attacks. U.S. ambassador to France Charles Bohlen had cautioned in January 1965 that Washington should "undertake a careful reexamination of the flow of American direct investment to Europe, especially that portion reflected in the balance of payments," in order to "mitigate the adverse effects of American investment as a whole on Atlantic political relation-

ships." This capital outflow was being portrayed as "American 'domination' and 'penetration' of European industry,"[24] producing widespread
resentment in Europe that went well beyond the Gaullists and the French.
Two days later, Bohlen warned that while "French action on gold purchases has essentially financial motivation," it was clear that de Gaulle
had embraced "Rueff's line that France, by holding large dollar balances,
was helping to finance take-over by American companies." The ambassador predicted that "1965 may be marked as the year General de Gaulle
began taking a serious interest in economics—or at least in economic
power." There were signs that de Gaulle was "beginning to take economic
power seriously and hence to apply his guiding principles—'Independence, grandeur, and the struggle against 'American Hegemony'" in the
field of international monetary relations. "It remains to be seen what de
Gaulle's peculiar capacity for destructiveness can achieve in this area, but
I believe we must be prepared for trouble."[25]

Days before the press conference, Bohlen and treasury official John
Leddy reported a rumor that one of the subjects of de Gaulle's speech
would be the "gold problem" and that "all indications are that it will be
critical in nature, possibly inspired by the well-known views of Jacques
Rueff."[26] This was a clear signal of trouble. Most of the economists within
the Johnson administration thought Rueff was "a nut" and believed his
ideas were "mistaken and dangerous."[27] Gardner Ackley, the chairman
of the Council of Economic Advisers, called Rueff "a fanatic." Ackley
pointed out that the old French economist was "not anti-U.S., nor anti-
U.K., but just pro–gold standard . . . he is an international menace,
through his influence on General de Gaulle."[28] It was now clear that Rueff,
not Giscard, was dominating French international monetary policy.

De Gaulle's attacks infuriated key administration officials. George Ball
warned that there were "a lot of very angry Congressmen and Senators"
who may "want to pass a Resolution, which they probably could unanimously, to have the French pay the four and a half billion dollars they owe
us" in defaulted loans from the First World War.[29] Ball told Secretary of
the Treasury Dillon that "the General should be treated as a wild boy."
State Department official Griffith Johnson told Ball that de Gaulle's statement was "as important" as his rejection of Britain's application to the
EEC two years earlier. "We should not pooh pooh this one, we should take
the offensive."[30] Ball told Francis Bator that a "strong statement from
Treasury" was needed, one that took into account that French policy
"involved political issues as well as financial."[31]

In response the administration dispatched Under Secretary of the Treasury Fred Deming to Europe. His first stop was the FRG, where he met with

financial officials on 19 and 20 February 1965. Deming was relieved when Karl Blessing, president of the Bundesbank, told him that there would be "no change in German policy, and that Germany would not embarrass the United States." State Secretary Rudolf Lahr assured Deming that "the United States can depend on German support." But there were also admonitions. Dr. Gocht, from the Ministry of Economics, warned, "[T]he U.S. deficit cannot last much longer and we should understand this. Europe will not take much more in dollar holdings." Blessing was just as blunt. The United States had accumulated a deficit of "about $25 billion" since 1957. If the dollar outflow was not eliminated, the "the number of people favoring a fundamental change in the system would grow rapidly." Worse, "within two years monetary groupings might emerge in Europe" that would lead to "exchange restrictions, destruction of international trade, and a repetition of the 1930's." While the FRG wanted to work through the Group of Ten, Blessing felt that no agreement could be reached until the U.S. "balance of payments problem has been resolved."[32]

Deming went next to Great Britain, where he warned his financial counterparts that "we might have a currency system imposed on us that is not to our liking." British treasury officials told American officials that de Gaulle's attack must be met with a strong response to avoid the danger of leaving "a vacuum" that would allow the "French ideas to be the focus of discussion at the September IMF meetings."[33] Deming returned from his trip convinced that the United States must take action, telling administration officials that "time was running out and that it was essential to correct the U.S. deficit within the next two years at most."[34] The administration would have to put forward a new proposal for international monetary reform to blunt de Gaulle's attack, while simultaneously ending the American deficit. Would Johnson be successful? De Gaulle, for one, was skeptical. "Reestablishing the equilibrium is a very difficult operation. A political power they lack would be required. The Johnson guy doesn't have what it takes. He cannot do it. Just like he cannot make peace with Asia."[35]

## A New American Approach

A week after de Gaulle's press conference, President Johnson indicated his interest in monetary reform in a message on the U.S. balance of payments. Johnson rejected de Gaulle's call for a return to a pure gold standard. "To go back to a system based on gold alone—to the system which brought us all to disaster in the early 1930s—is not an answer the world will, or should, accept."[36] But the administration would have to come up with some sort of policy to ward off French attacks. It was clear that the current global payments system had serious flaws. Though the administration saw de Gaulle's response as politically motivated, there was an obvious economic logic to French policy. Many economists believed the dollar *was* overvalued and if the American deficits continued, other Europeans would want gold.

It turned out that Henry Fowler, who replaced Douglas Dillon as secretary of the treasury, was far more open than his predecessor to international monetary reform.[37] But others in the administration were still not convinced the United States should make any bold proposals. Surprisingly, Gardner Ackley questioned "whether there is in fact such a need" for reform, and Walter Heller wondered if the United States would lose more by presenting a proposal the Europeans did not like. But as several key people pointed out, Deming's trip to Europe had revealed that the Europeans would be demanding a new system in the near future. Why not propose such a system now, when an improved U.S. balance of payments gave the administration far more leverage than it would have had only two or three years earlier?[38] The group decided that the administration should publicly spell out its vision for reforming the international monetary system within the next few months.

Johnson ordered Fowler to form a small, high-level group from the White House, Treasury and State Departments, the CEA, and the Federal Reserve to develop a "comprehensive U.S. position and negotiating strategy designed to achieve substantial improvement in international monetary arrangements."[39] Johnson wanted the group to confront three questions: how could the United States reduce its vulnerability to hostile monetary actions taken by surplus countries like France; how could large amounts of easily accessible credit be made available to finance deficit countries to facilitate the adjustment process without deflation; and how could reserve assets be provided in amounts that would facilitate growing world trade and payments? Johnson instructed Fowler to "explore the entire range of actions open to the United States which would bring to bear our economic strength, and our political strength, to secure reforms which would be desirable." American monetary policy no longer focused on eliminating the balance-of-payments deficit. The administration believed, incorrectly as it turned out, that it was well on its way to achieving that goal. Instead, American policy concentrated on halting French efforts to undermine the dollar.

This dramatic shift in American foreign economic policy was made public, with much fanfare, in a speech by Henry Fowler before the Virginia Bar Association on 10 July 1965. "I am privileged to tell you this evening that the president has authorized me to announce that the United States now stands prepared to attend and participate in an international monetary conference which would consider what steps we might jointly take to secure substantial improvements in international monetary arrangements."[40] The Treasury Department, which two years earlier had gone to great lengths to suppress any program of monetary reform, now warmly embraced it. Fowler claimed that the United States could no longer supply the majority of the world's liquidity through its balance of payments deficits, because to continue to do so would undermine confidence in the dollar. When the United States reduced and eventually eliminated its deficit, some new form of reserve asset or liquidity would have to be created to take the dollar's place. In a world where trade and capital movements were rapidly increasing, the combination of growth and stable exchange rates could only be maintained with larger amounts of liquidity. Fowler called for international negotiations to decide just how this new liquidity would be provided.

Fowler's speech elicited widespread acclaim in the financial community and in the major U.S. newspapers.[41] Reaction in France was less approving. Giscard pointed out that while Fowler's speech "bears witness to the fact that U.S. authorities have become aware of the defects" of the international monetary system, the French government has been "calling attention" to its flaws for "the last three years."[42] Johnson sent Deming and then Fowler (accompanied by a large entourage, including Ball and Bator) to reassure Europe and gauge the effect the Hot Springs speech had in France. Discussions with the French were, at least on the surface, "frank and friendly," and were conducted in an atmosphere of "mutual respect."[43] Behind the scenes, however, the French attitude was far from cooperative. Giscard told de Gaulle that Fowler "takes on the theme of international monetary reform as his, but without giving it any practical contents." De Gaulle was unimpressed, and it was clear that his position had hardened even further in the months since his press conference. "Americans think of themselves as the policeman of the currency world." He dismissed any possibility that the French and Americans could resolve their differences and create a new international reserve unit. "Reserve currencies, it's enough like this. We're not going to invent other ones! There is gold. The rest are stories, they are used to give us the runaround."[44]

## The SDR Negotiations and the Gold Problem

What was the debate about international reserve creation, and in particular, the SDR, all about? In a fixed exchange rate monetary regime, the transfer of some mutually acceptable asset must settle payment imbalances between countries. The Bretton Woods system allowed gold or dollars that were convertible into gold to serve this role. Because dollars could be used by foreign businesses and foreign central banks for reserve assets (liquidity) to settle payments imbalances, the balance-of-payments deficits were not solely the by-product of a lack of monetary discipline in the United States. In fact, much of the postwar U.S. payments deficit was not really a deficit in any real sense, because the dollars were demanded for purposes other than the purchase of American goods and services. (This is explained in detail in Appendix A.)

But after 1957 the demand for the dollar as a reserve asset was drying up. The deficit dollars kept coming, however, both in the form of increased American investments seeking to take advantage of higher European growth and government outlays for the defense of Europe. Many European central bankers believed this influx of overvalued dollars was exporting American inflation to their countries. The French accused the Americans of running deficits to finance American takeovers of European firms. This overabundance of dollars overseas, referred to at the time as the "dollar overhang," together with the ever increasing American payments deficits, undermined confidence in the convertibility of the dollar into gold. The dollar, even when earning interest, was no longer viewed as being as good as gold, and the United States could no longer settle its debts with its currency alone. Between 1958 and the first months of 1961, the United States lost $5.4 billion in gold, a rate that would have completely depleted America's gold stocks within the decade, if not sooner.

But that is not what happened. In the next three years, the U.S. lost less than $2 billion worth of gold, despite a payments deficit that averaged over $3 billion per year.[45] Overseas central bankers held on to over $11 billion in dollar liabilities because of the extraordinary efforts made by the Kennedy administration to dampen the demand for American gold. For example, both the Federal Reserve and the Treasury Department actively intervened in currency markets to stabilize the dollar through forward exchange purchases and swap agreements. Special medium-term bonds with higher interest rates were sold to central banks. West Germany and Japan were pressured into holding deficit dollars earned through U.S. defense expenditures, and other surplus countries were urged to do the same. The most important initiative was the gold pool agreement, which stipulated that the United States and major Western European countries would supply gold to the London market in order to maintain the price of $35 an ounce. This operation, established to avert a destabilizing increase in the free-market price of gold like the one that had threatened monetary stability in the summer and fall of 1960, was quite successful in dampening the private, speculative demand for gold. In spite of large payments deficits, the U.S. net gold position decreased by only $1.35 billion in the two years after the gold pool was started (1961–63).[46]

Despite the elaborate methods that were developed to suppress demand for gold, American financial authorities understood that they would eventually face renewed demand unless the United States eliminated or at least dramatically reduced its payments deficit. But if the U.S. deficit completely dried up, then gold would be the only source of liquidity to settle payments imbalances. Furthermore, while U.S. policy makers understood the advantages of the dollar being a reserve currency, the dollar's role came at a high cost. For example, when the United States had difficulty controlling its deficits, it could not adjust its exchange rate as easily as nonreserve currency. Other countries could devalue their exchange rate to achieve equilibrium, but the United States had to resort to economic policies that restricted American economic activity abroad or deflated the domestic economy. The United States did not want to change its par value; even if it did, every other country would simply shift its own par values to eliminate the benefits of devaluation. The United States could not control dollars held overseas or the overhang dollars held privately and by central banks. A loss of confidence, perhaps inspired by French efforts, could unleash a run to buy the entire American gold supply. To many American policy makers, the American gold supply was hostage to speculators and potentially hostile central banks in Europe.

To alleviate this burden while still guaranteeing adequate international liquidity, the United States proposed the creation of a new asset called the special drawing rights. The SDR would be international money allocated according to a ratio based on gold and dollar holdings. The Americans envisioned it not as a credit but as a real store of value that could be transferred like gold or dollars. The French protested this proposal vigorously. The SDR would not be convertible into gold or dollars on demand. In their view, any new instrument should be a credit that would eventually be paid back, or "reconstituted," into real money like gold. How could you create international money that was not backed by gold?[47] The French saw the SDR plan as an American ploy to force Western Europe to finance even more American balance-of-payments deficits.

The dispute was an acrimonious test of wills; both the United States and France leaned heavily on the major European countries to support their views. But as a result of the trilateral talks, chronicled in the next chapter, the Federal Republic of Germany agreed, albeit reluctantly, to support most of the American policy. The result was that something closer to the American vision of the SDR was accepted in September 1967. The

SDR was, at least in theory, a reserve asset that did not have to be reconstituted into gold. But it was unclear when and how the SDR would be activated and whether they would be widely used.[48]

There was something unreal about the SDR debate. By 1967 many academic economists, especially in the United States, were pointing out that the balance-of-payments and gold problem would disappear overnight if currencies were allowed to adjust naturally in a freely floating exchange rate system. But neither American nor European policy makers wanted this, for a number of reasons. First, there was a real sense that floating exchange rates would be unstable. This instability, it was feared, could disrupt trade and capital flows and deflate the world economy. Furthermore, some (though not all) American policy makers disliked a floating exchange rate system because they feared it would undermine the privileges the dollar had as a "key" currency. As a reserve currency, the United States could finance its deficit in ways nonreserve currencies could not. Finally, the Europeans did not want free-floating exchange rates, because that would lead to a devaluation of the dollar. That would decrease the value of their large dollar reserves and, more important, make American exports far more competitive in Europe.

## Troubles with Sterling, 1964–1966

While the United States battled the French over SDRs, the Johnson administration faced international monetary challenges on another front. America's closest ally, Great Britain, was plagued by balance-of-payments deficits even more threatening than those of the United States. And as Jeremy Fielding points out in his excellent dissertation on the subject, the Johnson administration saw England's problems as far more than an economic issue. Great Britain's monetary difficulties threatened its military positions in East Asia, the Middle East, and Germany, and pressure on sterling made all of these commitments vulnerable. But if the British pulled back because of their monetary woes, the Johnson administration feared that power vacuums would be created in strategic parts of the world that could easily be filled by Russia or China. On the other hand, a collapse of sterling would increase the vulnerability of the dollar and threaten the viability of the international monetary system. Sterling's difficulties forced the United States to make painful choices throughout the 1964–66 period: generously support sterling with very big aid packages, allow sterling to collapse, or see the British prune overseas military commitments the Americans thought vital to the West's Cold War efforts. Because the Johnson administration did not want to contemplate sterling devaluation or British withdrawal and did not possess much leverage to force the British to deflate their economy to improve the payments account, they had little choice but to bail out sterling in 1964, 1965, and 1966.

The government of Harold Wilson faced a choice as soon as his Labour Party took power in October 1964—devalue quickly and get the monetary unpleasantness behind him, or aggressively defend sterling. James Callaghan, who was named chancellor of the exchequer, and George Brown, who became first secretary of state, assisted Wilson in this difficult decision. Brown was also put in charge of a new organization, the Department of Economic Affairs, which was responsible for long-range planning. The DEA, like the CEA in the United States, acted as a powerful, progressive counterweight to the more conservative policies of the British Treasury.

Wilson felt that the Labour government had not been elected to deflate the economy, decrease social welfare spending, or stifle the unions. Quite the contrary. But Wilson did not want his first major act of policy to be devaluation. Labour governments had devalued sterling in 1931 and 1949, and Wilson did not want the party forever branded as the party of devaluation. Wilson and his advisers quickly decided to reject this course, telling Lyndon Johnson that devaluation had been ruled out "now, and for all time."[49] Instead, the Wilson government would pursue a neutral budget in the short term, plan for massive increases in productivity for the long term, and rely on American aid should sterling's woes continue. It was a strategy doomed to failure.

The markets perceived Callaghan's first budget, presented on 11 November 1964, as a poor response to sterling's weakness. After refusing to increase interest rates, the government was forced to raise them from 5 to 7 percent on 21 November.[50] The rise was too late to stem the outflow of sterling, and the Bank of England lost $213 million in reserves in one day. The Bank of England demanded deflation, but Wilson threatened to call a national election if the central bank tried to force policy. The bank backed down, and the Labour government decided to approach the Johnson administration for massive aid.[51] This was the first of several occasions when Wilson would ask the Americans to bail out sterling so that he could avoid politically unpopular action at home.

The Johnson administration was not pleased but approved a package that included large-scale aid and allowed Great Britain to impose import surcharges.[52] Aid and trade restrictions were far better than the alternatives: devaluation, an interest rate spike (which would attract capital out of the dollar and thus hurt the U.S. balance of payments), or reducing British military commitments abroad. The crisis in sterling, and the way Wilson handled it, did not lead to a successful first meeting with Johnson.

The president told the prime minister "our folks were damned tired of being told that it was their business to solve all the world's problems."[53] Secretary of the Treasury Dillon and Fed chairman Martin told their British counterparts that the $3 billion aid package would not save sterling unless the Labour government pursued a rigorous and comprehensive strategy to strengthen its currency.[54] But the Johnson administration had very little leverage, as Wilson could always point out that policies the United States abhorred, including devaluation or overseas military reductions, could also rectify Britain's balance of payments.

The administration's concerns were warranted. In June 1965 British trade figures weakened, and another run on sterling ensued. Sterling's difficulties could not have come at a worse time for Johnson, as the United States was both preparing its own international monetary reform proposal and escalating its military presence in Southeast Asia. A sterling devaluation would jeopardize "the entire structure of trade and payments which we have worked so hard to build since World War II."[55] Worse, by undermining the dollar, a collapse of sterling could threaten America's security policies in Europe and especially Southeast Asia. This meant that devaluation was "unthinkable" for the administration.[56] Just as important, British leaders made it clear that their own security commitments around the world would be jeopardized without American aid. The United States had little choice but to bail out the British for the second time in less than a year.

Still, the administration wanted to impose some conditions on aid. First, the package had to be multilateral. This was important, since European central bankers were likely to set down stricter terms than the Americans. There also had to be some evidence of a British plan to correct the underlying problems in the economy that were weakening sterling. Federal Reserve chairman Martin negotiated a plan with his counterpart at the Bank of England. The Cromer-Martin plan proposed a $2.5 billion bailout combined with moderate economic restraints at home. The announcement of the plan calmed foreign exchange markets. But the summer 1965 sterling crisis increased the bitterness Johnson felt toward Wilson, since it was believed that the prime minister had threatened devaluation in order to force the administration's hand.[57]

Less than a year later, a third and more serious sterling crisis erupted. Britain's currency was weakened by labor strife, troubles in Rhodesia, the escalating Vietnam War, and a loosening of the deflationary measures imposed in Great Britain after the August 1965 emergency. The 1966 crisis revealed deep splits within the Wilson government, between those who supported devaluation, those who supported deflation, and those who proposed that the United States bail out Britain once again. Some within the Wilson government advocated devaluation, and the prime minister had to go to great lengths to fight what essentially became a "no confidence" question within his own party.

The Johnson administration wondered if the Labour government could come up with a tough enough plan to save sterling and, by extension, the dollar and the international monetary system. The United States was in a bind: it was tired of bailing sterling out of trouble, especially since the dollar's performance had weakened considerably. The president would have preferred even stricter deflationary measures, but he understood that if the issue was forced, the British might simply devalue or end all of their east-of-Suez commitments. But to the administration's great relief, Wilson abandoned the high-growth National Plan and rammed through a deflationary package that included large cuts in both domestic and overseas expenditures. The new policy, announced on 20 July 1966, also included tourist restrictions and a wage and price freeze.

The Johnson administration lavished high praise on Wilson for having the courage to take these tough measures. The Labour government had avoided devaluation, preserved most of its overseas commitments, and promised to wrench out the inflationary pressures that were the underlying cause of sterling's weakness. The markets also responded favorably. Wilson's perceived political bravery also made the Johnson administration far more supportive of Britain's efforts to achieve a better offset deal with West Germany, a story told in the next chapter.

After the 1966 sterling crisis, both Great Britain and the United States finally seemed to be on the road to monetary stability. The Johnson administration was preparing a tough balance-of-payments program that it hoped would shrink the American deficit and restore confidence in the dollar among European central banks. The United States was on its way to defeating the French and winning approval of special drawing rights. In time, SDRs would supplement gold and dollars as reserve assets and remove the danger of a run on the American gold supply. It was hoped that a successful sterling program and SDR negotiations, combined with a tough U.S. payments program, would resolve the issue of the American payments deficit and gold outflow issues once and for all.

But it was not to be. Sterling's difficulties were far from over, and the next crisis would be far more crippling and stretch shrinking British gold reserves even further. SDRs would prove useless in the ensuing crisis. The next British monetary emergency would expose the fatal weakness of the dollar, forcing the United States to defend its own currency while scrambling to save the international monetary system.

## Chapter Six

# Defend Europe or the Dollar?

*Money and Security, 1964–1967*

In September 1966 Under Secretary of State George Ball sent President Lyndon B. Johnson a memo detailing his views on how the president should approach the foreign exchange offset issue during his upcoming meeting with West German chancellor Ludwig Erhard. Erhard, whose political survival depended on a successful meeting with the president, sought a drastic reduction in the current offset agreement and a complete and public decoupling of future offsets from the issue of American troop levels in Germany. Several of Johnson's advisers, including Secretary of Defense Robert McNamara and Secretary of the Treasury Henry Fowler, insisted that the FRG had to fulfill the agreement completely. Furthermore, they urged the president to reaffirm the link between full offset and troop levels. German military purchases were a critical part of the administration's policy to reduce the U.S. balance-of-payments deficit. To their mind, any reduction in German offset purchases had to be met with corresponding American troop withdrawals. Ball strongly disagreed, and contended that such a hard-line stand over the offset agreement would prove shortsighted.

Ball's memo, which has recently been declassified, warned the president that the atmosphere surrounding Erhard's visit would be "electric and ominous." The offset issue would pose "a major challenge to American statesmanship." Unless it was handled with understanding and sensitivity, the offset issue could "produce a crisis in our relations with Germany—and hence with Europe." A failed meeting would finish the Erhard government and might encourage forces that could lead Germany "down a dark and dangerous road." Ball pointed out that both German politicians and the German people were showing worrisome signs of "malaise . . . malaise which has been an early warning signal in German history on earlier occasions." The coupling of offset and troop withdrawals made Germans deeply suspicious of American leadership and led to a growing conviction that "de Gaulle is right and that the U.S. cannot be trusted." The American demand for full weapons offset had made Germany feel that it was "singled out" despite its support for a number of unpopular American policies, including the war in Vietnam and the Kennedy Round trade negotiations. Ball explained that because of their "unequaled capacity for feeling sorry for themselves," the Germans "have come to regard our demands as nagging and resentment against us is deepening." They "can easily develop neuroses that can be catastrophic for all of us. *They did it before and they can do it again.* . . . A neurotic, disaffected Germany could be like a loose ship's cannon in a high sea."[1]

Because of the enormous political stakes for American policy in Germany and Europe, Ball recommended that Johnson accommodate Erhard by softening the offset-troop link and reducing the current obligations. The under secretary of state thought that this was a small price to pay to avoid a public rupture with America's closest ally, especially at a time of great uncertainty within NATO. Despite his dark warnings, Ball was overruled and the president followed the hard line recommended by McNamara and Fowler. Erhard left the summit humiliated. The chancellor, who had often been characterized in Germany as America's "whipping boy,"[2] was ridiculed in Germany for being so naive in his dealings with the Johnson administration. Erhard weathered a barrage of attacks and insults at home until his government fell in November. The public atmosphere surrounding his collapse was marked by widespread demands for a reassessment of Germany's relationship with the United States.

Why was the foreign exchange offset issue so politically explosive? The most important point to make is that there was far more at stake than a simple financial arrangement. The offset agreement was a critical part of a larger security framework that had important political, strategic, and military components. This security framework was a series of largely tacit understandings that kept American troops in Germany, nuclear weapons out of the hands of Germans, and the Soviets out of West Berlin. A crucial part of this arrangement was the FRG's commitment to help strengthen the dollar and protect the U.S. gold supply by offsetting and neutralizing the foreign exchange cost of the American forces stationed in Germany. If this offset arrangement unraveled, the American payments deficit would balloon and gold losses would increase. This could force the Johnson administration to withdraw troops from Germany, increasing the pressure on the FRG to get its hand on a nuclear trigger and scaring the Soviet Union into a far more hostile posture. The détente and relative stability that had been created in Central Europe would be shattered.

This unraveling of the offset arrangement could not have come at a worse time. France had just left NATO and Great Britain was threatening to bring home its army on the Rhine. The MLF and proposed Non-Proliferation Treaty (NPT) were dividing the alliance. The military escalation in Vietnam and the Mansfield Resolution increased the pressure to return American troops from Europe.[3] Perhaps the most threatening development was the reemergence of the balance-of-payments deficit. The American deficit had decreased in 1964 and 1965, but was exploding because of the inflationary pressures of the Vietnam War and the Great Society programs. With international monetary and trade negotiations stalled, sterling in peril, and the French attacking the dollar, a six-division American presence in Germany was considered untenable without full offset. But the strategy of flexible response, the political stability of Germany and Central Europe, and the NATO alliance itself could be undermined by large withdrawals of American troops.

The monetary-security framework that kept U.S. troops in West Germany and made the rhetorical strategy of flexible response in Europe possible was delicate throughout the 1960s. The same questions that had consumed the Kennedy administration continued to plague the Johnson administration. Would the Germans accept their nonnuclear status? Would they continue to make onerous offset payments to relieve the foreign exchange costs of American troops? On the American side, would worsening balance-of-payments deficits and the war in Southeast Asia increase domestic pressures to redeploy troops? Could this three-layered game—deterring the Soviets, restraining the FRG, and winning domestic support for an expensive overseas commitment—be maintained in the face of an emerging U.S.-Soviet détente, increased German resentment, and domestic pressures to return American troops from Europe? Ironically, this "détente" only magnified the dilemmas surrounding America's military strategy in Europe, particularly the question of America's conventional force commitment to NATO.

What was the true significance of the offset arrangement and why did it fall apart, provoking such a deep crisis in U.S.-German relations? This chapter details the inextricable link between international monetary issues and security in German-American relations, beginning with Rusk's Frankfurt speech in the autumn of 1963 until the conclusion of the trilateral negotiations in the spring of 1967. It also focuses on the complicated nature of the "German problem," which combined with the nuclear-sharing issue to threaten the offset arrangement. The enormous tensions and pressures produced by the monetary-security link, and its impact on U.S. policy toward Europe, are examined in detail. A large part of this chapter takes up the decision to rework the monetary-security framework through the trilateral talks between the United States, Germany, and Great Britain. These arduous and painful negotiations successfully reformulated, at least for a time, the monetary-security link and managed to forestall a deepening of the strain in U.S.-German relations. Most important, these talks prevented the unraveling of the alliance that seemed all too probable throughout 1966.

### U.S.-German Monetary Cooperation and the Unraveling of Offset

Most American policy makers felt that the offset arrangement was the natural counterpart to the decision to stay in Europe with a large military presence. The reluctant decision to maintain six fully supplied combat divisions in Germany, spelled out in Rusk's Frankfurt speech, was driven by the political settlement in Europe that emerged in 1963 (Chapter 4). At the heart of this settlement was a security regime that kept the United States in Europe and maintained Germany's nonnuclear status while keeping the Soviets out of West Berlin. This regime went a long way toward stabilizing Central Europe after the crisis period of 1958–62 and the near revolt of Western Europe against the United States in 1963.[4] But this American military presence, especially the large combat troop deployments, enlarged the American balance-of-payments deficit. Both the Kennedy and Johnson administrations believed that it was essential for the surplus European countries to finance and/or neutralize the foreign exchange costs of U.S. military expenditures in Europe. To their mind this was only fair, because they benefited more than anyone from the American security regime. Minor agreements were reached with Italy and Japan, but only West Germany was expected to provide a full and open-ended offset. Both sides understood this regime was far more than a simple burden-sharing exercise.

It is important to remember that there were two components to German-American monetary cooperation during the Kennedy and early Johnson administrations. Military hardware purchased by West Germany, or the offset, was only one aspect of the arrangement. Less publicized but equally important was the informal agreement by the Bundesbank to hold its surplus dollars in interest-bearing securities instead of buying gold or selling them to others who might buy gold. This arrangement, which was initiated in 1961, almost came unglued at the end of 1963. Secretary of the Treasury Douglas Dillon warned the new president that there were signs of "restiveness" from the Bundesbank. "We have recently had numerous first-hand reports that the Bundesbank is considering the purchase of very substantial quantities of gold from us. . . . This would be most damaging to the dollar."[5] If the Germans made large purchases, confidence in the dollar would be severely undermined and a run on gold could ensue. Under Secretary of the Treasury Robert Roosa was dispatched to talk to Karl Blessing, head of the Bundesbank. Blessing informed Roosa that Erhard had intervened to make sure that the Bundesbank did not change its reserve management policy.[6] The Americans considered this arrangement critical to their own gold policy and hoped, mostly in vain, that other European surplus countries would follow the lead of the West German central bank and hold their dollars instead of purchasing gold.

Holding dollars, important as it was, did nothing to lessen the American balance-of-payments deficit. The Americans believed there was an agreement whereby Germany would fully offset the foreign exchange costs of the six U.S. divisions located in the FRG for as long in the future as was required. The briefing papers for the December 1963 meeting with Erhard implied that the United States *expected* full offset for as long as six divisions were in Germany. But Erhard did not formally commit to full offset beyond the 1963–64 agreements arrived at in 1962.[7] In fact, Dillon warned the president in December 1963 that the Germans would have trouble fulfilling the current agreement and had "put us on notice that it is unlikely . . . that they will be able to continue payments . . . which would full offset our defense expenditures in Germany."[8]

The Americans left no doubt in the minds of the Germans that there was a direct link between full offset and the troops. "The U.S. seeks German commitments to continue in 1963–1964 and for as many years as required an offset arrangement whereby the Germans will undertake both military orders *and payments* to the U.S. *fully equal* to the annual levels of U.S. military expenditures in Germany." To underscore the importance of this objective, the paper suggested describing to Erhard the heavy pressure the Johnson administration faced to reduce its overseas cost, including the well-known Eisenhower proposal to remove all but one American division from Europe. Erhard should be made to understood that full offset was an "absolute necessity" if six divisions were to remain in Germany.[9]

At the December meeting, Erhard agreed to fulfill the current offset agreement. But the chancellor was reluctant to accept a direct link between the six-division presence and a full, open-ended commitment to offset U.S. foreign exchange losses with purchases of American military hardware. In a discussion with John McCloy in 1966, Erhard pointed out that while he had agreed in 1963 to continue the arrangement, at the time there had been a "qualifying reservation, namely that the obligation was made conditional upon the budgetary situation permitting it."[10] Erhard claimed that this reservation had been mistakenly left out in ensuing offset discussions. Part of the problem came from the fact that neither the

United States nor Germany wanted a public and direct link between the troops and offset. The American troops would look like mercenaries or, worse, occupiers, and it would appear that the defense of Germany rested upon unseemly financial haggling. The final communiqué of the December 1963 meeting used the language of "mutual benefit," stating that the agreement was of "great value to both governments" and should be "fully executed and continued."[11]

The ambiguity of the offset-troop link created problems and misunderstandings almost immediately. In a memo six months after the December meeting, McGeorge Bundy told the president that Erhard did not want "a formal bargain that offset payments are a condition of our six-division presence," although he knew that "the connection exists." But even on the American side, there was some confusion as to how tight the link was and how loudly it should be spelled out to the Germans. Bundy suggested that Johnson "firmly but always privately" underline the linkage, but reported that "Dean Rusk wishes you wouldn't."[12] The ambiguity of the agreement was admitted several years later in a paper detailing the history of the offset agreement. While acknowledging that there was a "relationship between the levels of U.S. forces and the amounts of German offset procurement," the paper stated that the "precise character of this relationship" was never "agreed between the two governments."[13]

The offset arrangement came unglued in late 1965. Secretary of the Treasury Fowler sent a memo warning the president that the FRG was seriously behind in its payments. This seemed to be evidence that the Germans were trying to get out of the agreement. Fowler recommended that the United States take a hard-line approach: "If the FRG should seek to withdraw from its present offset commitments, it would be logical to assume that the FRG no longer considered it necessary to maintain U.S. combat troops in Germany at present levels. Such a conclusion seems reinforced by the fact that senior U.S. officials have repeatedly made clear to the FRG the relationship between German fulfillment of its offset commitments and U.S. ability to maintain present levels of forces in Germany."[14]

Whereas McNamara and the Defense Department supported Fowler, the State Department was opposed, arguing that insistence on a "fully automatic connection between the offset and the presence of troops in Germany would be dangerous in view of de Gaulle's persistent argument that U.S. forces will eventually be withdrawn from Europe."[15] Bundy, who normally took a hard-line view on offset, suggested that Johnson use his political skills "to get Fowler's result with Ball's politeness."[16] The issue was confused even further in May 1966, when McNamara and German defense minister Kai-Uwe von Hassel were unable to agree on the exact nature of the offset arrangement. McNamara reiterated the direct link between full offset and American combat troop levels in Germany. Unless a full offset was forthcoming, now and in the future, the "U.S. would be required to reduce its forces to the level of the offset goals." Von Hassel replied that it was the view of his government that the agreements entered into "only applied to specific periods of two years each."[17] Any further agreements, which were unlikely to contain full offset through armaments purchases, would have to be negotiated.

Why were the Germans so reluctant to make the full offset purchases as called for in the agreement? The argument given by FRG leaders at the time was that they faced budgetary problems caused by an unanticipated economic slowdown in West Germany. Furthermore, they claimed they did not need any more arms and had reached the limit of what they could usefully purchase from the United States. The Americans were skeptical. The size of the FRG budget was a matter of priorities—social spending was increased dramatically in the 1960s, while defense spending remained flat, and actually decreased as a percentage of German GNP (from 6 percent in 1963 to 5 percent in 1967). And McNamara vigorously disputed the contention that the German military had satiated its need for American military equipment. "With respect to German requirements to meet NATO standards, the German forces are seriously deficient. . . . German statements to the effect that they do not need the military items involved in the offset are therefore clearly untrue."[18]

Given the importance the Americans placed on offset and the state of chaos that the alliance was in during the summer of 1966, it is hard to believe that the chancellor's decision to abrogate the agreement was merely the result of a budget crunch.[19] If the offset agreement was popular and deemed politically important, the necessary funds to fulfill the agreement could have been found. But Erhard's popularity in Germany had plummeted. In addition to being blamed for the economic slowdown, he was being attacked by the German "Gaullists" for weakness in his dealings with the United States and his failure to accommodate France. U.S.-German relations were strained over a wide range of issues, including nuclear sharing, the proposed Non-Proliferation Treaty, American troop redeployments, and the response to France's withdrawal from NATO. By forcing the Johnson administration to decouple offset from the troop issue and obtaining concessions on the current offset agreement, Erhard believed he could demonstrate the value of his relationship with the Americans to the German electorate while avoiding a fight over tax increases needed to fund the offset obligation. "For Erhard, it may be essential to political survival to prove that he remains a special friend of Lyndon Johnson, but, at the same time, that he can successfully stand up to the Americans on bread-and-butter issues."[20] But this was an enormous miscalculation. Erhard's decision to end full offset provoked a serious rift with the Americans and led to a disastrous meeting with President Johnson.

### The Monetary-Security Arrangement Falls Apart

In July 1966 Chancellor Erhard sent a letter to President Johnson that touched on the two most sensitive and potentially troubling issues in American-German relations: nuclear proliferation and sharing, and offset. With regard to the offset issue, Erhard dropped a bombshell. The chancellor alerted the president that the FRG would have difficulty meeting its current obligations through military purchases. What's more, Erhard decoupled the offset and troop issue and implied that the link never existed. "In my view, which, I hope, is shared by you, this set of problems should . . . not be linked with the question of the future presence of U.S. troops in Germany."[21] This was a direct challenge to American policy, and the Johnson administration recognized that it had to decide whether to end the link or make corresponding troop withdrawals.

The issue of nuclear sharing and proliferation was even more complicated than offset. For some time, the United States had tried to find a way to include the FRG in the nuclear club without giving the Germans any real control or possession of atomic weapons. The idea was to ease the obvious discrimination against the FRG in nuclear affairs without unduly scaring Germany's neighbors. Early in the Kennedy administration, the United States had focused on the idea of a multilateral approach in which interested NATO members, including West Germany, would participate in a joint integrated nuclear force. It was hoped that by participating in this force, the West Germans would not feel the need to obtain unilaterally an independent atomic capability. But the idea had floundered on specifics. Would the weapons be on ships or submarines? Who would pay for it? Would the force be mixed-manned? Would the French resist? Would the Soviets object? Who besides the United States and Germany would participate? Would the U.S. Congress go along? Would the United States eventually drop its veto and allow a truly European force? Most important, who would make the decision to launch the weapons?

As negotiations dragged on, year after year, with no concrete results except increased tensions in the alliance, some in the Johnson administration—at first McGeorge Bundy and then Francis Bator—lost enthusiasm for what was labeled the "hardware" solution.[22] Several members of the administration thought that it might be worth trading the joint inte-

grated force and the European clause to obtain a nonprolifera[tion]
with the Soviets.[23] Some hoped that participating in a nuclea[r]
group could appease the Germans. Erhard's July 1966 letter[...]
these hopes by asking Johnson to guarantee that any nonproliferation
agreement not exclude the possibility of "establishing in the future a joint
integrated nuclear force."[24] This was the official American position at the
time, but the administration wanted flexibility on the proliferation issue
and did not want to be pinned down by a commitment to the FRG. But
now, Erhard was connecting West German monetary cooperation to
America's policy on proliferation, a dangerous linkage. This issue was
potentially explosive. As George McGhee, the U.S. ambassador to West
Germany, told Rusk, "Germany stands little hope" of participating in a
multilateral force and "no hope at all of ever obtaining a national nuclear
force." This was not because of "technical" or "expenditure" reasons but
because "we would not permit it." If West Germany undertook a unilateral effort to acquire a national nuclear capability, the United States
"would withdraw," the other NATO allies would "dissociate themselves
from Germany," and the Soviets would "make such efforts the subject of a
preemptive attack."[25]

Troubling events in Europe, including evidence that the Germans were
reassessing their relations with the United States, clouded both issues.
One example of this trend was the issue of French troops in Germany.
When France announced its decision to leave NATO, the Americans convinced Erhard to demand that French military forces remain under some
sort of NATO command during war or leave Germany. If the French
troops remained in Germany but were not part of NATO, they would look
like occupiers, especially given de Gaulle's public attacks on the United
States and his suspicious-looking visit to Moscow. But the so-called Gaullists in the FRG government, led by Strauss, undermined this position, and
convinced Erhard to accept the French troops without the conditions laid
out by NATO.[26] Erhard's capitulation to de Gaulle resurrected old fears of a
Franco-German bloc, outside of NATO, which excluded the United States.
This was just one of several issues that led the State Department to conclude that "[t]he Germans are in the process of reexamining their relations to the United States and to NATO."[27]

The administration had to decide how to deal with this array of explosive problems with West Germany. The first task was to respond to Erhard's letter. Bator recommended that the president ignore Erhard's plea
to reconfirm the American policy on nuclear proliferation because the
administration was so divided on the issue. The administration wanted
flexibility to negotiate with the Russians and did not want to be tied down

any further than it already was. On offset, Bator told Johnson that he faced a tough choice. Erhard could be told that full weapons offset was absolutely required to maintain six American combat divisions and that a failure to fulfill the agreement would lead to corresponding reductions. This was McNamara's and Fowler's position, and would be the appropriate step if the president wanted to use financial pressure "to maneuver the Germans into *asking* us to cut troops." McNamara believed that this would force the Germans to build up their own army, using weapons purchased from the United States. But McGhee, together with Ball, Rostow, and Bator, all recommended that Johnson send a gentle letter to Erhard that left some room for renegotiation of the offset agreements. To withdraw troops because of money would "confirm the opinion that NATO is falling apart," underscore de Gaulle's claim that the British and Americans are unreliable and "care more for their pocketbooks than for the safety of Europe," and "seriously unsettle German politics—with unpredictable results."

Bator recognized that the nuclear sharing and offset issues were related, and that it would be very dangerous to thwart Erhard on both counts. "If we are going to take risks with German politics, I would vote that we do so in connection with nuclear-sharing/non-proliferation, rather than with offset and U.S. forces in Europe." Frustrating the Germans on either issue carried risks, but Bator thought such a risk was worth it "to get Bonn to give up on hardware in order to test the Russians on non-proliferation." But Bator thought it would be foolish to play around with the "stability of German and alliance politics, and hence with our security in Europe," in order to achieve marginal balance-of-payments savings.[28] Despite the previous offset troop link, Bator believed that any shift in American security policy should be based on political and military factors.

These issues were made considerably more complicated when the British announced on 19 August that they would make large troop withdrawals from their army on the Rhine because of the collapse of the Anglo-German offset talks.[29] The Erhard government appeared unmoved by the announcement and even less inclined to fully offset British costs than American costs. The Johnson administration viewed this as a potentially devastating blow to an already reeling alliance. If the cuts were carried out, there would be strong pressures on the Europeans and Canadians to cut their own troops, "leading to a downward spiral of national force commitments to NATO."[30] Domestic pressure to withdraw American troops, already intense, would increase.

The administration now faced two immediate offset-related issues.

First, President Johnson had to decide whether to decouple offset from troop levels in order to give Erhard the breathing room he needed. Second, the administration had to dissuade the British from rushing into troop cuts in Germany that could "start an unraveling process in NATO."[31] Following an idea suggested by Assistant Secretary of State for European Affairs John Leddy, the president approved a plan to invite Britain and the FRG to participate in a trilateral discussion of important alliance issues. It was proposed that these talks could take up the nagging questions surrounding the U.S. and U.K. offset requirements, the debates over threat assessment and force posture, and the nuclear problem in NATO. Leddy argued that these talks were necessary because "these three problems had become public issues and fostered uncertainty abroad and at home about the US commitment in Europe and the fundamental unity of purpose of the three major NATO members, just at a time when de Gaulle was attacking the Alliance."[32] The president also decided to send only an interim reply to Erhard's July 1966 letter, holding him to his obligations for the current offset arrangements but suggesting that the administration was prepared to look at other offset options in future agreements.

British prime minister Harold Wilson quickly agreed to the talks, but Erhard hesitated, fearing it was an attempt by the United States and Britain to gang up on West Germany. Erhard sent a letter back telling Johnson that he would consider the issue but wanted to talk about it further during their meeting. The administration sensed that the chancellor was stalling and feared that Great Britain would not defer its troop cuts until the Erhard-Johnson meeting. With neither the current or future offset issues resolved, the stage was set for a disastrous summit. Erhard's effectiveness as the chancellor and as a useful ally to the Americans was quickly fading. "*For us*, it is important—even more than Erhard's survival—that we not appear the culprit if he fails."[33]

The president's advisers decided before the meeting with Erhard that the United States should keep the FRG to the original payments schedule but allow it to meet some of this obligation through the purchase of bonds. McNamara and Fowler agreed to stretch out the FRG's weapons orders, but Ball and Bator wanted these orders reduced by the amount of the bonds. For the long-term offset agreements, the administration reluctantly agreed that it would quietly drop the direct offset-troop link but would demand that Erhard participate in the U.S.-U.K.-FRG trilateral talks. These discussions would go beyond simple offset and include threat assessment, strategy, deployments, burden sharing, and foreign exchange neutralization. In a significant concession, the administration agreed that any cuts resulting from the talks would be represented in terms of defense, not money.[34] Still, it was unclear whether Erhard would accept either these new terms or the mechanism of trilateral negotiations.

### Reaction from West Germany

The West Germans only slowly recognized the hardening American attitude. In April, Foreign Minister Gerhard Schroeder warned McGhee that constant rumors about American troop withdrawals could "reveal a negative relation of the United States to Europe and Germany" that the press would play up. This "would become dangerous."[35] As had often been the case, McGhee assured the West German official that "specialists" had been withdrawn, but not essential combat troops, and that the action was a "regrouping" (*Umgruppierung*) and not a withdrawal. One month later, however, the administration was in no mood to reassure. Heinrich Knappstein, the FRG ambassador to the United States, complained to Rusk that McNamara was publicly threatening troop withdrawals if the offset was not met in full. Knappstein emphasized West Germany's concern about "the junction [*Junktim*] that McNamara established between stationing troops and the offset agreement." The ambassador argued that "American troops are stationed in Europe in the context of the joint defense of the Alliance and not because of financial agreement."

To Knappstein's great shock, Rusk, who was the most important voice within the Johnson administration *against* U.S. troop withdrawals, responded sharply. "There were strange contradictions in the attitudes of the allies." When the administration asked about the paltry contributions from Europe toward common defense, the United States was told that "they cannot undertake bigger defense efforts," and besides, "the danger in Europe has been reduced." But when "one mentions the U.S. efforts," Europe's attitude changed. "This would not be possible in the long run." Rusk emphasized that "[o]ne could not measure the efforts that are expected from the U.S. and that the Europeans make, with two standards, and one could not expect from the U.S. efforts that the Europeans do not want to make."[36]

The West German ambassador to the United States recognized that this was a major shift in the secretary of state's attitude. "Rusk's comments seem remarkable to me, since he did not at all attempt to weaken the position that McNamara had held during talks" with von Hassel. The insistence of "junction" between troops and offset reflected "a general ill-will" about the "contributions of the Europeans." West Germany, in particular, was singled out for "insufficient . . . efforts," which could have an effect that went beyond "the simple offset problem."[37]

Over the next few weeks, Knappstein prepared a series of reports for Bonn detailing the rapidly changing climate in Washington. The ambassador warned, "[W]e must expect that the American pressure on us will rather become stronger to continue" the full offset payments for a "virtually infinite time in an unaltered amount."[38] Many policy makers, including important senators, were publicly calling for large withdrawals of U.S. troops from Europe. Knappstein pointed out that the reasons for this attitude went beyond the balance of payments, including the Vietnam War, "increasing discontent" with U.S.-European attitudes, and even an alarming "neo-isolationist trend" suggesting that the United States "could defend itself only with the missile potential." Beyond these substantive issues, there was an "emotional position"—not entirely new but gaining "weight and momentum"—that the Europeans are "fat and lazy" and want to merely "enjoy their prosperity" under "the protection of the American nuclear shield." In the long term, these feelings would one day force the United States to confront seriously the question of a "substantial reduction of troops." Knappstein warned that "21 years after the end of World War II, the mood of the people is no longer simply to win in favor of further infinite stationing of troops. . . . The demand 'bring the boys back home' that Eisenhower successfully adopted . . . in 1952 . . . has still today an attractiveness that should not be underestimated."[39]

Still, before the administration proposed trilateral negotiations, West German officials believed that the American threat to withdraw was a bluff, at least in the short term. The secretary of defense's "repeated explanations, threats, and disclaimers" about troop withdrawals had been harmful, and it had been "extremely difficult to induce McNamara, who has extremely a mind of his own, to take a cooperative position."[40] But surely the secretary of defense would never undermine his own flexible response doctrine that he had finally, despite great difficulties, convinced the Federal Republic to embrace.[41] "McNamara is totally aware of the fact that the enemy's fighting strength has not decreased, but rather increased. If he would concede to the domestic policy pressure on decreasing the troops in Europe too early, his concept of defense would be questioned. This concept connects the forward defense with the idea of flexible response."[42] McNamara had not planned to "execute substantial decreases already before that time, because this would have contradicted his strategic concept."[43] Giving up on "the American concept of the flexible response and thus to a decrease of the nuclear threshold" through troop withdrawals could "mean the deathblow for NATO."[44]

McNamara was not bluffing—the secretary of defense was the loudest advocate of troop withdrawals from Europe in the administration. American rhetoric on flexible response was not backed by an *operational* commitment to the strategy at the highest political levels. Worse from the West German perspective, the trilateral negotiations suggested that the Americans were willing to bend their strategic concept to meet their balance-of-payments needs. "The proposal of the American President comes unexpectedly." West German officials felt that both the format and the subject of the negotiations were not in their interest, as their main purpose was to allow the United States and Great Britain to gang up and force "Germany to bigger efforts" in offset. If these negotiations failed, West Germany might be blamed for "the resulting weakening of the defense of Central Europe." Excluding other NATO countries from the negotiation would produce "ill-will" and "suspicion" aimed "primarily against us." These questions touched on fundamental questions of "the East-West relation and the European security" and should not be approached from the comparatively second-order perspective of "foreign exchange offset."[45] After receiving the proposal for trilateral negotiations, the West German foreign minister told George McGhee "he cannot see . . . the strategic, ideological, political, journalistic and psychological meaning of such trilateral negotiations." Such negotiations are "not very attractive."[46] Even the selection of someone as prestigious as John McCloy was not welcome: his dispatch, which "always automatically implicates considerations of prestige, is not really fortunate."[47] While both sides had a great interest in solving this vexing problem before the upcoming Erhard-Johnson meeting, neither could agree on the mechanism or procedure to end the offset dispute without rancor.

### The Erhard-Johnson Summit

How critical would the Erhard-Johnson negotiations over foreign exchange be for U.S.-FRG relations? McGhee contended that the "U.S. reaction to Erhard's appeal will, I believe, be one of the most important decisions the U.S. has faced in the post-war period." If the negotiations failed and the United States moved "to reduce our combat forces in Germany (a division or more) as a direct consequence of German failure to meet the offset . . . [t]he Erhard government would fall" and "Germany and America will tend to drift apart." Furthermore, it "would be necessary to review the concept of flexible response which we have promoted." Far more was at stake than addressing the U.S. balance of payments. Withdrawing troops because of the dollar and gold drain could fundamentally alter great-power politics in Europe:

Germany, which has until now depended almost entirely on the
U.S. for its security, would be forced to reorient its basic security
policy. This could take the form of increased dependence on
Gaullist France, a "go-it-alone" nationalism or efforts to accom-
modate itself with the Soviets. . . . Result: U.S. force reductions
would . . . be considered generally as a major shift in U.S. policy.
History would record it as the ebb point—the beginning of an
American withdrawal from Europe.[48]

Just as it appeared that things couldn't get any worse, Senate Majority
Leader Mike Mansfield offered a nonbinding resolution with twelve other
senators recommending unspecified cuts in U.S. forces in Europe. This
resolution was based on the Senate Democratic Policy Committee's unan-
imous recommendations. Both the Erhard and Johnson governments
were horrified by this unexpected development only weeks before the
summit. Johnson unleashed his anger in a phone call to Senator Russell
Long. "This is desperately unwise." The president needed the time and
the support to undergo negotiations so that the Germans would not conclude "we are pulling out completely," which could lead them to start "a
complete rearmament or blow up." Johnson knew better than anybody
that something had to be done about the dollar and gold outflow. But the
Mansfield Resolution was not the way to go about it: "I'm more anxious
than any man on that ▓▓▓▓▓ committee on balance of payments to
get troops out. But I sure as ▓▓▓ don't want to get them out with 22
divisions there and kick off World War III. And every ▓▓▓ man on that
resolution will run and hide, by ▓▓▓, when you say, 'You kicked this thing
off, you pulled a ▓▓▓▓▓▓ Chamberlain and you ran out and said you
were going to pull out, you're not interested anymore.' "[49]

Given the divisions within the administration, between Congress and
the president and, most important, between the American and West German positions, it was clear that the September summit would be a fiasco.
The chancellor began his meeting with the president with a thinly veiled
threat, pointing out that there were "trends in Germany to lean closer to
France." He contended that on both the offset and the nuclear-sharing
problems, the "German people wanted to know where exactly they stand
at this point in terms of security, how they would be protected in the
event of the conclusion of a non-proliferation treaty." Erhard told Johnson that he preferred bilateral, not trilateral, exchanges on these issues
first. Because of the economic slowdown in Germany, "it would not be
possible to fulfill all financial obligations under the current offset agree-

LBJ meeting with FRG chancellor Ludwig Erhard. The September 1966 summit between the two leaders was a disaster. When the West German chancellor told Johnson that "it would not be possible to fulfill all financial obligations under the current offset agreement to the full amount," the president exploded. Erhard, known in West Germany as America's "whipping boy," returned home humiliated, and his government fell weeks later. (Courtesy of the Lyndon B. Johnson Library and Museum)

ment to the full amount." The FRG had always been a loyal ally, especially when it came to supporting the U.S. balance of payments, and Erhard hoped that something could be arranged in a "business-like" way.[50]

Erhard seemed to be accusing Johnson of not being dependable, while West Germany was backing out of a signed agreement. The president exploded. If anything, "his problems were even more severe than those of the Chancellor." The president was not quite clear as to "what the essence of the Chancellor's remarks was. In the past he had always taken the German word for granted." The U.S. situation "was serious enough even if the Germans would keep their commitments." Did the chancellor mean to say he could not fulfill his military obligations or did he imply other things were included like buying bonds? How could he (Johnson) defend himself if the chancellor was not meeting his commitments?[51]

The summit deteriorated to the point that the president asked McNamara after one of the meetings to find out how much savings in the U.S. balance of payments a *complete and total withdrawal* of American troops from Western Europe would produce. "How much, when you pull *all your troops out of there*? Just suppose that you decided that we couldn't afford it." McNamara was taken aback by the request. "Of course, if we were going to pull them all out, it would be quite a difficult movement back because we just have . . . something like a million tons of equipment" in West Germany. Johnson was unfazed. "Looks to me, we ought to take advantage of this opportunity to make him tell us that he cannot afford to have our troops there."[52]

There was no further mention of a complete U.S. pullback and, in the end, a ragged compromise was worked out between Erhard and Johnson. But for the West German leader, the meeting was the worst of both worlds. In essence, Erhard obtained an important concession: a decoupling of full offset through military purchases from troop levels *in the future*. This was a significant U.S. compromise. But Erhard was in trouble *right now*. By failing to meet the current obligation, the chancellor seemed petty and ended up infuriating the president.

The real problem now was to come up with a way to keep British and American troops in Germany despite the enormous domestic and international pressures in both countries to bring the forces home. Although the preferred method of full offset through military purchases was no longer feasible, some method had to be found to ease the foreign exchange burdens of stationing American and British soldiers overseas. Without an acceptable formula, Great Britain would withdraw, with unknown consequences on the ailing alliance. The administration turned its energies toward the trilateral talks in the hopes of solving these complicated problems.

## Dangers for the United States and West Germany

The failure of Erhard and Johnson to solve the foreign exchange troop question put the West German–U.S. relationship in its worst crisis during the Cold War. The Federal Republic finally understood that the dollar and gold question was the key issue. "Therefore, the question about the foreign exchange balance is for the U.S. government of central importance. If they do not succeed to resolve it, the domestic policy pressure up to this date on decreasing the force in Europe could become irresistible." This would bring "dangers that are difficult to assess for us."[53] If large troop withdrawals went forward, "we have to expect a dangerous progressive development that could also affect our political position negatively as a whole—not only regarding questions of security."[54] Far more was at stake than money or even military strategy. The whole question of the relationship between security and German reunification "could be touched on from the view of the foreign exchange offset in a way that would not be without dangers."[55]

*at .ll US pullout*

The stakes for West Germany were enormous. Failure would risk the "withdrawal of the British troops" and "American troops"; the "the far-reaching collapse of our German politics up to now"; and "a lasting weakening of the Atlantic Treaty." West Germany would find itself alone. "In the face of the Soviet Union's extraordinarily big military means of power, this is a highly dangerous situation." Without American military protection, the Federal Republic "could not resist an increased pressure of the Soviet Union to change our German politics and to give up the goals of our German politics up till now."[56] The most important goal of the Federal Republic's policies, German reunification, would be shelved forever, and West Germany would be politically neutralized.[57]

The Americans, for their part, understood there were great dangers for them as well. McGhee told the State Department that it was realistic to describe "the present German state of mind with respect to the United States as clearly unhealthy." This was not "one of those sharp crises of confidence in which there was always an element of the synthetic," as was often the case during the Adenauer period. The problems "run somewhat deeper, are more widespread than in the past, and reflect in part the general sense of change (in) Europe by limited détente with the Soviets and de Gaulle's challenge to the post-war institutional structure." West Germany has "a nagging concern about the United States and a fading confidence in the clarity of our purposes in Europe, added to a feeling that the Germans are being victimized and are being treated by us in a way not consonant with their primary role as loyal allies or their future importance to a realization of U.S. policy objectives in Europe."[58] Behind all the talks of offset, nonproliferation, and U.S. troop withdrawals, the real fear was that the Johnson administration would sacrifice core German interests in order to achieve détente. "They see a number of mutual interests emerging between the U.S. and the Soviet Union, which they feel could bring about a realignment in the post-war security system."[59] The trilateral negotiations would not only have to amend the delicate monetary-security framework that was the basis of stability in Central Europe. These discussions would also have to repair the deeply strained and increasingly combustible relationship between the United States and the Federal Republic of Germany.

### The Trilateral Negotiations, Part I:
### September–December 1966

Once again, an American president was confronted with the difficult questions surrounding the balance-of-payments cost of U.S. combat troops in Germany. Most senior foreign policy advisers in the Johnson administration, with the possible exception of McNamara, understood the consequences for the NATO alliance if the trilateral negotiations failed. The administration was faced with enormous pressure to withdraw American forces in Europe. The United States was fighting an unpopular war in Vietnam with little support from Europe. Congress and the American public were clearly growing tired of the Europeans, and in time, the troop commitment could become politically unsustainable. European finance ministers and central bankers were blocking the trade negotiations and monetary reforms that the Americans felt they needed to protect the dollar. Far less, during a much more dangerous period, had caused Kennedy and Eisenhower to consider large troop withdrawals. The president signaled the importance of the talks by assigning John McCloy, former high commissioner of Germany, as the American negotiator to the trilateral negotiations.

The administration had decided not to look at the financial problem in isolation but to reassess the military threat and the forces required to deter and counter the Soviets. This would serve two purposes in the negotiations: to reassure the Germans that any military redeployments were strategically sound and militarily safe, and to rebuff British attempts to fall back on their long-held "plate glass" or "tripwire" strategy to justify large cuts of their own. These concerns were interrelated, as the Germans believed past negotiations had revealed that the British thought "a conventional defense in Europe is hopeless and therefore neither strong conventional forces nor war supply for more than 14 days are required in Central Europe."[60] If circumstances forced the Johnson administration to withdraw troops, they wanted to make sure that other NATO countries did not massively reduce their forces and completely undermine the flexible response posture.

To accomplish these goals, it would be necessary to convince the British (and others) that the Soviet threat to Europe was undiminished. But, surprisingly, a paper prepared by the State Department for John McCloy accepted the optimistic evaluations of the Soviet threat held by the Europeans. The report acknowledged that it was highly unlikely that the Soviets were going to use force in Europe any time soon.[61] The State Department paper ruled out a deliberate decision by the Soviets to launch a massive invasion. The mobilization of large numbers of Soviet divisions would eliminate any hope of surprise and of a quick victory. More important, the Soviets knew that a massive assault on Europe would risk, if not guarantee, a devastating response from the United States. Like President Kennedy four years earlier, the analysts judged a "limited land grab" highly unlikely, despite the Joint Chiefs of Staff's contention that "the

Soviets can also conduct maneuvers . . . and . . . make a land grab or city grab with little or no worrying. NATO must have adequate forces in the Central Region to cope with this kind of threat."[62] Ironically, the only scenario that was described as even remotely threatening was a *reduction* of Soviet troops in the GDR. This could reverse the trend toward "greater stability" in the GDR and prompt a Soviet intervention "with all the ramifications which that might have."[63]

The key question, from a military standpoint, was whether deterring the Soviets depended on large numbers of American combat troops. Surprisingly, the paper argued that this was not necessarily the case. In an interesting observation about the robust nature of strategic nuclear deterrence, the paper argued that "even in a circumstance when doubts about American reliability might cause widespread consternation in Western Europe, the Soviets would nevertheless almost certainly still remain deterred by the possibility of even a less-than-probable American involvement." The Soviets had little to gain from an invasion and could suffer potentially devastating consequences if they tried. "Indeed, not even the dissolution of NATO would altogether assure Moscow that the U.S. might not see an attack upon Western Europe as so great a threat to American vital interests to warrant American intervention."[64] Detailed military examination of the European theater confirmed McNamara's analysis that American troops could be brought home without endangering Europe. Even "a total reduction in NATO Central Region M-Day army manpower of 75–150,00 would not seriously weaken our conventional capabilities" to deal with the most likely contingencies.[65]

If, from a strictly military point of view, the large American combat troop presence could be considerably reduced without tempting the Soviets to intervene, then why were they needed at all?[66] A report on NATO prepared for the trilateral negotiations provided an answer that few policy makers would discuss in public. "If the relationship between Western Europe and the U.S. had been based merely on common defense against the Soviet threat, it might be logical to conclude that the basic raison d'être of the alliance was rapidly being eroded."[67] But the strong American presence in NATO, particularly the large deployment of U.S. troops in Germany, served a political purpose that was perhaps more important than its military function: "Western Europe (except France) continues to want the United States to exercise its political weight in the area for a number of reasons." One political function was to reduce the scope of "traditional power politics" as represented by de Gaulle's "hegemonic drive." But an even more important function was the contribution NATO and the U.S. presence made to "the German problem." U.S. power had allowed the FRG to be "integrated into the West European political fabric" without upsetting the region's internal balance. "This factor contributing to NATO's strength seems to be growing more important as time passes."[68]

A strong military presence in Germany was necessary to guard American political interests in Europe, which included but went well beyond rebuffing a Soviet attack. This was the meaning behind such euphemisms as "maintaining the cohesion" or "enhancing the stability of the alliance," which were given as the main purpose of the trilateral negotiations. Given that the Soviets were not going to invade Western Europe any time soon, this meant managing the "German problem." American troops in Germany guaranteed that the FRG would remain allied to the West and could be prevented from making any destabilizing moves toward the East. British troops guaranteed a U.K. role in the German problem. More important, a strong U.K. presence appeared to put the management of the "German problem" in a multilateral (and less coercive) context.[69] This is not to discount completely the military function of American troops in the mid-1960s. A Europe without a strong American combat troop presence could be pressured or even blackmailed by the Soviet colossus without a shot's being fired. A drift toward neutralism or, worse, a revival of intra-European rivalry and conflict might have resulted. But during a period of relative stability between the Eastern and Western blocs, the Soviet Union was unlikely to launch an attack, or even blackmail Europe, if the American presence were to be reduced by three divisions.

The political importance of the American presence was clear. But how much, in terms of the balance of payments, was the United States willing to pay for its presence in Europe? Under Kennedy and Johnson, the Germans had been told that full military offset was the sine non qua of a six-division American presence. But this bluff had been called, and the United States had to carry out its own threat to bring troops home or devise a new formula to neutralize the foreign exchange costs. Many different ideas were considered, including multilateral clearing schemes and nonmilitary offset purchases. Eventually a formula was found that focused on a combination of transactions: first, as much military procurement as possible; second, nonmilitary procurement; third, long-term special securities; and finally, a specific, detailed promise not to turn in surplus dollars for gold.[70] This was not a perfect combination: U.S. officials preferred military procurement far more than additional debt and a gold pledge that de facto already existed. But this new formula might provide the political cover necessary to keep troop withdrawals to a minimum. Still, it was startling how far the administration was forced to move away from the full military purchase offset formula. And there was no guarantee that the British and the Germans would accept the Johnson administration's views.

In spite of the extensive American preparations for the negotiations, the talks faced difficulties from the start. One issue involved the relationship of the talks between the United States, West Germany, and Great Britain to the NATO organization and the countries in the alliance that were not participating in the talks. The Belgians and Italians complained that the negotiations represented the formation of a "U.S.-U.K.-FRG directorate."[71] This concern seemed justified, given that the talks were dealing with such broad topics as threat, force levels, and burden sharing. Fortunately, McCloy gave a presentation to the North Atlantic Council that persuaded the rest of NATO that the talks were "ad-hoc" and "one-time" in nature.

The positions taken by McCloy's counterparts in the negotiations were more troubling. Ambassador McGhee warned Washington that "Erhard and Westrick have only the most general idea of what we consider the Trilateral Committee is supposed to do."[72] The Germans preferred dealing with the offset issue in a bilateral negotiation without involving the British. Furthermore, FRG officials were worried that threat assessment and force planning exercises would be used to justify financially driven redeployments. The British, for their part, only seemed interested in getting as much money out of the Germans as possible. "The U.K. clearly wants to adapt strategy and forces to fit its pocketbook, minimizing the threat and the value of conventional strength, and relying almost wholly on the nuclear deterrent."[73]

All of these problems were overshadowed by the weakness of the Erhard government, which had been grievously wounded by the failed summit with the Americans.[74] Erhard complained about his treatment at the hands of the Johnson administration, and pointed out that the FRG had "been very considerate and helpful in the US balance of payments situation." The chancellor claimed that his failure to obtain offset relief prompted questions in Germany about "whether the expenditures were really justified." Erhard argued that this was connected to larger problems facing Germany, including reunification and the nuclear question. Germans were asking questions "regarding the character of the security that would be achieved" through offset military purchases. The FRG had seen "certain recommendations, particularly those of Norstad, which had not been accepted and there had been other steps taken which had caused uneasiness." Many Germans felt that the emphasis on flexible response had been an attempt to play down the availability of the nuclear deterrent.

There was a fear in the FRG that these talks were "simply preparing the way for further reductions without true consultations," a concern that was producing "nervousness" and an "element of doubt." Erhard warned that his domestic opponents were arguing that the best way to strengthen Europe would be "to fall in with France and General de Gaulle."[75]

McCloy assured the chancellor that the trilateral exercises were not a pretext for removing troops without consultation and explained that the flexible response posture was necessary to avoid a choice between capitulation and Armageddon in a crisis with the Soviets. But all this was too late for Erhard. In late October, the Free Democratic Party (FDP) withdrew from Erhard's governing coalition when the chancellor proposed a tax increase to raise the revenue needed to fulfill the offset obligation. It took more than a month to form a new government, and the trilateral talks were brought to a halt. On 1 December, Kurt Georg Kiesinger, who advocated closer Franco-German ties, succeeded Erhard as chancellor.

This delay provoked complaints from Great Britain, which had been promised that the trilateral talks would be completed by December or January. In order to forestall a unilateral British withdrawal, at least until June 1967, the Johnson administration had to offer Britain a onetime $35 million weapons purchase order. It was also at this point that the Americans decided once and for all that they had to drop the short-lived offset formula that required the Germans to make military purchases equal to the U.S. foreign exchange burden. Military purchase would have to make up some of the offset, but the administration recognized that the difference would have to be made up through monetary cooperation and perhaps some sort of "multilateralizing" of costs within NATO. But even with these concessions, any German monetary deal was likely to be "$300–400 million" short on the American side and "$100–130 million" less than the foreign exchange costs of the troops. Would the administration pull out troops to make up the gap? McCloy wanted to maintain troop levels and "eat the difference," but no one in the administration thought this was politically possible. Rostow told the president that it was much easier to be pessimistic about the outcome of the talks. "At worst we shall be left with a choice between a sharp cut in the U.S. and U.K. troops, and absorbing a foreign exchange cost of $400–500 million."[76]

## The Trilateral Negotiations, Part II: January–May 1967

The West German government of Kurt Georg Kiesinger understood that "the hour of truth seems to have come" in the trilateral talks. The monetary-security negotiations had begun with hope, but the new government recognized that "the catastrophic developments" surrounding the 1967 FRG budget warranted a "very pessimistic assessment of our possibilities for the foreign exchange support" of both the United States and Great Britain. "There is every reason to fear that the Trilateral talks will come to an abrupt end, if our financial cards are put openly on the table." The result would be a "seriously increasing worsening of our relations with the United States and Great Britain." Far more was at stake than money. The "foreign exchange assistance is only the tail of the dog 'military-political balance.'" But this "tail 'foreign exchange assistance' wags this dog." The key question facing both the new chancellor and all the negotiators was: "can the dog survive if the tail is practically cut off?"[77]

After much deliberation within the new FRG government over whether to continue the trilateral negotiations, on 26 January 1967, the German Foreign Ministry told McGhee that the FRG government had decided to resume discussions, assigning Ambassador Georg Duckwitz to the task. But the government also informed McGhee that "it was necessary to advise the United States and the United Kingdom of the extraordinary difficulties faced by the German government on the offset question because of the budget situation."[78] More than five months had passed since the trilateral negotiations had been proposed, and the only thing that the Johnson administration had to show for its efforts was a $35 million procurement bribe paid to the British to postpone any British withdrawals until June 1967. Domestic pressure to redeploy troops had increased in the meantime.

McCloy needed instructions from the administration on how to proceed in the trilaterals on the issue of American troop withdrawals. There were three sharply divided positions in the administration. McNamara argued that withdrawing two divisions and six air wings would be safe. He did not believe that this would embolden the Soviets in Europe, and enough forces would remain in place to deal with the two most likely contingencies—an unexpected limited conflict or a large-scale conventional attack preceded by extensive political warning. In addition to yearly savings of $200 million in the balance of payments, the cut would have the advantage of making the U.S. military more mobile and flexible. Rusk suggested "rotating" one division and three air wings. The secretary of state would have preferred no cut at all, but he believed that both the domestic and international pressures would not allow the president to maintain the status quo on troops. McCloy, who had been present at the creation of NATO, was against any cuts at all. He shared the opinion held by the Joint Chiefs of Staff (JCS) that a large cut would be militarily unsafe. McCloy contended that if the Americans made a large cut, the

Europeans would soon follow with cuts of their own, until NATO was an empty shell. McCloy indicated that he could possibly stomach a one-division cut, but if Johnson followed McNamara's line and cut two divisions, he would resign as the American negotiator.[79]

The president's deputy special assistant for national security affairs, Francis Bator, told Johnson that, in strictly military terms, McNamara was right. Two divisions could be brought back to America without endangering NATO's military posture against the Soviet Union. Bator did not "share McCloy's view of the world, or the Chiefs." But the offset and redeployment issue was not just a military question; increasingly it was a question of alliance politics, particularly surrounding the "German problem." "Whatever we do, we are in for a year or two of poor weather in our relations with Germany and Europe. . . . Our job is to navigate these rough waters with a minimum of damage."[80] The question was which strategy would be in the long-term interests of U.S. policy in Europe. McNamara's "quick surgery" option of a two-division cut could put the nagging issue of U.S. redeployments to rest once and for all. McCloy's position of no cuts had little credibility and caused nervousness in Europe over future troop withdrawals. Even Rusk's one-division rotation scheme risked being seen as only a first step. On the other hand, Bator said an argument could be made for what he called "tranquilizers and rest," or no cut right now. U.S.-German relations were strained, and this was no time to make them worse with troop cuts. A one-division cut might be possible, but only if the administration promised not to cut again unless the Russians reciprocated.

Much of this decision would be based on what kind of formula was devised to neutralize the foreign exchange costs of the U.S. troops. Bator emphasized that there was no chance for a 100 percent military offset deal. But he believed that the reserve management agreements suggested by the Deming Group[81] could prove more valuable in the long run. In addition to publicly agreeing to hold their surplus dollars, the Germans would push other Europeans to do the same and would support the United States against France in the international monetary negotiations. Bator optimistically saw a chance to move most of the major dollar holders, minus France, into a de facto dollar standard. "It will mean recognition of the fact that, for the time being, the U.S. must necessarily play banker to the world and that the continuing threat to convert gold is simply unacceptable."[82] But Bator emphasized that the Germans would only agree to these policies if the United States cooperated with them on troop levels. A unilateral cut of two or even one division, without consultations, would preclude German cooperation on the money issue.

The decision would be serious for the president. Regardless of what happened with U.S. relations with Germany and Europe, he would be blamed. But because of the stakes involved, Bator urged the "tranquilizers and rest" policy: "My own view is that a large troop cut now, following U.K. troop cuts, non-proliferation, etc. will make you much more vulnerable to the charge that you played accomplice to de Gaulle in wrecking NATO and damaging 20 years of constructive relations with Europe. . . . This is *my* bad dream. . . . The truth is I fear another Skybolt, but with much greater domestic repercussions."[83]

The last thing Johnson wanted was another Skybolt, but he also understood the pressures on him to bring American troops home from Europe. The Germans had publicly reneged on their agreement, and in one of his first speeches the new chancellor accused the administration of failing to properly consult with the FRG. "If I had a dollar for every time I consulted the Germans, I'd be a millionaire." Johnson wanted to strengthen the alliance and do what he could to make the trilateral negotiations a success, but he was not going to commit to a force level until he knew what the British and Germans were going to do. "I know how I feel; I want to marry and live with the woman; but it is important to know how she feels; her decisions will have an important bearing here."[84] Johnson favored Rusk's one-division, three-air-wing rotation scheme, but refused to authorize McCloy to let Germany or Britain know what the U.S. decision on troop withdrawals would be. Johnson would only allow him to indicate that the decision would depend on the results of the talks, the U.K. decision, and the FRG proposals with respect to the American balance of payments.[85]

McCloy felt hamstrung by his instructions. To his mind, it gave the impression of U.S. indecision, when everyone knew that the administration had been working on the problem since October. McCloy argued, "NATO clearly needs a clear note on the trumpet" and asked if he could indicate to the Europeans that the president was very reluctant to make any withdrawals at this time. The president lit into McCloy. He wanted McCloy to remind the Europeans "we didn't create these problems." The Germans and British had caused this crisis by not carrying out their obligations. The United States would do all it could but the president believed that at this point the Rusk scheme was now only a best-case scenario. McCloy cautioned "that I think you are on the verge of the collapse of the alliance. We are going back to the old world of dog-eat-dog—each nation for itself." McCloy believed that if the president intervened, the Congress could be turned around. Johnson pointed out that neither McCloy nor Bator had any clue as to the domestic pressure he was under to make significant reductions. "You are wrong; you are an old and good banker; but it's one thing what a banker will tell you at a cocktail party; it's another when you go up to the window. I know ▓▓▓ well I don't have the votes; they're not there."[86]

When the negotiations resumed in early March, McCloy discovered that there had been little movement or progress in the German and U.K. positions, and the negotiations were clearly in danger of ending without a solution. McCloy told his counterparts that "the talks were not addressing the fundamental questions of how [to] preserve [the] Atlantic Alliance and maintain the deterrent."[87] Bickering, insults, and threats had poisoned the atmosphere of the talks, and the negotiations threatened to do more harm than good. McCloy emphasized that the U.S. position was that the security of the Atlantic alliance should not be sacrificed for financial reasons, and that force levels should be determined by mutual agreement. But McCloy insisted that the Germans recognize the unique balance-of-payments pressures faced by both the United States and Great Britain. This problem had to be handled in a spirit of cooperation. The United States no longer expected a full offset through military purchases for itself, but in addition to a cooperative reserve management policy, McCloy stressed that the gap between the U.K. demands and the German offer had to be filled.

Within the West German government, there was uncertainty as to how to proceed. The most basic questions of strategy and foreign policy were discussed. "What is our concept of defense politics?" If the British troops were essential to German security, then the chancellor argued that "it would be criminal not to find any solution for the question of foreign exchange." But Kiesinger was not convinced that the "British troops are necessary for our security." If the British withdrew their troops, would there be a "U.S. chain reaction?" West German policy makers understood that they were taking great risks with their hard-line position. "If one allows the British to withdraw" because of the offset question, "this will mean the dissolution of NATO."[88]

McCloy soon learned why the FRG was dragging its feet over the trilateral negotiations. Meeting with the new German chancellor for the first time, McCloy chided Kiesinger for his speech in which he accused the Americans of "complicity" for their overtures to the Soviets on the Non-Proliferation Treaty.[89] This had angered the president. McCloy then asked the chancellor to find some way to alleviate the foreign exchange difficulties faced by the Americans and British because of their troop commitments. Kiesinger was unmoved by McCloy's statement. The chancellor explained that the "complicity" comment had been misunderstood. But the Americans had to understand how upset the Germans were about American policies, particularly the foreign exchange offset and nuclear questions. Former chancellor Adenauer had publicly called the NPT proposals "the Morganthau Plan squared." Other FRG politicians were comparing it with the Treaty of Versailles. Right-wing parties were gaining strength through anti-American positions. "There was a rising feeling, however, in Germany, that something had 'gone wrong' with the former pattern of good relations between the U.S. and Germany. This was accompanied by a feeling that NATO was in danger of developing into a sort of 'shell with no real spirit left in it.' "[90] The chancellor pointed out that it was one thing for Germany to declare among its allies that it renounced the manufacture of atomic weapons, but quite another to "enter into a binding agreement with its major adversary limiting even further its capabilities in the nuclear field."[91] In this environment, it would be difficult for Kiesinger to produce a generous offset agreement: "For the first time in the history of the Federal Republic, the public opposes a proposal that comes from the United States . . . not only from them, but this is to a certain extent a joint plan between the United States and the one power that is our most determined opponent, which is the Soviet Union."[92]

McCloy did what he could to reassure the chancellor about the NPT negotiations and stressed that the United States was willing to be very accommodating on the offset deal. The result was a German offer involving $500 million in four- to five-year U.S. notes, an unspecified amount of military procurement, and a public Bundesbank letter promising not to convert its dollars into gold.[93] This deal, which was much less attractive for the Americans than the previous offset arrangement, was by no means guaranteed of making it through Kiesinger's cabinet. Strauss now controlled the Finance Ministry and the budget, and given his Gaullist sentiments, getting money out of him to finance a new agreement with the Americans would be difficult. To this end, Johnson sent a letter to Kiesinger, emphasizing the personal importance he placed on the successful outcome of the talks.[94]

The German cabinet, after a heated debate, approved the rather meager offset arrangement with the United States.[95] But two issues still threatened to sink the trilateral exercise—the British offset and the American rotation scheme. If the British did not achieve their offset target, they would remove as many troops as necessary to meet their target. The Wilson government had come down from its demand for a full offset, but there was still a $40 million gap between its minimum requirement and the highest German offer. Both sides said they had reached the limit of what they were prepared to do. How would this gap be filled? Some sort of additional American procurement in Britain seemed to be the only available solution. Second, the Germans worried that the American rotation scheme cut U.S. military strength too deeply. The FRG would accept the rotation of one division, but it felt that the return of 144 fighter aircraft to the United States was too large. The Germans hinted that unless this figure was reduced to 72 aircraft, the financial deal they had offered would not be forthcoming.

Johnson was understandably unhappy with having to both accept a steep reduction in German offset payments and finance part of the U.K.-German arrangement. And McNamara, who had been on the losing side over much of the offset discussions within the administration since the Erhard summit, was furious that the West German military was trying to dictate his force structure. But if the Americans did not concede, the whole deal could fall apart. A collapse of the negotiations would force the British out and increase the call for a large American withdrawal. "Since we are asking the Germans to 1) split with the French and support us on international money; 2) move in our direction in the Kennedy Round; 3) accept the non-proliferation treaty without a time limit, the question arises what we might offer them."[96] American concessions would have to come in the trilateral negotiations. The Johnson administration worked up a procurement plan to make up most of the $40 million U.K.-German gap and agreed to return only 96 planes to the United States.

These concessions sealed the trilateral negotiations. Great Britain withdrew only one brigade and the United States rotated only one division. The Germans purchased the medium-term securities and, more important, released a letter from Blessing to the Federal Reserve that promised to maintain Germany's no-gold pledge indefinitely.

The Americans successfully reworked the monetary-security regime with the Germans and, to a lesser extent, the British. But the deal that was reached was much less generous than the previous arrangement. The troop level and offset issues were publicly decoupled. And while there would be some military purchases, the Germans were not held to a specific target. The Americans even had to divert some of these purchases to the British, in addition to making their own purchases in Great Britain, in order to avoid large reductions in the army on the Rhine. Medium-term bonds, which were loans that had to be repaid, replaced purchases. The much-hailed centerpiece of the agreement, the Bundesbank no-gold pledge, was just a restatement of an agreement the Americans already tacitly had with the Germans. It certainly helped that the Blessing letter was made public. But the reserve management policy of the Bundesbank had not been a secret to other European central bankers. And while one

U.S. division and several air wings were rotated, the U.S. commitment to maintain a large conventional force in Germany remained in place. Overall, the Americans were forced to accept a rather dramatic retreat on the offset issue, a price the Johnson administration paid reluctantly to maintain a security regime that stabilized great-power politics in Europe.

Why did the Germans unilaterally abrogate the offset agreement, which was the heart of the monetary-security regime that stabilized Central Europe? It is hard to imagine that a German chancellor would undermine a key element of the 1963 political settlement because of a temporary budget shortfall. More likely, the German leadership was troubled by the constant rumors and hints that U.S. troops would be redeployed. They were unhappy with being singled out on the offset issue. They were concerned about the fracture in NATO-French relations. Alarmingly, the Americans were much less supportive of Germany on the unification and borders issues than in the past. But the issue that most nagged at the Germans during this period was the nuclear question. The failure of the multilateral force, coupled with the seeming willingness of the Americans to accommodate the Soviets on a nonproliferation treaty at the expense of the Germans, produced a sense that perhaps the security regime with the United States should be reassessed.

For their part, the Americans were faced with a choice. The Kennedy administration had reluctantly decided to station six combat divisions in Germany for as long as they were needed. But because this commitment exacerbated the American balance-of-payments deficit, it was thought essential that the Germans fully offset their foreign exchange costs through military purchases in the United States. In their mind, they had reached a bargain, and if the Germans failed to fully offset, American troops should be sent home. This was the position of McNamara, Fowler, and, to some extent, Bundy. But when actually confronted with the decision to reduce troops on a massive scale after the Germans reneged on the offset deal, the Americans hesitated. Although the military importance of American troops may have receded, their political importance had not. These troops, by both protecting and containing Germany, stabilized great-power politics in Europe, a situation the Americans did not want to undermine, even to alleviate the dollar and gold crisis.

*Chapter Seven*

# The End of Bretton Woods

*The Devaluation of Sterling
and the 1968 Gold Crisis*

In a May 1968 memo to President Johnson entitled "Explanation of Possible World Financial Crisis," CEA chairman Arthur Okun laid out a terrifying scenario for how the dollar and gold crisis could lead to a worldwide economic and political catastrophe.[1] Okun argued that if the Vietnam tax increase were not passed, the world would think "the United States is *not serious* about preserving the dollar." Foreign investors would conclude that their dollars were vastly overvalued, the price of gold would escalate, and central banks, uncomfortable with their growing supply of American currency, would start to demand "huge quantities of gold for their dollars." Sterling would collapse—again—but this time drag the dollar down with it, forcing the United States to suspend formally dollar-gold convertibility. "Thus, we would expect tremendous havoc and uncertainty in world finance." Okun claimed that this would be "a *major world political defeat for the United States.*" International trade would founder, employment would drop, and stocks and bonds would plummet. American leverage at a world monetary conference would be "pathetic." "Reactionaries at home would have a field day *attacking all Government programs.*" The Federal Reserve would be trapped between the traditional policy to fix a balance-of-payments crisis—"very tight money"—and the need to calm panicked financial markets with easy money. "Perhaps the most long-lasting consequence would be in the international political sphere. Our financial disaster would create pressures to *renege on our worldwide commitments.*"[2] Troops would be called back home, the Paris Peace talks would collapse, and a dangerous power vacuum would come into being. According to Johnson's chief economic adviser, every important Johnson administration policy—domestic and foreign—was threatened by the dollar and gold crisis.

Okun's alarmism was even more surprising because the administration had believed, months earlier, that it had solved the gold outflow and payments deficit issue. The arduous trilateral negotiations had been successfully concluded in the spring of 1967. The Germans promised to purchase military equipment and long-range bonds to offset some of the American foreign exchange costs surrounding the U.S. troop commitment. More important, the Bundesbank, the world's largest foreign holder of dollars, publicly agreed to keep its dollars and not buy gold from the United States. The administration hoped that other surplus countries could be persuaded to follow a similar no-gold policy. Furthermore, the negotiations to create a new international monetary asset, the SDR, ended with an American victory. Despite enormous objections from the French, the Johnson administration convinced the G-10 to create a new form of liquidity to supplement gold and the dollar. Both of these agreements had been hard won, and both were expected to alleviate the gold drain, which had plagued the United States since 1958. More important, these agreements were supposed to save a faltering Bretton Woods monetary system.

Things did not go as planned, however. This chapter chronicles a series of unexpected events that shook the international monetary system to its core in 1967 and 1968. In November 1967 the British government was forced to devalue sterling, weakening the dollar and sharply increasing overseas demand for gold. The deficit in the U.S. balance of payments, which had decreased in 1965, exploded by the end of 1967, driven by the inflationary strains of the Vietnam War and the Great Society programs. The most obvious candidate for balance-of-payments relief, troop withdrawals from Europe, was ruled out when it became clear the West Germans were losing confidence in the American security guarantee and were considering unsettling foreign policy shifts of their own. A program to improve the balance of payments through tax increases and restrictions on capital, trade, and tourist accounts met with harsh resistance from the U.S. Congress. There were no easy choices—they had already been made—if the Bretton Woods system was to be saved. The cautious optimism expressed in 1967 was replaced by panic in early 1968. By the end of the March 1968 gold crisis, the Bretton Woods system was, for all practical purposes, finished.

## The Devaluation of Sterling

Although the dollar was weak in late 1967, British sterling was weaker. Sterling had long been the most fragile link in the fixed exchange rate system. The Bretton Woods agreements had envisioned rapid current-account convertibility and the elimination of capital controls for the major world currencies soon after the war. Great Britain, as a founder of the Bretton Woods system, was expected to achieve this status immediately. But American planners had vastly overestimated the strength of the British economy, and the Attlee's Labour government had refused to cancel or renegotiate the enormous sterling debts held by Commonwealth creditors. These sterling debts were both an economic and a political albatross.

If they were canceled or unilaterally decreased, the Labour government feared the decline of London as a banking center and a rapid disintegration of the empire and Commonwealth. But if they remained, these sterling balances could be used to run down the British dollar and gold reserves and force a devaluation of sterling.

Despite massive American aid and extensive capital- and current-account controls, sterling remained weak in the immediate postwar period. The British, closely consulting with the Truman administration but in open violation of the rules of the International Monetary Fund, devalued sterling in 1949 by 30.5 percent, from $4.03 to $2.80. But this massive devaluation did not bring sterling any closer to full current-account dollar accountability. A push by the Churchill government to let the pound float and use American aid to stabilize sterling at a new exchange rate was rejected by the Eisenhower administration, and the British, along with other Marshall aid recipients, joined the European Payments Union and accepted its plan for a more gradual approach to convertibility. The success of the EPU allowed the major Western European currencies to achieve current-account dollar convertibility at the end of 1958.

Great Britain withstood serious monetary crises in 1957, after the Suez debacle, and 1961, and both times sterling was saved by American-led bailout efforts. Harold Wilson's Labour government faced a sterling crisis immediately upon entering office in 1964. In retrospect, Wilson himself admitted that devaluing sterling at that point would have been politically expedient because he could have blamed British monetary woes on the policies of the outgoing Conservative Party. But, instead, the government imposed a 15 percent import surcharge and arranged for a $3 billion line of credit with a consortium led by the Federal Reserve Bank of New York, the Bank for International Settlements, and the central banks of Canada, Japan, and each of the Common Market countries.

This large bailout program was only a reprieve. The Wilson government, elected on a program of increased social welfare spending, was understandably reluctant to initiate the austerity measures that were necessary to strengthen the pound. Sterling came under strong speculative attacks in the spring of 1967. The Middle East crisis closed the Suez Canal, which squeezed British exports and led Arab countries with large sterling deposits to exchange them for dollars. This produced the most serious sterling crisis since the 1949 devaluation.

The Johnson administration identified the weakness of sterling as the Achilles' heel of the Bretton Woods system. If the British government decided to devalue, international confidence in the ability of the United

States to hold the par value and maintain convertibility of the dollar into gold would be weakened. Massive capital flows out of the dollar into stronger European currencies might deplete the American gold supply, forcing the Johnson administration to suspend convertibility. If the administration could not prevent a devaluation of sterling, how could it prevent international monetary disorder?

After another run on sterling during the summer of 1966, the Division of International Finance at the Federal Reserve produced a top-secret study, laying out the consequences of a sterling devaluation.[3] The study also examined a wide array of possible American responses. Robert Solomon and Robert Young, advisers to the Federal Reserve Board, warned that, if sterling were devalued, "the foundations of the existing international monetary system would be shaken at best; beyond this, severe crisis with dire consequences for the international economy could not be ruled out." It was important that the U.S. government be prepared with possible responses well in advance, because whatever policy the United States followed would have "far-reaching implications for the stability of international commerce and finance, for domestic policies, and for economic welfare at home and abroad."[4]

The effect of a sterling devaluation on international monetary relations would depend, the report stated, on how large the devaluation was and whether the major industrial nations would accept the changed exchange rate structure or initiate their own devaluations. The Federal Reserve predicted that the devaluation had to be at least 10 percent to be credible and no more than 20 percent to avoid countervailing devaluations; 15 percent was considered the most likely number. Regardless of the amount, a devaluation of sterling would lead to a strong "bear" attack on the dollar, producing "serious market uncertainties about the viability of other exchange rates, including those of the dollar."[5] The greatest danger that the United States would face would be a massive capital flight. Short-term foreign and domestic funds would move out of the dollar and into some of the stronger currencies, especially those of the EEC. European central bankers, alarmed at the flood of dollars, would move quickly to redeem them for gold from the U.S. Treasury. Other central banks, anticipating dollar devaluation and an increase in the price of gold, would start to liquidate their existing dollar assets to purchase gold. In addition, foreign private funds would buy gold on the London market, gold that would have to be supplied by the gold pool countries. Many of the gold pool countries would hesitate at supplying the gold needed to maintain the open market price of thirty-five dollars an ounce, and the whole operation would collapse. With the gold pool defunct, the price of gold would increase, central banks would make a run on American gold, and international monetary cooperation would cease.

What policies could be developed to meet this threat? The report examined a wide array of options, all of which were at least considered by the Johnson administration a year later when sterling was devalued. The choices fell into three categories. The United States could try to adjust to the new situation without any change in par value for the dollar or other major currencies and without changing the role of gold. The authors of the report cautioned that maintaining the status quo would be very difficult and would require measures to restrict the anticipated capital flow out of dollars. In order to maintain the new exchange rates without changing the role of gold or the dollar, the United States would have to consider capital controls, ask the IMF to invoke the "scarce currency clause," and pressure the European surplus countries to revalue their currencies upward.

The second option the United States had in the event of a sterling devaluation was to change the role of gold in the international payments system while maintaining the new exchange rate structure. The United States could end its practice of selling gold to foreign central banks without necessarily abandoning the dollar's par value or its convertibility into other currencies. It could also design a "defensive ring" of cooperative central banks, which would manage gold convertibility among them while denying gold to unfriendly countries. It could also negotiate the closing of the private gold markets, end the gold pool operation and separate the private and central bank gold markets, or raise the official price of gold. Finally, the United States could decide to alter existing exchange relationships by establishing a new par value for the dollar, either through negotiations with the leading industrial countries or by allowing the dollar to float.

A radical version of this last option, which the Federal Reserve study entitled "Plan X," was perhaps the most intriguing possibility. Plan X suggested that a sterling devaluation could be used to American advantage, providing the United States with "a ready-made, welcome opportunity to get the gold and the balance of payments monkey off our back."[6] It would suspend all gold sales and purchases, and allow the dollar to float. "The object of this policy move would ostensibly be to make the Europeans fish or cut bait."[7] The United States would force the Europeans to decide whether they would support their currencies at the old exchange rate, and accumulate more dollars, or let their own currencies appreciate against the dollar. The study distinguished between those who wanted to use a dollar float as a temporary expedient to achieve a more reasonable

LBJ meeting with Walt Rostow and Secretary of the Treasury Fowler. Johnson claimed, "The biggest problem I've got outside of Vietnam is balance of payments." The administration believed that it had solved the problem in 1965, when Henry Fowler announced that the United States would hold a world monetary conference. Despite the strenuous efforts of the administration, by 1968 sterling had collapsed and the dollar was threatened. (Courtesy of the Lyndon B. Johnson Museum and Library)

par value, and those who wanted to end the Bretton Woods–IMF system in favor of a nonreserve, floating exchange rate regime. The former, the "temporary relapsers," believed that fixed exchange rates had to be re-established in order to maintain the dollar's reserve-currency role and the IMF's position as the overseer of international monetary relations. The "full-blown floaters" who would support Plan X believed that the IMF–Bretton Woods system was deeply flawed and wasted valuable resources. In a floating exchange rate regime, the whole issue of liquidity, adjustment, and par values would cease to be an issue for the United States.

Plan X is fascinating because it entertained the idea of abandoning fixed exchange rates and dollar-gold convertibility. It is also interesting, because there is extensive, and generally favorable, marginalia, apparently written by Johnson's assistant national security adviser, Francis Bator. Throughout the trilateral and payments discussions, Bator had told the president he had a trump card: the United States could go off gold or allow the dollar to float. Many of the ideas contained in Plan X were implemented five years later by the Nixon administration.

Few if anyone in the Johnson administration saw the sterling devaluation as an opportunity for a bold new course in international monetary policy. In November 1967, when it became clear that sterling was in serious trouble, Walt Rostow warned that devaluation could be dangerous. "The main point is the risks for us are just too great to be worth the gamble."[8] Henry Fowler told Johnson that "if sterling falls, there will be great monetary unrest. The dollar will be affected strongly."[9] Great efforts were made to put together yet another massive, multilateral bailout package for sterling.[10]

As it became increasingly clear that the Wilson government would devalue, however, the Johnson administration recognized that it had little choice but to accept the new exchange rates. Any public equivocation would unsettle the currency markets and increase the flight from the dollar. In his public statement on November 18, after the devaluation of the pound sterling from $2.80 to $2.40 was announced, Johnson declared that the new parity would allow the United Kingdom to "achieve the needed improvement in its ability to compete in world markets." The president reaffirmed the American commitment to "buy and sell gold at the existing price of $35 an ounce."

## The French, the United States, and the Gold Pool

Of course, the United States would not be buying any gold, at least at that price. The key question was whether the United States, with the help of the gold pool, could supply enough gold to the London market to keep the price of gold around thirty-five dollars an ounce. The administration believed that it could hold off a run on the dollar if the gold pool increased the amount of gold it was willing to sell in London. But the Europeans were getting restless; they were not prepared to accept an unlimited amount of dollars and lose gold to the London market at the same time. Complicating matters was the fact that the French appeared to be conspiring to unsettle the currency markets with rumors. France had dropped out of the gold pool during the summer of 1967, though it had never been publicly announced. The Americans just picked up France's share. But Paul Fabra, a financial writer for *Le Monde* who had close ties to de Gaulle's government, chose the week after the sterling devaluation to write that France had dropped out of the gold pool. Other items that were discussed in top-secret G-10 meetings also appeared in French newspapers at the time.[11]

In fact, the sterling devaluation, at least at first, seemed to be the monetary test of wills that the French had been seeking for some time. The French had pursued monetary and fiscal policies that would produce a large balance-of-payments surplus. Surplus dollars were used to purchase American gold. France also used its influence to "prevent the adoption of U.S. proposals for reforms of the international monetary system." By dropping out of the gold pool in June, France signaled that it was no longer interested in any further international monetary cooperation. According to a top-secret CIA report, the "French government attitudes, and the actions of some French officials, were important factors contributing to the massive speculation against the dollar and gold." But as the gold crisis intensified and the Americans considered taking drastic action, the French backed off. "By mid-December . . . the French government had become concerned about the deepening crisis and subsequently has generally refrained from unsettling actions."[12]

What about the other major European central banks? The Johnson administration calculated that the gold pool would have to supply as much as $3 billion in gold to maintain the London market price. Despite the fact that $1.8 billion of this would be provided by the United States, the Europeans did not want to lose over $1 billion in gold. The United States proposed a new scheme, which it called the gold certificate program. Any gold pool member who lost gold to the London market would receive a gold certificate that was to be treated like gold in official central bank transactions. The Europeans, however, were unwilling to replace real gold with paper gold.[13]

In the weeks that followed the devaluation, there was a strong feeling among European central bankers that the gold pool should be terminated before their losses got out of hand. But the administration felt this would lead to an increase in the official price of gold, validating de Gaulle's monetary policy. Fred Deming, under secretary of treasury for monetary affairs, was dispatched to Europe and negotiated a new gold pool arrangement that would maintain unity and continue to feed gold to the London market.[14] Rumors persisted, however, that the London market would be closed, that licensing measures or a gold tax would be introduced, or the gold pool had collapsed. Gold pool losses since the devaluation mounted, reaching $1.5 billion by the end of December. After meeting with European central bankers in Switzerland on 10 December, it was clear that support for the gold pool was deteriorating.[15] The meeting failed to produce a communiqué on the subject, and in the week that followed the gold pool lost $548 million.

Federal Reserve chairman Martin negotiated with his European counterparts to reach an agreement to continue the pool. Hubert Ansiaux of Belgium, speaking for himself and the Germans, Italians, Dutch, and Swiss, told Martin in a 15 December phone call that "we were strongly of the opinion until yesterday night, when you got in touch with all of us, to recommend that we should stop our intervention in the market."[16] But Ansiaux said the group would agree to continue the pool under two conditions: that the Americans reimburse the Europeans in gold for "excessive accumulations of dollars" and, more important, that the administration announce a strong balance-of-payments program within the next few weeks. "We very much hope that the program will be really very fundamental and substantial; not just a stop-gap measure; something really affecting the root of the matter."[17]

The Johnson administration had been working on a serious program throughout the fall of 1967, but now the stakes were much higher.[18] After the collapse of sterling, the gold pool countries made it clear that without drastic American action to reduce its payments deficit, they would end their cooperation. The news of such a pullout would drive the price of gold on the London market sky-high, and make it almost impossible for the Americans to maintain a price of thirty-five dollars an ounce. Nor would the Europeans accept anything that struck them as a gimmick, such as an immediate activation of the SDR or a gold certificate program.

What would a program to improve the balance of payments look like? The trade account could be adjusted with export rebates and import surcharges, but that would not produce the immediate results the Europeans wanted. There were three accounts that were causing most of the dollar outflow: the capital account, the tourist account, and the military expenditures account. Cutting any of the three would be controversial. Moving from voluntary to mandatory capital controls would be seen as overly intrusive by the banking and business community. Restricting tourism would hinder a fundamental freedom. Reducing military expenditures required an important policy shift—either ending the war in Vietnam or cutting the number of American troops stationed in Europe. In late 1967 it was inconceivable that the Johnson administration would simply end the Vietnam War to rectify the U.S. balance of payments. That meant that American expenditures in the NATO area were the most attractive targets for cuts. But for complex political and military reasons, cutting America's military expenditures in Europe would prove impossible. The savings would have to come from somewhere else.

## America, Germany, and the Balance of Payments

This was the most severe monetary crisis the United States faced in the postwar period. The balance-of-payments deficit for the 1967 fourth quarter alone would be worse than any year on record. There was a massive capital flight from the dollar. The gold pool operation, critical to keeping the gold price at thirty-five dollars an ounce, was disintegrating. Countries outside of the gold pool were turning in their dollars for gold at an alarming rate, and the gold level at the U.S. Treasury was near the minimum required by law to back the domestic currency. This gold could not be sold without legislation or piecemeal Federal Reserve waivers. The Johnson administration, paralyzed by domestic discontent and the Vietnam War, was incapable of producing any rapid, meaningful balance-of-payments relief that required congressional approval. Yet, despite these constraints, it was universally acknowledged that a dramatic program was needed to restore confidence in the dollar and avoid the complete collapse of the Bretton Woods system of fixed exchange rates. With few exceptions, policy makers within the administration feared that going off gold would set off a series of events that would result in competitive devaluations, capital controls and trade restrictions, economic blocs, and a seizing up of international liquidity that would bring an international depression. These fears may have been based on an incorrect reading of the history of the 1930s and a misunderstanding of international economics. But U.S. policy was made on the basis of these fears, and outside of a small group of academic economists and a handful of government officers, most responsible decision makers believed that no effort should be spared to maintain dollar-gold convertibility at thirty-five dollars an ounce.

Would these efforts include a radical paring down of U.S. political and military commitments around the world? The administration's easiest source of savings that could be achieved through executive order was to reduce the American troop presence overseas, especially in Western Europe. The proposal to withdraw troops from Europe was not new, and had been on the table since the Eisenhower administration. If anything, there was more public and congressional support for bringing troops back to the United States than ever before.

The severity of the monetary crisis seemed to make such a move unavoidable. Months before the crisis, Secretary of the Treasury Fowler had been furious that the financial and monetary aspects of U.S.-European relations had not received more scrutiny. In a May 1967 meeting called to discuss problems in the U.S. relationship with Western Europe, Fowler complained that no mention was made of what he felt was the most important issue of all, "the financial problem." Fowler had told the president that "the financial problem" with Western Europe "is our Achilles heel, which more than any of the specific problems listed in the State Department paper" is a "threat to our position in Western Europe and the effectiveness of our foreign policy in dealing with it." The primary cause of this problem was the "disparities in burden-sharing relative to *financial* strength that result from political, diplomatic and military arrangements."[19] It was bad enough that the West Europeans were uncooperative. Some of them, led by France, were pursuing overtly hostile policies aimed at harming the economic and political interests of the United States. By standing idly by without trying to stop the French, the rest of the Common Market was, according to Fowler, complicit in these destructive policies. The Common Market countries have "made less contribution to the common defense" than they should have; they have "continued to pile up international reserves," instead of embracing policies that promote international payments equilibrium; they have been "overly cautious" when considering American proposals for international monetary reform; and they have allowed their balance-of-payments receipts to be swollen from "U.S. military expenditures."[20] The devaluation of sterling, the upward pressure on gold in the London market, and the flight from the dollar added urgency to Fowler's position.

This line of argument was not new. The two previous secretaries of treasury, Douglas Dillon and Robert Anderson, had produced their own, almost identical proposals to do something about the balance-of-payments costs of the American military commitment to Europe. These policies had been considered by both Eisenhower and Kennedy but ultimately had been modified or rejected. But the circumstances in the second half of 1967 were changing dramatically. First, this monetary crisis was far worse than the ones faced by Eisenhower and Kennedy. Second, tensions with the Soviet Union over Europe had receded dramatically since 1963. Finally, U.S. relations with Western Europe were strained, perhaps even more than during the crisis year of 1963. France had pulled out of the NATO organization, Great Britain had been rejected for admission to the Common Market for the second time in four years, and there were almost universal misgivings in Europe about a whole range of American policies, from the balance of payments to nuclear strategy to Vietnam. There was widespread support for détente with the Soviet Union and mutual force reductions in Central Europe. Western European defense budgets, as a percentage of GNP, had fallen. Even West Germany was quietly demonstrating its discontent with the American commitment and the utility of NATO by striking out with its own initiatives toward East Germany and the Soviet Union.

After the acrimonious trilateral negotiations of 1966–67, however, the administration hesitated to reopen the controversial question of American troop withdrawals from Europe. At the same time that the administration was searching for a way to end the monetary crisis, the State

Department was trying to develop policies that would repair America's strained relations with Western Europe. The difficulty of this task was compounded by a sense, in late 1967 and early 1968, that the NATO alliance was in serious trouble. The State Department worried that ten years of American threats to withdraw troops from West Germany had undermined the FRG's faith in the American commitment. The rough treatment of Erhard over offset in the fall of 1966 and the difficult trilateral negotiations had exposed the widest rift in U.S.-German relations since the founding of the FRG.

A series of recently declassified documents from the Department of State Policy Planning Papers reveal how acute these concerns were. A 16 November 1967 report entitled "Implications of a More Independent German Foreign Policy" claimed "the mood underlying present FRG policies is, to a much greater extent than prior to 1966, one of uncertainty, resentment, or suspicion regarding the direction of U.S. policy." This was largely because the United States was threatening troop withdrawals from West Germany at the same time that it was initiating a conciliatory policy toward the Soviet Union. "Many Germans fear deeply that the U.S. will either progressively reduce its forces in Europe and thus make the Germans vulnerable to Soviet pressure, or strive increasingly for accords with the USSR at the expense of FRG interests, or both." The authors claimed that the typical American rebuttal, that "the Germans have no place to go," only applied when the FRG had "confidence in U.S. support for German security and reunification."[21] The Germans were starting to believe that this confidence was no longer warranted.

Another policy planning paper, written three months later, was even more pessimistic. "The Germans are convinced that the U.S. will in the relatively near future make further substantial and unilateral reductions in its forces in Germany." This report, entitled "Germany and the Future of Western Europe," predicted that FRG policy would be increasingly willing to make dangerous concessions to the Soviets to win liberalization in East Germany. The report suggested that such liberalization, let alone progress toward unification, was against Soviet interests. FRG security concessions would purchase nothing but disappointment and eventually resentment within West Germany. "Disillusion in West Germany might well set in and produce radical movements of the right and left." The fear of American troop withdrawals would make the West Germans feel "intensely isolated." They would also feel that they were being pressured into accepting a neutralized status in any event, one where the division of Germany would be permanently institutionalized, in effect, by East-West security control arrangements. In this frame of mind, almost any FRG government would fear it had to purchase confederation with the GDR from the Soviets at the price of neutralization, and perhaps make even more far-reaching concessions, as a desperate last chance for progress toward reunification and assurance of some security.[22]

This meant that troop withdrawals could no longer be contemplated to resolve the balance of payments. Redeployment could not even be threatened to squeeze more money out of the Germans. Almost ten years of uncertainty over the American conventional commitment had strained relations with West Germany. The trilateral talks had been held to resolve, once and for all, the relationship between troop levels, offset, and reserve management policies. The United States could not admit, six months after it was signed, that the trilateral agreement was a failure. The alliance could not withstand more threats and acrimony. Even Robert McNamara, the strongest advocate of troop reductions in Europe, agreed. "We cannot pull our troops out of Western Europe right now because it would mean the disintegration of NATO."[23] The Johnson administration would have to look elsewhere for savings to improve the U.S. balance of payments.

## The 1968 Balance-of-Payments Program

The Cabinet Committee on Balance of Payments met throughout December to design a credible plan to limit the flow of dollars overseas. Led by Secretary of the Treasury Fowler and attended by representatives from the Federal Reserve and cabinet officers including McNamara and Rusk, the group wanted to present a tough program to the world. A daily tourist tax, mandatory capital controls, limits on overseas spending, a border tax, and export rebates were considered. There were arguments over what accounts to target; the Commerce Department wanted to avoid mandatory capital controls, and the State Department worried that the trade and tourist measures would infuriate America's allies. But by late December, the committee had come up with a tough program for the president.[24]

Johnson did not like the political implications of much of the program. The border tax, while legal under the provisions of the General Agreement of Tariffs and Trade (GATT), could set off retaliatory measures by the countries most hurt by the policy. Wide-scale retaliation would eliminate any savings in the balance of payments and could spark a large trade war. Johnson argued that the balance of trade, which was in surplus, was not the problem, and that protectionist measures could stimulate speculative moves against the dollar. The president was not enthusiastic about the tourist provisions either. The tourist tax proposal was "complicated" and would advertise American "weakness," which could trigger currency speculators. Penalizing tourists inhibited the "good will which tourism builds" and would be "used by the Republicans in an election year."[25]

The program, announced on New Year's Day 1968, included the stringent capital and overseas lending controls.[26] Both of these provisions were favored by the Europeans, and despite anger on Wall Street and Main Street, neither program was likely to stir up much voter protest. Also provided were initiatives by the Commerce Department and the Export-Import Bank to encourage American exports. But on the questions of trade and travel, the president's message was vague. On both issues, Johnson promised to consult Congress and to enter into direct negotiations with countries overseas to achieve balance-of-payments savings.

The administration dispatched groups of high-level officials to Europe, Japan, and Canada to explain the plan and seek further concessions on trade, tourism, and offsets for military expenditures. Most foreign officials approved of the effort, although they universally emphasized the importance of getting a tax increase to narrow the U.S. budget deficit. There was a certain strangeness to the whole effort: here was the world's largest economy, representing over one-third of the world's total output, owning more than $110 billion of overseas assets, possessing 20 percent of the world's gold reserves, and it was forced to seek approval for a politically unpopular plan from countries like Italy and Belgium. There was a growing sense that these problems were to some extent unreal, more a product of an ineffective monetary system than a reflection of a broken American economy. This feeling moved to the foreground as it became clear the strict balance-of-payments program would not end American gold losses.

The foreign exchange markets had responded enthusiastically to the program at first, and gold pool losses were dramatically reduced in January. But the Tet offensive, which began on 31 January, shattered the calm on the London market. Tet made it clear that military expenditures overseas would balloon in 1968. General Earle Wheeler's ensuing request for 200,000 more men would explode the American payments deficit.[27] Congress showed no sign of passing the tax increase, the domestic gold cover had not been lifted, and the trade and capital accounts weakened despite the 1968 program. Worse, the United States was forced to draw on the IMF and sell gold in order to settle swap arrangements with gold pool countries.[28] This signaled to the market that other gold pool countries would not keep supplying gold to the London market indefinitely. As Rostow told Johnson in February: "The situation could turn into a crisis of confidence and feed on itself—much like a run on a bank. The end result could be a serious contraction of international liquidity and pressure on all countries to adopt restrictive economic policies—at home and abroad—to preserve their gold holdings."[29]

Rostow told the president that policies to correct the payments deficit would no longer be enough. The rules of the international monetary system would have to be changed or the system would suffer meltdown. Rostow offered the president three choices: create an international paper reserve that would substitute for gold; raise the price of gold, thereby increasing the value of world reserves; or abandon the fixed exchange rate system altogether.[30] According to Rostow, the first choice would be the best: the gold pool would be maintained, but a certificate that would serve the same reserve purposes as gold would replace losses by central banks. Maintaining the gold pool was necessary to demonstrate to private speculators that they were fighting not just the $12 billion gold supply of the United States but the combined $26 billion gold stock of all the gold pool members. But even this scenario was a fiction. Because the United States made good on some of the gold pool losses, the Americans supplied almost 75 percent of the total gold pool resources.[31] Rostow also suggested that the price band on gold could be increased so that the price could fluctuate at a range of thirty-two to thirty-eight dollars an ounce before the gold pool intervened.

Rostow found the other two options less appealing. Creating a two-price structure for gold—one determined by the London market and the other fixed by central banks at thirty-five dollars an ounce—was not likely to hold for long. Even if the gold pool countries refrained from buying or selling gold on the open market, central banks outside of the gold pool would have an enormous incentive to cash in all of their official dollar holdings when the price of gold in London started to rise. The final option—suspending dollar-gold convertibility—was to Rostow's mind the most risky. There were two variations on this option. The United States could maintain its fixed parity by selling and buying currencies in other exchange markets. But it might have to go to the IMF or sell its gold to obtain these currencies. The more radical variant would be to just let the dollar's exchange rate float. That would put the onus of decision on the Europeans. They could intervene in the exchange markets to maintain the value of the dollar, or they could let the dollar fall in value. The first option would be expensive, but the second option would make dollar exports more attractive and European imports more expensive. Rostow did not think the Europeans would allow this to happen without instituting exchange controls and trade and capital restrictions against the dollar.

Rostow believed this would be the first step on the road to ruin. "In the end world trade would decline and many countries would be under pressure to follow deflationary policies."[32]

## The March Gold Crisis and the End of Bretton Woods

The gold pool losses intensified in early March, with a total loss of $123 million in gold in the first week. The following Friday the gold pool lost $179 million in one day.[33] The Americans absorbed most of these losses. But the Johnson administration still held out hope that the gold pool could be maintained. Treasury Secretary Fowler told the president that among "the available options, our clear preference is to beat back the current speculative attack." This required the gold pool countries to act together "to show that they are determined to keep the present system going and will firmly oppose any increase in the price of gold." But if the Europeans dropped out of the gold pool, the Americans faced difficult choices. They could support the London market by themselves, they could establish the two-price market for gold, or they could start licensing gold sales. Fowler was even more concerned than Rostow about the consequences of a move off gold toward a dollar float. Fowler warned a "gold embargo would lead to exchange rate wars and trading blocs with harmful political as well as economic effects."[34]

But by the end of the second week in March, it was clear that the gold pool operation would not hold. Something dramatic had to be done. On 13 March, Rostow warned the president:

> The continuation of gold losses at the pace of recent months is untenable. As a political fact, we cannot go on selling gold indefinitely to speculators and hoarders. However rational such a course may be, there is a growing revulsion against it, here and in Europe. . . . Strong and dramatic international action is required to end the hysteria: —a visible mobilization of overwhelming force. . . . Unless we can take convincing international action to this effect very, very soon, we shall face a choice among even more difficult and disagreeable alternatives.[35]

After high-level discussions throughout 13–14 March, the administration settled on a plan to convene an emergency meeting of select central bankers. The London gold market would be closed on Friday, 15 March, and the bankers would meet in Washington, D.C., on the weekend of 16–17 March to hammer out new rules on gold and reserves. The administration would present a plan to the Europeans that would establish interim rules on gold, including a two-price scheme, measures to keep order in the financial markets, and a timetable for early activation of SDRs. If the Europeans rejected the plan, the administration would "have to suspend gold convertibility for official dollar holders, at least temporarily, and call for an immediate emergency conference."[36]

The administration went to work on two tracks, domestic and foreign. The State Department sent out an urgent wire to the European embassies ordering them to contact the most important central bankers, waking them from sleep if necessary. "You must track down these men at all costs."[37] All the major European central bankers agreed to come to Washington immediately. The administration had less success convincing Congress that it needed to take immediate steps, including passing the long-languishing tax bill, in order to ease the crisis. Congress had refused for months to raise taxes unless the Johnson administration made serious budget cuts. Rostow told Johnson that members of Congress did not realize that the gold crisis went "to the heart of the nation's capacity to carry its external commitments; maintain the world trade and monetary system; and avoid a serious domestic breakdown in our economy."[38]

The administration also anticipated difficulties with the European central bankers. There were two extreme positions that could surface during the conference. The Europeans could demand an immediate rise in the price of gold, thereby increasing the value of their reserves and ending the gold drain in London. But the Americans would never agree to this policy, which would represent a complete capitulation to the French position. The Americans could take the other extreme: a unilateral gold embargo and a floating rate for the dollar. This choice would move the burden of decision on the Europeans; they could either accept a devaluation of the dollar or support the dollar's exchange rate from their reserves.[39] Either position would symbolize the complete collapse of international monetary cooperation. There was a range of choices between these two extremes that would produce a successful meeting.

To the surprise of the American negotiators, the Europeans agreed to almost all the Johnson administration's suggestions. The central bankers accepted the two-price scheme for gold. The gold pool would be dissolved, but the central banks involved would declare that the gold they already possessed was sufficient for international monetary purposes. This meant that they would neither buy nor sell gold on the London market, in effect, demonetizing new gold production. If the global trading system needed more liquidity to achieve payment equilibrium, then SDRs would be activated. There was also the problem of central banks outside of the gold pool. The gold pool countries agreed not to sell gold to those countries that continued to sell gold in the private market.[40] The

Americans also sent telegrams to all the world's central bankers, strongly suggesting that it was in their best interest to refrain from exploiting any arbitrage situation made possible by the two-tier market.[41] France, the one country that might have caused problems, had seen its own balance of payments shift from surplus to deficit by 1968 and was in no position to buy gold from the United States.

### After the Gold Crisis: Would the System Hold?

The separation of the gold markets in March 1968 put the world on a de facto dollar standard. This outcome was the result of enormous American pressure. The world's leading central bankers were essentially given a choice: accept the demonetization of gold or be prepared for unilateral American action. Few central bankers wanted the Americans to close their gold window officially or allow the dollar to float. So they accepted the fiction that the price of gold between central bankers could remain the same while the price on private markets was allowed to rise.

This system would only work if central bankers agreed not to exploit the difference between the private and intragovernmental price of gold. It also depended upon the Americans drastically reducing the outflow of dollars. But the United States had failed to stem the dollar outflow in the past ten years, even at the cost of losing its gold. The Johnson administration had made it clear that large gold purchases would revive the threat of unilateral action. So the only real sanction against the Americans running large balance-of-payments deficits—the loss of gold—had been more or less removed.

Would this new system hold? In some ways, it was not a radical departure from the way the system had been working. Two of the largest dollar surplus countries, West Germany and Japan, had been holding dollars and not purchasing American gold for some time. France, which did not accept the new rules, had moved from a large balance-of-payments surplus to a deficit, and was no longer in a position to threaten the U.S. gold supply. The real question was exchange rate parities. Was the dollar overvalued in relation to the currencies of Western Europe and Japan, as many believed? And could these parities be maintained and defended in the face of ever increasing private capital flows?

The renewed commitment to fixed exchange rates was soon tested. Not surprisingly, the first currency challenged was the British pound. As always, the Americans paid close attention to what happened to sterling. If Great Britain could not maintain its exchange rate, less than a year after devaluing and receiving billions in international credit, then the exchange value of the dollar would also come into doubt. Sterling was being

Bill Mauldin, "The formula, gentlemen, is to work hard and to lose a war occasionally—but you must pick your enemies carefully." As global foreign exchange markets grew larger and more sophisticated, the par values of sterling, the dollar, and even the French franc were threatened. But the West German mark remained strong. (© 1968 by Bill Mauldin; reprinted with permission)

converted into dollars, and these new dollar holders wanted U.S. gold. Treasury Secretary Fowler told the president that they "needed to stop this process and remove the threat of sterling balance conversions." Federal Reserve chairman Martin warned that action was needed to "avoid a serious international monetary crisis."[42] By September, a $2 billion credit agreement prevented another sterling devaluation.[43]

Another, more serious foreign exchange rate crisis emerged from an unusual place. The May 1968 student disturbances in Paris were followed by workers' strikes that produced sharp increases in French wages in the summer and fall of 1968. By September, the French treasury had lost an astounding $3 billion in reserves. The Johnson administration was less concerned about the fate of the franc—de Gaulle's monetary difficulties must have seemed ironic, if not amusing, to Americans infuriated by years of attacks on the dollar—than by the effect a large French devaluation would have on the pound. If the French franc were devalued too much, then the market would lose confidence in sterling and might attack the dollar next. The administration organized a monetary conference to deal with the misalignment in Western Europe's currencies in a cooperative, multilateral setting. The French were told not to act capriciously or alone. Fowler warned that "the U.S. was not in a mood or position to accept any further disadvantages unilaterally arrived at."[44] The secretary of the treasury argued that a French devaluation was not really necessary. If the French decided to devalue, Fowler wanted the change in value to be small.

Most American officials believed that it was far more important for West Germany to revalue its currency upward. This would decrease the Federal Republic's enormous trade surplus and benefit not just the French but the British and Americans as well.

The Americans, the French, and the British put tremendous pressure on the West Germans to revalue their currency. The British even brandished the threat of troop withdrawals if the FRG did not act. But to the surprise of many, the normally cooperative Germans refused to enact more than a minor border tax adjustment. West German finance minister Franz Joseph Strauss contended that France's economic problems were not the Federal Republic's concerns and argued that the FRG needed a large surplus to meet its offset responsibilities to the United States. Strauss leveled exaggerated accusations at the United States. "The U.S. buys German companies at three to four times the price Europeans would pay. This makes it hard to understand U.S. balance of payments problems."[45] Fowler told the president that the multilateral negotiations had unleashed "considerable bitterness" among the Europeans.[46] Harold James has argued that the meeting was "poorly prepared in every sense" and provided "an unpromising prologue" to the bitter financial summits of the 1970s.[47]

In the end, de Gaulle announced that he would not devalue the franc.[48] But the bitter meeting signaled the end of even the small amount of cooperation that had marked the Western alliance's monetary relations in the late 1960s. Each of the most important participants, beginning with the United States during the March gold crisis conference, had signaled its intentions to look after its own interests instead of the interests of the system. Most surprising was the lack of intra-European cooperation. The French and the British had no problem brandishing political threats against the Federal Republic, and the West Germans did not hesitate to reject their pleas.

## Conclusion

From the immediate perspective of the Americans, the March 1968 emergency conference was a success. They did not have to float the dollar, reduce their overseas military commitments, or initiate deflationary measures at home. Instead, they were able to escape pressure through an obvious gimmick: separating the private gold market from the central bank gold market. As long as the central bankers of Europe and Japan did not ask for gold, the Americans were protected from the pressures of the market. Why did the Europeans agree to such a system? They were unwilling to continue the gold pool operation. A dollar float would have hurt their exports and helped American imports, and they would have had to run down their own gold supply to maintain the exchange rate of the dollar. And the Americans made it clear that they would not increase the price of gold. In the end, the central bankers of Belgium, Germany, Italy, the Netherlands, Switzerland, and the United Kingdom had little choice but to accept their present supply of gold and to minimize their conversions of excess dollars into gold.

It was clear, however, that this system could not last. If the price of gold rose dramatically on the London market, central bankers would be tempted to convert their dollars into gold and sell it on the open market. Maybe the Americans could prevent the other gold pool countries from pursuing such a step, but how could those outside of the system be stopped? By threatening not to sell gold to those central banks that sold gold on the private market, the Americans were essentially ending the gold convertibility pledge of the dollar. The system had become completely divorced from economic reality and, hence, thoroughly politicized. The fear of gold losses would no longer act as an incentive for the Americans to bring their payments deficit into equilibrium. If surplus countries grew tired of accepting dollars and tried to buy American gold, the United States could threaten to suspend convertibility and let the dollar float. This would leave the decision up to the surplus countries; they could buy gold but accept a floating dollar and cheaper American exports; or accept overpriced, surplus dollars and trade advantages. As much as Western Europe and Japan enjoyed the benefits of an overpriced dollar, it was inevitable that a time would come when they would be unable to accept the inflationary effect of unlimited American balance-of-payments deficits.

The agreement reached in March 1968 was a temporary reprieve for the terminal case of Bretton Woods. The reprieve lasted as long as it did because of American political pressure on surplus countries to accept dollars. The biggest surplus countries, West Germany and Japan, were the countries most vulnerable to this pressure because they depended on American military and political protection. Other traditional surplus countries of Western Europe, particularly France, suffered losses in their balance of payments in 1969 that prevented them from purchasing American gold. The American payments deficit, which actually narrowed in 1969, exploded during the first half of 1971. Richard Nixon's decision, on 15 August 1971, to suspend the gold convertibility should have surprised no one. The Bretton Woods system, if it ever really existed, had been on life support since its inception. Between 1958 and 1968, it had only been kept alive by a series of extraordinary measures that made little long-term, macroeconomic sense.

*Chapter Eight*

# Nixon and the New Era in Global Monetary Relations

Richard Nixon was far less interested in the subtleties of international monetary policy than his predecessors. He told his closest White House advisers, "I do not want to be bothered with international monetary matters. . . . I will not need to see the reports on international monetary matters in the future."[1] In the first year of his administration, Nixon stunned the international financial community by refusing to address the annual meeting of the IMF and World Bank.[2] And his treasury secretary, John Connally, neatly summed up the so-called policy of benign neglect toward the U.S. balance-of-payments deficit when he told world bankers that the "dollar may be our currency but it's your problem."[3]

It is not that Nixon did not care about America's economic position in the world. The president understood that during the last one-third of the twentieth century "economic power will be the key to other kinds of power."[4] Nor did Nixon want inaction. He told his close advisers on several occasions that "we need a new international monetary system."[5] The president simply wanted to make it clear that he would not let the dollar and gold problem interfere with his administration's goals in areas he considered more important, such as domestic economic recovery and détente with the Soviet Union. As Joanne Gowa and Allen Matusow have convincingly demonstrated, the Nixon administration's domestic and international economic policies were subordinated to one goal: reelection in 1972.[6]

There is little doubt that the Nixon administration was far harsher than its predecessors in its rhetoric and declarations of unilateralism. Both the sense of urgency and the spirit of multilateral cooperation from past administrations were gone. But in many ways, these were simply stylistic changes. Short of complete exchange controls and massive deflation, which would have been political suicide, there was little any administration, Democratic or Republican, could have done to save what little remained of the Bretton Woods monetary system after the March 1968 gold crisis. Even Henry Kissinger, the most cautious Nixon administration official regarding international monetary matters, admitted in June 1969 "we have already moved a long way towards suspension of the gold convertibility of the dollar."[7] While the timing and method were certainly dramatic, Richard Nixon's closing of the gold window on 15 August 1971 should have surprised no one who analyzed U.S. balance-of-payments statistics.

Why? The traditionally large U.S. trade surplus had declined from $6.8 billion in 1964 to only $600 million by 1968. By 1969, the overall current account deficit, which included trade, services, tourism, and government expenditures abroad, reached $1 billion. Throughout the 1960s, the American surplus on its current account partially balanced large losses on the capital outflow and government expenditures overseas. Inflation, declining U.S. productivity, an overvalued dollar, and worsening trade relations with both Western Europe and Japan made it highly unlikely this trend could be quickly reversed. This meant that weaknesses of the international monetary system would be exposed by increasingly large and volatile capital flows. The world was effectively on a de facto dollar standard after the separation of the private and central bank gold markets in 1968. But it was unrealistic to expect central bankers to absorb larger and larger quantities of these deficit dollars. With meaningful international monetary reform elusive, America's promise to convert dollars into gold at thirty-five dollars an ounce was unsustainable.

## Nixon Takes Over

A far smaller circle of advisers than in the Johnson and Kennedy administrations crafted Nixon's foreign economic policy, and especially international monetary policy. Part of this had to do with Nixon's personality and management style. He called his first secretary of the treasury a "cipher," hid from his budget director, avoided Arthur Burns, and told an aide that the Council of Economic Advisers did not "have any influence" on economic policy.[8] Furthermore, the voices of the State Department and the office of national security adviser were, despite their best efforts, marginalized during most debates over the dollar and gold question. Nixon's secretaries of the treasury, David Kennedy and especially John Connally, directed U.S. international monetary policy. But despite large egos, neither man fully understood the intricacies of the global payments system, and both relied heavily on their under secretary for international monetary affairs, Paul Volcker. Volcker chaired a small, interdepartmental working group that Nixon established to make recommendations on international monetary policy.[9] International monetary policy was also made in a far more ad hoc, sporadic way, since dollar and gold questions only rose to the highest levels in the White House during crises.

The change in tone was apparent immediately. A transition task force set up to look at the balance-of-payments problem for the incoming

Nixon and his economic team. He called his first secretary of the treasury a "cipher," hid from his budget director, avoided Arthur Burns, and told an aide that the Council of Economic Advisers didn't "have any influence" on economic policy. But the president understood that during the last one-third of the twentieth century "economic power will be the key to other kinds of power." (Courtesy of the Nixon Presidential Materials Project)

Nixon administration called for dramatic, if politically implausible, action. First, both the voluntary and mandatory capital controls imposed by the Johnson administration should be abolished. Such restraints were "wasteful and inefficient" and undermined the "free enterprise system." Foreign central bankers would oppose such a move, but several months later Treasury Secretary Kennedy told the president that "European reservations are not . . . a compelling reason to delay."[10] Second, the administration should move quickly to force a "significant realignment of parities of some currencies." The president should try to negotiate these changes but should not be afraid to take dramatic unilateral action if necessary. "If for any reason . . . a 'gold rush' develops, the United States should suspend gold convertibility" with an aim toward negotiating "new flexibility" into the international monetary system.[11] From the start, the Nixon administration demonstrated far more interest in exchange rate flexibility than any of its predecessors.

The administration's early studies and discussions highlighted the three questions that would dominate international monetary discussions within the Nixon administration during the first year. First, should the voluntary and mandatory capital controls instituted during the Johnson period be amended or rescinded? Nixon had campaigned against these controls, but if they were removed, there was concern that the U.S. balance-of-payments deficit would explode. The free-market conservatives in the administration wanted the controls ended, but the more cautious advisers like Kissinger and Volcker prevented their complete removal.[12] Second, how should the offset negotiations with the West Germans be pursued? Finally, should the United States propose dramatic international monetary reforms? Or should the administration remain passive in the face of increasing global monetary turbulence?

In approaching the offset question, the new administration recognized that the biyearly negotiations with the Federal Republic of Germany were upsetting a key geopolitical relationship. Nixon told his aides "we should not seek any substantial increase in the currently anticipated level of German military procurement and should not press the issue to the point of risking [a] possible row with FRG."[13] American negotiators offered to change the terms of the monetary link, deemphasizing offset if West Germany would revalue its currency and lend full support to U.S. efforts to reform the international monetary system. But with the FRG's new policy of Ostpolitik unsettling traditional U.S. geopolitical calculations in Europe, Nixon was not even prepared to use his political capital to achieve these modest goals. As Kissinger told his aides, the "one thing we *must* avoid is any arm-twisting of the Germans."[14] Despite an attempt to influence the West German cabinet, American efforts failed to produce the sought-after revaluation of the mark until months after the negotiations had finished.[15]

A deal was signed on 9 July 1969 that included far less military hardware purchases than previous agreements. Almost immediately, both the United States and the West Germans prepared for the next two-year negotiations. In June 1970 West German defense minister Helmut Schmidt told U.S. ambassador Kenneth Rush that his government could no longer accept even the watered-down offset arrangements and wanted to move burden-sharing questions to NATO as a whole (where it was certain they would be ignored). The American negotiators, on the other hand, suggested the controversial notion of direct budget support for U.S. troops in West Germany. But Nixon refused to use any political capital on the offset question.[16] An even weaker agreement was signed at the end of 1971, despite calls by some in the administration to get tougher on West Germany. This was one of the last such offset agreements to be signed until the whole controversial concept was dropped by the Ford administration.[17]

Nixon's reluctance to pursue offset did not, however, reduce the intense pressure from other quarters to withdraw U.S. troops from NATO. America's continued monetary woes, combined with détente with the Soviets and FRG chancellor Willy Brandt's policy of Ostpolitik, seemed to lessen the need for large U.S. conventional forces in Europe. Senator Mike Mansfield's reintroduced amendment to enact unilateral withdrawals was stopped only with help from an unlikely source—Soviet premier Leonid Breshnev. The Soviet leader understood that the U.S. troops were there as much to contain the West Germans as the Soviets, and his statement that he was willing to enter into mutual arms reductions in central Europe in May 1971 undermined congressional efforts to reduce U.S. troops. Nixon was in a much weaker position when the Jackson-Nunn amendment to the defense appropriation of 1973 and 1974 called for troop withdrawals from NATO Europe. Despite enormous congressional pressure, Nixon's policy sought to decouple troop levels from the balance of payments, exhibited by his NSC decision in late 1970 to avoid force withdrawals "except in the context of mutual reductions negotiated with the East."[18] Nixon sided with those in his administration who argued that "we should *never* reduce" U.S. troops "for balance of payments reasons."[19]

The administration took a far tougher line with the Europeans when it came to international monetary reform and, in particular, exchange rate flexibility. After months of inaction, Nixon called a meeting on 26 June 1969 to consider his options and coordinate the administration's options. Traditional policies to reduce a payments deficit in a fixed rate regime, such as domestic deflation and more exchange controls, were rejected outright. Nixon's economic advisers hotly debated radical proposals, including a unilateral closing of the gold window or an increase in the dollar price of gold. In the end, it was decided that the administration would demand larger allocations of the new SDRs, pressure Western Europe to revalue its currencies, and put the issue of greater flexibility of exchange rates on the international agenda. If other central bankers did not cooperate, then the United States could always force the world onto a de jure "dollar standard" by closing the gold window.[20]

The administration used the ensuing chaos in the monetary system to push its international monetary agenda. Paul McCracken, the chairman of Nixon's Council of Economic Advisers, urged the president to act aggressively. "A U.S. initiative on the exchange rate would be truly an achievement of your Administration."[21] But Treasury Secretary Kennedy pointed out that "there is widespread reluctance to deal with this issue" abroad.[22] This left the administration with an important policy choice. As Kissinger told the president in September 1969, Nixon could "attempt to forestall the development of a crisis or let it develop and respond after-wards."[23] If other countries were unresponsive to American plans, or if anyone pursued an uncoordinated devaluation or float, the administration could "suspend convertibility of the dollar into gold" and, if neces-sary, "double or triple the price of gold."

International events unfolded in such a way that the United States did not have to make extreme threats. After more than a year of trying to hold out against any change in its parity, France devalued the franc by 11.1 per-cent on 8 August 1969. Shortly thereafter, the West Germans revalued the mark upward. SDR allotments had been increased. By October, Kissinger told Nixon that his international monetary policy had been a success. By exploiting turmoil in the foreign exchange markets, the administration had accomplished "two of the three components" agreed to "at your June 26th" meeting—currency realignment and larger SDR allocations.[24] Yet the third, and arguably most important, policy goal—increased exchange rate flexibility—had not been achieved. None of the more radical policies that had been debated in June had been pursued, and once the currency markets calmed, the question of fundamental international monetary reform again faded into the background. But the Nixon administration had made it clear that it would consider any and all international mone-tary policies and was prepared to act unilaterally if necessary.

### Connally at Treasury

After the summer of 1969, international monetary relations settled down in the wake of the French devaluation and the German revaluation. Can-ada floated the dollar in May 1970, but for the most part foreign exchange markets were calmer in 1970. American policy makers used this time to push proposals for greater exchange rate flexibility but had little success. The European Economic Community was actually trying to *decrease* flex-ibility between its currencies in order to coordinate economic policy more effectively.

In early 1971 the Federal Reserve, now headed by Arthur Burns, eased monetary conditions in the United States. The European Community was outraged by the ensuing inflow of dollars into its central banks, and the West Germans even suggested a joint float against the dollar. But the French vetoed any deviation from fixed exchange rates, preferring infla-tion to a parity adjustment that would weaken the competitive position of their exports. The dollar inflows became so bad that most European cen-tral bankers closed their dollar operations on 5 May 1971, and when they opened again on 10 May, West Germany allowed the foreign exchange markets to determine the value of the mark. The Europeans were afraid that Nixon was not prepared to do anything about the increasing monetary chaos. Chancellor Willy Brandt complained to Nixon that the monetary crisis had "created great difficulties" for Germany and Europe.[25]

American policy makers were not sympathetic. In March, Federal Reserve Bank of New York governor Charles Coombs told the president that "the dollar was hopelessly overvalued" and that unilaterally suspending the dollar's convertibility would be much better than "arduous and possibly confrontational negotiations" for currency realignments. In May the Treasury Department produced a paper that ruled out any increase in the dollar price of gold, something the French insisted upon. Furthermore, it argued that the American deficit "was only partly due to U.S. economic policies" and that American military commitments and overseas barriers to trade were the real culprits. Most surprising, the Treasury Department now denied that the United States had any responsibility to the rest of the world to do anything about its monetary problems. "Other countries decided long ago to use the dollar as a reserve currency and to peg their currencies to the dollar." Doing this gave overseas central bankers the "responsibility for fixing exchange rates, leaving the U.S. in a passive position."[26]

The force behind much of this economic nationalism was the new secretary of the treasury, John Connally. Nixon's infatuation with the Texas Democrat and sometime LBJ protégé is well known.[27] The president clearly wanted to rid himself of annoying monetary crises before the 1972 election campaign began, and Connally could provide the bold leadership that neither McCracken at CEA, George Shultz at the Office of Management and Budget, or Volcker as under secretary could provide. Secretary Connally ruthlessly consolidated his monopoly over U.S. foreign economic policy during the spring and summer of 1971, further marginalizing the CEA and completely removing the State Department and national security adviser from the policy process.[28] And he publicly laid out the new spirit of American unilateralism in U.S. international monetary policy. On 28 May, Secretary Connally told an international group of bankers in Munich, Germany, that there "is a clear and present danger to our monetary system" and that the United States "would no longer engage in international actions in which the true long-run interests of the U.S. are not just as clearly recognized as those of the nations with which we deal."[29] The treasury secretary told a group of American ambassadors that the United States "should not and will not seek a solution" to the balance-of-payments deficit "by depressing the U.S. economy."[30] With

John Connally. Nixon was infatuated with John Connally, a Texas Democrat. The secretary of the treasury dominated U.S. foreign economic policy and claimed, "Foreigners are out to screw us. Our job is to screw them first." (Courtesy of the Nixon Presidential Materials Project)

the Europeans and Americans at loggerheads, Connally believed it was pointless to call an international monetary conference to solve the problem. "Foreigners are out to screw us. Our job is to screw them first."[31]

Already large inflows of dollars into foreign central banks exploded during the first weeks of August. The American payments deficit for the first six months of 1971 was an astounding $22 billion at an annualized rate. The administration began discussing a bold, comprehensive plan presented by Connally that would cap domestic wages, tax imports, provide targeted tax cuts, and close the gold window. Others in the administration were more cautious, and Nixon hesitated to take the "big steps." Early discussions indicated that the most likely time frame for announcing the program was the week after Congress reconvened in September.[32]

Turmoil on global currency markets, however, forced a far quicker timeline. On 6 August, Henry Reuss's House Subcommittee on International Exchange and Payments released a report that claimed that the "dollar is overvalued." The only way to solve the fundamental disequilibrium that was producing massive American deficits, according to the report, was to alter exchange rates. This report led to a new wave of dollar dumping. Foreign central banks intervened to prop up the dollar, but on 13 August, the Bank of England asked the Federal Reserve to guarantee part of its dollar holdings. It was clear that when markets opened on Monday, 16 August, the attack on the dollar would be unstoppable.

Nixon called his top economic policy makers to a meeting at Camp David the weekend of 14 and 15 August. No one from the State Department was invited, and Henry Kissinger was not even aware that the meeting was taking place. Given the perceived stakes for both the global economy and world politics, it was a surprisingly undisciplined and rushed exercise. There was much heated debate over what elements should be included in what was to become Nixon's "New Economic Policy." Fed chairman Arthur Burns was against closing the gold window. George Shultz protested the mandatory wage and price controls. Volcker did not think the 10 percent import tax was wise. But when the chairman of the Federal Reserve argued that the industrialized countries would retaliate against closing the gold window, Connally thundered, "[L]et 'em. What can they do?"³³

Throughout the weekend, Nixon deliberated. Would a comprehensive national program make the United States look weak, or would the president look strong? Should he wait before he did anything, announce each program one at a time, or should he forgo the closing of the gold window? The treasury secretary pushed Nixon to announce a large program immediately, which would give the impression Nixon "picked the time" to end America's economic problem. In the end, Nixon accepted Connally's advice to take a "big, bold approach" and included all elements of the proposal, announcing the plan in a nationwide television address on Sunday evening, 15 August.³⁴ Despite (or perhaps because of) such a big setback for currency and trade liberalization, the president's program was, at least at first, very popular with the American people.³⁵ Nixon had masterfully turned an apparent defeat—the formal end of Bretton Woods—into a victory for the U.S. economy and his administration.

For the most part, overseas central bankers decided to let their currencies float. France imposed extensive currency and capital controls. But Japan desperately tried to maintain the yen's 360-to-1 rate with the dollar, adding $4 billion to its reserves in only two weeks. By the end of August, the Bank of Japan gave up this futile effort and floated the yen. This highlighted another point—Japan had replaced Western Europe as the target of America's economic complaints. Given the economic uncertainty of the late 1960s and early 1970s, trade had become a far more combustible domestic political issue. Unlike monetary affairs, Nixon had expended a lot of time and political capital on trade disputes with Japan. Connally's strategy to end America's monetary woes permanently and revive the domestic economy demanded that exchange rates be readjusted to allow the United States to recapture the large trade surpluses it had enjoyed in the early 1960s.[36]

But what would happen to the international monetary system in the wake of Camp David? There were many unanswered questions. Would the dollar simply float against other currencies on the open market? Or would a new gold-dollar price be established? Volcker met with angry and confused central bankers the next day in London but had little to offer. "The U.S. had not spelled out any program in the president's message or elsewhere." The United States did not want a quick or easy solution that would only lead to the same problems later; nor did the administration want a large, unwieldy Bretton Woods-type conference. The United States would not change the gold price of its currency, nor would it intervene in the markets to maintain the dollar's fixed rate. "In the end our view is that after years of deficits, the U.S. is entitled to run surpluses."[37]

Connally had publicly vowed never to devalue the dollar. But as useful as Connally's economic nationalism was for Nixon's domestic political approval, the president did not want to see a trade and monetary war break out. In December the world's most important financial officials gathered at the Smithsonian Institution in Washington to negotiate wide-ranging currency realignments. West Germany agreed to revalue its currency upward by 13.57 percent and Japan grudgingly agreed to revalue the yen 16.9 percent. It was also agreed that currencies could trade within wider bands against each other—2.25 percent in either direction, as opposed to the 1 percent allowed under the original Bretton Woods arrangements. In exchange for these concessions, the United States agreed to devalue the dollar to thirty-eight dollars an ounce.[38]

None of these arrangements would last very long. Foreign exchange markets were volatile throughout 1972. In January 1973 the Nixon administration ended wage and price controls, and a massive outflow of dollars ensued. In February the crisis induced Paul Volcker to take a secret trip to negotiate new parities. In Tokyo, Volcker publicly demanded at least a 10 percent revaluation, and after closing its foreign exchange market, Japan allowed the yen to appreciate 17 percent in a float. European foreign exchange markets closed soon thereafter, and it became clear that it would be impossible to avoid a systemwide float. The new secretary of the treasury, George Shultz, was a student of Milton Friedman, and both had long advocated market-determined exchange rates. While Europe and Japan wanted to reestablish a fixed exchange rate regime, Shultz told the world that America's days as the caretaker of the global payments system were over. "Santa Claus is dead."[39] And after years on life support, so was the Bretton Woods monetary system.

*Conclusion*

# No Way to Build an Empire

For well over a decade, top American policy makers were obsessed with the U.S. balance-of-payments deficit and gold outflow. After the London gold crisis of 1960, the Eisenhower administration feared a complete economic meltdown of the Western alliance if the deficit was not ended. President Kennedy confessed that the payments deficit worried him as much as, and at times even more than, nuclear weapons. And Lyndon Johnson, despite his many other preoccupations, was haunted by the idea that if the dollar and gold problem got out of hand, a global depression could ensue. The dollar and gold question was the most important issue of American foreign economic policy from the late 1950s through the early 1970s—far more important than we have previously understood.

Furthermore, these monetary questions influenced fiscal policy, debates over America's military strategy in Europe, and U.S. relations within NATO. A fascinating document written by Averell Harriman in 1966 for President Johnson reveals even farther-ranging connections between the balance of payments and world politics. In it, Harriman lays out a plan to settle all of the Cold War's most troubling problems. The Russians will be told that the Germans would never get nuclear hardware, allowing the Soviets to sign a nonproliferation agreement. In return, the Russians would "commit themselves to getting Hanoi to make peace in Southeast Asia." Finally, the United States would "pay off the Germans by making balance of payments concessions." In the end, Walt Rostow argued against the proposal, in large part because it was "wrong to let the Germans off the hook on balance of payments offsets."[1] While it is hard to imagine that such a deal could have been arranged, it is even more amazing that a chance to end the Vietnam War and arrange a nuclear nonproliferation treaty was vetoed because it infringed on President Johnson's ability to carry out U.S. international monetary policy.

How does this story alter our understanding of U.S. foreign policy during this period? At first glance, the gold and dollar story appears to demonstrate the primacy of economic considerations during the Cold War. Many scholars have identified materialist and economic factors as the driving forces of U.S. foreign policy. At their most extreme, these arguments explain the Cold War as a product of the crisis in world capitalism and of the need for the American economy to expand abroad and support the military-industrial complex at home. Thirty-five years ago, Gabriel

Kolko claimed in *The Roots of American Foreign Policy* that "the dominant interest of the United States is in world economic stability, and anything that undermines that condition presents a danger to its present hegemony."[2] Thomas McCormick summed up the world systems view by claiming that "a single hegemonic power has a built-in incentive to force other nations to abandon their economic nationalism and protectionist controls to accept a world of free trade, free capital flows, and free currency convertibility."[3] Even scholars sympathetic to this international economic order believed it advanced American hegemony. According to the distinguished political scientist Robert Gilpin, the United States maintained its hegemonic power vis-à-vis Western Europe "based on the role of the dollar in the international monetary system and on the extension of its nuclear deterrent to include its allies."[4]

The foundation of this imperial power, according to these interpretations, was the Bretton Woods international monetary system. The United States exploited its position as a global hegemon "to create the Bretton Woods multilateral monetary system" to "make the world economy more unitary and interdependent." The result "was a golden age of capitalism between 1950 and 1973," an era "so prosperous that its chief beneficiaries, the great core states, saw no need to use war as a means to redistribute global resources and wealth."[5] Bretton Woods was especially successful in the 1960s because it "solved the fundamental problems of the world economy." Distribution issues were settled at both a national and international level, "national autonomy" questions never arose, and the "international regime" functioned effectively because the United States behaved responsibly and the issues the system faced "were relatively simple."[6] Most of "America's allies acquiesced in a hegemonic system that accorded the United States special privileges to act abroad unilaterally to promote U.S. interests."[7] Since the Bretton Woods system was "a prerequisite for continued American global hegemony,"[8] the United States would not "condone a structural reform" of the system that threatened "the continued preeminence of the dollar."[9]

The documents, as we have seen, reveal a different story altogether. The United States certainly benefited by being able to run deficits year after year. But as countries like France, West Germany, Japan, and others accumulated these deficit dollars, a sense of economic insecurity and vulnerability—not hegemony—developed among top U.S. policy makers. This feeling deepened as America's allies became increasingly willing to exploit their monetary power to signal their displeasure with U.S. security policies. Many government officials felt trapped by the system, because the United States could not unilaterally devalue, as other countries would

Herblock cartoon. When the Bretton Woods agreements were signed in 1944, the dollar was all-powerful. By 1971, U.S. balance-of-payments deficits and the outflow of American gold had left the dollar weak and vulnerable. (© 1971 Herblock; from *Herblock's State of the Union* [Simon and Schuster, 1972])

have surely followed with equal devaluations. This led top American policy makers as early as 1962—long before the escalation in Vietnam or the Great Society programs—to consider dramatic reforms that would have radically altered the international monetary system and in many cases curtailed the privileges enjoyed by the dollar.[10]

Furthermore, the international monetary system was chaotic and prone to destabilizing crises. The Bretton Woods system began breaking

down as soon as it really began to function—after most Western Europeans adopted current-account convertibility for their currencies at the
end of 1958. Governments worldwide, including the supposedly "open-
door" United States, responded to these crises by increasing restrictions
on trade and capital movements and generally accepting the restrictions
installed by others. This highlights an unrecognized but key point: the
Bretton Woods period *was not* a golden age of "open-door" capital mobility. The worldwide explosion of capital flows came *after* the Bretton
Woods system of fixed exchange rates and dollar-gold convertibility collapsed in the early 1970s. Only in the late 1970s did most countries begin
to abandon the array of capital controls that had been necessary to maintain strict par values. Exchange rate flexibility combined with deregula-
tion of the financial markets, improved technology, and the development
of innovative financial hedge instruments to protect against exchange
rate risks to encourage a massive increase in cross-border capital movements, particularly to East Asia and Latin America.

This new understanding of America's international monetary policy
casts doubt on overly simplistic "open-door," "empire," or "world systems" interpretations for this period. There is plenty of room for debate
over the motives and wisdom of America's foreign policy during the
second-half of the twentieth century. But if America's goal had been to
build a profitable economic empire during the Cold War, it could not have
gone about it in a worse way.[11] America's Cold War policies *encouraged*
major allies to install capital controls and form trade and currency blocs
that discriminated against dollar goods. Japan and Western Europe rebuilt
their war-devastated economies behind protectionist trade and monetary
walls, accepting billions in U.S. aid while avoiding expensive military
expenditures because of American security policies. How many empires
have watched their total share of world GDP drop so quickly as America's
from the end of World War II to the 1970s? While these policies may have
been geopolitically expedient, if the United States had been interested in
global economic domination, there were far more profitable ways to go
about it.[12]

Does this mean that this period could be better understood through a
"national security" framework alone? Again, the balance-of-payments
story provides ambiguous evidence. The gold and dollar crisis occurred
during the height of the Cold War competition with the Soviet Union,
and according to a Realpolitik framework, such "high" politics should
have easily trumped the "low" politics of payments deficit. Yet time and
time again, Eisenhower, Kennedy, and Johnson all considered pulling
back U.S. troops from NATO Europe in order to ease the U.S. foreign

exchange woes. When troops were not pulled back, it often had less to do with the Soviet threat in Europe or the so-called flexible response strategy than the need to neutralize the explosive "German" and "nuclear" questions with a large American force presence.

Perhaps the key point to emerge from the study is the extent to which alliance politics, monetary relations, and strategy were all so tightly intertwined. As we have seen, the politics of the balance of payments during this period cannot be understood in isolation from the question of America's overall relations with Europe. This meant that the dollar and gold question went far beyond monetary and trade policy and was inseparable from such fundamental political issues as U.S. policy toward NATO and, in particular, the German problem and the nuclear question. This underscores a crucial methodological point. We cannot look at questions of economic policy, strategy, and foreign policy in isolation from each other. To most American policy makers, the dollar and gold problem was a political issue at its core. This is an important lesson to remember, given how chaotic international monetary relations are today.

The revisionist perspective is correct about one important aspect of America's international monetary policy—it was deeply influenced by policy makers' understanding of the Great Depression. But this view was shaped less by the desire for profit or empire than by the fear that an international economic collapse would again lead to world war, an unthinkable possibility in the atomic age. The events that had turned a deep recession into a global disaster—the collapse of the Creditanstalt bank; Great Britain suspending sterling-gold convertibility; the failure of the 1933 London Economic Conference; the devaluation of the dollar; the rise of fascism, Nazism, and autarky; and, finally, global war—were seared into the collective consciousness of most policy makers. To most, there was a causal link between monetary relations and war: monetary chaos and devaluations let loose beggar-thy-neighbor policies and economic nationalism; economic nationalism produced dictatorships; and dictators unleashed global conflagration. In retrospect, the Great Depression analogy that drove America's monetary policy in the 1960s was as oversimplified and wrongheaded as the Munich analogy that helped usher in the disaster in Vietnam. But the analogy had a powerful grip on policy makers' imaginations.

From a macroeconomic standpoint, these fears were generally exaggerated. As we have seen (and as is detailed in Appendix A), a good portion of the deficit was not a deficit at all but comprised dollars demanded by central bankers and international businesses for reserve and intervention purposes. While flexible exchange rates have not realized all of the high hopes of their proponents, neither have they brought the disaster, depression, and political chaos many feared. Most important, monetary turmoil has not fueled war. Furthermore, flexible exchange rates have largely solved the two structural problems of the Bretton Woods system, the liquidity issue and adjusting payments imbalances. Still, the story of the politics of the American balance-of-payments deficit underscores how influential these generational lessons can be in policy debates. It also underscores how important it is for historians to scrutinize these lessons, so that myth can be separated from fact.

# Appendix A. *Analyzing the Numbers*

## *Breaking Down*
## *the U.S. Balance of Payments for 1960–1961*

When we talk about a payments surplus or deficit in a fixed exchange rate system, we are usually talking about a surplus or deficit within some particular group of accounts. The economic transactions between a country and the rest of the world can be broken down into several categories: *current account*, which includes all the goods and services bought and sold to or from abroad by the residents of a country but goes beyond trade to include items like tourism, investment income, and the controversial subcategory of military and other government expenditures in foreign countries; *unilateral transfers*, which either can be remittances by private citizens or firms or can be government transfers; and the *capital account*, which details both direct and portfolio foreign investment. In a fixed exchange rate regime, these three categories of transactions are autonomous in nature, meaning that they occur as a result of commercial incentives or political considerations that are given independently of the overall balance of payments or of particular accounts.[1]

If the sum total of the economic transactions of these three groups of accounts is in surplus or deficit, it must be settled by *balancing items*. In a fixed exchange rate regime, a country must fill any deficit arising from the first three categories of its balance of payments with either short-term official capital movements or the movement of an official reserve (for example, gold, or a reserve or "key" currency). How a deficit is financed depends on the rules of the international monetary system in question. Balancing items should be seen as "accommodating" in nature, because they arise out of the requirement that a payments gap must be filled. Balancing transactions *did not* occur automatically in the Bretton Woods regime, and were normally the responsibility of a nation's foreign exchange authority.

Throughout the 1950s and most of the 1960s, the United States ran a large current-account surplus. This surplus was lessened, but not eliminated, by large military and government expenditures abroad and, to a lesser extent, American tourism. For instance, the surplus on current account, *excluding military expenditures abroad*, was $4.6 billion in 1960, and $5.0 billion in 1961. But American military expenditures were $3.0 billion during each year, considerably reducing the overall current-account surplus. Military expenditure abroad was often seen as an inviting category to reduce the payments deficit, because it could be directly controlled by government policy or could be reduced by pressuring foreign governments to offset the foreign exchange cost.

The second category, unilateral transfers, was usually in deficit because of the large grants of American aid during this period, although this deficit was somewhat offset by the advance repayment on U.S. government loans by foreign governments. Foreign aid would have seemed a likely candidate for balance-of-payments relief, but the Kennedy and Johnson administrations had ambitious goals in the area of development aid and loans. Eventually, foreign aid was reduced and the United States required it be used ("tied") to purchase American goods and services.

The United States ran a large deficit in the third category, direct and portfolio foreign investment, throughout this period. American direct and long-term portfolio investment abroad was $2.5 billion in 1960 and $2.6 billion in 1961. Foreign direct and portfolio investment in the United States was only $.3 and $.4 billion during 1960 and 1961. This occurred for several reasons. Rapid growth in Western Europe and Japan offered more attractive investment opportunities for American capital than the more mature, slower-growing domestic economy. American companies could get around the Common Market's discrimination against dollar-denominated trade by building factories and expanding their businesses in EEC countries. Additionally, as the world's banker, the United States lent long and borrowed short. Foreign-held dollar accounts that were invested in short-term American financial instruments were counted as part of the deficit, as were the long-term loans and investments American banks and corporations made overseas. This meant that these dollars were counted twice in the deficit.[2] Furthermore, the United States retained investment and interest rate regulations that discouraged foreign investment in America.

The capital-account deficit was controversial. European governments wanted U.S. investment to promote higher growth and technology transfers but worried that this capital was a vehicle for American economic and political dominance. De Gaulle accused the Bretton Woods system of allowing American multilateral corporations to finance the takeover of European industries with U.S. deficits. American policy makers increasingly saw this category as a rich source of payments savings and legislated increasingly stricter controls on foreign investment, beginning with the Interest Equalization Act of 1963 and eventually resulting in the Monetary Control Program of 1968.

Combined, the deficit on the second and third categories was always considerably larger than any surplus the United States had on current accounts. For instance, the United States deficit on the first three categories was $3.9 billion in 1960 and $2.5 billion in 1961. According to balance-of-payments theory, this shortfall had to be met with *balancing items*, such as official short-term capital movements (loans) or reserve instruments (such as gold). But this did not always happen.

The American deficits were unique because the most important balancing item in the Bretton Woods system was the dollar. It hardly made sense to allow a debtor country to pay off his debts with a currency it could print at will. The system was supposed to be protected from such an inflationary outcome by the American guarantee to convert dollars into a fixed amount of gold. But, as we have seen, the United States was able to evade this pressure and, in fact, use its political clout to pressure surplus countries to hold dollars and not exchange them for gold. This pressure caused American policy makers to separate the issue of payments deficits and gold outflow from a political standpoint, although they were obviously closely linked in economic terms. Payments deficits were not a grave threat if the United States could convince surplus countries to hold dollars instead of gold. Some of the largest surplus countries, such as West Germany and Japan, agreed to accumulate dollars indefinitely. This allowed the United States to run deficits *and* protect its gold reserves.

## How Were American Deficits Financed?

Despite extensive and controversial attempts to reduce the deficit through capital controls, offset payments, tourist restrictions, and the like, a large American payments deficit persisted for years. Balancing items such as gold were used to cover some, but not all, of this deficit. But these reserve assets should have eventually run out. The rest of the deficit was filled by dollar liabilities in the form of very liquid, short-term bonds. This type of short-term financing was based on the willingness of creditors, such as West Germany or Japan, to lend. But chronic deficits should have made these creditors hesitant or unwilling to lend to the United States. Creditors could not be expected to accept dollars forever to cover the U.S. deficit. Why did the rest of the world continue to take dollars when their value was in doubt?

The persistent American deficit highlighted the unique role the dollar played in the international monetary system. This role brought certain advantages and disadvantages and made it very difficult to measure the actual balance-of-payments deficit of the United States. As a result of the rules by which the postwar international monetary system operated, the dollar served with gold as a balancing item for international transactions. This posed a problem that was not fully recognized when the system was set up. The dollar was demanded by foreign nations both as a reserve asset and to finance much of the world's trade. This demand for American dollars was in excess of the demand for American goods. In other words, some of the deficit might not actually be a deficit at all, as those excess dollars were desired, at least for a time, by central banks and entities involved in financing trade. Therefore, in the case of the United States, the equilibrium point for the balance of payments may not have been zero:

> Thus, if we assume that foreign dollar holdings will continue to expand to serve both trade financing and reserve purposes, the desirability of a zero balance on official reserve transactions may be subject to question. It does not follow of course that the liquidity balance should furnish the appropriate policy criterion. Rather what might be sought is a concept that would measure the provision to the rest of the world of dollar balances and monetary reserve assets by the U.S. in its capacity as a world banker and supplier of international reserve currency. We might call this the "net contribution to world liquidity."[3]

The dollar's unique role in world trade and reserve creation meant that a certain level of American balance-of-payments deficit could be desirable. Was the whole balance of payments deficit of the United States a reflection of the high demand for American dollars overseas? Not necessarily. Many of those deficit dollars were not held indefinitely by central banks but instead were used to buy gold from the U.S. Treasury. Buying gold indicated a desire to hold a reserve asset other than the dollar. Might that mean that the deficit was, in fact, equal to the sum of dollars used to buy gold? The United States lost $1.7 billion dollars in gold during 1960 out of a "deficit" of $3.9 billion. Does that mean that the rest of the deficit, $2.2 billion, was a result of the international demand for dollars?

Again, it is hard to say, because theoretically the remaining dollars could be turned in for gold at any time. As long as the dollar was "as good as gold," holding dollars in the form of short-term interest-bearing securities was probably preferable to buying gold, which earned no interest income and had high transaction costs. A preference for dollars over gold in the short-term is no indication that American dollars are demanded for reserve or trade purposes. These short-term securities were highly liquid and could be turned in for gold at any time, as they often were. But the so-called gold drain lessened considerably after the initial gold crisis of 1960, even as the American payments deficit ballooned.[4] The loss of American gold was linked to the size of the American payments deficit, but there were other independent political variables, which restricted the purchase of gold by America's creditors. By suggesting cooperation from important allies, American policy makers managed to make the payments deficit and gold loss distinct issues.

Short-term dollar liabilities dramatically increased throughout the 1960s, eventually exceeding the dollar value of the American gold stock upon which dollar convertibility was based. If one subtracted gold sales and international liquidity requirements from the basic deficit, would the American balance of payments be in equilibrium? As dollar liabilities increased and the dollar convertibility pledge came into doubt, there was a greater demand for gold as a balancing item. But vast political pressure on creditor nations by the United States often muted this demand. The largest holder of dollar liabilities, West Germany, had agreed to hold its dollars in interest-bearing securities and not purchase American gold. This agreement, which was secret until the release of the Blessing letter in 1967, was part of a controversial monetary agreement reached to relieve the American payment costs of troops stationed in West Germany. It was an arrangement that made the Bundesbank very uncomfortable, and the West German central bank would not have made such a deal unless the United States had linked the monetary arrangement to important political and security issues.

It was the overriding goal of the United States throughout this period to avoid a rapid depletion of American gold stocks. If the United States had no gold, then its promise to convert dollars was meaningless. In international terms, America would be bankrupt. This pledge was seen as the cornerstone of a healthy world economy. Therefore, political pressure was put on surplus countries to hold their dollars as reserves when they often would have preferred gold. It then becomes a push-pull question: did foreign countries want to hold dollars to finance trade or because of their utility as a reserve asset? Or were they being pressured to hold their dollars against their will, when they would have preferred gold instead? How could this push-pull dynamic be measured so as to come up with an accurate assessment of the true balance-of-payments disequilibrium?

Given the size of the American economy and its role as the world's banker, and the requirements of the postwar monetary regime, a certain amount of American payments deficit was to be expected. Certain capital-market efficiencies are involved in which the United States "lends long" and "borrows short." Trade in financial claims, as opposed to real goods and services, may have no real counterpart. Yet given the concern that American policy makers had for the deficit, and given the constant complaints of surplus countries during the 1960s about the American deficit, it is likely that the U.S. deficit went well beyond the international demand for dollars. How much the payments deficit went beyond this demand is hard to measure. But the more important question was: how could the United States run a payments deficit beyond the world demand for the dollar for trade finance and as a reserve asset? That part of the story was driven far more by larger political and strategic considerations than by economic factors. In essence, the United States forced certain surplus countries, specifically West Germany, to hold dollars in exchange for protection. Certain countries, namely France, refused to go along with this arrangement and bought gold with their dollars. American foreign economic policy during the 1960s focused on persuading the rest of the world to follow the German, and not the French, example.

Of course, the preceding description does not reflect how American policy makers always understood the problem. They viewed the balance-of-payments deficit as a product of American security commitments and saw the gold outflow as the result of hostile French policies combined with unscrupulous speculation by uncontrolled free markets. As the 1960s wore on, the thinking shifted to some extent, and policy makers began to focus on the export of American capital. But on some level, the deficit remained a mystery to American policy makers, given how the balance of payments resisted government pressures and policies. Official Washington was frustrated by the seemingly intractable nature of the payments deficit. These feelings were often vented toward the countries of the Atlantic alliance, whose nations had been protected and rebuilt with American dollars, and who now seemed unwilling to help the United States find a manageable solution to their monetary problems. As we have seen, the balance-of-payments deficit and gold outflow problems acted like an acid on the Western alliance, slowly fraying the political and military bonds that held it together.

# Appendix B. *Charts and Graphs*

Gold Holdings, 1948–1975 (in millions of U.S. dollars)

| | 1948 | 1949 | 1950 | 1951 | 1952 | 1953 | 1954 | 1955 | 1956 | 1957 | 1958 | 1959 | 1960 | 1961 | 1962 |
|---|---|---|---|---|---|---|---|---|---|---|---|---|---|---|---|
| United States | 24,399 | 24,563 | 22,820 | 22,873 | 23,252 | 22,091 | 21,793 | 21,753 | 22,058 | 22,857 | 20,582 | 19,507 | 17,804 | 16,947 | 16,057 |
| United Kingdom | 1,611 | 1,321 | 2,861 | 2,172 | 1,483 | 2,263 | 2,537 | 2,012 | 1,773 | 1,555 | 2,807 | 2,514 | 2,801 | 2,267 | 2,581 |
| France | 0.548 | 0.543 | 0.662 | 0.597 | 0.582 | 0.617 | 0.708 | 0.942 | 0.924 | 0.581 | 0.75 | 1,290 | 1,641 | 2,121 | 2,587 |
| Germany | 0 | 0 | 0 | 0.029 | 0.14 | 0.326 | 0.626 | 0.915 | 1.495 | 2.539 | 2.654 | 2,657 | 2,992 | 3,665 | 3,681 |
| Italy | 0.096 | 0.256 | 0.256 | 0.333 | 0.346 | 0.346 | 0.346 | 0.352 | 0.338 | 0.452 | 1,086 | 1,749 | 2,203 | 2,226 | 2,243 |
| Netherlands | 0.165 | 0.194 | 0.309 | 0.314 | 0.542 | 0.737 | 0.794 | 0.855 | 0.833 | 0.741 | 1,052 | 1,135 | 1,455 | 1,582 | 1,582 |
| Switzerland | 1,331 | 1,426 | 1,366 | 1,343 | 1,391 | 1,445 | 1,528 | 1,624 | 1,688 | 1,904 | 1,913 | 1,913 | 2,162 | 2,533 | 2,639 |
| Japan | 0.003 | 0.004 | 0.007 | 0.01 | 0.016 | 0.183 | 0.022 | 0.022 | 0.023 | 0.023 | 0.023 | 0.244 | 0.247 | 0.287 | 0.289 |

(cont.)

| | 1963 | 1964 | 1965 | 1966 | 1967 | 1968 | 1969 | 1970 | 1971 | 1972 | 1973 | 1974 | 1975 |
|---|---|---|---|---|---|---|---|---|---|---|---|---|---|
| United States | 15,596 | 15,471 | 14,065 | 13,235 | 12,065 | 10,892 | 11,859 | 11,072 | 10,206 | 10,487 | 11,652 | 11,652 | 11,599 |
| United Kingdom | 2,485 | 2,137 | 2,265 | 1,941 | 1,290 | 1,473 | 1,472 | 1,348 | 0.843 | 0.801 | 0.887 | n/a | 0.888 |
| France | 3,175 | 3,729 | 4,706 | 5,238 | 5,234 | 3,877 | 3,547 | 3,532 | 3,825 | 3,826 | 4,261 | 4,261 | 14,133 |
| Germany | 3,866 | 4.272 | 4,403 | 4,317 | 4,228 | 4,540 | 3,983 | 3,993 | 4,494 | 4,363 | 5,179 | 5,810 | 5,338 |
| Italy | 2,342 | 2,107 | 2,403 | 2,414 | 2,400 | 2,923 | 2,957 | 2,887 | 2,884 | 3,130 | 3,482 | 3,482 | 3,482 |
| Netherlands | 1,602 | 1,692 | 1,752 | 1,724 | 1,714 | 1,695 | 1,710 | 1,789 | 2,110 | 2,116 | 2,424 | 2,732 | 2,547 |
| Switzerland | 2,790 | 2,697 | 3,010 | 2,812 | 3,057 | 2,596 | 2,614 | 2,703 | 3,093 | 3,093 | 3,666 | 4,682 | 4,539 |
| Japan | 0.289 | 0.305 | 0.328 | 0.33 | 0.339 | 0.356 | 0.413 | 0.533 | n/a | 0.802 | 0.891 | 0.905 | 0.865 |

*Source:* International Monetary Fund, 〈www.imfstatistics.org〉.

U.S. Balance of Payments, Net Totals, 1958–1972

| | 1958 | 1959 | 1960 | 1961 | 1962 | 1963 | 1964 | 1965 | 1966 | 1967 | 1968 | 1969 | 1970 | 1971 | 1972 |
|---|---|---|---|---|---|---|---|---|---|---|---|---|---|---|---|
| *Balance of payments[a]* | | | | | | | | | | | | | | | |
| Goods/services/transfers | −132 | −2,290 | 1,515 | 3,027 | 2,406 | 2,963 | 5,883 | 4,364 | 2,492 | 2,243 | −336 | −885 | 2,782 | −323 | −6,180 |
| Trade balance, fob | 3,312 | 972 | 4,436 | 5,416 | 4,442 | 4,993 | 6,831 | 4,951 | 3,926 | 3,860 | 624 | 638 | 2,159 | −2,722 | −6,987 |
| Military expenditures/sales | −3,135 | −2,805 | −2,713 | −2,552 | −2,308 | −2,238 | −2,133 | −2,122 | −2,935 | −3,138 | −3,140 | −3,335 | −3,377 | −2,907 | −3,605 |
| Other services | 2,029 | 1,967 | 1,828 | 2,722 | 3,009 | 2,930 | 3,882 | 4,293 | 4,334 | 4,519 | 5,008 | 4,646 | 4,000 | 5,306 | 4,411 |
| Remittances/pensions | −722 | −791 | −672 | −705 | −738 | −826 | −809 | −950 | −923 | −1,196 | −1,121 | −1,190 | −1,060 | −1,063 | −1,052 |
| Government grants | −1,616 | −1,633 | −1,664 | −1,854 | −1,919 | −1,896 | −1,888 | −1,808 | −1,910 | −1,802 | −1,707 | −1,644 | −2,047 | −2,430 | −2,576 |
| Capital excluding reserves | −3,171 | −405 | −4,035 | −3,316 | −3,536 | −4,631 | −6,329 | −5,075 | −1,711 | −4,574 | 2,490 | 6,518 | −9,923 | −16,878 | 534 |
| U.S. government | | | | | | | | | | | | | | | |
|  Advance repayments | | 435 | 53 | 696 | 681 | 326 | 123 | 221 | 429 | 6 | 269 | −87 | 244 | 227 | 137 |
|  Other long-term | −632 | −432 | −630 | −1,366 | −1,530 | −1,538 | −1,781 | −1,803 | −1,698 | −2,637 | −2,600 | −2,186 | −2,253 | −2,771 | −1,633 |
|  Short-term | −339 | −356 | −528 | −261 | −245 | −445 | −19 | −16 | −265 | 209 | 62 | 89 | −16 | 182 | 166 |
| Direct investment | −1,083 | −1,134 | −1,533 | −1,526 | −1,522 | −1,893 | −2,333 | −3,411 | −3,575 | −2,879 | −2,890 | −2,238 | −3,380 | −5,058 | −3,133 |
| Other private long-term | −1,463 | −455 | −574 | −651 | −1,087 | −1,351 | −2,137 | −1,166 | 1,021 | −33 | 4,060 | 2,324 | 1,952 | 677 | 3,036 |
| U.S. private short-term | −311 | −77 | −1,348 | −1,556 | −553 | −734 | −2,147 | 753 | −415 | −1,209 | −1,087 | −716 | −1,132 | −3,429 | −3,009 |
| Foreign commercial banks | 37 | 1,140 | 104 | 595 | −129 | 438 | 1,454 | 116 | 2,697 | 1,272 | 3,387 | 9,434 | −6,508 | −6,908 | 3,716 |
| Other foreign short-term | 626 | 474 | 421 | 748 | 849 | 566 | 511 | 231 | 95 | 697 | 1,289 | −102 | 1,170 | 202 | 1,254 |
| Net errors and omissions | 488 | 412 | −772 | −998 | −1,111 | −339 | −1,118 | −576 | −514 | −1,088 | −514 | −2,924 | −458 | −9,776 | −1,854 |
| Official reserves, net | | | | 1,347 | 2,702 | 2,011 | 1,564 | 1,289 | −266 | 3,405 | −1,641 | −2,739 | 9,839 | 29,753 | 10,358 |
| Gold (purchases) | | | | | | 461 | 125 | 1,406 | 830 | 1,170 | 1,173 | −967 | 787 | 866 | 594 |
| Fund gold tranche position | | | | | | | 266 | 165 | 278 | −94 | −870 | −1,034 | 389 | 1,350 | 170 |
| Foreign exchange | | | | | | | −220 | −349 | −540 | −1,024 | −1,183 | 814 | 2,152 | 381 | 35 |
| Liabilities to foreign official | | | | | | | 1,393 | 67 | −834 | 3,366 | −761 | −1,521 | 7,362 | 27,405 | 10,322 |
| SDR holding | | | | | | | | | | | | | −851 | −249 | −763 |
| *Government finance[b]* | | | | | | | | | | | | | | | |
| Deficit (−) or surplus | −1.58 | −13.09 | 0.75 | −2.3 | −5.8 | −4.01 | −5.91 | −1.67 | −3.61 | −8.81 | −25.16 | 3.23 | −3 | −23 | −23 |
| *Additional statistics[c]* | | | | | | | | | | | | | | | |
| Government bond yield | | | | | | | | | | | | | | | |
|  Medium-term | 2.79 | 4.44 | 3.98 | 3.5 | 3.45 | 3.65 | 4.03 | 4.26 | 5.2 | 5.03 | 5.75 | 7.02 | 7.32 | 5.56 | 5.61 |
|  Long-term | 3.43 | 4.07 | 4.02 | 3.9 | 3.95 | 4 | 4.15 | 4.21 | 4.66 | 4.85 | 5.26 | 6.12 | 6.58 | 5.74 | 5.63 |
| Industrial share prices | 100 | 124 | 120 | 142 | 133 | 149 | 117 | 127 | 124 | 135 | 117.7 | 116.4 | 100 | 118.7 | 133.4 |
| Exports | | | | | | | | | | | | | | | |
|  Excluding military aid | 17,920 | 17,643 | 20,584 | 21,000 | 21,688 | 23,249 | 25,834 | 26,753 | 29,494 | 31,035 | 34,063 | 37,332 | 42,659 | 43,549 | 49,219 |
|  Including military aid | 16,377 | 16,416 | 19,635 | 20,190 | 20,960 | 22,329 | 26,652 | 27,532 | 30,434 | 31,627 | 34,636 | 38,006 | 43,224 | 44,130 | 49,778 |
| Imports, fob | 13,387 | 15,690 | 15,075 | 14,758 | 16,464 | 17,213 | 18,750 | 21,430 | 25,621 | 26,893 | 33,226 | 36,043 | 39,952 | 45,563 | 55,583 |

*Source*: International Monetary Fund, *International Financial Statistics*.

[a] In millions of U.S. dollars

[b] In billions of U.S. dollars

[c] Percent or index numbers

U.S. Gold Holdings

Amount in Millions of U.S. Dollars

30,000
25,000
20,000
15,000
10,000
5,000
0

1948 1949 1950 1951 1952 1953 1954 1955 1956 1957 1958 1959 1960 1961 1962 1963 1964 1965 1966 1967 1968 1969 1970 1971 1972 1973 1974 1975

Source: International Monetary Fund, (www.imfstatistics.org).

NATO: Military Expenditures as a Percentage of GDP

| | 1952 | 1953 | 1954 | 1955 | 1956 | 1957 | 1958 | 1959 | 1960 | 1961 | 1962 | 1963 | 1964 | 1965 | 1966 | 1967 | 1968 | 1969 | 1970 | 1971 | 1972 |
|---|---|---|---|---|---|---|---|---|---|---|---|---|---|---|---|---|---|---|---|---|---|
| United States | 13.6 | 13.4 | 11.6 | 10 | 9.8 | 9.9 | 10 | 9.4 | 8.9 | 9.1 | 9.3 | 8.8 | 8 | 7.5 | 8.4 | 9.4 | 9.2 | 8.6 | 7.8 | 6.9 | 6.6 |
| Canada | 7.7 | 7.8 | 7 | 6.6 | 6.1 | 5.6 | 5.2 | 4.6 | 4.3 | 4.3 | 4.2 | 3.7 | 3.6 | 3 | 2.8 | 3 | 2.6 | 2.4 | 2.4 | 2.3 | 2.2 |
| Belgium | | 4.8 | 4.8 | 3.8 | 3.5 | 3.6 | 3.6 | 3.5 | 3.4 | 3.3 | 3.3 | 3.4 | 3.4 | 3.2 | 3.1 | 3.1 | 3.2 | 2.9 | 2.9 | 2.8 | |
| Denmark | 2.7 | 3.4 | 3.2 | 3.2 | 3 | 3.1 | 2.9 | 2.6 | 2.7 | 2.6 | 3 | 3 | 2.8 | 2.8 | 2.7 | 2.7 | 2.8 | 2.5 | 2.3 | 2.5 | 2.3 |
| France | 8.6 | 9.1 | 7.3 | 6.4 | 7.7 | 7.3 | 6.8 | 6.6 | 6.4 | 6.2 | 6 | 5.6 | 5.3 | 5.2 | 5 | 5 | 4.8 | 4.4 | 4.1 | 3.9 | 3.7 |
| FR Germany | 5.8 | 4.2 | 4 | 4.1 | 3.6 | 4.1 | 3 | 4.4 | 4 | 4 | 4.8 | 5.2 | 4.6 | 4.3 | 4.1 | 4.3 | 3.6 | 3.6 | 3.3 | 3.4 | 3.5 |
| Greece | 6.5 | 5.2 | 5.5 | 5.2 | 6 | 5.1 | 4.8 | 4.9 | 4.9 | 4.9 | 4.1 | 3.9 | 3.7 | 3.6 | 3.7 | 4.5 | 4.8 | 4.9 | 4.9 | 4.8 | 4.7 |
| Italy | 4.5 | 3.8 | 4 | 3.7 | 3.6 | 3.5 | 3.4 | 3.3 | 3.3 | 3.1 | 3.2 | 3.3 | 3.3 | 3.3 | 3.4 | 3.1 | 3 | 2.7 | 2.7 | 3 | 3.1 |
| Luxembourg | 2.4 | 2.9 | 3.3 | 3.2 | 1.9 | 1.9 | 1.9 | 1.8 | 1.1 | 1.1 | 1.4 | 1.3 | 1.5 | 1.4 | 1.4 | 1.2 | 1 | 0.9 | 0.8 | 0.9 | 0.9 |
| Netherlands | 5.6 | 5.6 | 6 | 5.7 | 5.7 | 5.2 | 4.7 | 4 | 4.1 | 4.5 | 4.5 | 4.4 | 4.3 | 3.9 | 3.7 | 3.9 | 3.7 | 3.6 | 3.5 | 3.5 | 3.4 |
| Norway | 4 | 5.1 | 5 | 3.9 | 3.5 | 3.6 | 3.5 | 3.6 | 3.2 | 3.3 | 3.6 | 3.5 | 3.4 | 3.7 | 3.5 | 3.4 | 3.6 | 3.6 | 3.5 | 3.4 | 3.3 |
| Portugal | | 4 | 4.2 | 4.2 | 4 | 4 | 4 | 4.3 | 4.2 | 6.4 | 6.9 | 6.5 | 6.7 | 6.3 | 6.3 | 7.2 | 7.5 | 6.9 | 7.2 | 7.6 | |
| Turkey | 5.1 | 4.9 | 5.4 | 5.1 | 4.7 | 4.1 | 3.8 | 4.5 | 4.7 | 5 | 4.9 | 4.6 | 4.6 | 4.8 | 4.3 | 4.4 | 4.6 | 4.4 | 4.3 | 4.5 | 4.3 |
| United Kingdom | 10 | 10 | 8.8 | 8.2 | 7.8 | 7.2 | 7 | 6.6 | 6.5 | 6.3 | 6.4 | 6.2 | 6.1 | 6 | 5.7 | 5.8 | 5.5 | 5.1 | 4.9 | 5.1 | 5.4 |

Source: SIPRI Yearbook, 1974.

France Balance of Payments, Net Totals, 1958–1971

| | 1958 | 1959 | 1960 | 1961 | 1962 | 1963 | 1964 | 1965 | 1966 | 1967 | 1968 | 1969 | 1970 | 1971 | 1972 |
|---|---|---|---|---|---|---|---|---|---|---|---|---|---|---|---|
| *Balance of payments*[a] | | | | | | | | | | | | | | | |
| Good and services | | 702 | 673 | 912 | 808 | 351 | 20 | 481 | 16 | 39 | −77 | −741 | 637 | 1,837 | 1,901 |
| Trade balance | | 427 | 92 | 417 | 485 | 119 | −89 | 388 | −38 | 275 | 68 | −859 | 320 | 1,105 | 1,275 |
| Transfers | | | | | | | | | | | | | | | |
| Private | | 32 | 46 | 115 | 89 | 110 | 129 | 100 | 86 | 67 | −524 | −713 | −568 | −852 | −894 |
| Government | | −1 | −85 | −55 | −95 | 89 | −62 | −63 | −69 | −78 | −458 | −344 | −221 | −460 | −723 |
| Net errors/omissions | | 108 | 8 | 54 | 11 | 127 | 60 | 152 | 159 | 83 | −35 | 288 | 363 | 161 | 134 |
| *Government finance*[b] | | | | | | | | | | | | | | | |
| Deficit (−) or surplus | −6.98 | −6.28 | −4.17 | −4.36 | −6.1 | −8.26 | −1.57 | 0.18 | −2.03 | −6.34 | −9.47 | −0.341 | 3.68 | −3.45 | 6.32 |
| Revenue | 51.78 | 60.44 | 65.55 | 70.49 | 78.02 | 88.41 | 98.52 | 105.78 | 112 | 120.8 | 129.8 | 153.17 | 169.88 | 180.2 | 205.42 |
| Expenditures | 58.76 | 66.72 | 69.72 | 74.85 | 84.13 | 96.68 | | | | 127.2 | 139.3 | 156.58 | 166.2 | 183.65 | 199.1 |

Source: International Monetary Fund, *International Financial Statistics.*

a In millions of U.S. dollars

b In billions of francs

West Germany Balance of Payments, Net Totals, 1958–1972

| | 1958 | 1959 | 1960 | 1961 | 1962 | 1963 | 1964 | 1965 | 1966 | 1967 | 1968 | 1969 | 1970 | 1971 | 1972 |
|---|---|---|---|---|---|---|---|---|---|---|---|---|---|---|---|
| *Balance of payments*[a] | | | | | | | | | | | | | | | |
| Goods and services | 7,870 | 7,389 | 8,015 | 7,217 | 2,914 | 5,837 | 1,383 | −13 | 1,708 | 4,075 | 4,684 | 3,768 | 3,646 | 4,184 | 5,395 |
| Trade balance | 4,880 | 5,104 | 5,310 | 6,491 | 2,984 | 5,875 | 1,351 | 248 | 1,878 | 4,166 | 4,485 | 3,901 | 3,954 | 4,560 | 6,065 |
| Transfers | | | | | | | | | | | | | | | |
| Private | −1,890 | −3,247 | −3,395 | −4,442 | −5,128 | −4,956 | −544 | −739 | −863 | −780 | −794 | −1,043 | −1,648 | −2,163 | −2,619 |
| Government | −1,890 | −3,247 | −3,395 | −4,442 | −5,128 | −4,956 | −786 | −866 | −718 | −829 | −1,035 | −1,121 | −1,019 | −1,129 | −1,737 |
| Net errors/omissions | −400 | −104 | 1,679 | 434 | 925 | −528 | 498 | 706 | 141 | 4 | 734 | 458 | 903 | 413 | 366 |
| *Government finance*[b] | | | | | | | | | | | | | | | |
| Deficit (−) or surplus | −0.22 | −4.85 | −1.36 | 0.32 | −1.54 | −3.14 | −0.56 | −1.55 | −2.2 | −8.37 | −3.91 | 1.68 | −0.56 | −1.36 | −3.64 |
| Revenue | 31.31 | 33.93 | 39.29 | 43.65 | 48.51 | 51.43 | 56.64 | 61.17 | 64.7 | 66.6 | 71 | 82.6 | 86.47 | 96.11 | 106.29 |
| Expenditure | 31.53 | 38.78 | 40.65 | 43.33 | 50.05 | 54.57 | 57.2 | 62.72 | 67 | 75 | 74.9 | 80.92 | 87.03 | 97.47 | 109.93 |

*Source:* International Monetary Fund, *International Financial Statistics.*

[a] In millions of deutschemarks

[b] In billions of deutschemarks

U.K. Balance of Payments, Net Totals, 1958–1972

| | 1958 | 1959 | 1960 | 1961 | 1962 | 1963 | 1964 | 1965 | 1966 | 1967 | 1968 | 1969 | 1970 | 1971 | 1972 |
|---|---|---|---|---|---|---|---|---|---|---|---|---|---|---|---|
| *Balance of payments*[a] | | | | | | | | | | | | | | | |
| Goods and services | 412 | 230 | −166 | 106 | 235 | 263 | −586 | 370 | 762 | −131 | −106 | 1,603 | 2,155 | 3,098 | 870 |
| Trade balance | 41 | −102 | −386 | −127 | −72 | −49 | −1,453 | −664 | −204 | −1,446 | −1,543 | −338 | 28 | 737 | 1,675 |
| Investment income | 297 | 270 | 234 | 244 | 329 | 377 | 1,106 | 1,238 | 1,064 | 1,018 | 761 | 1,082 | 1,236 | 1,138 | 1,142 |
| Transfers | | | | | | | | | | | | | | | |
| Private | 5 | 3 | 6 | 9 | 1 | −14 | −64 | −90 | −137 | −173 | −230 | −185 | −81 | −33 | −188 |
| Government | −72 | −80 | −98 | −116 | −121 | −136 | −456 | −496 | −504 | −769 | −1,032 | −420 | −413 | −480 | −473 |
| Net errors/omissions | 49 | −67 | 256 | −29 | 84 | −111 | −31 | 89 | −73 | 581 | −194 | 669 | 278 | 731 | −1,451 |
| *Government finance*[b] | | | | | | | | | | | | | | | |
| Deficit (−) or Surplus | −100 | −136 | −301 | −221 | 82 | −123 | −423 | −597 | −521 | −1,134 | −755 | 1,116 | 678 | −562 | −1,429 |
| Revenue | 5,547 | 5,781 | 5,933 | 6,435 | 7,136 | 6,927 | 9,392 | 10,522 | 11,644 | 12,766 | 14,791 | 17,116 | 18,160 | 19,426 | 20,881 |
| Expenditures | 5,054 | 5,244 | 5,619 | 6,116 | 6,461 | 6,610 | 8,975 | 9,832 | 10,649 | 12,247 | 13,779 | 14,458 | 15,787 | 17,699 | 20,269 |

*Source:* International Monetary Fund, *International Financial Statistics.*

[a] In millions of pounds sterling

[b] In billions of pounds sterling

214 Appendix B

SDR Holdings (in millions)

| | 1970 | 1971 | 1972 | 1973 | 1974 | 1975 |
|---|---|---|---|---|---|---|
| United States | 0.8506 | 1.193 | 1.957 | 2.166 | 2.374 | 2.334 |
| United Kingdom | 0.2657 | 0.6415 | 0.6562 | 0.7242 | 0.8425 | 0.8151 |
| France | 0.1714 | 0.3777 | 0.6303 | 0.0878 | 0.2476 | 0.286 |
| Germany | 0.2576 | 0.4934 | 0.8928 | 1.673 | 1.762 | 1.698 |
| Italy | 0.0767 | 2.474 | 0.3707 | 0.4136 | 0.2213 | 0.0971 |
| Netherlands | 0.144 | 0.6188 | 0.7053 | 0.5734 | 0.5947 | 0.6092 |
| Japan | 0.1462 | 0.307 | 0.4608 | 0.5128 | 0.5286 | 0.5196 |

*Source:* International Monetary Fund, ⟨www.imfstatistics.org⟩.

# Notes

## Abbreviations

CAB   Cabinet Memoranda
CIA   Central Intelligence Agency
DDE   Dwight D. Eisenhower
DDEL  Dwight D. Eisenhower Presidential Library
*DDRS*  *Declassified Documents Reference Service*
FO    Foreign Office
FOIA  Freedom of Information Act
*FRUS*  U.S. Department of State, *Foreign Relations of the United States*
HSTL  Harry S. Truman Presidential Library
JFKL  John F. Kennedy Presidential Library
LBJL  Lyndon B. Johnson Presidential Library
NSF   National Security File
POF   President's Office Files
PREM  Prime Minister's Office Files
PRO   Public Records Office
RG    Record Group
SML   Seeley Mudd Library
UPA   University Publications of America (microfilm)
USNA  United States National Archives
WHCF  White House Central Files

## Introduction

1. Ian Fleming, *Goldfinger*.

2. Telegram, Joseph Califano to Johnson, 22 December 1967, "The 1968 Balance of Payments Program," NSF, NSC History, box 54, LBJL.

3. Minutes of the Cabinet Committee on Balance of Payments, 21 December 1967, "The 1968 Balance of Payments Program," NSF, NSC History, box 54, LBJL.

4. Telegram, Johnson to Califano, 23 December 1967, "The 1968 Balance of Payments Program," NSF, NSC History, box 54, LBJL.

5. Ibid.

6. "January 1, 1968, Statement by President Johnson Outlining a Balance of Payments Action Program," in "Maintaining the Strength of the United States Dollar in a Strong Free World Economy: A 1968 Progress Report," UPA, Administrative History, Department of the Treasury.

7. Friedman, "The Price of the Dollar," 240.

8. Undated memo, Barbara Ward Jackson, NSF, box 53, LBJL.

9. Ackley for Johnson, 1 January 1968, NSF, box 53, LBJL.

10. Rostow for Johnson, 23 January 1968, NSF, box 53, LBJL.

11. The gold pool was a 1961 agreement between Switzerland, West Germany, Italy, the Netherlands, France (for a time), Belgium, and Britain whereby each country agreed, in conjunction with the United States, to utilize a portion of its gold stocks to hold down the price of gold on the market in London. When the price would rise, the gold pool agreed to sell gold until the price returned to thirty-five dollars an ounce.

12. The SDRs were first proposed by the Johnson administration in 1965 to augment and perhaps replace gold and dollars as the world's reserve currency. SDRs would be international money allocated according to a ratio based on gold and dollar holdings. The Americans envisioned it not as a credit but as a real store of value that could be transferred like gold or dollars but would not be convertible

into gold or dollars on demand. A watered-down version of the SDR proposal was accepted in September 1967 (see Chapters 5 and 7).

13.  Also see Gavin, "The Myth of Flexible Response."

14.  Kunz, *Butter and Guns*, 99. For similar interpretations, see Chapter 3, note 3.

15.  Cohen, *Organizing the World's Money*, 97.

16.  Discussion between Kennedy, William McChesney Martin, Chairman of the Federal Reserve, and Theodore Sorensen, 16 August 1962, 5:50–6:32 P.M., tape 13, POF, JFKL.

17.  Gowa, *Closing the Gold Window*, 52.

18.  Kunz, *Butter and Guns*, 192.

19.  For the leading work on empire by invitation, see Lundestad, "Empire by Invitation? The United States and Western Europe, 1945–1952," and *Empire by Integration*. For a good definition of informal empire, see Doyle, *Empires*, 43–44.

20.  Gilpin, *The Political Economy of International Monetary Relations*, 134.

### Chapter One

1.  The best economic analyses are Cooper, *The International Monetary System*, and de Grauwe, *International Money*.

2.  During the nineteenth century, if a nation lost gold because of a trade deficit, deflation was often avoided because of investment and loans from France and especially England. The surplus country of the interwar period, the United States, did not supply loans and investments out of its current-account surplus during the 1930s. This was due to its bad experience with overseas investment and loans made during the 1920s, and because restrictions on trade and capital that prevailed throughout much of the world at the time. For an especially good account of nineteenth- and early twentieth-century international monetary relations, see Gallarotti, *The Anatomy of an International Monetary Regime*.

3.  See John Ikenberry, "The Political Origins of Bretton Woods," in Bordo and Eichengreen, *A Retrospective on the Bretton Woods System: Lessons for International Monetary Reform*, and Gardner, *Sterling-Dollar Diplomacy in Current Perspective*.

4.  For a description of Keynes's original monetary plans, see *Collected Writings*, vol. 25.

5.  Shelton, *Money Meltdown*, 17.

6.  Keynes, *Collected Writings*, 25:42.

7.  Ibid., 267 and 445.

8.  See "Hearings before the Committee on Banking and Currency," House of Representatives, 79th Cong., 1st sess., HR 2211; IMF and International Bank, 570–75, 588–91.

9.  Memorandum by the President of the Board of Trade, "The Future of Multilateral International Economic Cooperation," 12 September 1949, 4, CP (49) 188, PRO.

10.  For an excellent description of the political and economic causes of capital flight, see Brown, *The Flight of International Capital*, 1–15.

11.  The impact of this outlook should not be underestimated. There was really only one voice calling for free exchange rates during the 1950s, and that was Milton Friedman. His ideas were completely ignored until the 1960s, when other economists started to doubt the wisdom of the Bretton Woods system. See Friedman, "The Case for Flexible Exchange Rates."

12.  Stern, *The Balance of Payments*, 152.

13.  Ibid.

14.  For an excellent account of the origins and implementation of the Anglo-American loan, see Woods, *A Changing of the Guard*.

15.  For the origins of the European Recovery Plan, or Marshall Plan, see Milward, *The Reconstruction of Western Europe*, and Hogan, *The Marshall Plan*.

## Chapter Two

1. Memorandum from Karl Brandt of the Council of Economic Advisers to the President's Special Assistant (Randall), 21 September 1960, and circulated 12 October, *FRUS*, 1958–60, 14:64–66.

2. President Dwight D. Eisenhower, Memorandum of Discussion at the 465th Meeting of the National Security Council, 31 October 1960, Whitman File, NSC Records, DDEL.

3. Memorandum of Discussion at the 465th Meeting of the National Security Council, 31 October 1960, Whitman File, NSC Records, DDEL.

4. Memorandum of Conference with President Eisenhower, 4 November 1959, Whitman File, DDE Diaries, DDEL.

5. The exception is Kaufman, *Trade and Aid*. Several scholars have looked at the economic influence of the balance of payments during the late Eisenhower administration, but none has looked at the strategic impact or made the connection to the Berlin crisis. Some political background is given in Strange, *International Monetary Relations of the Western World*, 26–64. Donfried discusses the origin of the German offset agreements in her dissertation, "The Political Economy of Alliance: Issue Linkage in the West German American Relationship," 46–104.

6. Telegram from Embassy in Washington to British Foreign Office, 2 December 1956, PREM 11/1826, XC 7840, PRO. Great Britain was forced to submit to the dictates of American policy because it could not defend its exchange rate without massive help from the United States. Without this help, Great Britain would have to devalue sterling relative to other currencies, an option that would threaten sterling's role as a key currency used in international trade and finance. In order to regain the "invisible" earnings that Great Britain had used to build its political and military strength during the nineteenth and early twentieth centuries, postwar British governments aspired to return London to its historical role as world's banker. Without confidence that sterling would retain its value, it was unlikely that London could ever regain this position.

7. See Memorandum of Conversation, "World Financial Problems," 24 February 1958, *FRUS*, 1958–60, 14:76–80.

8. See Treasury memo, "U.S. Gold Situation," 30 October 1958, *FRUS*, 1958–60, 14:91–93. The British were advocates of this solution, but the Americans refused to consider this option, not the least because the Soviets would be the biggest beneficiary of the increase.

9. Anderson to Eisenhower, 30 December 1958, *FRUS*, 1958–60, 14:97–99.

10. See Southard to Treasury Secretary Anderson and Acting Secretary of State Dillon, "The Issue of Dollar Discrimination," 18 May 1959, *FRUS*, 1958–60, 14:107–9.

11. Henry C. Wallich of the Council of Economic Advisers to Secretary of the Treasury Anderson, 10 March 1959, RG 56, Records of the Department of Treasury, Subject Files, Commerce Department, USNA.

12. In the end, even Wallich suggested no more than eliminating the 25 percent domestic gold reserve requirement of the Federal Reserve in order to make more gold available for international liabilities.

13. Memorandum of Discussion at the 409th Meeting of the National Security Council, 4 June 1959, Whitman File, NSC Records, DDEL.

14. "International Payments Position of the United States," paper prepared in the Department of State, 24 July 1959, *FRUS*, 1958–60, 14:116.

15. Ibid., 118.

16. Minutes of a Cabinet Meeting, 7 August 1959, Whitman File, Cabinet Series, DDEL.

17. See Trachtenberg, *History and Strategy*, and *A Constructed Peace*.

18. Memorandum of Conference with President Eisenhower, 24 August 1959, Whitman File, DDE Diaries, DDEL.

19. Khrushchev accepted Eisenhower's invitation to visit the United States in September 1959 to discuss, among other things, the ongoing crisis over Berlin. The talks, held at Camp David, were friendly but did not resolve the major differences between the United States and the Soviet Union.

20. Memorandum of Conference with President Eisenhower, 4 November 1959, Whitman File, DDE Diaries, DDEL.

21. Memorandum of Conversation, 24 October 1959, *FRUS*, 1958–60, 7, pt. 1: 488–94.

22. Ibid., 494.

23. Memorandum from the Assistant Secretary of State for Policy Planning to Secretary of State Herter, 29 October 1959, *FRUS*, 1958–60, 7, pt. 1: 494–96.

24. Ibid.

25. Ibid., 496 (emphasis in original).

26. Memorandum of Conversation on NATO Problems, 24 November 1959, *FRUS*, 1958–60, 7, pt. 1: 520.

27. Eisenhower, *Waging Peace*, 606.

28. Memorandum of Conference among Eisenhower, Herter, Reinhardt, Merchant, and Kohler, drafted 22 October 1959, Whitman File, DDE Diaries, DDEL.

29. For an account of the capital flight during the summer and fall of 1960, see Brown, *The Flight of International Capital*.

30. This arbitrage situation, where gold could be bought for thirty-five dollars in the United States and sold in London for more than forty dollars, was like a pure money machine. In today's open markets, American gold would have been gone within hours, not months. This was as risk-free an investment as one could find, as there was always the possibility that the United States would raise the dollar price of gold, a possibility that investors thought more and more likely as the London price increased. As long as the United States maintained its gold guarantee, there was virtually no chance that the price the United States paid for gold would be lowered.

31. Memorandum for the Record by the President's Assistant, "Meeting with the President, Regarding Recent Developments in the London Gold Market, 2:30 P.M., Tuesday, October 25, 1960," 25 October 1960, *FRUS*, 1958–60, 14:129.

32. Letter from President Eisenhower to Chancellor Adenauer, 7 October 1960, *FRUS*, 1958–60, 9:692.

33. Ibid., 693.

34. Telegram from the Embassy in Germany to the Department of State, 20 October 1960, with a translation of Chancellor Adenauer's reply to President Eisenhower's letter of 7 October 1960, *FRUS*, 1958–60, 9:695.

35. Memorandum of Discussion at the 465th Meeting of the National Security Council, "Long-Range Military Assistance Plans," 31 October 1960, *FRUS*, 1958–60, 14:520–38.

36. Ibid., 529.

37. Ibid.

38. Memorandum from Secretary of State Herter to Eisenhower, "Future Military Assistance for the Netherlands, Italy, Belgium, and Japan," 13 November 1960, *FRUS*, 1958–60, 14:539.

39. Memorandum from Secretary of the Treasury Anderson to Eisenhower, "Future Military Assistance for the Netherlands, Italy, Belgium, and Japan," undated, *FRUS*, 1958–60, 14:540–42.

40. Memorandum of Conference with Eisenhower, 9 November 1960, *FRUS*, 1958–60, 14:130.

41. Memorandum of Conference with Eisenhower in Augusta, Georgia, 15 November 1960, *FRUS, 1958–60*, 14:134.

42. Cable to Herter from Dillon, copy of cable to the President from Anderson, 23 November 1960, UPA, DDE Office Files, Administration-International Series, Anderson.

43. Ibid.

44. See "Communiqué on Anderson-Dillon Talks with W. German Leaders Indirectly Admits Failure of Mission," *New York Times*, 23 November 1960.

45. Memorandum of Conference with Eisenhower, 28 November 1960, *FRUS, 1958–60*, 14:142–47. The West Germans pointed out that it was unfair that they should have to make such efforts to relieve the U.S. deficit when the American government could not get its own companies to help. Of course, the British told Anderson that they planned to turn the dollars right around for gold from the United States.

46. Ibid.

47. Ibid., 143.

48. Ibid., 143–44. Dillon's presence on this trip had a further complication. He later became the secretary of the treasury for the Kennedy administration. Given the fact that a rumor to this effect was already in the air, and given the concern European leaders had for who would fill this position in the next administration, was Dillon the right person to send over as an advocate of Eisenhower's policy? Note the following on p. 144: "Mr. Dillon said that the press had been carrying stories that Senator Kennedy wants him to be his Secretary of the Treasury. The President stated that Kennedy had told Mr. Nixon that he would like to have Dillon and Lodge in his administration, but that they would not be given policy positions. Mr. Dillon seemed somewhat surprised at this."

49. Memorandum of Conference with Eisenhower, 28 November 1960.

50. Memorandum of Conference with Eisenhower, 30 November 1960, *FRUS, 1958–60*, 14:544.

51. Eisenhower, *Waging Peace*, 715.

52. "We believe Soviets probably implementing calculated policy of gradually turning over their responsibilities re Berlin to East German regime with a view to creating situation of fact which will weaken Western negotiating position," quoted from Telegram from the Department of State to the Embassy in Germany, 10 October 1960, *FRUS, 1958–60*, 9:606. "Foreign Minister von Brentano began by stressing the nature of the present Communist actions against Berlin which were calculated through step-by-step harassment to prepare for the eventual loss of the city without ever precipitating a show-down with the Western Powers on a clear issue understandable to public opinion." Memorandum of Conversation, "German and Berlin Problems and Forthcoming United Nations Session," 18 September 1960, *FRUS, 1958–60*, 9:571.

53. For the concern over Western unity, especially on the part of the German leadership during autumn 1960: "Macmillan visit to Moscow in March 1959, followed by Geneva conferences that year, created doubts and forebodings in minds of chancellor and of others (including Willy Brandt) which have never been entirely dispelled, and which, in my judgment, will be rekindled unless West finds means within next few months to assume a more vigorous, confident and united posture than it is now displaying." The document also goes on to state that "many Germans tend, as does Chancellor, to question degree of determination and solidarity, apart from public exhortation, which their Western Allies (in particular the U.K. and more recently France) are willing to display" and "I fear that we are at this moment experiencing a decline in German confidence that the West is willing to make effort required by German problem." See Telegram from the Embassy in Germany to the Department of State, 21 September 1960, *FRUS, 1958–60*, 9:580–81.

54.   "Free World response has been slow and limited, both in scope and effectiveness. Its purpose of causing the Soviets to decide to stop has not succeeded, nor
do the actions so far adopted seem apt to do so. The military strength of a free
Berlin is incomparably high. The U.S. guarantee of continued free existence for
West Berlin is the keystone of our worldwide alliance structure." Memorandum
for the Joint Chiefs of Staff (C.N.O. Arleigh Burke) to Secretary of Defense Gates,
JCSM-439-60, "Berlin Countermeasures," *FRUS*, 1958–60, 9:594.

55.   Memorandum of Conference with Eisenhower, 16 August 1960, Whitman File,
DDE Diaries, DDEL.

56.   Ibid.

57.   Ibid.

58.   Memorandum of Discussion at the 457th Meeting of the National Security
Council, 25 August 1960, Whitman File, NSC Records, DDEL.

59.   Memorandum of Discussion at the 467th Meeting of the National Security
Council, 17 November 1960, Whitman File, NSC Records, DDEL.

60.   Ibid.

61.   Cable from the Secretary of State to Eisenhower, 14 December 1960, *DDRS* 1990.

62.   Airgram from the delegation at the North Atlantic Council Ministerial Meeting
to the Department of State, 17 December 1960, containing the text of the secretary's speech to the NATO Ministerial Meeting, entitled "NATO Long-Range
Planning," *FRUS*, 1958–60, 7, pt. 1: 674–82.

63.   Ibid., 678.

64.   For an excellent account of how the strategy of massive retaliation was chal-
lenged from within the administration almost from its inception, see Gaddis,
"The Unexpected John Foster Dulles: Nuclear Weapons, Communism, and the
Russians," 49–58.

65.   Memorandum for the Record by Secretary of the Treasury Anderson, "Meeting
with President-Elect Kennedy and Secretary of the Treasury Anderson, December 6, 1960," 6 December 1960, *FRUS*, 1958–60, 14:147–51.

66.   "Report to the Honorable John F. Kennedy by the Task Force on the Balance of
Payments," 25 February 1963, Acheson Papers, HSTL.

67.   Ibid., 12–23. Of the Eisenhower administration's measures to correct the payments deficit, the report says on p. 26, "Some were restrictionist and of doubtful
wisdom."

68.   Ibid., 25–26.

### Chapter Three

1.   See Schlesinger, *A Thousand Days*, 601; Rostow, *The Diffusion of Power*, 136;
George Ball Oral History, #2, AC 88-3, p. 29, LBJL; and Memo of Conversation
between Kennedy and Adenauer, 24 June 1963, *FRUS*, 1961–63, 9:170. Schlesinger also quotes Kennedy as saying, "What really matters is the strength of
the currency. It is this, not the force de frappe, which makes France a factor."

2.   Beschloss, *The Crisis Years*.

3.   See Borden, "Defending Hegemony: American Foreign Economic Policy," 83–
85; Calleo, *The Imperious Economy*, 23; Calleo, *Beyond American Hegemony*, 13,
44–52; Costigliola, "The Pursuit of Atlantic Community: Nuclear Arms, Dollars,
and Berlin," 24–56; Kennedy, *The Rise and Fall of the Great Powers*, 434; Kunz,
*Butter and Guns*, esp. 94–108. Despite the promising title of her book, Kunz does
not link the dollar crisis to the political crisis between the Kennedy administration and its NATO allies. For interpretations that see Kennedy's monetary policy as a series of "ad hoc" expedients designed to maintain the privileged place
the dollar held in the postwar "capitalist world-system," see Borden, "Defending Hegemony," 57–62, 84; Calleo and Rowland, *America and the World Political
Economy*, 88–89; Odell, *U.S. International Monetary Policy*, 88; Strange, *International Monetary Relations*, 82, 207.

4.  Again, the professional literature on international monetary economics is quite large, but for the best works see Stern, *The Balance of Payments*; Cooper, *The International Monetary System*; de Grauwe, *International Money*.

5.  For the idea that the U.S. government was firmly committed to a NATO system based on a strong, permanent American presence, even in the Eisenhower period, see what has become the classic work on American foreign policy during the Cold War: Gaddis, *Strategies of Containment*, 168.

6.  For the conventional wisdom on the Kennedy's flexible response policy, see ibid., 198–236, and Stromseth, *The Origins of Flexible Response*.

7.  At first glance, McNamara's Office of the Secretary of Defense seems an odd ally for the Treasury Department's troop withdrawal policies. But as will become clear, while McNamara supported a conventional buildup by Western Europe, he also supported downsizing America's conventional forces in Europe. George Ball claims that McNamara was almost as obsessed with the balance of payments as the president: "Because Bob was prepared to distort any kind of policy in order to achieve some temporary alleviation to the balance of payments, which again to my mind was a function of his preoccupation with quantification." See George Ball Oral History, #2, AC 88-3, p. 19, LBJL. For additional evidence of McNamara's willingness to distort budgetary and security policy because of the balance of payments, see Shapley, *Promise and Power*, 225–26.

8.  Sorensen, *Kennedy*, 406. See also John Kenneth Galbraith's letter to the President from October 1960, in his *Letters to Kennedy*, 29–31.

9.  Reeves, *President Kennedy*, 23.

10. "Report to the Honorable John F. Kennedy by the Task Force on the Balance of Payments," 27 December 1960, from file AP/SD & WNA/Report to the President on the Balance of Payments, 25 February 1963, Acheson Papers, HSTL.

11. Reeves, *President Kennedy*, 27–28.

12. For a discussion of how the Kennedy administration consciously set out to create a different foreign-policy-making structure than Eisenhower's, see Mayer, *Adenauer and Kennedy*, 9. For Kennedy's difficulty making decisions about long-term policy, see Ball, *The Past Has Another Pattern*, 167–68.

13. The French were convinced that Kennedy had no idea of what he was doing concerning the balance of payments. See Alphand's comments about Kennedy in Lacouture, *De Gaulle*, 381, and Alphand, *L'étonnement d'être*, 381.

14. For an excellent account of America's trade policies during the 1960s, see Zeiler, *American Trade and Power during the 1960s*.

15. Memcon, 4 January 1961, "Federal Republic Procurement of Military Equipment in the U.S. to Assist in the Latter's Balance of Payments Problems," *DDRS* 1991, 2559.

16. Ibid. See also Dowling to State, 13 January 1961, *DDRS* 1991, 1849.

17. Kennedy to Rusk, undated (probably early February 1961), UPA, State, POF, reel 23.

18. Dowling to State, 18 March 1961, *DDRS* 1991, 1382.

19. See "The Report to the Honorable John F. Kennedy by the Task Force on the Balance of Payments," 27 December 1960, Acheson Papers, State Department and White House Adviser, Report to the President on the Balance of Payments, 25 February 1963, HSTL.

20. Rusk to Kennedy, "German Balance of Payments Proposals and Your Meeting with German Foreign Minister von Brentano on February 17," UPA, NSF, Western Europe, 1961–63, Germany, reel 9, 363.

21. "Points which the President may wish to emphasize in discussion with foreign minister von Brentano," 16 February 1961, UPA, POF, Part 5, Germany, reel 8, 738.

22. "Draft Aide Memoire for Brentano," 16 February 1961, UPA, POF, Germany, reel 8, 731.

23. Rusk to Kennedy, "Recent German Measures Relating to United States Balance of Payments," 9 July 1961, *FRUS*, 1961–63, 9:120–21.

24. For a detailed account of the shift in negotiations, see Zimmerman, "Offset and Monetary Policy in German-American Relations during Kennedy's Presidency, 1961–1963."

25. Dillon to Kennedy, 14 September 1961, POF, Departments and Agencies: Treasury, 89, JFKL.

26. Heller to Ball, "A 'Reverse Lend-Lease' Approach to an Intensified U.S.-Germany Payments Imbalance," 8 August 1961, UPA, POF, CEA, 7.

27. Heller to Kennedy, "Balance of Payments and Berlin," 17 August 1961, UPA, POF, CEA, 7. See also Richard Cooper to Walter Heller, "Reaction of Other Agencies to the Proposal for a 'Mutual Support Loan' from Germany to the United States," 30 August 1961, UPA, POF, CEA, 7.

28. Heller to Kennedy, "Current Status of 'Lend-Lease' or 'Mutual Support' Plan for Financing U.S. Troop Costs in Germany," 8 September 1961, UPA, POF, CEA, 7.

29. Dillon to Kennedy, "Fourth Quarterly Report on the Balance of Payments," 12 March 1962, *FRUS*, 1961–63, 9:17; Dillon to Kennedy, "Report on Measures to Improve the Balance of Payments," undated (sometime in late 1962 or early 1963), Acheson Papers, State Department and White House Adviser, Report to the President on the Balance of Payments, 25 February 1963, 2–4, HSTL.

30. A forward exchange contract is an agreement whereby one party agrees to buy or sell foreign currency on a fixed future date, or during a period expiring on a fixed future date, at a fixed rate of exchange. The other party undertakes to pay or receive the foreign currency in terms of the contract in exchange for the settlement currency.

31. For a description of these strategies, and the argument that they were not ad hoc but part of a coordinated, if by necessity muted, plan, see Robert Roosa, "The New Convertible Gold-Dollar System," 9 August 1962, UPA, POF, Treasury, 25; and Roosa, "International Liquidity," and cover sheet from Dillon to the President, 20 July 1962, UPA, POF, Treasury, 25.

32. Strange, *International Monetary Relations*, 65–90.

33. Memo for the President, "International Monetary Reform," 18 March 1961, UPA, POF, CEA, 7.

34. Triffin observed that the large U.S. payments deficit could lead to a crisis of confidence in the dollar and spark a mass conversion into gold, rendering the dollar unusable as a reserve currency and in the process destroying a large portion of the world's liquidity. This problem came to be known as the "Triffin Dilemma." Triffin, *Gold and the Dollar Crisis*.

35. Ibid.

36. Heller to Kennedy, "The Balance of Payments Dilemma," 28 November 1961, UPA, POF, CEA, 8.

37. Ibid., 3.

38. For evidence that the Franco-German bloc came into existence in 1962 and that its policies were meant as a rejection of Kennedy's Berlin and nuclear-sharing policies, see Schwarz, *Konrad Adenauer*, esp. 590 and 605.

39. For the best account of both the dispute over Berlin policy and nuclear sharing from the European side, see Soutou, *L'alliance incertaine*, 203–65; see also Mayer, *Adenauer and Kennedy*, esp. 43–74; Schwarz, *Konrad Adenauer*, 513–712. Schwarz's account is somewhat unbalanced; he calls Kennedy's Berlin strategy the "appeasement" strategy and credits Adenauer for saving Berlin (even while admitting that the German chancellor was prepared to let Berlin fall without a war). For the American side of the story, see Trachtenberg, *A Constructed Peace*. For another good source, see the diary entries for 1962 and 1963 in Sulzberger, *The Last of the Giants*.

40.  For a summary of the nuclear question from the European response to the flexible response doctrine, see Schwarz, *Konrad Adenauer*, 663-65, and Soutou, *L'alliance incertaine*, 214-29.

41.  See Gavin, "The Myth of Flexible Response." For evidence that Kennedy had moved away from supporting MLF by late 1962, see McNamara's comments, "Anglo-American Meeting," 20 December 1962, PREM 11/4229, PRO; Anglo-American Meeting, 19 December 1962, *FRUS*, 1961-63, 13:1097. See also the apparent willingness to trade MLF away if the Soviets offered something meaningful: *FRUS*, 1961-63, 7, pt. 1: 728 notes, 732, 735, 780-81, 790. Note that Kennedy himself called the MLF a "facade"; see *FRUS*, 1961-63, 13:499, and 173, 367, 502-3.

42.  For details on all these points, see Gavin, "The Myth of Flexible Response."

43.  Dillon to Kennedy, 25 May 1962, NSF Files, Departments and Agencies: Treasury, box 289, JFKL.

44.  Jones to State Department, 13 June 1962, UPA, POF, Treasury, 25.

45.  Memo of Meeting between Kennedy, Ambassador Alphand, M. Malraux, and McGeorge Bundy, 11 May 1962, *FRUS*, 1961-63, 13:695-701.

46.  Gavin to the State Department, 16 May 1962, *FRUS*, 1961-63, 13:702-3.

47.  Kennedy to Gavin, 18 May 1962, *FRUS*, 1961-63, 13:704.

48.  Gavin to the State Department, 28 May 1962, *FRUS*, 1961-63, 13:705-7.

49.  See Rueff, *Le lancinant problème des balances de paiements*.

50.  Press Conference, 4 February 1965, from de Gaulle, *Discours et messages*, vol. 4.

51.  De Gaulle's biographer, Jean Lacouture, argues that de Gaulle was interested in attacking the privileges during the Kennedy period. See Lacouture, *De Gaulle*, 381.

52.  Alphand, *L'étonnement d'être*, 380-81.

53.  Much of this section is based on Gavin and Mahan, "Hegemony or Vulnerability?," 61-84. I would like to thank Erin Mahan for her excellent suggestions and use of her French archival materials.

54.  On Baumgartner's attitude toward cooperating with the United States, see Entretien biographique de Claude Pierre-Brossolette, interview 4, 23, Comité pour l'historie économique et financière de la France, Ministère de l'Économie, des Finances, et d'Industrie, Paris, France, from Gavin and Mahan, "Hegemony or Vulnerability?"

55.  For Baumgartner's reaction to Rueff's views that *all* surplus dollars should be converted into gold, see, for example, Baumgartner to Rueff, letter, 27 June 1961, Wilfrid Baumgartner Papers, box 3BA34, folder Dr 7, from Gavin and Mahan, "Hegemony or Vulnerability?" For figures on French conversion of gold, see "Tableau des transactions en or des États-Unis avec les pays étrangers," in Bourguinat, "Le général de Gaulle et la réforme du système monétaire international," 125, cited in Gavin and Mahan, "Hegemony or Vulnerability?"

56.  Entretien biographique de Claude Pierre-Brossolette, interview 4, 18-22.

57.  On the French bureaucratic schism, see ibid., 32-33.

58.  Note, Olivier Wormser, 30 May 1961, Wilfrid Baumgartner Papers, box 3BA48, folder Dr 2. See also C. W. Sanders (British Board of Trade), "Points for Meeting," 26 June 1961, FO 371/158179, PRO. Cited in Gavin and Mahan, "Hegemony or Vulnerability?"

59.  Berstein, *The Republic of de Gaulle*, 101-24; Loriaux, *France after Hegemony*, 168-74.

60.  Jacques Rueff to Charles de Gaulle, 5 May 1961, Wilfrid Baumgartner Papers, box 3BA34, folder Dr 5, Fondation des sciences politiques, Paris, France. For Rueff's articles, see "Un danger pour l'occident: Le Gold-Exchanges standard," *Le Monde*, 27 June 1961; "Deux Pyramides du credit sur le stock d'or des Etats-Unis," ibid., 23 June 1961; and "Comment sortir du système?," ibid., 29 June 1961. Cited in Gavin and Mahan, "Hegemony or Vulnerability?"

61.    Rueff to Wilfrid Baumgartner, 26 June 1961, Wilfred Baumgartner Papers, box 3BA34, folder DR 7, FNSP, Paris, cited in Gavin and Mahan, "Hegemony or Vulnerability?"

62.    For Giscard's views on the Bretton Woods system, see, for example, Giscard, Speech before the National Assembly, 17 May 1962, sur le projet de loi relatif au renforcement des ressources du FMI, Direction des Affaires économiques et financières, papiers dirécteurs: Olivier Wormser, 63:388–404. On French concerns about the U.S. stock market crash, see Note d'information, René Larre (Conseiller financier, Embassy in Washington), 15 June 1962, Fonds Trésor: Vol. 15, Rélations bilaterales avec les Etats-Unis Côte B10915, folder: Budget, 1956–65. On Giscard's delicate balancing act, see de Lattre, *Servir aux finances*, 150. Cited in Gavin and Mahan, "Hegemony or Vulnerability?"

63.    Conversation between Giscard d'Estaing and James Tobin, 1 June 1962, Walter Heller Papers, reel 24: European budget study file. For Heller's study of French economic planning, see, for example, Heller, "Capital Budgeting Experience in Five European Countries," May 1962, ibid., reel 21: Budget (federal) file; and memorandum, Bundy to Heller, 14 May 1962, ibid., reel 24: European budget study file. Cited in Gavin and Mahan, "Hegemony or Vulnerability?"

64.    Bundy to Heller, 14 May 1962, Walter Heller Papers, reel 24: European budget study file. For French perception of Kennedy's motives, see Jacques Rueff to Philip Cortney, 31 May 1962, ibid.: Ribicoff file. Cited in Gavin and Mahan, "Hegemony or Vulnerability?"

65.    For figures on French dollar conversion, see United States Net Monetary Gold Transactions with Foreign Countries and International Institutions, 1 January 1962–30 June 1962, Fonds Trésor: Vol. 15, Rélations bilaterales avec les Etats-Unis Côte B10915, folder: Budget, 1956–65. On debt repayment, see Note pour le ministre, 3 July 1962, Direction des Affaires économiques et financières, papiers dirécteurs: Olivier Wormser, 119:252. Cited in Gavin and Mahan, "Hegemony or Vulnerability?"

66.    Jacques Reinstein (Minister-Counselor, U.S. Embassy Paris), circular telegram, 29 June 1962, RG 84, France, box 64, folder: Investment of Capital, cited in Gavin and Mahan, "Hegemony or Vulnerability?"

67.    De Lattre, *Servir aux finances*, 150.

68.    Maurice Perouse (Le Directeur du Trésor) to Giscard d'Estaing, Compte-rendu de la 8ème réunion du Groupe de Travail No. 3 du Comité de politique économique de l'O.C.E.D., 16–17 April at Château de la Muette, Fonds 9: Institutions Financières Internationales Côte B54754, cited in Gavin and Mahan, "Hegemony or Vulnerability?"

69.    Gavin to Rusk, 12 July 1962, UPA, NSF, Western Europe, France. See also Heller, Memo to the President, 16 July 1962, UPA, POF, CEA, 9.

70.    Ball to Kennedy, "Visit of French Finance Minister," 18 July 1962, UPA, NSF, Western Europe, France.

71.    No record of Giscard's meeting with Kennedy alone has been found in either U.S. or French archives. Kennedy mentions some of the points he discussed in a later meeting with Federal Reserve Chairman William Martin. Discussion between Kennedy, William McChesney Martin, Chairman of the Federal Reserve, and Theodore Sorensen, 16 1962, 5:50–6:32 P.M., tape 13, Presidential Recording, International Monetary Relations, POF, JFKL (transcribed by Francis J. Gavin). For the meeting with multiple participants, see Memcon, "Payments Arrangements among the Atlantic Community," 20 July 1962, *FRUS*, 1961–63, 13:733; and Memcon (luncheon meeting), 21 July 1962, UPA, JFK NSF, reel 2: 154–55.

72.    Alphand, *L'étonnement d'être*, 381. See also Entretien biographique de Alain Prate, entretien 4, Comité pour l'historie économique et financière de la France. Rueff's other strong ally, Foreign Minister Maurice Couve de Murville, was also preoccupied with strategic issues. While Giscard was in Washington, Couve was in Geneva for talks with the Soviets on Laos and Berlin. See Entretien Couve-

Gromyko in Geneva, 21 July 1962, Secrétariat général, Entretiens et messages, 1956–66, 16:179–81. Dinner of the four ministers of foreign affairs in Geneva, 21 July 1962, Secrétariat général, Entretiens et messages, 1956–66, 16:190–95. Cited in Gavin and Mahan, "Hegemony or Vulnerability?"

73. Memo, the President for the Secretary of the Treasury and Administrator, Aid, 20 June 1962, UPA, POF, Treasury, 25; Bundy for the President, 22 June 1962, UPA, POF, Treasury, 25; the President for the Secretary of the Treasury, 22 June 1962, UPA, POF, Treasury, 25.

74. In September 1962, Giscard began talking about a CRU, a proposal that was debated intermittently until 1965. See, for example, Loriaux, *France after Hegemony*, 185–86. See also Cohen and Smoute, *La politique de Valéry Giscard d'Estaing*, 146–48; and Bourguinat, "Le général de Gaulle et la réforme du système monétaire international," 116–17.

75. Coppock to Johnson, 1 August 1962, *DDRS* 1993.

76. Kaysen to Kennedy, 6 July 1962, *FRUS*, 1961–63, 9:138.

77. Ball to Kennedy, "A Fresh Approach to the Gold Problem," 24 July 1962, Ball Papers, box 15b, "Memorandum to the President on the Gold Problem," SML.

78. Ibid., 4–5.

79. Ibid., 5. Ball argued that "what we must tell our European allies is, therefore, clear enough: if we are to continue to carry our heavy share of the Free world burdens we can do so only under the conditions where our exertions in the common cause do not imperil the dollar and in fact, the whole international payments system. To create those conditions is the first and most urgent task for the Atlantic partnership."

80. Ibid., 10.

81. Presidential Recording, tape 14, 20 August 1962: 4:00–5:30 P.M., International Monetary Relations, POF, JFKL (transcribed by Francis J. Gavin).

82. Ball to Kennedy, "A Fresh Approach to the Gold Problem," 24 July 1962, 14.

83. James Tobin, "A Gold Agreement Proposal," 24 July 1962, Acheson Papers, State Department and White House Adviser, Report to the President on the Balance of Payments, 25 February 1963, HSTL.

84. Memo for the President, "An Interim International Monetary Arrangement," 9 August 1962, Acheson Papers, State Department and White House Adviser, Report to the President on the Balance of Payments, 25 February 1963, HSTL.

85. Heller to Kennedy, "Why We Need an Interim International Monetary Agreement," 9 August 1962, *FRUS*, 1961–63, 9:139.

86. Carl Kaysen and Kermit Gordon, "Gold Guarantees," 18 July 1962, UPA, POF, Treasury, 25.

87. Dillon to Kennedy, 7 August 1962, Acheson Papers, State Department and White House Adviser, Report to the President on the Balance of Payments, 25 February 1963, HSTL.

88. Fowler to Dillon, "The Need to Couple High Level Political Negotiations for More Equitable Burden Sharing . . . with any Political Negotiations for Interim Arrangements Designed to Defend U.S. Gold Reserves," 7 August 1962, Acheson Papers, State Department and White House Adviser, Report to the President on the Balance of Payments, 25 February 1963, HSTL. These memos indicated that the Treasury Department had no idea how important the American troops stationed in West Germany were to the stability and security of Europe.

89. "Appraisal of Problems in the Proposal for an 'Interim Monetary Arrangement,'" 16 August 1962 (no author given but included with a cover letter to Ball from W. N. Turpin, Dillon's Special Assistant), Acheson Papers, State Department and White House Adviser, Report to the President on the Balance of Payments, 25 February 1963, HSTL.

90. Ibid., 4–5.

91. William McChesney Martin Jr., Chairman of the Board of Governors, Federal Reserve System, "Commentary on 'An Interim International Monetary Arrangement' Presented by Chairman Martin," UPA, POF, Treasury, 25, 1.

92. Roosa, "The New Convertible Gold-Dollar System," and Roosa, "International Liquidity."

93. Bundy to Kaysen, 21 August 1962, NSF, Departments and Agencies, Treasury, 6/62–4/63, 289, JFKL. Bundy asked Kaysen, "Is Doug Dillon pinning us to his position by such public statements?"

94. Presidential Recording, tape 14, 20 August 1962: 4:00–5:30 P.M., International Monetary Relations, POF, JFKL (transcribed by Francis J. Gavin).

95. Presidential Recording, tape 11, 10 August 1962: 11:20–12:30 P.M., International Monetary Relations, POF, JFKL (transcribed by Francis J. Gavin).

96. Presidential Recording, Tape 14, 20 August 1962.

97. Ibid.

98. Memo, the President for the Secretary of the Treasury, Under Secretary of State, and Chairman of the CEA, 24 August 1962, NSF, Departments and Agencies, Treasury, 6/62–4/63, 289, JFKL.

99. Giscard d'Estaing to the finance ministers of the Group of 10, 12 September 1962, Direction des Affaires économiques et financières, papiers dirécteurs: Olivier Wormser, 132:347–50. Cited in Gavin and Mahan, "Hegemony or Vulnerability?"

100. Memo from Dillon and Ball to Kennedy, 12 September 1962, with attachment, Memo for Dillon and Ball from Johnson and Leddy, 10 September 1962, FRUS, 1961–63, 9:146.

101. Kaysen to Kennedy, 18 September 1962, FRUS, 1961–63, 9:149.

102. Dillon to Kennedy, 18 September 1962, FRUS, 1961–63, 9:152.

103. United States Net Monetary Gold Transactions with Foreign Countries and International Institutions, 1 January 1963–30 June 1963, Fonds Trésor, vol. 19, Rélations monétaires—Etats-Unis, 1962–78, Côte Z 9984, folder: Transactions d'or monétaire avec l'éntranger. Cited in Gavin and Mahan, "Hegemony or Vulnerability?"

104. For these fears in 1963, see Gavin, "The Gold Battles within the Cold War: American Monetary Policy and the Defense of Europe, 1960–1963," 61–94.

105. See Grin, "L'évolution du système monétaire international dans les années 1960," 389.

## Chapter Four

1. Memo for the Secretary of the Treasury, 19 January 1963, UPA, POF, Treasury, 25.

2. Summary Record of NSC Executive Committee Meeting, No. 38 (Part II), 25 January 1963, FRUS, 1961–63, 13:488.

3. For the issues surrounding de Gaulle's 14 January 1963 press conference, including France's rejection of Great Britain's application to enter the Common Market and de Gaulle's rejection of Kennedy's offer of nuclear assistance, see Soutou, L'alliance incertaine, 230–40. In large measure, de Gaulle was reacting to the results of the Anglo-American Nassau conference, where Kennedy offered British prime minister Harold Macmillan the Polaris missile system to replace the Skybolt missile, which had been canceled. Kennedy offered de Gaulle the same weapon, but since he did not have the submarines to fire the weapon, he considered the offer worthless. It turns out that Kennedy was willing to discuss any aspect of the offer, including helping de Gaulle build the submarines. Marc Trachtenberg argues that the French were genuinely interested in this offer until George Ball essentially sabotaged Kennedy's policy during his January meeting with de Gaulle. See Trachtenberg, A Constructed Peace, ch. 9. Kennedy

commissioned Richard E. Neustadt to write an in-house history and analysis of the events that led to the disastrous Nassau meeting and subsequent de Gaulle press conference. See "Skybolt and Nassau: American Policy-Making and Anglo-American Relations," 15 November 1963, Bator Papers, LBJL.

4. For the origins, meaning, and implications of the Franco-German Treaty, see Lacouture, *De Gaulle*, 333–62; Schwarz, *Konrad Adenauer*, 662–75; and Soutou, *L'alliance incertaine*, 241–59.

5. This discussion of the U.S. policies in Western Europe, and de Gaulle's attempt to weaken American influence, is based on Trachtenberg, *A Constructed Peace*.

6. For shared American and Soviet concerns about a rearmed West Germany intervening in East Germany, see Averell Harriman, "Outlook for Future Discussions with USSR," 30 July 1963, 2–3, NSF, Carl Kaysen: Test Ban and Related Negotiations, box 376, JFKL; and Memcon, Kissinger and Strauss, 10 May 1961, 5, NSF, box 320, JFKL.

7. This interpretation is based on Trachtenberg, *A Constructed Peace*, 360–68. In addition, see Murray, *Kennedy, Macmillan, and Nuclear Weapons*. For a challenge to Trachtenberg's interpretation of the Skybolt and Nassau affair, see Middeke, "Anglo-American Nuclear Weapons Cooperation after the Nassau Conference," 69–96.

8. Summary Record of NSC Executive Committee Meeting, No. 39, 31 January 1963, *FRUS*, 1961–63, 13:158.

9. Summary Record of NSC Executive Committee Meeting, No. 38 (Part II), 25 January 1963, *FRUS*, 1961–63, 13:490.

10. State to Bundy, "A Proposal for Strengthening Our International Financial Position," 24 January 1963, RG 59, SF 1963, FN 12, box 3451, USNA.

11. Remarks of President Kennedy to the National Security Meeting, 22 January 1963, *FRUS*, 1961–63, 13:486.

12. Summary Record of NSC Executive Committee Meeting, No. 38 (Part II), 25 January 1963, *FRUS*, 1961–63, 13:486–87.

13. Summary Record of NSC Executive Committee Meeting, No. 39, 31 January 1963, *FRUS*, 1961–63, 13:159–61.

14. Summary Record of NSC Executive Committee Meeting, No. 40, 5 February 1963, *FRUS*, 1961–63, 13:178.

15. Memorandum for the Record, "Joint Chiefs of Staff Meeting with the President, February 28, 1963—Force Strengths in Europe," 28 February 1963, *FRUS*, 1961–63, 13:517.

16. For the idea that U.S.-Soviet relations moved toward "détente" during 1963, which made it possible for the superpowers to cooperate on a range of issues, from Berlin to nuclear proliferation, to the consternation of the Germans, see Mayer, *Adenauer and Kennedy*; Zubok and Pleshakov, *Inside the Kremlin's Cold War*, esp. 236–74; Schwarz, *Konrad Adenauer*, esp. the chapter entitled "We Are the Victims of American Détente Policy," 687–99; Trachtenberg, *A Constructed Peace*, esp. ch. 9. Note the following analysis of superpower relations after the Cuban Missile Crisis from p. 271 of Zubok and Pleshakov: "By the end of the crisis, Khrushchev began to lean on the idea of joint management of the world with the United States much more than his Communist creed and his—albeit very crude—sense of social justice permitted. . . . The taming of the Cold War, fifteen years after its inception, and almost a decade after Stalin's death, finally happened." As Schwarz points out on p. 666, Adenauer saw these developments as a threat to the Federal Republic's security: "Adenauer again complained bitterly about the Americans: they would deceive no-one, but they were a people at the mercy of such changing moods! . . . Adenauer's immediate entourage was very familiar with his obsession that the Kennedy administration . . . was prepared to come to an American-Soviet arrangement over Berlin and Germany, despite the Cuba crisis. He became more and more obsessed with this idea fixe as 1963 advanced. Every event aroused his deepest distrust . . . the lowest point

in relations with the United States was reached in August 1963 during the quarrel about the GDR signing the Test Ban Treaty."

17.  Rostow to Kennedy, "Balance of Payments Problem," 4 February 1963, *FRUS*, 1961–63, 9:161.

18.  Dillon to Kennedy, 11 February 1963, *FRUS*, 1961–63, 9:163.

19.  Reeves, *President Kennedy*, 431.

20.  Dean Acheson Oral History, 31, JFKL.

21.  Tobin to Acheson, 20 February 1963, UPA, POF, CEA, 10.

22.  "In this whole discussion I have not mentioned the possibility of a change in the rate of exchange of the dollar. This is not because there is anything in the nature of the universe or the Constitution or good common sense to prevent the consideration of this matter at an appropriate time . . . I do not think that time is now . . . I did not want you, however, to think I thought this subject unmentionable." Acheson to Kennedy, cover letter for Dean Acheson, "Recommendations Relating to United States International Payments Problem," 25 February 1963, POF, 27, Special Correspondence Series, JFKL.

23.  Acheson Oral History, JFKL.

24.  Ibid., 31–32.

25.  Acheson, "Recommendations Relating to United States International Payments Problem," 24.

26.  "Meeting between the President and Mr. Dean Acheson, February 26, 1963, 11 A.M., on Balance of Payments," 27 February 1963, *FRUS*, 1961–63, 9:46.

27.  Ibid.

28.  It is hard to understand how Acheson thought that Dillon and the State Department had views that were not far apart. Roosa is a more interesting case. By the autumn of 1963, Roosa was advocating monetary reform, and it is possible that when Acheson talked to him he was of two minds on the matter. Neither Roosa nor other treasury officials were as doctrinaire in their views on reform as Dillon.

29.  Acheson Oral History, 33, JFKL.

30.  Heller to Kennedy, 6 April 1963, UPA, POF, CEA, 10, 4.

31.  Kennedy to the Cabinet Committee on the Balance of Payments, 10 April 1963, POF, Departments and Agencies, Treasury, 4/63, 90, 1, JFKL.

32.  Ibid., 2.

33.  Dillon to Kennedy, "Overall Recommendations on Balance of Payments," 17 April 1963, POF, Departments and Agencies, Treasury, 4/63, 90, 2–3, JFKL.

34.  Ball to Kennedy, "Negotiations at Political Level for Supplementary Financing of Balance of Payments Deficit," Ball Papers, box 15b, 2–3, SML.

35.  Ibid., 12.

36.  Rostow to Ball, "Negotiating Posture Balance of Payments," 26 March 1963, UPA, POF, State, 24, 1.

37.  Ball to Kennedy, "Negotiations," 22–25.

38.  Memorandum for the Record, "Meeting with the President, April 18, 1963, 10:00 A.M. to 12 Noon—Balance of Payments," 24 April 1963, NSF, Meetings with the President, 4/63, 317, 4, JFKL.

39.  Ibid., 2.

40.  Ibid., 5. For Ball's proposal to restrict the sale of foreign securities in the United States, see George Ball, Memorandum for the President, "The Possible Restriction of the Sale of Foreign Securities in United States Markets," 16 April 1963, Ball Papers, box 15b, SML.

41.  Ibid., 5.

42.  Memorandum from Kennedy to the Cabinet Committee on the Balance of Payments, 20 April 1963, POF, Departments and Agencies, Treasury, 4/63, 90, JFKL.

43.   Ibid., 1.
44.   "Meeting with the President, April 18, 1963, 10:00 A.M. to 12 Noon—Balance of
      Payments," 24 April 1963, 11.
45.   Ibid.
46.   Schaetzel to Kitchen, "Balance of Payments and Force Withdrawal," 24 July
      1963, FRUS, 1961–63, 8: microfiche supplement, document 336.
47.   Kaysen to Bundy, 20 May 1963, FRUS, 1961–63, 8: microfiche supplement, docu-
      ment 326.
48.   Klein to Bundy, 10 May 1963, FRUS, 1961–63, 8: microfiche supplement, docu-
      ment 323 (emphasis in original).
49.   Taylor to McNamara, "Preliminary Comments on the Department of Defense
      FY '63 Budget and 1963–1967 Program," NSF, Departments and Agencies, box
      275, 2, JFKL.
50.   Rusk to Taylor, 29 October 1961, FRUS, 1961–63, 8:191.
51.   Kaysen to Bundy, "Secretary McNamara's Memorandum on the Defense Budget
      Dated October 6, 1961," 13 November 1961, NSF, box 275, 1, JFKL.
52.   Kaysen to Taylor, 23 January 1962, FRUS, 1961–63, 8: microfiche supplement,
      document 258.
53.   JCS Meeting with the President, 27 December 1962, FRUS, 1961–63, 8:453.
54.   JCS Meeting with the President, "Force Strength in Europe," 28 February 1963,
      FRUS, 1961–63, 13:517.
55.   See, for example, Kennedy-Bundy-Rusk-McNamara meeting, 10 December
      1962, FRUS, 1961–63, 13–15: microfiche supplement, document 27; Kennedy-
      McNamara-JCS meeting, 27 December 1962, FRUS, 1961–63, 8:449; and Memo-
      randum for the Record, "Joint Chiefs of Staff Meeting with the President, Febru-
      ary 28th, 1963—Force Reductions in Europe," 28 February 1963, FRUS, 1961–63,
      vol. 13.
56.   Kennedy-Bundy-Rusk-McNamara meeting, 10 December 1962, FRUS, 1961–63,
      13–15: microfiche supplement, document 27, 3.
57.   Memorandum from William Y. Smith to Taylor, 9 August 1962, FRUS, 1961–63,
      15:268–69. It should be pointed out that this is an area where Kennedy and
      McNamara saw things much differently. During this same meeting, McNamara
      said it was "wrong to assume the early use of nuclear weapons" since all NATO
      heads of government would want to be contacted first. This disparity—between
      Kennedy's assumption that nuclear weapons would be used almost immedi-
      ately if the Soviets attacked the West, and McNamara's views that nuclear weap-
      ons should not be used at all—was never resolved.
58.   Conversation between Kennedy and Eisenhower, 10 September 1962, Presiden-
      tial Recordings, JFKL (transcribed by Erin Mahan). Earlier in the conversation,
      Kennedy told Eisenhower that de Gaulle would "be perfectly right in talking
      about our immediate use of nuclear weapons, it seems to me, if we didn't have
      [the] Berlin problem, because then obviously any Soviet intrusion across the
      line would be a deliberate one and would be a signal for war." See also Meeting,
      Kennedy and Mayor Willy Brandt, 5 October 1962, FRUS, 1961–63, 15: docu-
      ment 128, 347: "The Geography of Berlin was such that the disadvantage lay
      with us because it was we who would have to make the first military move. This
      detracted from the credibility of our threat of nuclear war and made necessary
      readiness to use our conventional forces."
59.   Conversation between Kennedy, Maxwell Taylor, Robert McNamara, George
      Ball, Averell Harriman, Gen. Lyman Lemnitzer, William Bundy, Michael For-
      restal, and others, 25 September 1962, JFKL (transcribed by George Eliades).
60.   Kennedy-Bundy-Rusk-McNamara meeting, 10 December 1962, FRUS, 1961–63,
      13–15: microfiche supplement, document 27, 3.
61.   JCS Meeting with the President, "Force Strength in Europe," 28 February 1963,
      FRUS, 1961–63, 13:517. See also Memcon, Kennedy and Couve de Murville,
      9 October 1962, FRUS, 1961–63, 15: document 130.

62. Summary of President's Remarks to the NSC, 7 January 1962, NSF, box 313, NSC Meetings, 1962, JFKL.
63. Memcon, Kennedy and Mayor Willy Brandt of West Berlin, 5 October 1962, *FRUS*, 1961–63, 15:347.
64. In fact, if West Berlin was *attacked* by the Soviets, as opposed to simply cut off, there would be *no flexibility* in the American response. When McNamara asked what would happen if U.S. troops in West Berlin were run over, George Ball stated "it's perfectly clear" that the United States would "go to general war." When Kennedy asked if that meant a nuclear exchange, an unidentified speaker told him "that's right." Transcript of Meeting, Thursday, 18 October 1962, 11:00 A.M., in May and Zelikow, *The Kennedy Tapes*, 144. Kennedy reaffirmed this strategy the next day. If the Soviets take "Berlin by force," then he would have "only one alternative": to "fire nuclear weapons" and "begin a nuclear exchange." Transcript of Meeting, Friday, 19 October 1962, 9:45 A.M., in ibid., 176. Kennedy repeated this scenario in his meeting with the congressional leadership three days later. If Berlin were seized, "our war plan at that point has been to fire our nuclear weapons at them." See POF, Presidential Recordings, tapes 33.2 and 33A.1, Monday, 22 October 1962, 5:30–6:30 P.M., JFKL.
65. Chiefs of Staff Committee, Joint Planning Staff, "Reductions in NATO Deployed Forces," 2 May 1963, DEFE 6/84, PRO.
66. "Remarks by Secretary McNamara, NATO Ministerial Meeting, 5 May 1962, Restricted Session," 5 May 1962, OSD-FOIA, 79-481, 12. "In short, then, weak nuclear capabilities, operating independently, are expensive, prone to obsolescence, and lacking in credibility as a deterrent. It is for these reasons that I have laid such stress on unity of planning, concentration of executive authority, and central direction."
67. Kohler to Rusk, "Secretary McNamara's Views on Nuclear Sharing," 12 April 1962, 1 (emphasis added), RG 59, 740.5611, USNA. See also Minutes of Meeting, the President, Rusk, McNamara, and Bundy, 16 April 1962, 2–4.
68. See Minutes of the 505th Meeting of the NSC, 20 October 1962, in *FRUS*, 1961–63, 11:126–36; and Minutes of the 506th Meeting of the NSC, 20 October 1962, in *FRUS*, 1961–63, 11:141–49.
69. "A USSR-US Enforced Non-Proliferation Agreement—the Probable Positions of the FRG, France, Italy, Norway, Belgium, and the Netherlands," undated (presumably June 1963), NSF, Carl Kaysen, Nuclear Energy Matters, 6/63, box 376, 3, JFKL. See also "On Nuclear Diffusion, Volume II," NSF, Carl Kaysen, Briefing Book, vol. II, box 376, 3, JFKL.
70. Interview, Joseph E. O'Conner with Carl Kaysen, 11 July 1966, 131, JFKL. Sulzberger, *The Last of the Giants*, 1004–5, suggests that the administration may have offered France nuclear assistance if it agreed to sign the partial test ban treaty.
71. For a detailed examination, see Gavin, "The Myth of Flexible Response," 847–75.
72. See, for example, Brussels to State, 28 May 1963, RG 59, SF 1963, Def 6, box 3747, USNA; Paris to State, 23 May 1963, RG 59, SF 1963, Def 6, box 3747, USNA.
73. Kitchen to Johnson, "Present Status of Defense Balance of Payments Problems Affecting State Department's Interests," 4 March 1963, RG 59, SF 1963, FN 12, box 3451, 2, USNA.
74. Rusk to Missions in the NATO Capitals, 18 June 1963, *FRUS*, 1961–63, 9:596–97.
75. Johnson to Rusk, "Political Effect of Troop Withdrawals from Europe," 17 May 1963, and attached report, "The Implications for US National Interests of American Military Retrenchment in Europe," RG 59, SF 1963, Def 6-8, box 3749, USNA.
76. McNamara to Kennedy, "Reduction in Department of Defense Expenditures Entering the International Balance of Payments," 16 July 1963, *FRUS*, 1961–63, 9:73.
77. Memo for the Record, "Troop Withdrawals," 4 September 1963, RG 59, SF 1963, Def 6-8, box 3749, USNA.
78. Memo for the Record, 12 September 1963, *FRUS*, 1961–63, 9:87.

79.  Ibid., 87–88.

80.  Rusk to Kennedy, "Department of Defense Proposals for Further Reductions in Balance of Payments Drain," undated, *FRUS*, 1961–63, 9:89–93. See also Popper to Schaetzel, "Points for Discussion with Ambassador Finletter," 19 September 1963, RG 59, SF 1963, Def 6, box 3747, USNA.

81.  "Meeting on Defense Proposals for Further Reductions in Balance of Payments Drain, September 19, 1963, 4 P.M.," 23 September 1963, *FRUS*, 1961–63, 9:98.

82.  Remarks by Roswell Gilpatric, Deputy Secretary of Defense, at the Annual UPI Editors and Publishers Conference, 19 October 1963, RG 59, SF 1963, Def 6-8, box 3749, 6, USNA.

83.  John G. Norris, "Pentagon to Seek Showdown on Basic NATO Strategy," *Washington Post*, 29 October 1963, A15.

84.  Johnson to Rusk, "U.S. Policy on Our Public Position on Troop Withdrawals," 21 October 1963, RG 59, SF 1963, Def 6-8, box 3749, 1, USNA.

85.  Bundy to Gilpatric, 18 October 1963, NSF, Departments and Agencies: Defense, box 274, JFKL.

86.  Ibid., 2. See also Weiss, Memorandum for the Record, 24 October 1963, RG 59, SF 1963, Def 6, box 3747, USNA.

87.  Visit to the United States, 9–17 September 1962, DEFE 13/323, PRO.

88.  Telegram, State Department to Embassy in Germany, 30 July 1963, *FRUS*, 1961–63, 9:184–85. See also p. 184, n. 1. See also Telegram, State Department to Embassy in Germany, 11 July 1963, *FRUS*, 1961–63, 9:176.

89.  Memo of Conversation, "Military Offset Arrangements; Developmental Assistance Activities," 15 November 1962, *FRUS*, 1961–63, 9:157.

90.  Donfried, "The Political Economy of Alliance: Issue Linkage in the West German–American Relationship," 110.

91.  Tape No. 102/A38, 30 July 1963 meeting, second side of cassette no. 1, right after first excision (43:26), JFKL.

92.  Gesprach des Botschafters Freiherr von Welck mit Staatspräsident Franco in Madrid, 29 May 1963, *Akten zur Auswartigen Politik*, 1963, 1:185.

93.  Ibid., n. 9.

94.  Memo of Conversation, "Trade and Fiscal Policy Matters," 24 June 1963, *FRUS*, 1961–63, 9:170.

95.  Memorandum of Conversation, "U.S. Troop Reductions in Europe," 24 September 1963, *FRUS*, 1961–63, 9:187.

96.  Gesprach des Bundeskanzlers Adenauer mit dem amerikanischen Verteidigungsminister McNamara, 31 July 1963, *Akten zur Auswartigen Politik*, 1963, 2:257.

97.  Another irony, common to alliance politics, was that as the Soviets and Americans moved away from the possibility of conflict and toward accommodation, America's leverage over its allies, especially the West Germans, increased, because it could no longer be assumed that the Kennedy administration would simply leave U.S. troops in Europe.

98.  Kennedy-Bundy-Rusk-McNamara meeting, 10 December 1962, *FRUS*, 1961–63, 13–15: microfiche supplement, document 27, 3.

99.  See Schwarz, *Konrad Adenauer*, 688: "This was linked to a situation of considerable change in the international political scene, which was considerably altered in the spring of 1963. Kennedy and Khrushchev drew the same conclusions from the Cuban crisis. After they had stared into the abyss of nuclear war, they believed it advisable to turn to detente. . . . [T]his meant, that in Europe, the Soviet Union must also be prepared not to make any more threats to the Western allies' enclave of Berlin. The acceptance of the GDR and the Wall were also the price of detente. U.S. and British readiness for an agreement in arms control also had to be taken into account; *this would be at the cost of basic German positions that until then had been vigorously defended*" (emphasis added).

100.   In the wake of de Gaulle's press conference and the Franco-German Treaty in January 1963, the United States put enormous pressure on West Germany to re-affirm its allegiance to NATO while distancing itself from de Gaulle. See ibid., 673–76, and Trachtenberg, *A Constructed Peace*, 374–79.

101.   For a document showing the Germans analyzing and weighing all their foreign policy options, but suggesting that the FRG had little choice but to follow the American line, see "Aufzeichnung des Staatssekretars Carstens," 16 August 1963, *Akten zur Auswartigen Politik*, 1963, 2:306.

102.   McGhee Papers, 1988 add, box 1, Memorandum on von Hassel Rusk talks, 10 October 1963, Georgetown University.

103.   Background Paper, "Germany and the U.S. Balance of Payments," 20 December 1963, NSF, Country File, Germany, box 190, 1, LBJL. See also Soutou, *L'alliance incertaine*, 265.

104.   Brief Talking Points on Offset Agreement, 26 December 1963, NSF, Country File, Germany, box 190, LBJL.

105.   The story of the battle within the West German CDU/CSU parties over foreign policy is told in Schwarz, *Konrad Adenauer*, 676–98. There were many other is-sues involved in Adenauer's removal from the chancellorship in the fall of 1963, including the infamous "Spiegal" affair. But it is clear that Ludwig Erhard un-derstood the implications of Adenauer's turn toward France, a policy he re-versed upon entering office. Part of this reversal included an affirmation of the U.S. troop-offset link, at least for the time being.

106.   "Excerpt from Proposed Speech by Secretary Rusk at Frankfurt, Germany, on Sunday, October 27, 1963," RG 59, SF 1963, Def 6-8, box 3749, USNA.

107.   "President's news conference statements on US Troop levels was widely covered in Saturday's German press under such headlines as; 'Kennedy puts an end to speculation' (Die Welt); Kennedy decides against troop withdrawals from Ger-many' (Frankfurter Allgemeine Zeitung); and 'Troops remain in Germany' (Deutsche Zeit Ung)." Bonn to Secretary of State, 2 November 1963, RG 59, SF 1963, Def 6-8, box 3749, USNA.

108.   McNamara to the President, 19 September 1966, Bator Papers, box 21, 1, LBJL. Also in NSF, Trilateral Negotiations and NATO, box 50.

109.   National Security Memorandum, No. 270, 29 October 1963, RG 59, SF 1963, Def 6-8, box 3749, USNA; also in *FRUS*, 1961–63, 13:624–26, and *FRUS*, 1961–63, 9:98–100.

110.   "A USSR-US Enforced Non-Proliferation Agreement—the Probable Positions of the FRG, France, Italy, Norway, Belgium, and the Netherlands," 12 June 1963, NSF, Carl Kaysen: Test Ban and Related Negotiations, box 376, 4–6, JFKL.

111.   "On Nuclear Diffusion," 20 June 1963, NSF, Carl Kaysen: Test Ban and Related Negotiations, box 376, 5, JFKL.

112.   Kennedy to Dillon, 19 September 1962, with attached Galbraith to the Presi-dent, 18 September 1963, UPA, POF, Treasury, 25.

113.   Galbraith to Kennedy, 28 August 1963, *FRUS*, 1961–63, 9:78–86.

114.   Dillon to Kennedy, 23 September 1963, UPA, POF, Treasury, 25.

115.   Ackley to Kennedy, 11 September 1963, UPA, POF, CEA, 11.

116.   Tobin to Kennedy, 11 September 1963, UPA, POF, CEA, 11. Tobin's memo is the most interesting. As in an earlier memo to Acheson, Tobin does not eliminate the possibility of floating exchange rates, nor did he characterize such a system as necessarily disastrous.

## Chapter Five

1.   For Roosa's views, see Oral History, Robert Roosa, 28 April 1968, 10–30, LBJL.

2.   Heller to Johnson, "Background Series on International Monetary Problems—Part III: Solutions and Remaining Problems," 5 August 1964, WHCF, FO 4, box 32, 3, LBJL.

3.   Kaysen to Johnson, "Report of the President's Task Force on Foreign Economic Policy," 25 November 1964, *DDRS* 1993, 1769.

4.   Ibid., 30–34.

5.   Dillon, Ball, and Bundy to Johnson, "Task Force Report on Foreign Economic Policy," 11 December 1964, Bator Papers, box 32, LBJL.

6.   By mid-1967, there were $27 billion in surplus dollars overseas, $12 billion in the hands of central bankers. If all other dollar holders followed de Gaulle's policy, the American gold supply could be quickly run down, even if the U.S. balance-of-payments deficit was eliminated.

7.   For the best work on the origins and implications of de Gaulle's *double-non* in January 1963, see Mahan, *Kennedy, de Gaulle, and Western Europe.*

8.   "L'imperialisme americain le plus insidieux est celui du dollar," Salon dore, 27 fevrier 1963, in Peyrefitte, *C'etait de Gaulle*, 74.

9.   "Nous payons les Americains pour qu'ils nous achetent," Conseil du 20 octobre 1965, in Peyrefitte, *C'etait de Gaulle*, 77.

10.   "Sans independence economique, il n'y a plus d'indendance tout court," Conseil du 19 novembre 1964, in Peyrefitte, *C'etait de Gaulle*, 76.

11.   "A la fin des fins, la dignité des homes se revoltera," Salon dore, 4 janvier 1963, in Peyrefitte, *C'etait de Gaulle*, 15–16.

12.   "Nous payons les Americains pour qu'ils nous achetent," Conseil du 20 octobre 1965, in Peyrefitte, *C'etait de Gaulle*, 77.

13.   "A la fin des fins, la dignité des homes se revoltera," Salon dore, 4 janvier 1963, in Peyrefitte, *C'etait de Gaulle*, 15–16.

14.   "Sans independence economique, il n'y a plus d'indendance tout court," Conseil du 19 novembre 1964, in Peyrefitte, *C'etait de Gaulle*, 76.

15.   "A la fin des fins, la dignité des homes se revoltera," Salon dore, 4 janvier 1963, in Peyrefitte, *C'etait de Gaulle*, 15–16.

16.   "Les Americains poussent les Allemands a faire de notre traité une coquille vide," apres le Conseil du 13 fevrier 1963, in Peyrefitte, *C'etait de Gaulle*, 227.

17.   "A la fin des fins, la dignité des homes se revoltera," Salon dore, 4 janvier 1963, in Peyrefitte, *C'etait de Gaulle*, 15–16.

18.   "L'imperialisme americain le plus insidieux est celui du dollar," Salon dore, 27 fevrier 1963, in Peyrefitte, *C'etait de Gaulle*, 74–75.

19.   Ibid., 75.

20.   "Le dollar decrochera un jour ou l'autre de l'or," Salon dore, 18 septembre 1963, in Peyrefitte, *C'etait de Gaulle*, 78.

21.   "Il faut rendre à l'or son role de support essentiel," Conseil du 16 septembre 1964, in Peyrefitte, *C'etait de Gaulle*, 78–79.

22.   "Nous ne sommes pas assez riches pour nous ruiner," Salon dore, 3 fevrier 1965, in Peyrefitte, *C'etait de Gaulle*, 80–81.

23.   "Salle des fêtes de l'Elysée," 4 fevrier 1965, in Peyrefitte, *C'etait de Gaulle*, 81.

24.   Telegram from Ambassador Bohlen to Under Secretary Ball and Treasury Secretary Dillon, 6 January 1965, NSF, Country File, France, box 170, LBJL.

25.   Telegram from Ambassador Bohlen to McGeorge Bundy, 8 January 1965, Section 2 of 2, NSF, Country File, France, box 170, 2, LBJL.

26.   Telegram from Ambassador Bohlen and Leddy to Under Secretary Ball and Secretary Dillon, 2 February 1965, NSF, Country File, France, box 170, 1, LBJL.

27.   Memorandum for the President from Gardner Ackley, 17 April 1965, Re: Jacques Rueff and Gold, WHCF Confidential, box 144, LBJL.

28.   Memorandum for the President from Gardner Ackley, Re: French Views on the International Monetary System, 12 April 1965, WHCF Confidential, box 144, LBJL.

29.   Ball to Dillon, 4 February 1965, Ball Papers, box 3, LBJL.

30. Griff Johnson to Ball, 4 February 1965, 2 P.M., Ball Papers, box 3, LBJL.

31. Ball to Bator, 4 February 1965, 3:25 P.M., Ball Papers, box 3, LBJL.

32. Summary of Conversations of Under Secretary for Monetary Affairs Deming with German Financial Officials, 19 and 20 February 1965, NSF Agency File, Department of Treasury, box 65, 1, LBJL.

33. Summary of Conversation of Frederick L. Deming, Under Secretary of Treasury, with UK Financial Officials in London, 22 February 1965, NSF Agency File, Department of Treasury, box 65, 6, 18C, LBJL.

34. Memorandum from Under Secretary of Treasury Deming to Secretary Dillon, George Ball, Willaim McChesney Martin, Garner Ackley, and McGeorge Bundy, Re: Financial Talks in the UK and Germany, 9 March 1965, NSF Agency File, Department of Treasury, box 65, 1, LBJL.

35. "Retablir l'equilibre, c'est une operation terrible," Salon dore, 17 fevrier 1965, in Peyrefitte, C'etait de Gaulle, 82.

36. Administrative History, U.S. Department of the Treasury, ch. 12, "International Monetary Negotiations and the SDR Plan," UPA, LBJ, Economy, 52.

37. Fowler to Ball, "International Monetary Reform," 30 April 1965, Administrative History of the Department of State, 1:box 3, ch. 9, sections B and C, LBJL.

38. Frank Schiff to the CEA, "Meeting of CEA Consultants on International Monetary Reform," 10 May 1965, Bator Papers, box 7, 1–5, LBJL.

39. Memo from the President, "Terms of Reference for Study of Monetary Arrangements," 2 June 1965, DDRS 1993, 2373, 1. See also Johnson to the Secretary of the Treasury, "Forward Planning in International Finance," 16 June 1965, DDRS 1993, 2375.

40. "Remarks by the Honorable Henry H. Fowler, Secretary of the Treasury, before the Virginia State Bar Association at the Homestead, Hot Springs, Virginia, Saturday, July 10, 1965, 6:00 P.M.," Bator Papers, box 7, 10, LBJL.

41. "Fowler Succeeds in Maneuvering the U.S. to High Ground on World Liquidity," Weekly Bond Buyer; "U.S. Backing for Conference on Monetary Reform Praised," Washington Post, 13 July 1965; "Fowler Plans Win Support of Wilson," Washington Post, 12 July 1965 (in the Washington Post article U.K. prime minister Wilson reiterated the U.S. position on the dire consequences of failing to reform the monetary system in favor of maintaining an adequate level of liquidity, stating, "There is a danger of the world economy grinding to a standstill . . . if we don't insure that monetary arrangements are adequate to deal with trading possibilities"); "Fowler Proposes a Global Parley on Money System," New York Times, 11 July 1965; Fowler Papers, box 25, International Economy–International Monetary Conference Newsclips 1965, LBJL.

42. Memorandum from Henry H. Fowler for the President, 19 July 1965, Bator Papers, box 7, LBJL.

43. Telegram from the U.S. Embassy in Paris to the State Department, 31 August 1965, LBJL.

44. "Les Americaines se prennent pour les gendarmes du monde monétaire," Conseil du 1 septembre 1965, in Peyrefitte, C'etait de Gaulle, 82–83.

45. During the period 1957–63, the total U.S. deficit totaled $18.4 billion. During the same period, the United States lost $7.3 billion in gold, most of it during the 1957–61 period.

46. Administrative History, U.S. Department of the Treasury, "International Financial and Monetary Cooperation," UPA, LBJ, Economy, ch. 10.

47. Memo, "Informal Report on Ministerial Meeting of the Group of Ten," 7 September 1967, NSF, Fried Files, box 1, LBJL.

48. For an account of the SDR negotiations, see Administrative History, U.S. Department of the Treasury, "International Monetary Negotiations and the SDR Plan," UPA, LBJ, Economy, ch. 12.

49. Wilson to Johnson, 24 October 1964, *FRUS*, 1964–68, 8:27.

50. Chronology of Events, T171/769, PRO.

51. Meeting Notes, 24 November 1964, PREM 13/261, PRO.

52. Fielding, "The Currency of Power," 97.

53. Ibid., 102.

54. Notes of Meeting, 7 December 1964, PREM 13/252, PRO.

55. Fowler to Johnson, 28 July 1965, *FRUS*, 1964–68, 8:175–76.

56. Francis Bator, 28 July 1965, NSF, box 207, LBJL.

57. Fielding, "The Currency of Power," 125–26.

### Chapter Six

1. Ball to Johnson, "Handling the Offset Issue during Erhard's Visit," 21 September 1966, Bator Papers, Erhard—9/66, box 21, LBJL, 1–2a (emphasis added).

2. State to Johnson, "Visit of Chancellor Erhard, September 26–27, 1966," *DDRS* 1993, 3191. Ambassador McGhee revealed that the West Germans were complaining that the Americans were making them the "Pruegelknabe," or whipping boy. See McGhee to State, 17 August 1966, *FRUS*, 1964–68, 15:390.

3. Senate Majority Leader Mike Mansfield introduced a resolution on 31 August 1966 calling for a "substantial" reduction of U.S. forces stationed in Europe.

4. Trachtenberg, *A Constructed Peace*, ch. 9.

5. Dillon to Johnson, "West Germany and Our Payments Deficit," 13 December 1963, NSF, Country File, Germany, box 190, 3, LBJL.

6. Dillon to Johnson, "Late Report on Germany and Our Payments Deficit," 20 December 1963, NSF, Country File, Germany, box 190, 1, LBJL. Apparently there had been some confusion in the Bundesbank over reserve management policy because of Blessing's absence in the last half of 1963; he had suffered a heart attack and apparently those below him were not aware of the arrangements with the United States.

7. Dillon to Johnson, "West Germany and Our Payments Deficit," 13 December 1963, 3–4.

8. Dillon, "German Offset Agreement," 13 December 1963, NSF, Country File, box 190, 1, LBJL.

9. Brief Talking Points on Offset Agreement, 26 December 1963, NSF, Country File, Germany, box 190, 1, LBJL.

10. Embtel 4833 (Bonn), McCloy to Johnson, 21 October 1966, NSF, Trilateral Negotiations and NATO, box 50, 2, LBJL.

11. McNamara to Johnson, 19 September 1966, Bator Papers, box 21, 1, LBJL. Also in NSF, Trilateral Negotiations and NATO, box 50, LBJL.

12. Bundy to Johnson, "Check List for Your Talk with Chancellor Erhard," 12 June 1964, NSF, Country File, Germany, box 191, 1, LBJL.

13. Background Paper, "U.S./German Military Offset Relationship," 5 November 1966, NSF, Trilateral Negotiations and NATO, box 51, 5, LBJL.

14. Fowler to Johnson, "Erhard Visit: Military Offset Agreement," 9 December 1965, NSF, Country File, Germany, box 190, 3, LBJL.

15. Position Paper, "Visit of German Chancellor Erhard, December 19–21, 1965-US/FRG Offset Agreement," 15 December 1965, NSF, Country File, Germany, box 192, 3, LBJL.

16. Bundy to Johnson, "Your Meeting with Chancellor Erhard," 19 December 1965, NSF, Country File, box 191, LBJL.

17. Background Paper, "U.S./German Military Offset Relationship," 5 November 1966, 5.

18. "The Chairman of the Joint Chiefs of Staff and USCINCEUR have concurred in a report which indicated some $4 billion in German requirements for initial

equipping, modernizing and training and for reserve stocks. By way of comparison: The US has a division slice of more than 41,000 men in Europe while the Germans have 27,000; the US has been maintaining 90 days of war reserve stocks in Europe while the Germans barely meet 30 days on some items and considerably less than that in the major equipment area; the US is at 100 percent of equipment levels in all its divisions while the Germans are not only less fully equipped, but equipped with less modern arms." McNamara to Johnson, 19 September 1966, Bator Papers, box 21, 1–2, LBJL. Also in NSF, Trilateral Negotiations and NATO, box 50, LBJL. See also Memcon, "UK Defense Review— NATO Area," 27 January 1966, FRUS, 1964–68, 13:303–5.

19.    This is not to say that the FRG did not have budgetary problems, nor does this deny that there were not certain financial and constitutional restrictions that made fulfilling the arrangement difficult. But the Germans had to know, after years of badgering on the subject, what a political cost abrogating the arrangement would have. In 1961 members of the Adenauer government had used the same excuses to avoid full offset until the Berlin crisis worsened, at which point the FRG decided that it was important to find a way around its difficulties to meet the American demands.

20.    Bator to Johnson, 25 September 1966, NSF, Trilateral Negotiations and NATO, box 50, 1, LBJL.

21.    Chancellor to Johnson, 5 July 1966, NSF, Trilateral Negotiations and NATO, box 50, 2–3, LBJL.

22.    See, for example, Bundy to Kennedy, "The MLF and the European Tour," 15 June 1963, FRUS, 1961–63, 13:592–95; Bundy to Ball, "The Politics of MLF," 25 November 1964, FRUS, 1961–63, 13:121–22; Bundy to Johnson, "MLF—An Alternative View," 6 December 1964, FRUS, 1961–63, 13:134–37; no author (probably by Bundy or Bator), "The Case against Offering the Germans Ownership in Nuclear Hardware," 9 December 1965, DDRS 1993, 3189; Bator to Johnson, "Further Reply to Erhard Letter of July 5: Two Major Decisions," 11 August 1966, NSF, Trilateral Negotiations and NATO, box 50, LBJL. President Kennedy was himself ambivalent over MLF, and at times McNamara was against the force.

23.    The European clause was a proposed provision of the multilateral force that would remove the American veto over the launching of weapons if the Western European nations came together, pooled their sovereignty, and became a "United States" of Europe. This provision, while unrealistic, was strongly supported by the West Germans because it did not completely shut the door on the Federal Republic, as part of a larger European entity, possessing nuclear weapons.

24.    Chancellor to Johnson, 5 July 1966, 2.

25.    McGhee to Rusk, 25 August 1966, FRUS, 1964–68, 15:395.

26.    "We have supported them in the clear stand outlined in the FRG declaration. . . . Since de Gaulle's visit to Bonn in July, however, German support for this position has come increasingly into question. . . . the German government formally and publicly established another basic reason in addition to the military one for the continued presence of the forces; namely, because they serve as a symbol of close Franco-German political cooperation. . . . The pre-eminence accorded to this political reason for the French presence . . . has the clear practical effect of subordinating the military aspects of the issue to the political. . . . This development represents a clear victory of the FonMin for those within the CDU/CSU who are against a hard line toward France. The turning point came in a party meeting on July 18, called by Erhard at the initiative of Strauss. . . . Barzel, Heck, Gertenmaier and Krone reportedly gave strong support to Strauss' insistence on a retreat from the Schroeder position, and won the Chancellor over." McGhee to State, 3 September 1966, FRUS, 1961–63, 13:461–62. See also Knappstein to Schroeder, "France and NATO," Akten zur Auswaertigen Politik, 1966, 2: document 160.

27.  Memo for the President, "Visit of Chancellor Erhard, September 26–27," undated, *DDRS* 1993, 3191.

28.  Bator to Johnson, "Further Reply to Erhard Letter of July 5: Two Major Decisions," 11 August 1966, NSF, Trilateral Negotiations and NATO, box 50, 3, LBJL.

29.  For two excellent dissertations that cover aspects of this subject, see Fielding, "The Currency of Power," and Zimmerman, "Dollars, Pounds, and Transatlantic Security."

30.  "Analysis of Major Decisions in Trilateral Talks," undated, NSF, Trilateral Negotiations and NATO, box 50, 1, LBJL.

31.  Bator to Johnson, "Agenda for Meeting on European Policy," 23 August 1966, NSF, Trilateral Negotiations and NATO, box 50, 1, LBJL.

32.  "Analysis of Major Decisions in Trilateral Talks," 2.

33.  Bator to Johnson, "Erhard Visit, September 26–27, 1966," 25 September 1966, NSF, Trilateral Negotiations and NATO, box 50, 1, LBJL.

34.  Erhard Visit, "Summary Talking Points," undated, Bator Papers, box 21, LBJL.

35.  Conversation between Federal Minister Schroeder and the American Ambassador McGhee, 29 April 1966, *Akten zur Auswaertigen Politik*, 1966, 2: document 125.

36.  Knappstein to the Office of Foreign Affairs, "American Troops in Germany—Offset Agreement," 24 May 1966, *Akten zur Auswaertigen Politik*, 1966, 2: document 161.

37.  Ibid.

38.  Knappstein to Schroeder, "German-American Offset-Agreement," 2 June 1966, *Akten zur Auswaertigen Politik*, 1966, 2: document 176.

39.  Knappstein to Schroeder, 10 June 1966, *Akten zur Auswaertigen Politik*, 1966, 2: document 189.

40.  Knappstein, "Conversation with Secretary of State Rusk; Here, New Rumors about Troop Withdrawal," 23 July 1966, *Akten zur Auswaertigen Politik*, 1966, 2: document 233.

41.  Note of the Secretary of State Carsten, Conversation with General Heusinger, 31 May 1966, *Akten zur Auswaertigen Politik*, 1966, 2: document 171. But West Germany was still very suspicious of the real intent behind the strategy: note how critical Erhard was of flexible response in his meeting with LBJ. "Chancellor Erhard followed this by pointing out the relative security felt by the people during the period of 'massive retaliation,' when nobody ever criticized extra expenses in the defense sector, as opposed to the insecurity felt since the introduction of the flexible response strategy with its 'thresholds' and 'pauses.' " Memcon, 25 September 1966, *FRUS*, 1964–68, 15:427. A month later, Erhard told McCloy that "flexible response is no longer believed in." Conversation between Federal Chancellor Erhard and American Special Envoy McCloy, 20 October 1966, *Akten zur Auswaertigen Politik*, 1966, 2: document 342.

42.  Envoy Lilienfeld, Washington, to the Office of Foreign Affairs, 19 September 1966, *Akten zur Auswaertigen Politik*, 1966, 2: document 294.

43.  Envoy Lilienfeld, Washington, to the Office of Foreign Affairs, "The NATO Defense Plan and Trilateral Talks," 19 October 1966, *Akten zur Auswaertigen Politik*, 1966, 2: document 338.

44.  Knappstein to Schroeder, 10 June 1966.

45.  Note of Ambassador Schnippenkoetter, "Strength of Troops and Foreign Exchange," 1 September 1966, *Akten zur Auswaertigen Politik*, 1966, 2: document 270.

46.  Conversation between Federal Minister Schroeder and the U.S. Ambassador McGhee, 7 September 1966, *Akten zur Auswaertigen Politik*, 1966, 2: document 275.

47.  Envoy Lilienfeld, Washington, to the Office of Foreign Affairs, 19 September 1966.

48. McGhee to State, 20 September 1966, *FRUS*, 1964–68, 15:417–19.

49. Telephone Conversation between Johnson and Senator Russell Long, 1 September 1966, *FRUS*, 1964–68, 15:398–404.

50. Transcript, "Offset and Troop Levels, Chancellor Ludwig Erhard, President Lyndon B. Johnson," 26 September 1986, NSF, Trilateral Negotiations and NATO, box 50, 1–4, LBJL.

51. Ibid., 5.

52. Telephone Conversation between Johnson and Secretary of Defense McNamara, 26 September 1966, *FRUS*, 1964–68, 15:434–35 (emphasis added).

53. Lilienfeld to the Office of Foreign Affairs, "The Chancellor's Visit to Washington; The Question about the American Troops in Europe, Especially in Germany, and about the Foreign Exchange Balance," 20 September 1966, *Akten zur Auswaertigen Politik*, 1966, 2: document 294.

54. Envoy Lilienfeld, Washington, to the Office of Foreign Affairs, "The NATO Defense Plan and Trilateral Talks," 19 October 1966.

55. Lilienfeld to the Office of Foreign Affairs, "The Chancellor's Visit to Washington; The Question about the American Troops in Europe, Especially in Germany, and about the Foreign Exchange Balance," 20 September 1966.

56. Note of Secretary of State Carstens, "Imminent Danger for Our Overall Situation of Foreign Politics," 5 October 1966, *Akten zur Auswaertigen Politik*, 1966, 2: document 312.

57. Note of the Secretary of State Carstens, "German Foreign Policy," 14 November 1966, *Akten zur Auswaertigen Politik*, 1966, 2: document 367.

58. McGhee to State, 17 August 1966, *FRUS*, 1964–68, 15:389. There were troubling signs on the West German domestic front as well. See Ambassador Knappstein, Washington, to Federal Minister Schroeder, Only for the Federal Minister and the Secretary of State, 11 November 1966, *Akten zur Auswaertigen Politik*, 1966, 2: document 366. "The Advisor of the President, Walt Rostow, called me this morning and said the following to me: The President put him in charge to contact me and to say to me that he, the President, is deeply concerned about the fact that the Federal Minister of Interior Luecke talked about the Versailles Treaty and the reparations in an analysis of the Hessian election success of the NPD in connection with the offset problem." See also n. 4, ibid., p. 1500. "During the elections of the Landtag in Hesse on November 6, 1966, the NPD got 7.9 percent of the votes and 8 mandates in the Landtag. In a contribution to the daily newspaper 'Die Welt,' the Federal Minister Luecke related the election success of the NPD among others to the fact that the 'propagandists of the NPD' cleverly used the ill-will and the disappointment of the voters of all democratic parties: 'The democratic parties were defamed as the "45-ers" in a similar way as the "system parties" and the "abstinence politicians" were sworn at 40 years ago. The NDP was successful not least thanks to their anti-American polemic in the Hessian election campaign. The arguments of the election speakers were: the Western Forces force us to purchase out-dated, useless weapons for dear money, while the German industrial workers must be laid off.'" Compare the article "After the Success of the NPD: What Is Now to Do?," *Die Welt*, no. 263, 10 November 1966, 2.

59. McGhee to State, 25 February 1967, *FRUS*, 1964–68, 15:493. For the widening gap between Soviet and *East* German interests, see the comments of Willy Brandt and Couve de Murville, Memcon, Quadripartite Dinner Discussion of East-West Relations; Berlin; The German Question, 14 December 1966, *FRUS*, 1964–68, 15:467 and 469.

60. Note of Ambassador Schnippenkoetter, 4 January 1967, *Akten zur Auswaertigen Politik*, 1967, document 6.

61. Garthoff and Sonnefeldt, "Soviet Intentions: Possible Soviet Uses of Military Force in Europe," 24 October 1966, NSF, Trilateral Negotiations and NATO, box 51, LBJL.

62. Memcon, "Memorandum of Conversation between General Wheeler and Mr. McCloy," 25 October 1966, NSF, Trilateral Negotiations and NATO, box 51, 1, LBJL.

63. Garthoff and Sonnefeldt, "Soviet Intentions: Possible Soviet Uses of Military Force in Europe," 10. Presumably, this meant a possible intervention by West Germany, dragging NATO into a confrontation with the Soviets over the GDR.

64. Ibid., 4.

65. "The Threat: Warsaw Pact Capabilities in the Central Region," undated (likely late 1966–early 1967), NSF, Trilateral Negotiations and NATO, box 51, 15, LBJL. The report also pointed out (p. 8) that it was the "threat of nuclear response" that has "provided and will continue to provide a highly effective deterrent against massive Soviet non-nuclear attack."

66. The West Germans strongly disagreed with the U.S. argument that American troops could be withdrawn without danger. See Note of the Ministry Director Ruete, "Long-Term Defense Planning; Here: Consequences of Potential Troop Reductions of the U.S. and Great Britain in Germany," 14 September 1966, *Akten zur Auswaertigen Politik*, 1966, 2: document 287, 1192–205.

67. Background Paper, "Political Significance of NATO: US Protection of and Political Predominance in Western Europe Exercised through NATO," 18 November 1966, NSF, Trilateral Negotiations and NATO, box 51, 3, LBJL. The rather provocative subtitle has only recently been declassified.

68. Ibid., 4. The section on Germany has only recently been declassified.

69. The British were even less concerned about the military consequences vis-à-vis the Soviets if NATO's conventional capability was downsized. In a passage that has only recently been declassified, an American background paper pointed out that the British believed that while "Soviet capabilities have not receded, the USSR has no intention to attack Europe today. Soviet Doctrine is based on the use of nuclear weapons from the outset. Therefore, a long conventional war in Europe is unlikely; any conflict there is likely to escalate to an all-out nuclear exchange very quickly. Even in the unlikely event of a Soviet attack with conventional forces, NATO forces would be compelled to use tactical nuclear weapons within days, if not hours." The British did recognize the *power political* implications of a troop withdrawal, however: "London fully realizes that its contribution to NATO forces enables it to participate in Allied efforts to control West Germany's present and future place in Europe. . . . Some London editorialists have recently expressed concern that withdrawal of British (and U.S.) troops would lead Bonn to argue that they should be replaced by Germans and 'properly' armed with nuclear weapons." Background Paper, "Factors Arguing for and against UK Troop Cutbacks in Germany," undated (probably November 1966), Trilateral Negotiations and NATO, box 51, 1–4, LBJL.

70. Winthrop Knowlton, Assistant Secretary of the Treasury, to McCloy, "Deming Group Paper on Future German Offset Arrangements," 8 November 1966, NSF, Trilateral Negotiations and NATO, box 51, LBJL. See also Colman to Hinton, "Payments Stabilization Arrangement with Germany," 26 October 1966, box 51, LBJL.

71. Embtel 59292, Rusk to All NATO Capitals, 4 October 1966, NSF, Trilateral Negotiations and NATO, box 50, 2, LBJL.

72. Embtel 4168 (Bonn), McGhee to State, 6 October 1966, NSF, Trilateral Negotiations and NATO, box 50, 1, LBJL.

73. Embtel 4835 (Bonn), McCloy to Johnson, 21 October 1966, NSF, Trilateral Negotiations and NATO, box 50, 2, LBJL.

74. The preliminary talks to begin the negotiations did not begin well. During a postsummit meeting, Erhard and McGhee apparently got into a shouting match about whether or not the FRG had promised to fulfill the current offset arrangement, and Erhard stormed out of the meeting. Conversation between Federal Chancellor Erhard and the American Ambassador McGhee, 6 October 1966, *Akten zur Auswaertigen Politik*, 1966, 2: document 315. Foreign Minister

Schroeder warned McGhee that the Johnson administration's postsummit insistence on complete fulfillment of the current offset arrangement had produced a "significant worsening of the entire mood with all unforeseen consequences. There would be a total ill-will to reach further agreements with America, this means agreements in all areas including the financial area." Conversation between Federal Minister Schroeder and the American Ambassador McGhee, 6 October 1966, *Akten zur Auswaertigen Politik*, 1966, 2: document 325.

75. Embtel 4833 (Bonn), McCloy to the President, 21 October 1966, NSF, Trilateral Negotiations and NATO, box 50, 2, LBJL.

76. Rostow to Johnson, 23 November 1966, NSF, Trilateral Negotiations and NATO, box 50, 5, LBJL.

77. Notes of Ministerial Director Harkort, 17 January 1967, *Akten zur Auswaertigen Politik*, 1967, document 23.

78. History, The Trilateral Negotiations and NATO, undated, NSF, Trilateral Negotiations and NATO, box 50, 5, LBJL.

79. Bator to Johnson, "U.S. Position in the Trilateral Negotiations," 23 February 1967, NSF, Trilateral Negotiations and NATO, box 50, LBJL.

80. Ibid., 3.

81. Led by Under Secretary of the Treasury for International Monetary Affairs Fred Deming, this interdepartmental group was established in June 1965 to investigate how best to reform the international monetary system.

82. Bator to Johnson, "U.S. Position in the Trilateral Negotiations," 23 February 1967, 6.

83. Ibid., 5.

84. Memo for the President, "President's Conversation with John McCloy concerning U.S. Position in Trilateral Negotiations," 2 March 1967, NSF, Trilateral Negotiations and NATO, box 50, 2, LBJL.

85. "Negotiator's Presentation," undated (likely the end of February 1967), NSF, Trilateral Negotiations and NATO, box 50, LBJL.

86. Memo for the President, "President's Conversation with John McCloy concerning U.S. Position in Trilateral Negotiations," 2 March 1967.

87. Embtel 7114 (London), "Trilateral Talks," 3 March 1967, NSF, Trilateral Negotiations and NATO, box 50, 1, LBJL.

88. Notes of Secretary of State Lahr, 2 March 1967, *Akten zur Auswaertigen Politik*, 1967, document 79.

89. See Conversation between the Federal Chancellor Kiesinger and the American Special Envoy McCloy, 4 March 1967, *Akten zur Auswaertigen Politik*, 1967, document 87. Furthermore, Kosygin had made a statement while in London to the effect that the Germans had no choice but to accept the NPT. The Germans were outraged that no British official contradicted or disagreed with Kosygin's statement.

90. Embtel 10266/2 (Bonn), 5 March 1967, NSF, Trilateral Negotiations and NATO, box 50, 3, LBJL.

91. Embtel 10266/3 (Bonn), 5 March 1967, NSF, Trilateral Negotiations and NATO, box 50, 1, LBJL.

92. Conversation between the Federal Chancellor Kiesinger and the American Special Envoy McCloy, 4 March 1967.

93. Bator to Johnson, 8 March 1967, NSF, Trilateral Negotiations and NATO, box 50, 1, LBJL.

94. Letter from Johnson to Kiesinger, 11 March 1967, NSF, Trilateral Negotiations and NATO, box 50, LBJL.

95. Embtel 10754 (Bonn), McGhee to State, 15 March 1967, NSF, Trilateral Negotiations and NATO, box 50, LBJL.

96.     Bator to Rostow for the President, "What We Want from the Germans, Part 3: Overall U.S. Priorities," 24 April 1967, NSF, Trilateral Negotiations and NATO, box 50, 1, LBJL.

**Chapter Seven**

1.      Okun to Johnson, 21 May 1968, WHCF, Ex Fi 10/11/66, box 2, 1-2, LBJL (emphasis in original).

2.      For quotations, see ibid., 1-3.

3.      Division of International Finance, Federal Reserve Board, "Contingency Planning—Sterling," 20 September 1966, Bator Papers, box 8, LBJL.

4.      Ibid., preface.

5.      Ibid., I-4.

6.      Division of International Finance, Federal Reserve Board, "Contingency Plan X: A Proposal to Force Major Surplus Countries to Support the Dollar at Present Parities or to Allow a Relative Appreciation of Their Currencies," 21 September 1966, Bator Papers, box 8, IX-2, LBJL.

7.      Ibid., IX-3.

8.      Rostow to Johnson, 13 November 1967, NSF, Gold Crisis, box 53, LBJL.

9.      Fowler to Johnson, "The Gold Situation," 13 November 1967, NSF, Gold Crisis, box 53, LBJL.

10.     Memo for the President, "Additional Assistance to the U.K. in Support of Sterling," 19 October 1967, NSF, 1968 Balance of Payments Program, box 54, LBJL; Rostow to Johnson, "Contingency Support for Sterling," 19 October 1967, NSF, 1968 Balance of Payments Program, box 54, LBJL; Fowler to Johnson, "Sterling Crisis," 12 November 1967, NSF, Gold Crisis, box 53, LBJL.

11.     "Paris Press on Gold Situation," 8 December 1967, NSF, Gold Crisis, box 53, LBJL. See also Central Intelligence Agency, Directorate of Intelligence, "French Actions in the Recent Gold Crisis," 20 March 1968, CIA, Washington, D.C.

12.     Central Intelligence Agency, Directorate of Intelligence, "French Actions in the Recent Gold Crisis," 20 March 1968, CIA.

13.     "Some Questions and Answers on the Gold Certificate Plan," 24 November 1967, NSF, Gold Crisis, box 53, LBJL; Board of Governors of the Federal Reserve System, "Talking Paper on the Relationship between the Gold Certificate Plan and the Financing of the U.S. Balance of Payments Deficit," 5 December 1967, NSF, Gold Crisis, box 53, LBJL.

14.     Ackley to Johnson, "The Gold Situation," 24 November 1967, NSF, Gold Crisis, box 53, LBJL.

15.     "The Gold Crisis: Nov. 1967–March 1968," 1967, NSF, Gold Crisis, box 53, 4, LBJL.

16.     15 December 1967, NSF, Gold Crisis, box 53, LBJL.

17.     Ibid., 1. See also Rostow to Johnson, 15 December 1967, NSF, Gold Crisis, box 53, LBJL.

18.     For earlier discussions, see Winthrop Knowlton, "1968 Balance of Payments Program: Status and Strategy," 12 October 1967, NSF, Fried Files, box 1, LBJL; Robertson to the Cabinet Committee on the Balance of Payments, 19 October 1967, NSF, Fried Files, box 1, LBJL; Cabinet Committee on the Balance of Payments, 8 November 1967, NSF, Fried Files, box 1, LBJL.

19.     Fowler to Johnson, "Problems Ahead in Europe," 25 May 1967, NSF, NSC Meetings File, box 51, 1, LBJL.

20.     Fowler to Johnson, "U.S.-European Relations," 23 May 1967, NSF, NSC Meetings File, box 51, 1, LBJL.

21.     Department of State Policy Planning Council, "Implications of a More Independent German Foreign Policy," 16 November 1967, Bator Papers, box 22, 3, LBJL. See also Department of State Policy Planning Council, "The Future of NATO: A

Pragmatic View," 1 November 1967, Bator Papers, box 22, LBJL; no author, "Key Issues in U.S.-European Relations," 8 November 1967, Bator Papers, box 22, LBJL.

22. Department of State Policy Planning Council, "Germany and the Future of Western Europe," 23 February 1968, Bator Papers, box 22, 1, LBJL.

23. Minutes of the Cabinet Committee on Balance of Payments, 21 December 1967, NSF, 1968 Balance of Payments Program, box 54, 7, LBJL.

24. For the development of this program and the debate within the administration, see Califano to Johnson, 18 November 1967, NSF, 1968 Balance of Payments Program, box 54, LBJL; Califano to Johnson, 14 December 1967, NSF, 1968 Balance of Payments Program, box 54, LBJL; Rostow and Califano to Johnson, "Balance of Payments Program," 18 December 1967, NSF, 1968 Balance of Payments Program, box 54, LBJL; Cabinet Committee on the Balance of Payments, "An Action Program for Maintaining the Strength of the United States Dollar in a Strong Free World Economy," 18 December 1967, NSF, 1968 Balance of Payments Program, box 54, LBJL; Minutes of the Cabinet Committee on Balance of Payments, 21 December 1967, NSF, 1968 Balance of Payments Program, box 54, LBJL; Fowler to Johnson, "Action Program for the Balance of Payments," 25 December 1967, NSF, 1968 Balance of Payments Program, box 54, LBJL; Califano for the President, 26 December 1967, NSF, 1968 Balance of Payments Program, box 54, LBJL; Califano to Johnson, 30 December 1967, NSF, 1968 Balance of Payments Program, box 54, LBJL.

25. Johnson to Califano, 23 December 1967, NSF, 1968 Balance of Payments Program, box 54, LBJL.

26. President Johnson, "Message to the Nation on the Balance of Payments," 21 December 1967, NSF, 1968 Balance of Payments Program, box 54, LBJL.

27. According to Clark Clifford, the effect this call-up would have on the U.S. balance-of-payments deficit was one of the factors that caused him to recommend that the request not be met. See Clark Clifford Oral History Interview III, 14 July 1969, by Paige Mulhollan, LBJL.

28. History, "The Gold Crisis," undated, NSF, Gold Crisis, box 53, 7, LBJL.

29. Rostow to Johnson, 14 February 1968, NSF, Gold Crisis, box 53, 2, LBJL.

30. Ibid., 2.

31. Ibid., 3.

32. Ibid., 6.

33. Memo for the President, "Gold Problem," 4 March 1968, NSF, Gold Crisis, box 53, LBJL; Memo for the President, 8 March 1968, NSF, Gold Crisis, box 53, LBJL.

34. Memo for the President, "Gold Problem," 4 March 1968.

35. Memo, "Next Steps in International Monetary Policy," 13 March 1968, NSF, Gold Crisis, box 53, 1, LBJL.

36. Rostow to Johnson, "Gold," 14 March 1968, NSF, Gold Crisis, box 53, 1, LBJL.

37. State to American Consul in Frankfurt, Embassy in Brussels, Rome, Bern, and Bonn, 15 March 1968, NSF, Gold Crisis, box 53, LBJL.

38. Rostow to Johnson, "Gold," 14 March 1968.

39. Fried, "Resolving the Gold Issue," undated, NSF, Gold Crisis, box 53, 5, LBJL.

40. History, "The Gold Crisis," 12–13.

41. These telegrams are located in NSF, Gold Crisis, box 53, LBJL.

42. "Meeting with the President—Sterling Balances Problem," 1 July 1968, NSF, Subject File, Balance of Payments, vol. V (1 of 2), box 3, LBJL.

43. Fowler to Johnson, "Agreement on Sterling Credit Package," 10 September 1968, NSF, Subject File, Balance of Payments, vol. V (1 of 2), box 3, LBJL.

44. Telegram, Embassy in Germany to the White House, 18 November 1968, NSF, Subject File, Monetary Crisis, November, 1968, Cables and Memos, 1:box 22, LBJL.

45.   Telegram, Embassy in Germany to the White House, 21 November 1968, NSF, Subject File, Monetary Crisis, November, 1968, Cables and Memos, 1:box 22, LBJL.

46.   Memo, 23 November 1968, NSF, Subject File, Monetary Crisis, November, 1968, Cables and Memos, 1:box 22, LBJL.

47.   James, *International Monetary Cooperation since Bretton Woods*, 193.

48.   The franc was devalued on 9 August 1969. For the reaction of the Nixon administration, see McCracken to Nixon, "Weekly Report on International Finance: The French Devalue," 9 August 1969, WHCF, FO 4-1, box 44, Nixon Presidential Materials Project, USNA.

### Chapter Eight

1.    Nixon to Haldeman, Ehrlichman, and Kissinger, 2 March 1970, NPM, NSC Files, box 341, *FRUS*, 1969–72, 1:95 n. 38.

2.    The NSC expert on international monetary relations, Fred Bergsten, told National Security Adviser Henry Kissinger that Nixon's decision not to address the meeting was "a needless affront to these two valuable organizations" and that no "U.S. President in history has heretofore failed to address the meetings personally when they were in Washington." Bergsten to Kissinger, 27 September 1969, NPM, NSC Files, box 289, *FRUS*, 1969–72, 1:374 n. 7.

3.    Volcker and Gyohten, *Changing Fortunes*, 81.

4.    James, *International Monetary Cooperation since Bretton Woods*, 210. Joan Hoff has convincingly argued that Nixon understood economics far better than his critics have claimed. See Hoff, *Nixon Reconsidered*, 142.

5.    Nixon to Haldeman et al., 2 March 1970.

6.    Gowa, *Closing the Gold Window*; Matusow, *Nixon's Economy*.

7.    Kissinger to Nixon, 25 June 1969, NPM, NSC Files, box 215, *FRUS*, 1969–72, 1:345.

8.    Matusow, *Nixon's Economy*, 11–33.

9.    National Security Study Memorandum 7, 21 January 1969, Department of State Lot Files, Lot 80 D 212, *FRUS*, 1969–72, 1:290. The "Volcker Group" was the successor to the "Deming Group," which had served a similar role during the Johnson presidency. In the end, Nixon ended up ignoring much of Volcker's cautious advice.

10.   Kennedy to Nixon, 11 April 1969, *FRUS*, 1969–72, 1:37.

11.   Summary of the Report of the Task Force on U.S. Balance of Payments Policies, undated, NPM, Transitional Task Force Reports, 1968–69, *FRUS*, 1969–72, 1:1.

12.   See Matusow, *Nixon's Economy*, 130; Kissinger to Nixon, 17 March 1969, NPM, NSC, box 309, *FRUS*, 1969–72, 1:29–30.

13.   National Security Decision Memorandum 12, 14 April 1969, part of which is found in *FRUS*, 1969–72, 1:49 n. 18.

14.   Kissinger to Bergsten and Sonnefeldt, 22 May 1969, NPM, NSC Files, box 681, *FRUS*, 1969–72, 1:63 n. 24. See also Bergsten to Kissinger, 24 March 1969, NPM, NSC Files, box 681, *FRUS*, 1969–72, 1:31–35.

15.   Kennedy to Nixon, 10 May 1969, NPM, NSC Files, box 309, and *FRUS*, 1969–72, 1:332 n. 2.

16.   See *FRUS*, 1969–72, 1: editorial notes 24, 45, and 50.

17.   Foreign exchange offset was less relevant in a flexible exchange rate regime, since deficits could be adjusted by shifting currency values.

18.   Hoff, *Nixon Reconsidered*, 191–94.

19.   Bergsten to Kissinger, 3 December 1970, NPM, NSC Files, box 309, *FRUS*, 1969–72, 1:119.

20.   For the debate and discussion surrounding this key meeting on U.S. international monetary policy, see Kennedy to Nixon, 23 June 1969, NPM, NSC Files,

box 215, *FRUS*, 1969–72, 1:341–44; Action Memorandum from Kissinger to Nixon, 25 June 1969, NPM, NSC Files, box 215, *FRUS*, 1969–72, 1:345–53.

21. McCracken to Nixon, 8 September 1969, NPM, NSC Files, box 215, *FRUS*, 1969–72, 1:368.

22. Kennedy to Nixon, 19 September 1969, NPM, NSC Files, box 289, *FRUS*, 1969–72, 1:369–70.

23. Kissinger to Nixon, 24 September 1969, NPM, NSC Files, box 215, *FRUS*, 1969–72, 1:372–73.

24. Kissinger to Nixon, 14 October 1969, NPM, NSC Files, box 216, *FRUS*, 1969–72, 1:375.

25. Brandt to Nixon, 12 May 1971, *FRUS*, 1969–72, 1:433 n. 155.

26. Paper Prepared in the Department of the Treasury, 9 May 1971, *FRUS*, 1969–72, 1:427–29.

27. Hoff, *Nixon Reconsidered*, 55, and Matusow, *Nixon's Economy*, 84–87.

28. For Connally seizing power, see Connally to Nixon, 29 March 1971, *FRUS*, 1969–72, 1:142–43; Connally to Nixon, 8 June 1971, *FRUS*, 1969–72, 1:440–41; Huntsman to Connally, 8 June 1971, NPM, NSC Files, box 216, *FRUS*, 1969–72, 1:442–43, esp. where Nixon says, "The Connally 1-man responsibility route is the best." For the absence of State and NSC at Camp David, see *FRUS*, 1969–72, 1: 466–67 n. 168.

29. Speech, Secretary of the Treasury, 28 May 1971, International Banking Conference of the American Bankers Association, Munich, Germany, *FRUS*, 1969–72, 1:433.

30. Department of State to Certain Posts—For Ambassador from Treasury Secretary Connally, "U.S. Balance of Payments," 12 April 1971, National Archives, RG 59, *FRUS*, 1969–72, 1:151.

31. Quotation from Connally, in James, *International Monetary Cooperation since Bretton Woods*, 210.

32. *FRUS*, 1969–72, 1:453–60 n. 164.

33. Safire, *Before the Fall*, 515.

34. Ibid.

35. Matusow, *Nixon's Economy*, 156.

36. Paper Prepared in the Department of the Treasury, 10 September 1971, "Requirements for a Secure U.S. Balance of Payments Position," *FRUS*, 1969–72, 1:179–83.

37. Memcon, "President's New Economic Program," 16 August 1971, *FRUS*, 1969–72, 1:469–78.

38. James, *International Monetary Cooperation since Bretton Woods*, 236–38.

39. Ibid., 241–43.

## Conclusion

1. Rostow to the President, cover letter for Harriman memo, "Negotiations," 4 October 1966, NSF, LBJL.

2. Kolko, *The Roots of American Foreign Policy*, 55. For Kolko's view that the Bretton Woods agreements were instruments of America's "open-door" foreign policy, see Kolko, *The Politics of War*, 255–58, 265.

3. McCormick, "World Systems," 94.

4. Gilpin, *The Political Economy of International Monetary Relations*, 134.

5. McCormick, "World Systems," 94.

6. Gilpin, *The Challenge of Global Capitalism*, 67. Gilpin's assessment is representative of a large conventional wisdom surrounding international monetary relations during the 1960s.

7. Cohen, *Organizing the World's Money*, 97.

8.  Kunz, *Butter and Guns*, 99.
9.  Gowa, *Closing the Gold Window*, 52.
10. This highlights the point that the dollar and gold problem was not simply a product of the Great Society programs and the U.S. escalation in Vietnam. For example, during 1965 and 1966, and 1969, the dollar and gold problem was far less pressing than in 1960 or 1963.
11. Consider U.S. policy in Vietnam. In his Bernath Lecture, historian Robert Buzzanco claimed that America's actions in Southeast Asia were motivated by economic gain. But Buzzanco also correctly pointed out the Vietnam War was an economic disaster for the United States, and that the Federal Reserve chairman, William McChesney Martin, and many mainstream business leaders were against further escalation by the end of Lyndon Johnson's term. It is hard to understand how you can have a foreign policy driven by domestic economic gain when that policy worsens your domestic economy, especially when the policy is resisted by the same "elite" that supposedly drove these policies—bankers, corporate leaders, and the Federal Reserve. See Buzzanco, "What Happened to the New Left?," 593–96.
12. Furthermore, few major economies have ever been less dependent on global markets and resources for their well-being than the United States in 1945. Even today, at the height of globalization, a collapse of world trade would hit the United States far less hard than most of the rest of the world. Because rich countries rarely trade with poorer countries, America's economic interaction with the developing world as a percentage of total GDP has *always* been very small. As for the fearsome industrial-military complex that purportedly drove America's foreign policy, it did not have the power to stop sudden and dramatic cuts in military procurement in the immediate postwar period (1946–50), the 1970s, and the 1990s. Dozens of defense contractors have gone out of business in the last fifty years. Nor did this military-industrial complex have any influence over U.S. troop withdrawals overseas.

### Appendix A

1.  Stern, *The Balance of Payments*, 3.
2.  To some extent, this double counting was misleading. The desire by Europeans to hold short-term dollar bonds indicated a short-term liquidity preference but not necessarily an unwillingness to acquire dollars. Europeans wanted to invest dollars but in ways which, because of their liquidity preference, counted negatively against the American balance of payments.
3.  Stern, *The Balance of Payments*.
4.  Much of this reduced gold outflow was due to the operation of the gold pool, a group made up of the largest Western economies. The gold pool countries agreed in 1961 to supply gold to the London market in order to maintain a private market price of thirty-five dollars an ounce and avoid a market breakout like the one that occurred in the summer and fall of 1960.

# Bibliography

**Manuscript Collections**
*Great Britain*
Public Record Office, Kew, England
  CAB 128 and 129: Cabinet meetings and memoranda
  FO 371: Foreign Office, Political Correspondence
  PREM 10, 11, and 13: Prime Minister's office files

*United States*
Dwight D. Eisenhower Library, Abilene, Kansas
  Administration Series
  Dwight D. Eisenhower Diary Series
  Papers of Dwight D. Eisenhower as President (Ann Whitman File)
  International Series
  National Security Council Series
  White House Office, International Trips and Meetings Series
Georgetown University, Washington, D.C.
  George McGhee Papers
Lyndon Baines Johnson Library, Austin, Texas
  George Ball Papers
  Francis Bator Papers
  Henry Fowler Papers
  Edward Fried Files
  National Security Files
  Oral History Collection
  Recordings and Transcripts of Conversations and Meetings, Recordings of
    Telephone Conversations, White House Series
  White House Central Office Files
John F. Kennedy Library, Boston, Massachusetts
  George Ball Papers
  Roswell Gilpatric Papers
  John F. Kennedy Library Presidential Recordings Collection
  National Security Files
  Oral History Collection
  President's Office Files
Seeley Mudd Library, Princeton University, Princeton, New Jersey
  George Ball Papers
Harry S. Truman Library, Independence, Missouri
  Dean Acheson Papers
United States National Archives, College Park, Maryland
  Nixon Presidential Materials Project, White House Central Files
    Name File and Subject File

Record Group 56: Department of Treasury Files
Record Group 59: Department of State Central Files

**Microform Sources**

*Declassified Documents Reference Service*. Declassified documents on microfiche and printed index, compiled periodically. Washington, D.C.: Carollton Press.

*The Diaries of Dwight D. Eisenhower: 1953–1961*. Documents and printed index. Frederick, Md.: University Publications of America, 1987.

*Minutes and Documents of the Cabinet Meetings of President Eisenhower*. Documents and printed index. Frederick, Md.: University Publications of America, 1980.

*President Dwight D. Eisenhower's Office Files, 1953–1961, part 1: Eisenhower Administration Series*. Documents and printed index. Frederick, Md.: University Publications of America, 1991.

*President Dwight D. Eisenhower's Office Files, 1953–1961, part 2: International Series*. Documents and printed index. Frederick, Md.: University Publications of America, 1991.

*President John F. Kennedy's Office Files, 1961–1963, part 3: Departments and Agencies File*. Documents and printed index. Bethesda, Md.: University Publications of America, 1989.

*John F. Kennedy National Security Files—Western Europe: National Security Files, 1961–1963*. Documents and printed index. Frederick, Md.: University Publications of America, 1987.

*Lyndon B. Johnson National Security Files—Western Europe: National Security Files, 1963–1969*. Documents and printed index. Frederick, Md.: University Publications of America, 1993.

*The National Economy under President Johnson*. Documents and printed index. Frederick, Md.: University Publications of America, 1983.

**Published Documents**

*Foreign Relations of the United States*

*FRUS*, 1958–60:

Volume 4: *Foreign Economic Policy*. Washington, D.C.: GPO, 1992.

Volume 7, Part 1: *Western European Integration and Security; Canada*. Washington, D.C.: GPO, 1993.

Volume 7, Part 2: *Western Europe*. Washington, D.C.: GPO, 1993.

Volume 8: *Berlin Crisis, 1958–1959*. Washington, D.C.: GPO, 1993.

Volume 9: *Berlin Crisis, 1959–1960; Germany; Austria*. Washington, D.C.: GPO, 1993.

*FRUS*, 1961–63:

Volume 7: *Arms Control and Disarmament*. Washington, D.C.: GPO, 1995.

Volume 8: *National Security Policy*. Washington, D.C.: GPO, 1996.

Volume 9: *Foreign Economic Policy*. Washington, D.C.: GPO, 1995.

Volume 13: *West Europe and Canada*. Washington, D.C.: GPO, 1994.

Volume 14: *Berlin Crisis, 1961–1962*. Washington, D.C.: GPO, 1993.

Volume 15: *Berlin Crisis, 1962–1963*. Washington, D.C.: GPO, 1994.

*FRUS*, 1964–68:

Volume 8: *International Monetary and Trade Policy*. Washington, D.C.: GPO, 1998.

Volume 12: *Western Europe*. Washington, D.C.: GPO, 2001.

Volume 13: *Western Europe Region*. Washington, D.C.: GPO, 1995.

Volume 15: *Germany and Berlin*. Washington, D.C.: GPO, 1999.

*FRUS*, 1969–72:

Volume 1: *International Monetary and Trade Policy*. Washington, D.C.: GPO, 2002.

*Akten zur Auswartigen Politik der Bundesrepublik Deutschland*

1963. Edited by Rainer Blasius, Mechhild Lindermann, and Ilse Dorothee Pautsch. Munich: Oldenbourg Verlag, 1994.

1966. Edited by Matthias Peter and Harold Rosenbach. Munich: Oldenbourg Verlag, 1997.

1967. Edited by Jurgen Klockler, Ilse Dorothee Pautsch, Matthias Peter, and Harold Rosenbach. Munich: Oldenbourg Verlag, 1998.

### Secondary Sources

Aldcroft, D. H. *From Versailles to Wall Street: The International Economy in the 1920s*. Berkeley: University of California Press, 1977.

Alphand, Herve. *L'étonnement d'être: Journal*. Paris: Fayard, 1977.

Anderson, B. L., and P. L. Cottrell, eds. *Money and Banking in England: The Development of the Banking System, 1694–1914*. Newton Abbot: David & Charles, 1974.

Argy, Victor. *The Postwar International Money Crisis: An Analysis*. London: George Allen & Unwin, 1981.

Aronson, Jonathan David. *Money and Power: Banks and the World Monetary System*. Sage Library of Social Research, vol. 66. London: Sage Publications, 1977.

Ball, George. *The Past Has Another Pattern*. New York: W. W. Norton, 1972.

Bergsten, Fred. *The Dilemmas of the Dollar*. New York: Council on Foreign Relations, 1975.

Bernholz, Peter. *Flexible Exchange Rate in Historical Perspective*. Princeton Studies in International Finance, no. 49. Princeton: Princeton University Press, 1982.

Berstein, Serge. *The Republic of de Gaulle, 1958–1969*. Translated by Peter Morris. Cambridge: Cambridge University Press, 1993.

Beschloss, Michael R. *The Crisis Years: Kennedy and Khrushchev, 1960–1963*. New York: Harper Collins, 1991.

Best, Richard. *"Cooperation with Like-Minded Peoples": British Influences on American Security Policy, 1945–1949*. New York: Greenwood Press, 1986.

Block, Fred L. *The Origins of International Economic Disorder: A Study of United States International Monetary Policy from World War II to the Present*. Berkeley: University of California Press, 1977.

Bloomfield, Arthur. *Monetary Policy under the International Gold Standard, 1880–1914*. New York: Federal Reserve Bank of New York, 1959.

Borden, William S. "Defending Hegemony: American Foreign Economic Policy." In Thomas G. Paterson, ed., *Kennedy's Quest for Victory: American Foreign Policy, 1961–1963*, 83–85. New York: Oxford University Press, 1989.

Bordo, Michael D., and Barry Eichengreen, eds. *A Retrospective on the Bretton Woods System: Lessons for International Monetary Reform*. Chicago: University of Chicago Press, 1993.

Bordo, Michael, and Anna Schwartz, eds. *A Perspective on the Classical Gold Standard, 1821–1931*. Chicago: University of Chicago Press, 1984.

Bourguinat, Henri. "Le général de Gaulle et la réforme du système monétaire international: La contestation manquée de l'hégémonie du dollar." In *De Gaulle en son siècle*. Paris: Institut Charles de Gaulle, 1992.

Brown, Brendan. *The Flight of International Capital: A Contemporary History*. London: Routledge, 1987.

Buzzanco, Robert. "What Happened to the New Left? Toward a Radical Reading of American Foreign Relations." *Diplomatic History* 23, no. 4 (Fall 1999): 575–607.

Cairncross, A. *Years of Recovery: British Economic Policy, 1945–1951*. London: Methuen, 1985.

Cairncross, A., and B. Eichengreen. *Sterling in Decline: The Devaluations of 1931, 1949, and 1967*. Oxford: Blackwell, 1983.

Calleo, David P. *Beyond American Hegemony: The Future of the Western Alliance*. New York: Basic Books, 1987.

——. *The Imperious Economy*. Cambridge, Mass.: Harvard University Press, 1982.

Calleo, David P., and Benjamin M. Rowland. *America and the World Political Economy: Atlantic Dreams and National Realities*. Bloomington: Indiana University Press, 1973.

Capie, Forrest, and Geoffrey Wood, eds. *A Monetary History of the United Kingdom, 1870–1982*. Vol. 1, *Data Sources and Methods*. London: Macmillan, 1986.

Casey, Kevin. *Saving International Capitalism during the Early Truman Presidency: The National Advisory Council on International Monetary and Financial Problems*. New York: Routledge, 2001.

Cassis, Youssef. *Finance and Financiers in European History, 1880–1960*. Cambridge: Cambridge University Press, 1992.

Chernow, Ron. *The House of Morgan: An American Banking Dynasty and the Rise of Modern Finance*. New York: Simon & Schuster, 1990.

Clapham, John. *The Bank of England: A History*. 2 vols. Cambridge: Cambridge University Press, 1945.

Clarke, Richard. *Anglo-American Economic Collaboration in War and Peace, 1942–1949*. Edited by Alec Cairncross. Oxford: Clarendon Press, 1982.

Clarke, Stephen V. O. *The Reconstruction of the International Monetary System: The Attempts of 1922 and 1933*. Princeton Studies in International Finance, no. 33. Princeton: Princeton University Press, 1973.

Cohen, Benjamin J. *Organizing the World's Money: The Political Economy of International Monetary Relations*. New York: Basic, 1977.

Cohen, Samy, and Marie-Claude Smoute. *La politique de Valéry Giscard d'Estaing*. Paris: Fondation des sciences politiques, 1985.

Coombs, Charles. *The Arena of International Finance*. New York: Wiley Press, 1976.

Cooper, Richard N. *The International Monetary System: Essays in World Economics*. Cambridge, Mass.: MIT Press, 1987.

Corden, W. M. "The Geometric Representation of Policies to Attain Internal and External Balance." In Richard N. Cooper, ed., *International Finance*, 256–90. Baltimore: Penguin Books, 1969.

——. *Inflation, Exchange Rates and the World Economy: Lectures on International Monetary Economics*. Chicago: University of Chicago Press, 1985.

Costigliola, Frank. "The Pursuit of Atlantic Community: Nuclear Arms, Dollars, and Berlin." In Thomas G. Paterson, ed., *Kennedy's Quest for Victory: American Foreign Policy, 1961-1963*, 24-56. New York: Oxford University Press, 1989.

Curtis, Michael. *Western European Integration*. New York: Harper and Row, 1965.

Davis, Lance E., and Robert A. Huttenback. *Mamon and the Pursuit of Empire: The Political Economy of British Imperialism, 1880-1913*. Cambridge: Cambridge University Press, 1986.

De Cecco, Marcello. *The International Gold Standard: Money and Empire*. 2nd ed. London: Frances Pinter, 1984.

de Gaulle, Charles. *Discours et messages*. Vol. 4, *Pour l'effort, Aout 1962-Decembre 1965*. Paris: Omnibus/Plon, 1993.

de Grauwe, Paul. *International Money: Post-War Trends and Theories*. Oxford: Clarendon Press, 1989.

de Lattre, André. *Servir aux finances*. Paris: Comité pour l'histoire économique et financière de la France, 1999.

de Vries, Margaret Garritsen. *Balance of Payments Adjustment 1945 to 1986: The IMF Experience*. Washington, D.C.: International Monetary Fund, 1987.

———. *The International Monetary Fund, 1966-1971: The System under Stress*. Vols. 1-2. Washington, D.C.: International Monetary Fund, 1976.

Diebold, William, Jr. *Trade and Payments in Western Europe: A Study in European Economic Cooperation*. New York: Harper & Bros., 1952.

Donfried, Karen E. "The Political Economy of Alliance: Issue Linkage in the West German-American Relationship." Ph.D. dissertation, Fletcher School of Law and Diplomacy, Tufts University, 1991.

Doyle, Michael. *Empires*. Ithaca: Cornell University Press, 1986.

Drummond, I. M. *British Economic Policy and the Empire: 1919-1939*. London: Allen & Unwin, 1972.

Eckes, Alfred E. *A Search for Solvency: Bretton Woods and the International Monetary System, 1941-1971*. Austin: University of Texas Press, 1975.

Eichengreen, Barry. *Elusive Stability: Essays in the History of International Finance, 1919-1939*. Cambridge: Cambridge University Press, 1990.

———. *Globalizing Capital: A History of the International Monetary System*. Princeton: Princeton University Press, 1996.

———. *Golden Fetters: The Gold Standard and the Great Depression*. New York: Oxford University Press, 1992.

———. *International Monetary Arrangements for the Twenty-first Century*. Washington, D.C.: Brookings Institution, 1994.

Eisenhower, Dwight D. *Waging Peace: 1956-1960*. Garden City, N.Y.: Doubleday, 1965.

Feis, Herbert. *The Diplomacy of the Dollar: First Era, 1919-1932*. Baltimore: Johns Hopkins Press, 1950.

Fielding, Jeremy. "The Currency of Power: Anglo-American Economic Diplomacy and the Making of British Foreign Policy, 1964-1968." Ph.D. dissertation, Yale University, 2000.

Fischer, Stanley. "Stability and Exchange Rate Systems in a Monetarist Model of the Balance of Payments." In Robert Aliber, ed., *The Political Economy of Monetary Reform*, 59-73. London: Macmillan, 1977.

Fleming, Ian. *Goldfinger*. New York: Signet, 1959.

Fleming, J. Marcus. "Domestic Financial Policies under Fixed and under Floating Exchange Rates." In Richard N. Cooper, ed., *International Finance*, 291–303. Baltimore: Penguin Books, 1969.

Friedman, Milton. "The Case for Flexible Exchange Rates." In *Essays in Positive Economics*, 157–204. Chicago: University of Chicago Press, 1953.

——. *Money Mischief: Episodes in Monetary History*. New York: Harcourt Brace Jovanovich, 1992.

——. "The Price of the Dollar." In *Dollars and Deficits: Inflation, Monetary Policy and the Balance of Payments*. Englewood Cliffs, N.J.: Prentice-Hall, 1968.

Friedman, Milton, and Anna Jacobson Schwartz. *A Monetary History of the United States: 1867–1960*. Princeton: Princeton University Press, 1963.

Gaddis, John Lewis. *Strategies of Containment: A Critical Appraisal of Postwar American National Security Policy*. Oxford: Oxford University Press, 1982.

——. "The Unexpected John Foster Dulles: Nuclear Weapons, Communism, and the Russians." In Richard Immerman, ed., *Dulles and the Diplomacy of the Cold War*, 49–58. Princeton: Princeton University Press, 1990.

Galbraith, John Kenneth. *Letters to Kennedy*. Cambridge, Mass.: Harvard University Press, 1998.

Gallarotti, Giulio. *The Anatomy of an International Monetary Regime: The Classical Gold Standard, 1880–1914*. New York: Oxford University Press, 1995.

Gardner, Richard N. *Sterling-Dollar Diplomacy: The Origins and the Prospects of Our International Economic Order*. New York: McGraw-Hill, 1969.

Gavin, Francis J. "The Gold Battles within the Cold War: American Monetary Policy and the Defense of Europe, 1960–1963." *Diplomatic History* 26, no. 1 (2002): 61–94.

——. "The Myth of Flexible Response: American Strategy in Europe during the 1960s." *International History Review* 23 (December 2001).

Gavin, Francis J., and Erin Mahan. "Hegemony or Vulnerability? Giscard, Ball, and the Gold Standstill." *Journal of European Integration History* 6, no. 2 (December 2000): 61–84.

Gilbert, Martin. *Quest for World Monetary Order: The Gold-Dollar System and Its Aftermath*. New York: John Wiley & Sons, 1980.

Gillingham, John R. *Coal, Steel, and the Rebirth of Europe, 1945–1955: The Germans and French from Ruhr Conflict to Economic Community*. Cambridge: Cambridge University Press, 1991.

Gilpin, Robert. *The Challenge of Global Capitalism: The World in the Twenty-first Century*. Princeton: Princeton University Press, 2000.

——. "The Nature of Political Economy." In Robert J. Art and Robert Jervis, eds., *International Politics*, 275–90. Boston: Little, Brown, 1985.

——. *The Political Economy of International Monetary Relations*. Princeton: Princeton University Press, 1987.

——. *U.S. Power and the Multinational Corporation*. New York: Basic, 1975.

Goodhardt, Charles. *The Evolution of Central Banks*. Cambridge: Cambridge University Press, 1989.

Gowa, Joanne. *Closing the Gold Window: Domestic Politics and the End of Bretton Woods*. Ithaca: Cornell University Press, 1983.

Grin, G. "L'évolution du système monétaire international dans les années 1960: Les positions des économistes Robert Triffin et Jacques Rueff." *Relations Internationales* (Winter 1999).

Grubel, Herbert G. *The International Monetary System: Efficiency and Practical Alternatives*. New York: Penguin Books, 1984.

Haberler, Gottfried, and Thomas Willet. *U.S. Balance of Payments Policies and International Monetary Reform: A Critical Analysis*. Washington, D.C.: American Enterprise Institute, 1968.

Hanrieder, Wolfram P. *Germany, America, Europe: Forty Years of German Foreign Policy*. New Haven: Yale University Press, 1989.

Hardach, Gerd. "The Marshall Plan in Germany, 1948–1952." *Journal of European Economic History* 16 (Winter 1987): 433–85.

Hathaway, Robert M. *Ambiguous Partnership: Britain and America, 1944–1947*. New York: Columbia University Press, 1986.

Helleniner, Eric. *States and the Reemergence of Global Finance: From Bretton Woods to the 1990s*. Ithaca: Cornell University Press, 1994.

Hirsch, Fred, Michael Doyle, and Edward L. Morse. *Alternatives to Monetary Disorder*. New York: Council on Foreign Relations, 1977.

Hitchcock, William. *France Restored: Cold War Diplomacy and the Quest for Leadership in Europe, 1944–1954*. Chapel Hill: University of North Carolina Press, 1998.

Hoff, Joan. *Nixon Reconsidered*. New York: Basic Books, 1994.

Hoffman, Stanley, and Charles Maier, eds. *The Marshall Plan: A Retrospective*. Boulder, Colo.: Westview, 1984.

Hogan, Michael J. *Informal Entente: The Private Structure of Cooperation in Anglo-American Economic Diplomacy, 1918–1928*. Columbia: University of Missouri Press, 1977.

——. *The Marshall Plan: America, Britain and the Reconstruction of Western Europe, 1947–1952*. Cambridge: Cambridge University Press, 1987.

Horsefield, Keith J. *The International Monetary Fund, 1945–1965: Twenty Years of International Monetary Cooperation*. Washington, D.C.: International Fund, 1969.

Howson, Susan. "The Management of Sterling, 1932–39." *Journal of Economic History* 40 (1980): 53–60.

Ikenberry, John G. "A World Economy Restored: Expert Consensus and the Anglo-American Postwar Settlement." *International Organizations* 46, no. 1 (Winter 1992): 289–321.

James, Harold. *International Monetary Cooperation since Bretton Woods*. New York: Oxford University Press, 1996.

Johnson, H. G. "Theoretical Problems of the International Monetary System." In Richard N. Cooper, ed., *International Finance*, 304–36. Baltimore: Penguin Books, 1969.

——. "Towards a General Theory of the Balance of Payments." In Richard N. Cooper, ed., *International Finance*, 237–55. Baltimore: Penguin Books, 1969.

——. "The Transfer Problem and Exchange Stability." In Richard N. Cooper, ed., *International Finance*, 62–86. Baltimore: Penguin Books, 1969.

Johnson, Peter A. *The Government of Money: Monetarism in Germany and the United States*. Ithaca: Cornell University Press, 1998.

Kaiser, D. *Economic Diplomacy and the Origins of the Second World War*. Princeton: Princeton University Press, 1980.

Kaplan, Jacob J., and Gunter Schleiminger. *The European Payments Union: Financial Diplomacy in the 1950s*. Oxford: Clarendon, 1989.

Kaufman, Burton I. *Trade and Aid: Eisenhower's Foreign Economic Policy, 1953–1961.* Baltimore: Johns Hopkins University Press, 1982.

Kelly, Janet. "International Monetary Systems and National Security." In Klaus Knorr and Frank N. Trager, eds., *Economic Issues and National Security.* Lawrence: Regent's Press of Kansas, 1977.

Kenen, Peter. *British Monetary Policy and the Balance of Payments, 1951–1957.* Cambridge, Mass.: Harvard University Press, 1960.

Kenen, Peter, Francesco Papadia, and Fabrizio Saccomanni, eds. *The International Monetary System.* Cambridge: Cambridge University Press, 1994.

Kennedy, Paul. *The Rise and Fall of the Great Powers: Economic Change and Military Conflict from 1500 to 2000.* New York: Random House, 1987.

Keohane, R. *After Hegemony: Cooperation and Discord in the World Political Economy.* Princeton: Princeton University Press, 1984.

——. "The Theory of Hegemonic Stability and Changes in International Regimes, 1967–1977." In O. Holsti, R. Siverson, and A. George, eds., *Change in the International System.* Boulder, Colo.: Westview, 1980.

Keynes, John M. *The Collected Writings of John Maynard Keynes.* Vol. 25. Edited by Donald Moggridge. London: Macmillan, 1980.

——. *The Collected Writings of John Maynard Keynes.* Vol. 26. Edited by Donald Moggridge. London: Macmillan, 1980.

——. *The Economic Consequences of the Peace.* New York: Harcourt, Brace and Howe, 1920.

Kindleberger, Charles. *Europe and the Dollar.* Cambridge: MIT Press, 1966.

——. *A Financial History of Western Europe.* 2nd ed. Oxford: Oxford University Press, 1993.

——. *The World in Depression, 1929–1939.* Berkeley: University of California Press, 1973.

Kirshner, Jonathan. *Currency and Coercion: The Political Economy of International Monetary Power.* Princeton: Princeton University Press, 1995.

Kolko, Gabriel. *The Politics of War: The World and United States Foreign Policy, 1943–1945.* New York: Random House, 1968.

——. *The Roots of American Foreign Policy.* Boston: Beacon Press, 1969.

Krasner, S. D. "State Power and the Structure of International Trade." *World Politics* 28 (1976): 317–47.

Kuisel, Richard. *Capitalism and the State in Modern France: Renovation and Economic Management in the Twentieth Century.* New York: Cambridge University Press, 1981.

Kunz, Diane. *Butter and Guns: America's Cold War Economic Diplomacy.* New York: Free Press, 1997.

——. *The Economic Diplomacy of the Suez Crisis.* Chapel Hill: University of North Carolina Press, 1991.

Lacouture, Jean. *De Gaulle: The Ruler, 1945–1970.* New York: W. W. Norton, 1992.

Landes, David. *The Unbound Prometheus: Technological Change and Industrial Development in Western Europe from 1750 to the Present.* Cambridge: Cambridge University Press, 1969.

Lewis, Arthur. *Growth and Fluctuations, 1870–1913.* London: Weidenfeld and Nicolson, 1978.

Lindert, Peter. *Key Currencies and Gold: 1900–1913.* Princeton Studies in International Finance, no. 24. Princeton: Princeton University Press, 1969.

Loriaux, Michael M. *France after Hegemony: International Change and Financial Reform*. Ithaca: Cornell University Press.

Lundestad, Geir. *Empire by Integration: The United States and European Integration, 1945–1997*. Oxford: Oxford University Press, 1998.

———. "Empire by Invitation? The United States and Western Europe, 1945–1952." In Charles S. Maier, ed., *The Cold War in Europe*. New York: Markus Wiener Publisher, 1994.

Machlup, Fritz. "The Cloakroom Rule of International Reserves: Reserve Creation and Resources Transfer." In Richard N. Cooper, ed., *International Finance*, 337–57. Baltimore: Penguin Books, 1969.

Mahan, Erin. *Kennedy, de Gaulle, and Western Europe*. New York: Palgrave, Macmillan, 2002.

Maier, Charles. *Recasting Bourgeois Europe: Stabilization in France, Germany and Italy in the Decade after World War I*. Princeton: Princeton University Press, 1975.

———. "The Two Postwar Eras and the Conditions for Stability in Twentieth-Century Western Europe." *American Historical Review* 86 (April 1981): 327–52.

Mallalieu, William C. *British Reconstruction and American Policy, 1945–1955*. New York: Scarecrow Press, 1956.

Manderson-Jones, R. B. *The Special Relationship: Anglo-American Relations and Western European Unity, 1947–1956*. London: Weidenfeld & Nicolson, 1972.

Matthews, R. C., C. H. Feinstein, and J. Odling-Smee. *British Economic Growth, 1856–1973*. Stanford: Stanford University Press, 1982.

Matusow, Allen J. *Nixon's Economy: Booms, Busts, Dollars and Votes*. Lawrence: University Press of Kansas, 1998.

May, Ernest, and Philip Zelikow, eds. *The Kennedy Tapes: Inside the White House during the Cuban Missile Crisis*. Cambridge, Mass.: Harvard University Press, 1997.

Mayer, Frank A. *Adenauer and Kennedy: A Study in German-American Relations, 1961–1963*. New York: St. Martin's, 1996.

McCloskey, Donald, and Richard Zecher. "How the Gold Standard Worked, 1880–1913." In J. A. Frenkel and H. G. Johnson, eds., *The Monetary Approach to the Balance of Payments*, 357–88. Toronto: University of Toronto Press, 1976.

McCormick, Thomas J. "World Systems." In Michael Hogan, ed., *Explaining the History of American Foreign Relations*. Cambridge: Cambridge University Press, 1991.

McGhee, George. *At the Creation of a New Germany*. New Haven: Yale University Press, 1989.

McNeil, William C. *American Money and the Weimar Republic: Economics and Politics on the Eve of the Great Depression*. New York: Columbia University Press, 1986.

Mee, Charles L. *The Marshall Plan: The Launching of Pax Americana*. New York: Simon & Schuster, 1984.

Meier, Gerald M. *The Problems of a World Monetary Order*. 2nd ed. Oxford: Oxford University Press, 1982.

Meyer, Richard. *Banker's Diplomacy: Monetary Stabilization in the Twenties*. New York: Columbia University Press, 1970.

Middeke, Michael. "Anglo-American Nuclear Weapons Cooperation after the Nassau Conference: The British Policy of Interdependence." *Journal of Cold War Studies* 2, no. 2 (2000): 69–96.

Milward, Alan S. *The Reconstruction of Western Europe, 1945-1951.* London: Methuen, 1984.

———. "Was the Marshall Plan Necessary?" *Diplomatic History* 13 (Spring 1989): 231-53.

Moggridge, D. E. *British Monetary Policy, 1924-1931: The Norman Conquest of 1468.* Cambridge: Cambridge University Press, 1972.

Murray, Donnette. *Kennedy, Macmillan, and Nuclear Weapons.* Basingstoke: Macmillan, 2000.

Nevin, Edward. *The Mechanism of Cheap Money: A Study of British Monetary Policy, 1931-1939.* Cardiff: University of Wales Press, 1955.

Newton, Scott. "The 1949 Sterling Crisis and British Policy toward European Integration." *Review of International Studies* 11 (July 1985).

———. "The Sterling Crisis of 1947 and the British Response to the Marshall Plan." *Economic History Review* 37 (August 1984): 391-408.

Ninkovich, Frank. *Germany and the United States: The Transformation of the German Question since 1945.* New York: Twayne, 1995.

Nitze, Paul. *From Hiroshima to Glastnost: At the Center of Decision—A Memoir.* New York: Grove Weidenfeld, 1989.

Nurkse, R. "International Investment Today in Light of Nineteenth-Century Experience." In Richard N. Cooper, ed., *International Finance,* 358-74. Baltimore: Penguin Books, 1969.

Odell, John. "Bretton Woods and International Political Disintegration: Implications for Monetary Diplomacy." In R. Lombra and W. Witte, eds., *The Political Economy of International and Domestic Monetary Relations,* 39-58. Ames: Iowa State University Press, 1982.

———. *U.S. International Monetary Policy: Markets, Power, and Ideas as Sources of Change.* Princeton: Princeton University Press, 1982.

Ovendale, Richie. *The English-Speaking Alliance: Britain, the United States, the Dominions and the Cold War, 1945-1951.* London: George Allen & Unwin, 1985.

Parrini, C. *Heir to Empire: United States Economic Diplomacy, 1916-1923.* Pittsburgh: University of Pittsburgh Press, 1969.

Paterson, Thomas, ed. *Kennedy's Quest for Victory: American Foreign Policy, 1961-63.* New York: Oxford University Press, 1989.

Peyrefitte, Alain. *C'etait de Gaulle: La France reprend sa place dans le monde.* Paris: Fayard, 1997.

———. *C'etait de Gaulle: Tout le monde a besoin d'une France qui marche.* Paris: Fayard, 2000.

Pollard, Robert A. *Economic Security and the Origins of the Cold War, 1945-1950.* New York: Columbia University Press, 1985.

Reeves, Richard. *President Kennedy: Profile of Power.* New York: Touchstone, 1993.

Rostow, Walt W. *The Diffusion of Power.* New York: Macmillan, 1972.

Rothwell, Victor. *Britain and the Cold War, 1941-1947.* London: Jonathan Cape, 1982.

Rowland, Benjamin M., ed. *Balance of Power or Hegemony: The Interwar Monetary System.* New York: New York University Press, 1976.

Rueff, Jacques. *Balance of Payments: Proposals for Resolving the Most Pressing World Economic Problem of Our Time.* New York: Macmillan, 1967.

———. *Le lancinant problème des balances de paiements.* Paris: Payot, 1965.

Safire, William. *Before the Fall*. Garden City, N.Y.: Doubleday, 1975.

Schlesinger, Arthur. *A Thousand Days: John F. Kennedy in the White House*. New York: Fawcett Premier, 1965.

Schreiber, J. J. Servan. *The American Challenge*. Translated by Ronald Steel. New York: Atheneum, 1968.

Schubert, Auriel. *The Credit-Anstalt Crisis of 1931*. Cambridge: Cambridge University Press, 1991.

Schuker, Stephen. *American "Reparations" to Germany, 1919–33: Implications for the Third World Debt Crisis*. Princeton Studies in International Finance, no. 61. Princeton: Princeton University Press, 1980.

———. *The End of French Predominance in Europe*. Chapel Hill: University of North Carolina Press, 1976.

Schwarz, Hans-Peter. *Konrad Adenauer: German Politician and Statesman in a Period of War, Revolution, and Reconstruction*. Providence: Berghahn Books, 1997.

Schwartz, Thomas. *Lyndon Johnson and Europe: In the Shadow of Vietnam*. Cambridge, Mass.: Harvard University Press, 2003.

Shapley, Deborah. *Promise and Power: The Life and Times of Robert McNamara*. Boston: Little, Brown, 1993.

Shelton, Judy. *Money Meltdown: Restoring Order to the Global Currency System*. New York: Free Press, 1994.

Solomon, Robert. *The International Monetary System, 1945–1976: An Insider's View*. New York: Harper & Row, 1977.

Sorensen, Theodore C. *Kennedy*. New York: Harper and Row, 1965.

Soutou, Georges-Henri. *L'alliance incertaine: Les rapports politico-strategiques franco-allemands, 1954–1996*. Paris: Fayard, 1996.

Stern, Robert M. *The Balance of Payments: Theory and Economic Policy*. Chicago: Aldine, 1973.

Strange, Susan. *International Monetary Relations of the Western World, 1959–1971*. Vol. 2. London: Oxford University Press, 1976.

———. *Sterling and British Policy: A Political Study of an International Currency in Decline*. New York: Oxford University Press, 1971.

Stromseth, Jane E. *The Origins of Flexible Response: NATO's Debate over Strategy in the 1960s*. New York: St. Martin's, 1988.

Sulzberger, C. L. *The Last of the Giants*. New York: Macmillan, 1970.

Temin, Peter. *Did Monetary Forces Cause the Great Depression?* New York: Norton, 1976.

———. *Lessons from the Great Depression*. Cambridge, Mass.: MIT Press, 1989.

Tew, Brian. *The Evolution of the International Monetary System, 1945–1988*. London: Hutchinson, 1988.

Trachtenberg, Marc. *A Constructed Peace: America and the Making of the European Settlement, 1945–63*. Princeton: Princeton University Press, 1999.

———. *History and Strategy*. Princeton: Princeton University Press, 1991.

Treverton, Gregory. *America, Germany, and the Future of Europe*. Princeton: Princeton University Press, 1992.

———. *The Dollar Drain and American Forces in Germany: Managing the Political Economics of Alliance*. Athens: Ohio University Press, 1978.

Triffin, Robert. *Europe and the Money Muddle: From Bilateralism to Near-Convertibility, 1947–1956*. New Haven: Yale University Press, 1957.

——. *Gold and the Dollar Crisis: The Future of Convertibility*. New Haven: Yale University Press, 1960.

——. "The Myth and Realities of the So-Called Gold Standard." In Richard N. Cooper, ed., *International Finance*, 38–61. Baltimore: Penguin Books, 1969.

Tsiang, S. C. "The Role of Money in Trade-Balance Stability: Synthesis of the Elasticity and Absorption Approaches." In Richard N. Cooper, ed., *International Finance*, 135–64. Baltimore: Penguin Books, 1969.

Van der Beugel, Ernst. *From Marshall Aid to Atlantic Partnership: European Integration as a Concern for American Foreign Policy*. New York: Elsevier, 1966.

Van der Wee, Herman. *Prosperity and Upheaval: The World Economy during 1945–80*. New York: Penguin Books, 1985.

Van Dormael, Armand. *Bretton Woods: Birth of a Monetary System*. New York: Holmes & Meier, 1978.

Van Helten, J. J., and Y. Cassis, eds. *Capitalism in a Mature Economy: Financial Institutions, Capital Exports and British Industry, 1870–1939*. Aldershot: Edward Elgar, 1990.

Vilar, Pierre. *A History of Gold and Money, 1450–1920*. London: New Left Books, 1976.

Volcker, Paul A., and Toyoo Gyohten. *Changing Fortunes: The World's Money and the Threat to American Leadership*. New York: Times Books, 1992.

Wexler, Imanuel. *The Marshall Plan Revisited: The European Recovery Program in Economic Perspective*. Westport, Conn.: Greenwood, 1983.

Wilson, Joan Hoff. *American Business and Foreign Policy, 1920–1933*. Boston: Beacon Press, 1971.

Wood, Robert. *From Marshall Plan to Debt Crisis: Foreign Aid and Development Choices in the World Economy*. Berkeley: University of California Press, 1986.

Woods, Randall. *A Changing of the Guard: Anglo-American Relations, 1941–1946*. Chapel Hill: University of North Carolina Press, 1990.

Wright, Harrison, ed. *The "New Imperialism": Analysis of Late Nineteenth-Century Expansion*. 2nd ed. Lexington: D. C. Heath, 1976.

Young, John W. *Britain, France, and the Unity of Europe, 1945–1951*. Leicester: Leicester University Press, 1984.

Zeiler, Thomas W. *American Trade and Power during the 1960s*. New York: Columbia University Press, 1992.

Zimmerman, Hubert. "Dollars, Pounds, and Transatlantic Security: Conventional Troops and Monetary Policy in Germany's Relations to the United States and the United Kingdom, 1955–1967." Ph.D. dissertation, European University, Florence, 1997.

——. "Offset and Monetary Policy in German-American Relations during Kennedy's Presidency, 1961–1963." Unpublished manuscript.

Zubok, Vladislav, and Constantine Pleshakov. *Inside the Kremlin's Cold War: From Stalin to Khrushchev*. Cambridge, Mass.: Harvard University Press, 1996.

# Index

Acheson, Dean, 98–100; on troop withdrawal, 61, 95

Ackley, Gardner, 5, 124, 126

Adenauer, Konrad: and refusal to help Eisenhower, 46–47, 50–52; and disagreement with U.S., 61, 73–74, 110–12, 227 (n. 16), 231 (n. 99), 232 (n. 105); and "Morgenthau Plan squared," 162

Anderson, Robert: and troop withdrawal recommendation, 34, 47–50; and Anderson-Dillon mission, 50–53

Anglo-American loan, 20

Ansiaux, Hubert: gold pool and, 172

Balance of payments: program of 1968, 2–7, 165, 177–80; ending as primary goal of U.S. foreign economic policy, 7; effect on grand strategy, 14; definition of, 26–27, 203; effect on U.S. foreign policy, 35, 197, 201–2; crisis of 1971, 191–96; and different accounts, 203–5

—deficit: and Bretton Woods system, 2–3, 7, 21, 30, 31, 33–34; recommendations to end, 3–7, 173, 177; as source of international liquidity, 3, 18, 22–23, 69, 99, 102; and pressure to withdraw U.S. troops from Europe, 8–9, 47–50, 64, 65, 93, 113; deflation as tool to correct, 17–18; how adjusted, 26–27, 30; foreign investment as cause of, 70, 121–22; American policy makers obsessed with, 197; how financed, 205–8

Ball, George, 59, 72, 78–80, 99; on troop withdrawals, 61, 63; proposal to reform Bretton Woods, 81–82, 101–3; disagreement with Dillon, 84–86, 99, 101–3; on seigniorage, 85; on de Gaulle, 124; on German offset, 135–36

Bator, Francis: and hardware solution, 142; and nuclear nonproliferation, 143–44; and offset, 144; and trilateral negotiations, 159

Baumgartner, Wilfrid, 76

Berlin crisis: 15, 34, 52, 53, 61, 73–74; Soviet pressure during, 34, 44, 219 (n. 52); effect on price of gold, 45; exposes rifts within alliance, 53, 219 (n. 53); prevents troop withdrawals, 57; and offset negotiations, 66; American and Soviet negotiations, 73; effect on U.S. military policy, 105–6, 229 (nn. 57, 58), 230 (n. 64); lessening of tensions, 112

Bohlen, Charles: on U.S. investments abroad, 123–24

Bowie, Robert, 53

Brandt, Karl, 33

Bretton Woods: as gold exchange standard, 3; agreements, 9, 14, 17–21, 28; flaws in, 9–11, 21–31, 87, 98–99, 198–200; proposed reform of, 10–11, 70–71, 78, 81–82, 84, 87–88, 99–103, 127, 199; as source of U.S. vulnerability, 10, 198–200; scarce currency clause, 20; and liquidity, 22, 23, 27–28; adjustment process, 26–27; U.S. advantages under, 85; Kennedy's opinion of, 88; collapse of, 166, 180; sterling devaluation and, 167; March 1968 crisis and, 185; formal end of, 195–96; as "golden age of capitalism," 198, 200

Brookings Institute: monetary reform proposal, 101–2, 107, 116

Bundy, McGeorge, 77, 78–79, 85, 109, 140, 142, 164

Cabinet Committee on the Balance of Payments: 1968 program, 2–5, 173, 177–80

Califano, Joseph, 2

Capital controls, 3, 18, 30, 75, 98, 99, 101, 103, 115, 168, 177, 188–90, 200; policies to avoid, 38; and 1968 gold crisis, 179; and overseas response to "New Economic policy," 195

Cold War: and international monetary relations, 11–13; revisionist interpretation of, 197–200; "realist" interpretation of, 200–201

Collective Reserve Unit (CRU), 80, 119; Heller's rejections of, 119

Common Market. See European Economic Community

Connally, John, 187, 193–96

Creditanstalt bank: collapse of, 13, 201

Current account: large U.S. surplus, 34, 38, 203–4; surplus decreases, 188

De Gaulle, Charles: disagreement with U.S. security policy, 61, 73–75; on the dollar, 75, 120–23; on threat of withdrawals, 75; on Britain's EEC entry, 92, 93–94, 226 (n. 3); tensions with U.S., 93–94, 120–23; and Bretton Woods, 120–24; and dollar/gold exchange, 120; and 4 February 1965 press conference, 120; and U.S. reactions to press conference, 121; and attack against U.S., 121; and French reactions to press conference, 123; and gold pool, 171–72; and franc crisis, 183–84, 192

Deflation: as tool to correct balance-of-payments deficits, 17–18; fear of, 71

Deming, Fred: trip to Europe, 124–25, 127; and 1968 gold crisis, 172

Dillon, Douglas: as Eisenhower's under secretary of state, 47–48, 50–52; and Anderson-Dillon mission, 50–53; as treasury secretary, 61–63, 67–68, 71–72, 74; on troop withdrawals, 61, 95; opposition to reform, 84, 97, 100–101; opposition to gold standstill, 87; and offset, 138

Dollar: and dilemmas as reserve currency, 23–26, 30, 130, 205–8; gold convertibility of, 24; and gold price, 37; and devaluation, 72, 84, 98, 228 (n. 22); French complaints about, 75, 120–24; hegemony of, 82; seigniorage, 85–86; and overhang, 99, 128–29; and economists' concern with overvalue, 126; and agreement with Bundesbank, 138; and trilateral negotiations, 159; and sterling devaluation, 168; March 1968 crisis, 182; convertibility suspended, 185, 194–95

Dual containment, 8. See also German question

Eisenhower, Dwight D.: on balance of payments, 33–57 passim; desire to withdraw U.S. troops from Western Europe, 40–44, 47–50, 52; on replacing gold with uranium, 49; and Bowie Report, 53–55; as advisor to Kennedy, 55–57

England. See Great Britain

Erhard, Ludwig, 113; and offset, 135, 139, 141–57 passim; on flexible response, 237 (n. 41). See also Erhard-Johnson summit

Erhard-Johnson summit, 149–51; and German security, 149; and nonproliferation treaty, 149; and troop withdrawals, 150

European Economic Community (EEC), 75, 80; British entry into, 92, 93; French attitude towards, 92, 93; and tariffs, 93, 94; and burden sharing, 175

European Payments Union, 29–30

European Recovery Act. See Marshall Plan

Federal Republic of Germany (FRG): gold policy of, 6, 66, 69, 94, 110–13, 162, 166, 207; promise to hold dollars, 31; and U.S. gold purchase, 36; and rising dollar balances, 41, 192; refusal to pay troop support costs, 51–52; and nuclear weapons, 61, 73, 91, 92, 93, 110; Bundeswehr, 64–65, 235 (n. 18); offset policy of, 64–65, 66–67, 113, 146, 162, 236 (n. 19); tensions with U.S., 72, 73, 110–12, 135–38, 142–48, 162, 176, 238 (n. 58); non-nuclear status of, 112, 114, 138, 164; acceptance of U.S. offset demands, 112–13; rejection of de Gaulle's policies, 113, 232 (n. 105); and NATO, 143; and NPT,

162, 164, 240, (n. 89); and U.S., French, and British pressures to revalue currency, 184; and Ostpolitik, 191; revalues mark, 192, 196. See also Adenauer, Konrad; Erhard, Ludwig; Franco-German alliance; German question; Kiesinger, Kurt Georg

Fixed exchange rates: difficulties in maintaining, 22, 24–25, 28

Flexible exchange rates, 13; adjustment and liquidity under, 12, 27, 30; and fear of competitive devaluations, 49; Nixon administration support for, 189, 196; and capital movements, 200

Flexible response: 73–74, 104–7, 232 (n. 116); myth of, 9, 60, 228 (nn. 57, 58), 230 (n. 64); under Eisenhower, 53–55, 74; Adenauer and de Gaulle's attitude towards, 73; effect of troop withdrawals on, 96; limited war contingencies, 106; McNamara's undermining of, 147. See also United States of America—military strategy of

Floating exchange rates. See Flexible exchange rates

Fowler, Henry, 84; Virginia Bar Association speech, 126–27, 234 (n. 41); and German offset, 135, 140; and 1968 gold crisis, 174; concerns about dollar float, 180

France, 6, 41, 46, 60, 64, 72; and franc, 11, 83; gold policy of, 69, 77, 83, 94; tensions with U.S., 72, 73–75, 78, 89–90, 120–24, 171–72; and nuclear weapons, 73, 90, 92, 95, 107; and dollar conversion, 76, 88, 120–24; economic policies of, 76, 120–24, 183–84; and CRU, 80; attitude towards Bretton Woods, 88, 120–24; and gold pool, 171–72; withdrawal from NATO, 175; and franc crisis, 183–84, 192; and devaluation of 1969, 192. See also De Gaulle, Charles; Franco-German alliance

Franco-German alliance, 15, 61, 75, 81, 89–90, 94, 110, 112–13, 115, 222 (nn. 38, 39)

Free exchange rates. See Flexible exchange rates

Friedman, Milton, 4, 216 (n. 11)

Galbraith, John Kenneth, 62, 115

General Agreement of Tariffs and Trade (GATT), 177

General Arrangements to Borrow (GAB), 25, 28

German question, the, 12, 14, 90–92, 153–55; and international monetary relations, 8–9, 200–201; and nuclear weapons, 12, 138; effect of troop withdrawal on, 96, 114; and nuclear weapons, 110, 142, 144; and NATO, 154

Germany. See Federal Republic of Germany

Gilpatric, Roswell, 61, 67, 109–10

Giscard d'Estaing, Valery, 76, 77; visit to U.S.

(1962), 78–80, 86–87; reaction to Fowler speech, 127

Gold: convertibility, 3, 24, 81, 84, 101, 115; London gold market and, 6, 45, 46, 62, 171; dollar price, 37, 62, 85; outflow, 36–37, 71, 89, 95, 114; standstill, 72, 80–81, 82, 83, 84–85; holdings, 79; concerns with price of, 171.

Gold crisis of 1960, 15, 33–34, 43, 45–50, 69–70

Gold crisis of 1968, 2–7; political consequences of, 165; and certificate proposal, 172; and troop withdrawals, 174; and London gold market, 178; and attempts to maintain gold pool, 179; and free exchange rates, 179; and separation of gold market, 181; and de facto end of dollar convertibility, 185

Goldfinger, 1–2

Gold Pool, 25, 28, 69, 85, 128, 179; crisis in, 168, 171, 215 (n. 11); U.S. efforts to prevent collapse of, 169; French withdrawal from, 171; European threats to withdraw from, 173; and 1968 gold crisis, 179; and gold outflow, 180

Gold standard, 3, 21, 30; differences from Bretton Woods system, 17

Gordon, Kermit, 84

Great Britain: and Bretton Woods, 17–21; and postwar deficits, 18; and EEC, 76; and Anglo-American loan, 20; and scarce currency clause, 20–21; and Skybolt affair, 92, 107; and troop withdrawals, 144, 163; and trilateral negotiations, 157, 239 (n. 69). See also Sterling

Great Depression, 7; and similarities to 1968 crisis, 5; avoiding another, 8, 24, 67, 84–85, 197; and beggar-thy-neighbor policies, 13, 25, 49, 201; lessons of the past and, 13–14, 201–2; as analogy, 14, 201–2

Harriman, Averell, 62

Hassel, Kai-Uwe von, 111

Heller, Walter, 63, 66–67, 70–71, 77, 100–101

Herter, Christian, 42–43, 48, 54–55

Humphrey, George, 35–36

International Monetary Fund (IMF), 17–18, 25, 28–29, 37, 69, 101, 102, 103; criticism of, 70, 78; annual meeting of, 87, 187

Jackson, Barbara Ward, 5

Japan, 10, 56, 68; and promise to hold dollars, 31; replaces Western Europe as economic competitor to U.S., 195–96; and yen revaluation, 196

Johnson, Lyndon Baines: and 1968 gold crisis, 2–7, 180–82; reaction to cabinet committee on balance-of-payments report, 2–

5; and gold standard, 3, 125; difference between Kennedy and, 117; and Kaysen report, 118–20; and de Gaulle, 120–30; and proposal for international monetary reform, 125–30; and Great Britain, 130–33, 145, 157, 162–63, 166–71; and trilateral talks, 145–46, 152–64 passim; and Mansfield Resolution, 149; See also Erhard-Johnson summit

Kaysen, Carl, 63, 72, 84; on flexible response, 104–5

Kaysen Report. See Task Force on Foreign Economic Policy

Kennedy, David, 188–89, 191

Kennedy, John F., 4, 9–10, 13, 45, 52; transition meeting with Eisenhower, 55–57; and transition task force on balance of payments, 56; and debates within administration over international monetary policy, 59, 61@62, 67–73, 80–88, 89–90, 94–104; on de Gaulle, 59; on Adenauer, 60, 111; on flexible response, 60, 104–7, 229 (nn. 57, 58), 230 (n. 64); on troop withdrawal, 60, 95–96, 104–10; on offset, 63, 64–65; and tensions with France, 74, 111; on seigniorage, 86; on standstill, 86; speech to IMF, 87; on Bretton Woods, 88; and fear of Franco-German attack on the dollar, 94, 97; on monetary reform, 101, 107

Keynes, John Maynard, 17–20, 29; and currency union plan, 19–20; similarity to Kaysen Report, 119

Kiesinger, Kurt Georg, 157–58, 161–62

Kissinger, Henry, 187, 190, 192, 195

Knappstein, Heinrich: and offset negotiations, 146–47

Leddy, John, 84, 86, 87, 124, 145

Limited Test Ban Treaty (1963), 107

London Economic Conference (1933), 13, 33, 201

London gold market, 4, 6, 45–46, 62, 218 (n. 30); effect of Tet offensive on, 178

Long Range International Payments Committee, 118

Macmillan, Harold, 33

Malraux, Andre, 74–75

Mansfield resolutions, 136, 149, 191

Marshall Plan, 29–30

Martin, William McChesney: and standstill agreement, 85; and Martin-Cromer plan, 132; and 1968 gold crisis, 172

McCloy, John: and trilateral negotiations, 153, 157–58; and troop withdrawals, 160

McCracken, Paul, 191, 193

McGhee, George, 110, 152

McNamara, Robert, 5, 9, 68, 74; and troop

withdrawals, 61, 63, 103–4, 107–9, 111–12, 146–48, 221 (n. 7); on flexible response, 104–7, 147, 229 (n. 57); and German offset, 135; meeting with Kai-Uwe von Hassel, 141; and U.S. arms sales to FRG, 141; and trilateral negotiations, 158, 160–61

Multilateral Force Proposal (MLF), 15, 74, 92, 236 (n. 26)

Murville, Couve de, 75, 76

Nassau Conference, "New Economic Policy," 195

Neustadt, Richard, 62

Nitze, Paul, 55

Nixon, Richard, 11, 62; primacy of domestic political considerations for, 187; unilateralism of, 187–88; disinterest in international monetary relations, 188; and gold window closure, 188, 195–96; and 1971 Camp David meeting, 195

Norstad, Lauris, 40–41, 55

North Atlantic Treaty Organization (NATO): threat of gold crisis to, 33–34; Bowie report on strategy of, 53–55; Herter's speech to, 55; and troop withdrawals, 137; and negotiations, 159

Nuclear Non-Proliferation Treaty (NPT), 15, 161–62, 197

Nuclear Weapons: and German question, 9, 12, 136, 142–43, 161–62; and international monetary relations, 9; effect on U.S. strategy, 39–40, 112, 114, 229 (nn. 57, 58); and military balance, 39–40; and nuclear sharing, 73–74, 90, 91, 92, 93, 107. See also Federal Republic of Germany: and nuclear weapons; France: and nuclear weapons

Offset arrangements, 3, 6, 50–51, 63, 64–65, 68, 69; and arms purchases, 64; during Berlin crisis, 66–67; FRG–U.S. tensions about, 135; unraveling of, 136; troop deployments and, 139–40; trilateral negotiations and new formula for, 161–62; U.S.–FRG resolution on, 162; Nixon's new policy towards, 190–91

Okun, Arthur, 165

Organization for Economic Cooperation and Development (OECD), 70, 78

Pegged-rate exchange. See Fixed exchange rates

Peyrefitte, Alain, 121–23

Plan X, 169; and end of dollar-gold convertibility, 170; and flexible exchange rates, 170

Redeployments. See United States of America—troop withdrawals of

Roosa, Robert, 67–69, 103, 228 (n. 28); on troop withdrawal, 61, 85; and swap agreements, 68–69; and Long Range International Payments Committee, 118

Rostow, Walt, 1, 5–6, 63, 197; on the dollar, 97; and 1968 gold crisis, 178–79, 180–81

Rueff, Jacques, 75; attack on the dollar, 76–77; on de Gualle's press conference, 124

Rusk, Dean, 65; on flexible response, 104; on withdrawals, 107; Frankfurt speech, 113; and trilateral negotiations, 158

Schroeder, Gerhard, 110, 111

Shultz, George, 193, 195–96

Skybolt affair, 92, 107, 226 (n. 3)

Smith, Gerard, 42–44

Smithsonian Institution meeting (December 1971), 196

Soresen, Ted, 97

Sterling: 1967 devaluation of, 2, 130, 166–71; 1931 devaluation of, 13; and 1947 suspension of convertibility, 28–29; 1949 devaluation of, 29; weakness after Suez crisis, 35–36, 217 (n. 6); U.S. options for combating devaluation of, 130, 167–71; and aid from U.S., 131, 167, 183; and 1964 outflow, 131; link to U.S. security policy, 132; and Cromer-Martin plan, 132, 133; and Bretton Woods, 167; devaluation history of, 167; and consequences for international monetary relations, 168; tested after March 1968 crisis, 182–83

Special Drawing Rights (SDRs), 25; initiation of, 6; French protest against, 117, 129; Johnson proposal for, 117; and failure to produce liquidity, 118, 215 (n. 12); U.S. hopes for, 129

Strauss, Franz Joseph, 67; and French economic problems, 184; and offset, 184

Swap agreements, 25, 28, 68–69, 83, 85

Task Force on Foreign Economic Policy, 118, 119–20

Taylor, Maxwell, 104, 105–6

Tobin, James, 77, 78–79, 82, 98, 232 (n. 116)

Trade: controls, 18, 200; and U.S. pressure for European tariff reductions, 63, 66, 93; and disputes with Japan, 195–96; import tax imposed on, 195

Triffin, Robert, 70, 222 (n. 34)

Trilateral negotiations, 152–64; LBJ's proposal for, 145; and the dollar, 150; McCloy report on, 153, 157–58; problems with, 156, 239 (n. 74); and Great Britain, 157, 239 (n. 69); and McNamara, 158, 160–61; and Rusk, 158; and troop withdrawal, 158–59, 163, 175; similarity to Skybolt affair, 160; LBJ's dissatisfaction with, 163; new formula for, 165

United Kingdom. *See* Great Britain
United States of America: and ambivalence towards empire, 3, 4, 12–13, 74–
75, 197–200, 245 (nn. 11, 12); and foreign
aid, 68; and tensions with France, 73–75,
78, 89–90, 120–24, 171–72; and tensions
with FRG, 73, 75, 110–12, 135–38, 142–
48, 162, 176, 238 (n. 58); and support for
Bretton Woods reform, 87, 101, 107, 125–
30
—military strategy of, 90–91; and need for
forward defense of Western Europe, 34–35;
and calls for more conventional forces, 39–
40; and differences within Eisenhower
administration, 39–45, 53–55; effect of
nuclear weapons on, 39–40, 112, 114;
Eisenhower's resistance to changes in, 39–
45; at odds with finance under Eisenhower, 39–45; and Bowie report, 53–55;
and flexible response, 104–7, effect of
troop withdrawals on, 107–8; importance
of Berlin on, 108, 229 (nn. 57, 58), 230
(n. 64); and Operation Big Lift, 109–10;
and NATO, 154; and Soviet deterrence,
154; U.S. political influence in Western
Europe on, 154

—troop withdrawals of, 93, 96–97, 98, 103–4,
106, 107–13; fear that balance-of-payments
deficit would force, 8, 9, 31; Eisenhower's
threat to enact, 43–44, 49, 52; threat of as
bargaining strategy, 69, 75, 84, 86; effect
on nuclear guarantee, 93; effect on nuclear
posture, 105–6, 108; calls for, 109; potential consequences of, 118, 137; Rusk's Frankfurt speech and, 118; effect on German
question, 142, 144, 149, 151–52, 154–55,
176–77, 239 (n. 39); and Great Britain, 144,
239 (n. 69); and Rusk-Knappstein talks,
146; and trilateral negotiations, 158–59,
163, 175; and 1968 gold crisis, 174; Nixon's
policies to avoid, 190–91
USSR: emerging détente with, 96, 112, 227
(n. 16), 231 (n. 99); deterrence relationship
with, 106

Vietnam, 82, 245 (n. 11)
Volcker, Paul, 188, 190, 193, 195–96

West Germany. *See* Federal Republic of
Germany
White, Harry Dexter, 17–20
Wilson, Harold, 131–34, 145, 162, 167, 171

# The New Cold War History

FRANCIS J. GAVIN
*Gold, Dollars, and Power: The Politics of International Monetary Relations, 1958–1971*
(2003)

WILLIAM GLENN GRAY
*Germany's Cold War: The Global Campaign to Isolate East Germany 1949–1969*
(2003)

MATTHEW J. OUIMET
*The Rise and Fall of the Brezhnev Doctrine in Soviet Foreign Policy*
(2003)

PIERRE ASSELIN
*A Bitter Peace: Washington, Hanoi, and the Making of the Paris Agreement*
(2002)

JEFFREY GLEN GIAUQUE
*Grand Designs and Visions of Unity: The Atlantic Powers and the Reorganization of Western Europe, 1955–1963*
(2002)

CHEN JIAN
*Mao's China and the Cold War*
(2001)

M. E. SAROTTE
*Dealing with the Devil: East Germany, Détente, and Ostpolitik, 1969–1973*
(2001)

MARK PHILIP BRADLEY
*Imagining Vietnam and America: The Making of Postcolonial Vietnam 1919–1950*
(2000)

MICHAEL E. LATHAM
*Modernization as Ideology: American Social Science and "Nation Building" in the Kennedy Era*
(2000)

QIANG ZHAI
*China and the Vietnam Wars, 1950–1975*
(2000)

WILLIAM I. HITCHCOCK
*France Restored: Cold War Diplomacy and the Quest for Leadership in Europe, 1944–1954*
(1998)

2326297

Made in the USA